Smart Services: Artificial Intelligence in Service Systems

Smart Services: Artificial Intelligence in Service Systems

Editors

Marlene Amorim
Yuval Cohen
João Reis

MDPI • Basel • Beijing • Wuhan • Barcelona • Belgrade • Manchester • Tokyo • Cluj • Tianjin

Editors

Marlene Amorim
University of Aveiro
Aveiro
Portugal

Yuval Cohen
Afeka Tel-Aviv College of Engineering
Tel-Aviv
Israel

João Reis
Lusofona University
Lisbon
Portugal

Editorial Office
MDPI
St. Alban-Anlage 66
4052 Basel, Switzerland

This is a reprint of articles from the Special Issue published online in the open access journal *Applied Sciences* (ISSN 2076-3417) (available at: https://www.mdpi.com/journal/applsci/special_issues/AI_Ser).

For citation purposes, cite each article independently as indicated on the article page online and as indicated below:

LastName, A.A.; LastName, B.B.; LastName, C.C. Article Title. *Journal Name* **Year**, *Volume Number*, Page Range.

ISBN 978-3-0365-6283-4 (Hbk)
ISBN 978-3-0365-6284-1 (PDF)

Contents

About the Editors . . . . **vii**

Preface to "Smart Services: Artificial Intelligence in Service Systems" . . . . **ix**

Yuval Cohen, Marlene Amorim and Joao Reis
Artificial Intelligence Trends and Applications in Service Systems
Reprinted from: *Appl. Sci.* **2022**, *12*, 13032, doi:10.3390/app122413032 . . . . **1**

Muchun Su, Diana Wahyu Hayati, Shaowu Tseng, Jiehhaur Chen and Hsihsien Wei
Smart Care Using a DNN-Based Approach for Activities of Daily Living (ADL) Recognition
Reprinted from: *Appl. Sci.* **2021**, *11*, 10, doi:10.3390/app11010010 . . . . **5**

Jieh-Haur Chen, Mu-Chun Su, Vidya Trisandini Azzizi, Ting-Kwei Wang and Wei-Jen Lin
Smart Project Management: Interactive Platform Using Natural Language Processing Technology
Reprinted from: *Appl. Sci.* **2021**, *11*, 1597, doi:10.3390/app11041597 . . . . **17**

Constâncio António Pinto, José Torres Farinha, Sarbjeet Singh and Hugo Raposo
Increasing the Reliability of an Electrical Power System in a Big European Hospital through the Petri Nets and Fuzzy Inference System Mamdani Modelling
Reprinted from: *Appl. Sci.* **2021**, *11*, 2604, doi:10.3390/app11062604 . . . . **31**

Jorge Fernandes, João Reis, Nuno Melão, Leonor Teixeira and Marlene Amorim
The Role of Industry 4.0 and BPMN in the Arise of Condition-Based and Predictive Maintenance: A Case Study in the Automotive Industry
Reprinted from: *Appl. Sci.* **2021**, *11*, 3438, doi:10.3390/app122413032 . . . . **57**

Ana Malta, Mateus Mendes, and Torres Farinha
Augmented Reality Maintenance Assistant Using YOLOv5
Reprinted from: *Appl. Sci.* **2021**, *11*, 4758, doi:10.3390/app11114758 . . . . **73**

João Reis, Yuval Cohen, Nuno Melão, Joana Costa and Diana Jorge
High-Tech Defense Industries: Developing Autonomous Intelligent Systems
Reprinted from: *Appl. Sci.* **2021**, *11*, 4920, doi:10.3390/app11114920 . . . . **87**

Maurice Preidel and Rainer Stark
SemDaServ: A Systematic Approach for Semantic Data Specification of AI-Based Smart Service Systems
Reprinted from: *Appl. Sci.* **2021**, *11*, 5148, doi:10.3390/app11115148 . . . . **101**

Balduíno Mateus, Mateus Mendes, José Torres Farinha, António Marques Cardoso
Anticipating Future Behavior of an Industrial Press Using LSTM Networks
Reprinted from: *Appl. Sci.* **2021**, *11*, 6101, doi:10.3390/app11136101 . . . . **133**

Adriane Cavalieri, João Reis and Marlene Amorim
A Conceptual Model Proposal to Assess the Effectiveness of IoT in Sustainability Orientation in Manufacturing Industry: An Environmental and Social Focus
Reprinted from: *Appl. Sci.* **2022**, *12*, 5661, doi:10.3390/app12115661 . . . . **149**

Shai Rozenes and Yuval Cohen
Artificial Intelligence Synergetic Opportunities in Services: Conversational Systems Perspective
Reprinted from: *Appl. Sci.* **2022**, *12*, 8363, doi:10.3390/app12168363 . . . . **167**

Syed Asad Abbas Bokhari and Seunghwan Myeong
Artificial Intelligence-Based Technological-Oriented Knowledge Management, Innovation, and E-Service Delivery in Smart Cities: Moderating Role of E-Governance
Reprinted from: *Appl. Sci.* **2022**, *12*, 8732, doi:10.3390/app12178732 . . . . **185**

About the Editors

Marlene Amorim

Marlene Amorim is professor of Operations and Service Management at the University of Aveiro. She is the Coordinator of the Research Line in Competitiveness Innovation and Public Policies at the GOVCOPP center. She served as Pro-Rector for Internationalization at the University and as Director and then Vice-Director for the Master in Industrial Engineering and Management. Marlene received her PhD in Management from IESE Business School of University of Navarra in Spain and conducts research in the area of service operations and service quality, notably in topics related to service process design and customer participation in service delivery.

Yuval Cohen

Professor (Ph.D) Yuval Cohen is a Senior Faculty Member at the Industrial Engineering department of the Afeka Tel-Aviv College of Engineering. Previously, he was the Head of the Industrial Engineering program at the Open University of Israel. His areas of expertise are in the intersection of: intelligent and advanced manufacturing, Industry 4.0, operations management, logistics and operations research. He has published more than 70 papers on these subjects. Prior to is academic career, Professor Yuval Cohen served several years as a Senior Operations Planner at FedEx Ground (USA) and was responsible for the five-year plan for the 24 hubs and 400 terminals. He received several awards for his contributions to the hub and terminal network planning. In 2001, he returned to Israel to establish and manage the Industrial Engineering program, and in 2014, he moved to Afeka Tel-Aviv Academic College of Engineering. He received his PhD from the University of Pittsburgh (USA), his MSc from the Technion, Israel Institute of Technology, and BSc from Ben-Gurion University. Dr Cohen is a Fellow of the Institute of Industrial Engineers (IIE) and a Full Member of the Institute for Operations Research and Management Sciences (INFORMS).

João Reis

João Reis is a Professor of Service Science, Operations Management and Supply Chain Management. He received a Doctoral Diploma in Industrial Engineering from the University of Aveiro (Portugal-EU). In recent years, he has been conducting scientific research in the fields of service science, industrial engineering and operations management. He is a Research Fellow at the Research Center on Industrial Engineering, Management and Sustainability (EIGeS) and at the GOVCOPP.

Preface to "Smart Services: Artificial Intelligence in Service Systems"

We encounter artificial intelligence (AI) chatbots daily on our phones and in our homes, such as Siri and Alexa. AI can also be found in the background of services such as Netflix and Facebook. AI completes computerized tasks typically reserved for humans, including answering technical questions and recommending movies to watch.

It is a contemporary trend to adopt advanced technology in various ways, and professional services deploy artificial intelligence (AI) as part of their information systems. These applications are expected to have a profound effect on services and carry implications for professional work. However, most of the AI potential for service provision is waiting to be developed and explored.

The main goal of this Special Issue is to address the recent advances and problems in the applications of artificial intelligence to various services. The presented papers cover AI implementations in wide range of service fields such as: healthcare, tourism, education, finance, retail, governmental services and much more. They also present the state of the art of AI deployment in services and predict the ways AI will develop in these types of services. A wide variety of AI techniques are presented in the papers of this issue. For example: deep neural networks (DNN), natural language processing (NLP), augmented reality (AR), autonomous systems, chatbots, machine learning (ML) and many more.

We believe that in this issue, the readers will be exposed to cutting-edge research in AI deployment in services and the issues that arise with this deployment.

Finally, we would like to take this opportunity to express our most profound appreciation to the MDPI staff, the editorial team of Applied Sciences journal, especially Ms. Christine Zhang, the assistant editor of this Special Issue, the talented authors, and the hardworking and professional reviewers.

Marlene Amorim, Yuval Cohen, and João Reis
Editors

applied sciences

MDPI

Editorial

Artificial Intelligence Trends and Applications in Service Systems

Yuval Cohen [1,*], Marlene Amorim [2] and Joao Reis [3]

[1] Department of Industrial Engineering, Afeka Tel-Aviv College of Engineering, Tel-Aviv 69988, Israel
[2] Department of Economics, Management, Industrial Engineering and Tourism (DEGEIT) and GOVCOPP, University of Aveiro, 3810-143 Aveiro, Portugal
[3] Department of Industrial Engineering and Management, Faculty of Engineering, Lusofona University and EIGeS, Campo Grande, 1749-024 Lisbon, Portugal
* Correspondence: yuvalc@afeka.ac.il

1. Introduction

Artificial intelligence (AI) has been increasingly adopted in service production systems. Many aspects of modern service delivery are progressively being automated, opening up opportunities for experimentation with new AI applications technologies across multiple industries. AI technologies are driving the service industry and have had promising results in reducing the service costs and error occurrences, as well as reducing service lead times. Future studies should contribute to strengthening the theoretical production. With increased availability of virtual channels, new approaches to resource management are required for effective service delivery. The Special Issue on "Artificial Intelligence Trends and Applications in Service Systems" features recent research paper submissions in this promising application area for artificial intelligence. The Special Issue includes a wide range of papers covering recent AI applications and new technologies across service companies. The papers cover managerial and customer challenges, technologies, service robotics, and research trends. Overall, the Special Issue offers insights to broaden the adoption of AI in services and inspire management decision and innovation in the field.

Citation: Cohen, Y.; Amorim, M.; Reis, J. Artificial Intelligence Trends and Applications in Service Systems. *Appl. Sci.* **2022**, *12*, 13032. https://doi.org/10.3390/app122413032

Received: 12 December 2022
Accepted: 15 December 2022
Published: 19 December 2022

2. Service Application Use of Advanced Technologies and Artificial Intelligence

A seminal paper on AI in service [1] defines four intelligences required for service tasks: mechanical, analytical, intuitive, and empathetic. Currently, AI integration primarily involves mechanical and analytical intelligences, and is mainly performed at the task level rather than the job level. Eventually, the progression of technology will lead to the inclusion of more intelligences and AI capabilities to replace more sophisticated tasks and, ultimately, to some job replacements [1]. Robots are good example for the use of mechanical intelligence and are used in service for simple and homogeneous tasks, compared to human tasks [2]. A good literature review on the use of AI in services could be found in Reis et al. [3]. A more recent review [4,5] focuses on the use of AI in tourism and hospitality services. In addition, it is becoming common to find articles corroborating the fact that, for environments with high customer contact, service robots tend to outperform humans in standardized tasks [6]. However, in most cases, service robots have not yet reached the technological maturity that allows them to adequately replace humans [6], which justifies the need for further scientific research. Therefore, managers facing difficult decisions about whether AI-enabled service robots are capable of replacing human labor or whether to invest in mixed options such as human–robot systems should have scientific studies to back them up. Other articles, beyond hospitality and tourism, are dealing with chatbots for healthcare and oncology [7,8], for online marketing and sales [9,10], finance and banking [11] and more. Therefore, it can be easily inferred that the combination of AI and services is rapidly evolving. In light of the above, this Special Issue is presented to collect the latest research on relevant topics and, more importantly, to address current challenging issues with AI integration and service delivery.

3. The Special Issue Contributions

In this section, we briefly present the papers of the Special Issue and their contributions.

The first paper [12] deals with serving the elderly population. It develops automatic recognition of elders and seniors' activities of daily living as the first step to solve the healthcare issues faced by seniors in an efficient way. The paper describes a deep neural network (DNN)-based recognition system aimed at facilitating smart care, which combines activities of daily living (ADL) recognition, image/video processing, motion calculation and DNN.

The second paper [13] uses natural language processing to serve as a communication bridge between different parties or subcontractors to solve communication interaction problems in large projects. Communication problems often arise between different organizations, different organizational units, or different parties. These problems are rampant and often lead to litigation. The solution uses an interactive concept of natural language processing technology embedded in a common project management platform.

The third paper [14] deals with a large hospital in the health sector. The research aims at increasing the reliability of an electrical power system in a large European hospital through the use of Petri nets and fuzzy inference system modelling. Inference provides solutions for places where poor reliability has been detected.

The fourth paper [15] deals with increasing the reliability of industrial and service systems by integrating predictive maintenance (PdM) and condition-based maintenance (CBM) into business process management (BPM) and business process model and notation (BPMN) methodologies. A case study in Renault illustrates how the concepts are applied in real-life cases.

The fifth paper [16] proposes a task assistant model based on a deep learning neural network. A YOLOv5 network is used to recognize some of the new parts as part of a maintenance assistant's augmented reality system.

The sixth paper [17] characterizes the activities of autonomous intelligent systems development in high-tech defense industries. Three categories are discovered: fully autonomous operations, partially autonomous operations, and smart autonomous decision-making. It was also found that autonomous systems are more related to tactical rather than strategic issues.

The seventh paper [18] deals with a systematic approach for semantic data specification of AI-based smart service systems. The paper presents the developed and proposed SemDaServ system. SemDaServ provides a three-step process and five accompanying artifacts. Using domain knowledge to specify data is critical and creates additional challenges. Therefore, the SemDaServ approach systematically captures and semantically formalizes domain knowledge in SysML-based models for information and data.

The eighth paper [19] deals with the predictive maintenance of an industrial press. It uses neural networks to anticipate future behavior of the industrial press. Data are pre-processed and neural networks are optimized to minimize prediction errors. The results show the effective prediction of up to a month ahead of time.

The ninth paper [20] adopts an environmental and social perspective in a proposed conceptual model to evaluate the effectiveness of IoT in guiding towards sustainability in the manufacturing industry.

The tenth paper [21] examines and discusses synergetic opportunities for integrating different AI capabilities into conversational systems in services: two case studies of service systems are presented to illustrate the importance of synergy. A special focus is given to the conversation part of these service systems: the first case presents an application with high potential to integrate new AI technologies into its AI portfolio, while the second case illustrates the advantages of a mature application that has already integrated many technologies into its AI portfolio.

The eleventh paper [22] explored factors affecting E-service delivery in smart cities. In particular, it examined the significance of innovation as a mediator between knowledge management and e-service delivery. It also investigated the moderating impact of e-governance on the relationship between innovation and e-service delivery. Both innovation and E-governance were found to be powerful factors affecting service delivery in smart cities.

4. Conclusions

While this Special Issue is now closed, more in-depth research into the use of AI in services is expected. It can be anticipated that more advanced AI and new technologies will be available in the future for enhanced service delivery. This Special Issue covers current advances in the next generation of AI technologies that are revolutionizing the service delivery systems (SDS). The scalability of digital AI (e.g., chatbots) allows us to dramatically increase its availability to the public. Thus, the motivation to develop and test Service AI capabilities and to integrate AI in the delivery of digital services grows.

Author Contributions: Conceptualization, Y.C., M.A. and J.R.; methodology, Y.C., M.A. and J.R.; validation, Y.C., J.R. and M.A.; investigation, Y.C.; writing—original draft preparation, Y.C.; writing—review and editing, J.R.; supervision, M.A. All authors have read and agreed to the published version of the manuscript.

Acknowledgments: This issue would not have been possible without the contributions of various talented authors, hardworking and professional reviewers, and dedicated editorial team of *Applied Sciences*. Congratulations to all the authors—we are convinced that the reviewers' comments and suggestions, as well as the editorial decisions, were in the direction of presenting a more solid contribution and we hope that the authors were proud of the final version of the articles. We would like to take this opportunity to record our sincere gratitude to all reviewers. Finally, we would also like to place on record our gratitude to the editorial team of *Applied Sciences*.

Conflicts of Interest: The authors declare no conflict of interest.

References

1. Huang, M.; Rust, R. Artificial intelligence in service. *J. Serv. Res.* **2018**, *21*, 155–172. [CrossRef]
2. Wirtz, J.; Patterson, P.; Kunz, W.; Gruber, T.; Lu, V.; Paluch, S.; Martings, A. Brave new world: Service robots in the frontline. *J. Serv. Manag.* **2018**, *29*, 907–931. [CrossRef]
3. Reis, J.; Amorim, M.; Cohen, Y.; Rodrigues, M. Artificial intelligence in service delivery systems: A systematic literature review. In *Trends and Innovations in Information Systems and Technologies. WorldCIST 2020*; Rocha, Á., Adeli, H., Reis, L., Costanzo, S., Orovic, I., Moreira, F., Eds.; Advances in Intelligent Systems and Computing; Springer International Publishing: Cham, Switzerland, 2020; pp. 222–233.
4. Li, M.; Yin, D.; Qiu, H.; Bai, B. A systematic review of AI technology-based service encounters: Implications for hospitality and tourism operations. *Int. J. Hosp. Manag.* **2021**, *95*, 102930. [CrossRef]
5. Rawal, Y.; Soni, H.; Dani, R.; Bagchi, P. A Review on Service Delivery in Tourism and Hospitality Industry Through Artificial Intelligence. In *Proceedings of Third International Conference on Computing, Communications, and Cyber-Security*; Lecture Notes in Networks and Systems; Springer International Publishing: Singapore, 2023; pp. 427–436.
6. Reis, J.; Melão, N.; Salvadorinho, J.; Soares, B.; Rosete, A. Service robots in the hospitality industry: The case of Henn-na hotel, Japan. *Technol. Soc.* **2020**, *63*, 101423. [CrossRef]
7. Palanica, A.; Flaschner, P.; Thommandram, A.; Li, M.; Fossat, Y. Physicians' perceptions of chatbots in health care: Cross-sectional web-based survey. *J. Med. Internet Res.* **2019**, *21*, e12887. [CrossRef]
8. Xu, L.; Sanders, L.; Li, K.; Chow, J. Chatbot for health care and oncology applications using artificial intelligence and machine learning: Systematic review. *JMIR Cancer* **2021**, *7*, e27850. [CrossRef] [PubMed]
9. Chung, M.; Ko, E.; Joung, H.; Kim, S. Chatbot e-service and customer satisfaction regarding luxury brands. *J. Bus. Res.* **2020**, *117*, 587–595. [CrossRef]
10. Chen, J.; Tran-Thien-Y, L.; Florence, D. Usability and responsiveness of artificial intelligence chatbot on online customer experience in e-retailing. *Int. J. Retail. Distrib. Manag.* **2021**, *49*, 1512–1531. [CrossRef]
11. Khan, S.; Rabbani, M. Artificial Intelligence and NLP-based Chatbot for Islamic Banking and Finance. *Int. J. Inf. Retr. Res.* **2021**, *11*, 65–77. [CrossRef]
12. Su, M.; Hayati, D.; Tseng, S.; Chen, J.; Wei, H. Smart Care Using a DNN-Based Approach for Activities of Daily Living (ADL) Recognition. *Appl. Sci.* **2021**, *11*, 10. [CrossRef]

13. Chen, J.; Su, M.; Azzizi, V.; Wang, T.; Lin, W. Smart Project Management: Interactive Platform Using Natural Language Processing Technology. *Appl. Sci.* **2021**, *11*, 1597. [CrossRef]
14. Pinto, C.; Farinha, J.; Singh, S.; Raposo, H. Increasing the Reliability of an Electrical Power System in a Big European Hospital through the Petri Nets and Fuzzy Inference System Mamdani Modelling. *Appl. Sci.* **2021**, *11*, 2604. [CrossRef]
15. Fernandes, J.; Reis, J.; Melão, N.; Teixeira, L.; Amorim, M. The Role of Industry 4.0 and BPMN in the Arise of Condition-Based and Predictive Maintenance: A Case Study in the Automotive Industry. *Appl. Sci.* **2021**, *11*, 3438. [CrossRef]
16. Malta, A.; Mendes, M.; Farinha, T. Augmented Reality Maintenance Assistant Using YOLOv5. *Appl. Sci.* **2021**, *11*, 4758. [CrossRef]
17. Reis, J.; Cohen, Y.; Melão, N.; Costa, J.; Jorge, D. High-Tech Defense Industries: Developing Autonomous Intelligent Systems. *Appl. Sci.* **2021**, *11*, 4920. [CrossRef]
18. Preidel, M.; Stark, R. SemDaServ: A Systematic Approach for Semantic Data Specification of AI-Based Smart Service Systems. *Appl. Sci.* **2021**, *11*, 5148. [CrossRef]
19. Mateus, B.; Mendes, M.; Farinha, J.; Cardoso, A. Anticipating Future Behavior of an Industrial Press Using LSTM Networks. *Appl. Sci.* **2021**, *11*, 6101. [CrossRef]
20. Cavalieri, A.; Reis, J.; Amorim, M. A Conceptual Model Proposal to Assess the Effectiveness of IoT in Sustainability Orientation in Manufacturing Industry: An Environmental and Social Focus. *Appl. Sci.* **2022**, *12*, 5661. [CrossRef]
21. Rozenes, S.; Cohen, Y. Artificial Intelligence Synergetic Opportunities in Services: Conversational Systems Perspective. *Appl. Sci.* **2022**, *12*, 8363. [CrossRef]
22. Bokhari, S.; Myeong, S. Artificial Intelligence-Based Technological-Oriented Knowledge Management, Innovation, and E-Service Delivery in Smart Cities: Moderating Role of E-Governance. *Appl. Sci.* **2022**, *12*, 8732. [CrossRef]

applied sciences

Article

Smart Care Using a DNN-Based Approach for Activities of Daily Living (ADL) Recognition

Muchun Su [1], Diana Wahyu Hayati [2], Shaowu Tseng [1], Jiehhaur Chen [2,3,*] and Hsihsien Wei [4]

1 Department of Computer Science and Information Engineering, National Central University, Jhongli, Taoyuan 32001, Taiwan; muchun@csie.ncu.edu.tw (M.S.); shaowu@g.ncu.edu.tw (S.T.)
2 Department of Civil Engineering, National Central University, Jhongli, Taoyuan 32001, Taiwan; dwh.diana@gmail.com
3 Research Center of Smart Construction, National Central University, Jhongli, Taoyuan 32001, Taiwan
4 Department of Building and Real Estate, Hong Kong Polytechnic University, Hong Kong, China; hhwei@polyu.edu.hk
* Correspondence: jhchen@ncu.edu.tw; Tel.: +886-3-422-7151 (ext. 34112); Fax: +886-3-425-0675

Abstract: Health care for independently living elders is more important than ever. Automatic recognition of their Activities of Daily Living (ADL) is the first step to solving the health care issues faced by seniors in an efficient way. The paper describes a Deep Neural Network (DNN)-based recognition system aimed at facilitating smart care, which combines ADL recognition, image/video processing, movement calculation, and DNN. An algorithm is developed for processing skeletal data, filtering noise, and pattern recognition for identification of the 10 most common ADL including standing, bending, squatting, sitting, eating, hand holding, hand raising, sitting plus drinking, standing plus drinking, and falling. The evaluation results show that this DNN-based system is suitable method for dealing with ADL recognition with an accuracy rate of over 95%. The findings support the feasibility of this system that is efficient enough for both practical and academic applications.

Keywords: activities of daily living (ADL); pattern recognition; deep neural network (DNN); skeletal data processing; image processing

Citation: Su, M.; Hayati, D.W.; Tseng, S.; Chen, J.; Wei, H. Smart Care Using a DNN-Based Approach for Activities of Daily Living (ADL) Recognition. *Appl. Sci.* **2021**, *11*, 10. https://dx.doi.org/10.3390/app11010010

Received: 13 November 2020
Accepted: 19 December 2020
Published: 22 December 2020

1. Introduction

The proportion of the elderly in the population in most advanced countries now exceeds 15% [1], and the problems associated with aging including dementia and chronic illnesses are also increasing year by year. The care of the elderly is important but is especially difficult for those living alone. The situation is made worse given the current serious shortage of healthcare personnel. The concept of the Activities of Daily Living (ADL) first emerged in the 1950s in the field of healthcare as a tool to assess the daily self-care activities of disabled, and physically or mentally handicapped patients, such as those with dementia or chronic mental health problems. ADL usually include ordinary activities such as eating, shifting position, mobility, bathing, dressing, etc. These are typically rated on some scale such as the Barthel Index, Katz Index or Karnofsky Index, with the Barthel Index being most commonly used as a basis for evaluation of home care [2–5]. Motion recognition is a common technology today which has found applications in games, interactive computer-human interfaces, telepresence technology, and medical care. In the medical field it is currently used in remote rehabilitation systems, which enable a virtual rehabilitation teacher to evaluate the effectiveness of at home rehab and alleviate the problem of lack of medical resources in remote areas [6,7]. Motion recognition methods that focus on the description of image features have inspired researchers to improve the efficiency of the technology. ADL recognition for years has been discussed for years and some work has been carried out to improve sensor ability [8]. Recent studies have mostly concentrated on the development of methodologies, including machine learning, probabilistic finite, entropy-based, and knowledge-driven approaches [9–11]. The processing of data for ADL is also important in order to improving recognition accuracy [12–14]. It is desirable to deal to use a comprehensive methodology that provides solutions for the recognition of human behaviors, image processing, and movement calculation to achieve the goal of smart care.

This paper describes a Deep Neural Network (DNN)-based recognition system that combines ADL recognition, image/video processing, movement calculation, and DNN for the purpose of achieving smart care. It utilizes skeletal data obtained from color images from webcams or surveillance records, using the DNN for ADL recognition. The system takes advantage of low-cost and easy-to-install color cameras for monitoring indoor environments and incorporates a feature extraction method for motion recognition.

2. Related Applications for Neural Networks

Typically, neural networks (NN) perform well when dealing with simple problems, such as back-propagation (BP), where choosing the appropriate features is important [15–17]. However, this methodology may not be sufficient to deal with complex architectures and high-dimensional data. Complex architectures can be avoided by application of the concept of deep learning utilizing unsupervised learning methods to extract features from the data and then moving on to the process of supervised learning for labelling data [18,19]. In 2012, the Google Brain team applied deep learning to process YouTube videos [13]. They also developed the Tensor Processing Unit (TPU) [20–23], a customized special Integrated Circuit (IC) application. There are more and more examples of system architectures for the application of deep learning including DNN, Deep Belief Networks (DBN) and Convolutional Neuron Networks (CNN) [24,25]. CNN focuses on feature extraction and its classifier where the data are processed in its convolutional layer and connected in the pooling layer for full classification. The Convolutional Architecture for Fast Feature Embedding (Caffe) is another typical deep learning framework [26]. It has the advantages of being easy to use, fast training, and modularity [26,27]. In recent years, the use of Caffe version 2 has spread to being used in mobile devices with Android and IOS systems [28–30]. The above-studies demonstrate that DNN-oriented approaches and applications have become more efficient.

3. Data Collection and Processing

Easy acquisition and availability to the general population is the key to simulating real ADL. The ADL camera, available to most users must have the following basic prerequisites: resolution of 640 by 480, length of recorded video from 10 to 20 s and Frames Per Second (FPS) = 30. These conditions are essential for practical purposes. Therefore, the following criteria are set for the evaluations: (1) the video capture to the subject angle and distance can vary by 30 degrees from left to right, front to back; (2) the subjects can range in height 160–180 cm with a mean height around 173 cm. This range includes 80% of the population in Taiwan. (3) The top 10 most common ADL are selected including standing, bending, squatting, sitting, eating, raising one hand, raising two hands, sitting plus drinking, standing plus drinking, and falling [31–33]. Each subject performs one common ADL for 10 to 20 s for 4 times, giving 40 videos in total for training. Snap shots of each common ADL are illustrated in Figure 1. Based on the policy requested by Ministry of Science and Technology (MOST), Taiwan, every individual participating the research has signed the agreement and been permitted.

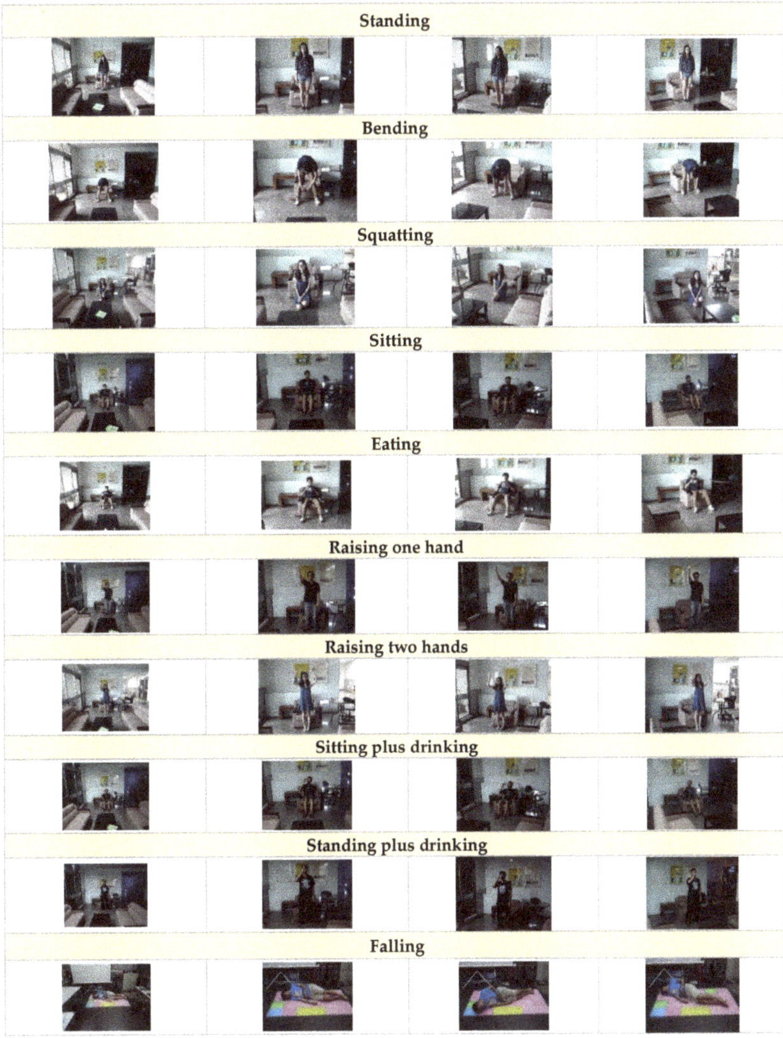

Figure 1. Ten most common ADL.

For indoor ADL determination one usually needs to consider consistent changes in the position of the human body as well as human skeletal information even for the same individual. It is necessary to normalize the skeletal information for pre-processing to generate features to facilitate neural network identification. The process of database normalization is divided into two parts, data translation and data scaling. Data translation is the translation of the neck as the new origin O_t', where each joint point $j_x(t)$ is subtracted from the coordinates of the neck $j_{Neck}(t)$ to perform translation, substituting the relevant nodes into the new joint point $j_x'(t)$. It can be expressed as follows:

$$j_x'(t) = j_x(t) - j_{Neck}(t), \tag{1}$$

where $j_x'(t)$ is the new coordinate of the joint point x at time t; $j_x(t)$ is the coordinate of the joint point at time t; $j_{Neck}(t)$ is the coordinate point of the neck at time t. During data scaling the skeleton is captured on a 2D image. The original length of the limbs is not known but the coordinates of the skeleton on the 2D image are pointed out. Consider the distance from the center of the hip joint to the neck at time *t* as the unit length. The algorithm is formulated as in Equation (2) where it can be seen that the proportion of *h*(*t*) in the whole body when bending over is smaller than that in the whole body when standing:

$$h(t) = \| \frac{(j_{LHip}(t) + j_{RHip}(t))}{2} - j_{Neck} \| . \tag{2}$$

Now, *s*(*t*) is solved for in Equation (3) using the two limb lengths as the basis for normalization:

$$s(t) = \| \frac{j_{LShoulder}(t) + j_{RShoulder}(t)}{2} - j_{Neck}(t) \| . \tag{3}$$

The maximum value for *s*(*t*) and *h*(*t*) is expressed as the unit length *U*(*t*) in Equation (4). By dividing the skeletal coordinate points, the new zooming joint coordinate point $S_x(t)$ can be obtained in Equation (5):

$$U(t) = max(h(t), s(t)); \tag{4}$$

$$S_x(t) = (\frac{j'_x(t)}{U(t)}). \tag{5}$$

The computation of the joint angle and changes in length from wrist to joint for extracting the features including the angle of the limb joint, angle between the end of the limb and the horizontal, and change in length from wrist to joint are described below.

3.1. Limb Joint Angle

The upper limbs are comprised of a combination of the left elbow, left shoulder, neck, right shoulder and right elbow. Similarly, the lower limbs have joint angles for the left knee, left hip joint, right hip joint, and right knee. A joint angle can be calculated using three selected points $p_1 - p_3$, where p_2 is the center point for calculation of the vectors $\vec{v}$ and $\vec{u}$, as shown in Equations (6) and (7):

$$\vec{v} = p_1 - p_2; \tag{6}$$

$$\vec{u} = p_3 - p_2. \tag{7}$$

The angle is calculated with *arctan*2 and the horizontal axis is from $-\pi$ to π so the value of *arctan*2 must be converted from $-\pi$ to 0 to π to 2π as in Equation (8):

$$va(\vec{s}) = \begin{cases} arctan2(\vec{s}), if\ 0 \geq arctan2(\vec{s}) > \pi \\ \pi + arctan2(\vec{s}), if\ 0 > arctan2(\vec{s}) \geq -\pi \end{cases}, \tag{8}$$

where $\vec{s}$ is the input vector and *arctan*2. The inverse tangent function is used to calculate the angle. Substituting $\vec{v}$ and $\vec{u}$ into Equations (6) and (7) we obtained Equation (8) in order to yield the angles *i* and *j*. The angle *a*(*i*, *j*) relative to $\vec{u}$ can be found by

$$a(i,j) = (i - j) \times \frac{180}{\pi}. \tag{9}$$

The angles calculated above are shown in Figure 2 where $\theta1$ to $\theta5$ are the upper limb joint angles, and $\theta6$ to $\theta10$ are the lower limb joint angles.

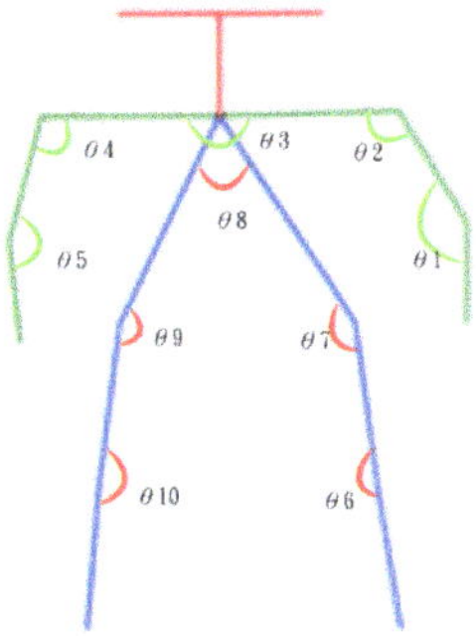

Figure 2. Joint angle diagram.

3.2. *Angle between the Limb End and the Horizontal*

The human skeleton is closely related to the nearby space while the individual is moving. The computation of the angles between the limbs and the horizontal axis is the same as for the joint angles, by plugging the vectors into Equation (8). There are a total of four angles shown in Figure 3.

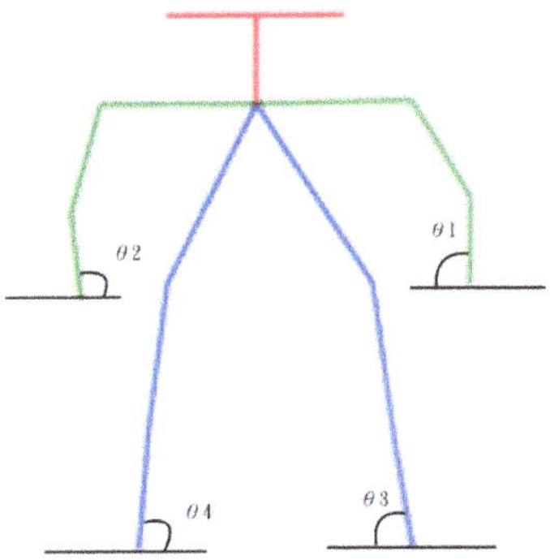

Figure 3. Four limb angles.

3.3. *Length Change for Wrist to Joint*

The position/height from the wrists to the joints can be clearly recognized in postures such as raising the hands, sitting, and squatting. Assuming that the shoulder and knee joints are taken as the reference points with which to calculate the change in positions known as the height difference in the y-axis. The calculation process is expressed as:

$$U_y(t) = \| \left(j^y_{LHip}(t) - j^y_{RHip}(t) \right) - j^y_{Neck}(t) \|, \quad (10)$$

where $j^y_x(t)$ represents the position of the $y-$axis for the joint point; and $U_y(t)$ is the length from the hip joint to the neck. The computation to determine the relative distance between the wrist and check point c is shown in Equation (11) below:

$$VL(p,c,t) = \begin{cases} p - c, if\ abs(p-c) < U_y(t) \\ U_y(t), if\ (p-c) > U_y(t) \\ -U_y(t), if\ (p-c) < U_y(t), \end{cases} \quad (11)$$

where p is the y-axis position of the wrist; c is the y-axis position of the check point in a given space.

Next, we adopt the sliding window concept to filter out noise. All input images are classified into [0, 1] and sorted in a sequence. When a pre-terminated window is set at time = *t*, e.g., 3 slots, there are two images labeled "0" and one labeled "1". The movement in the image is labeled "0" by voting from the count of "0" and "1". At time = *t* + 1, voting again determines the movement in the image which is labeled "1", as shown in Figure 4.

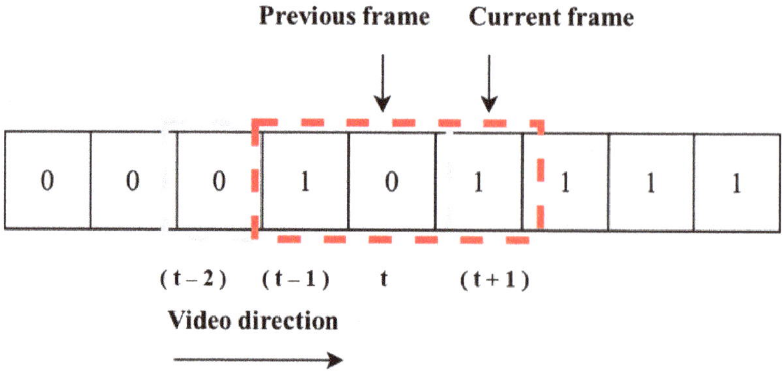

Figure 4. Sliding window concept.

4. DNN-Based Systems for ADL Recognition

The most commonly used neural networks to solve practical problems are the single layer BPNN, multi-layer BPNN, CNN, and DNN. This study develops a recognition system for ADL using DNN and compares it with the single layer BPNN, multi-layer BPNN, and CNN methods to evaluate the feasibility of the proposed system. We start with consideration of the parameters for these neural networks, using the following suggested parameter settings [34–36]: (1) activation functions = sigmoid; (2) learning rate = 0.8 for BP neural networks and 0.01 for DNN; (3) optimal method = gradient correction for BP neural networks and Adam optimization for DNN; (4) five hidden layers with 5–50 neurons in each layer for DNN, e.g., DNN with a [20, 20, 20, 20, 20] classifier; (5) two fully connected classifiers for CNN to deal with 2048 dimensions, 384 neurons for the first hidden layers, 192 neurons for the second hidden layers since the kernel size of convolution layer = 5 by 5 with step = 1 by 1 and pooling layer = 3 by 3 with step = 2 by 2.

The feature extraction for recognition of ADL is examined for comparison among the four methods. Comparison is conducted using 3-fold cross-validation. As can be seen in Figure 5, all four methods have recognition accuracy rates of greater than 98% at least. The DNN with a [30, 30, 30, 30, 30] classifier and CNN systems perform even better, reaching and accuracy rate of over 99%. Next, we carry out multi angle tests using these four methods. In reality, it is not guaranteed that we can obtain front facing video of every subject. We shoot side and front footage twice in each practice session, and then randomly mix these videos together for system recognition. As can be seen in Figure 6, DNN with a [30, 30, 30, 30, 30] classifier and CNN systems have almost the same test results, with an accuracy rate of approximately 97.5%, slightly better than for the multi- and single layer BPNNs. To check whether the ADL recognition process works for most subjects, to meet the initial three requirements, we randomly select video footage of different subjects with different combinations of movement for 3-fold cross-validation. Frankly speaking, all the NN applications perform well for ADL recognition. As shown in Figure 7, all four systems have high accuracy rates greater than 98% for training. The DNN system with a [30, 30, 30, 30, 30] classifier has the highest accuracy rate, around 95%, for testing, among these four systems. The results confirm that the DNN-based system for ADL recognition performs the best among the major NN applications.

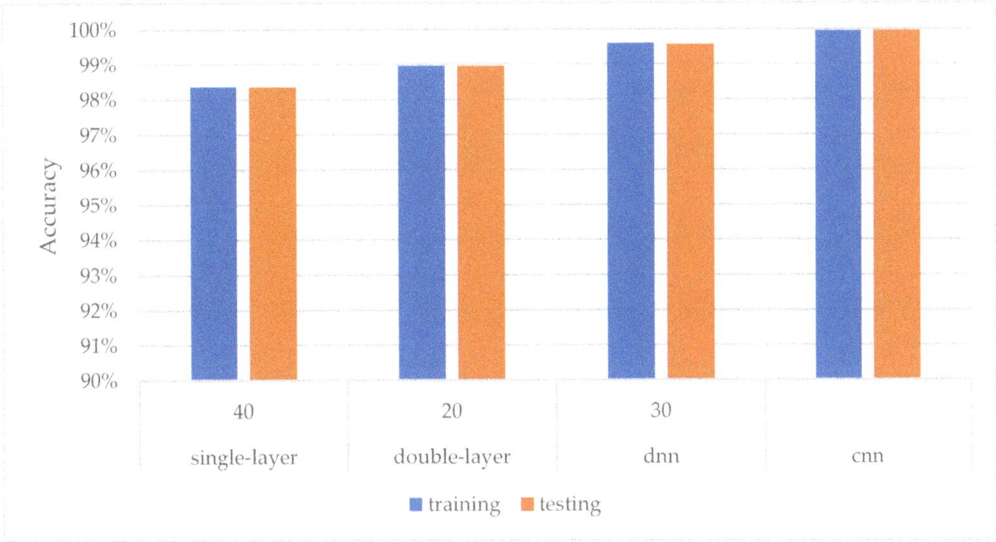

Figure 5. Feature extraction comparison among the four major NN methods.

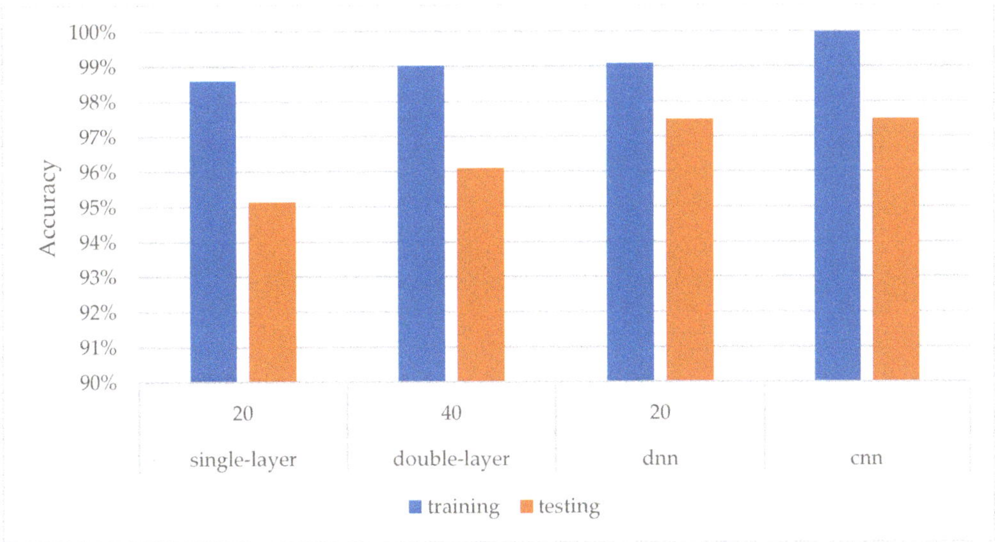

Figure 6. Multi shooting angle comparison among the four major NN methods.

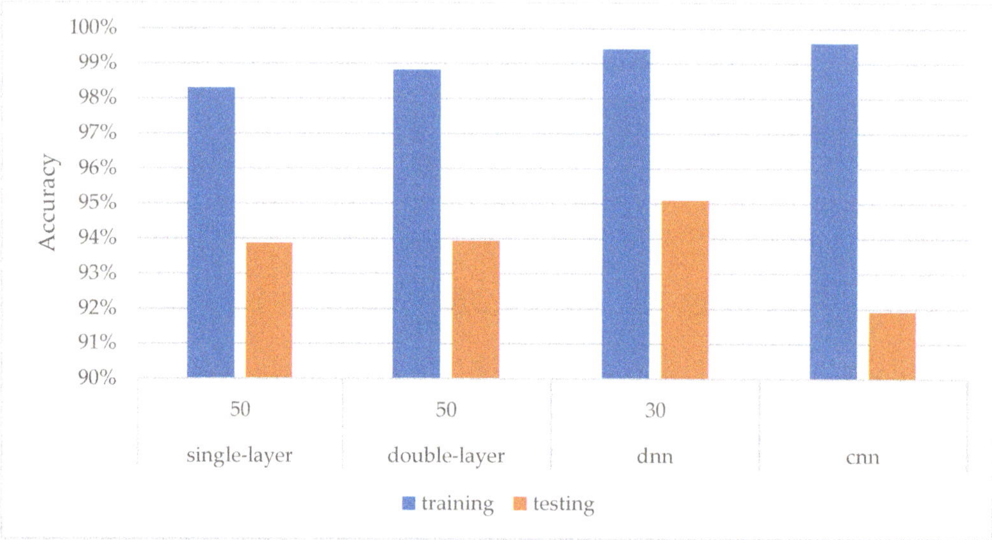

Figure 7. Scenario comparison among the four major NN methods.

An important step to ensure better efficiency and accuracy for DNN-based recognition system is to determine the size of the sliding window. The frame in the Figure 4 is an example for a 3-click window. A small window can reduce the computation/processing time but may not be able to yield high accuracy. On the other hand, a relatively large window may provide a higher accuracy rate but will usually cause system lags in recognition, sometimes significant enough to render the system impractical. Figure 8 exhibits a [30, 30, 30, 30, 30] DNN classifier with window sizes of 1, 3, 5, 7, and 9. When the click number increases, the computational penalty for the size of the window leads to computational lag, because too much information may contain enough noise to reduce the accuracy of the results. It is clear that the best accuracy is obtained with a 7-click sliding window. The developed ADL recognition system is completed using a [30, 30, 30, 30, 30] DNN classifier with a 7-click sliding window to filter out noise, to facilitate recognition, to increase efficiency, and to yield higher accuracy.

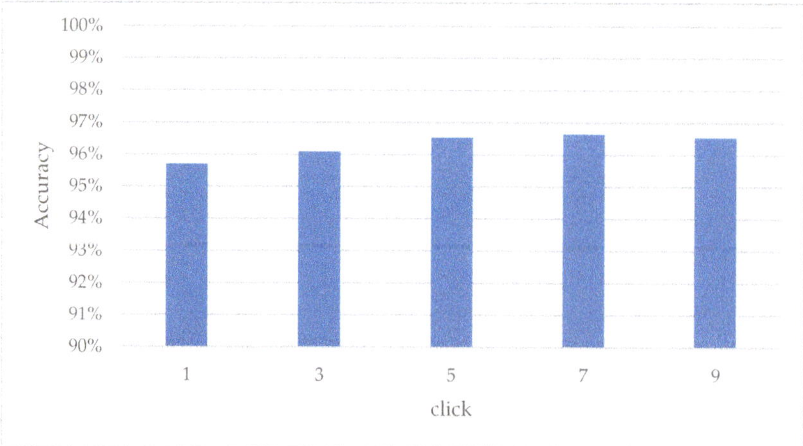

Figure 8. Accuracy comparison among 1–9 click sliding windows.

5. Evaluation and Results

The proposed system is empirically evaluated by adopting lengthier video footage with various ADL than that used in the previous section. A 5-min video containing all 10 types of the most common ADL was used. Each type of ADL appeared randomly 3 to 5 times in the footage. Each ADL was manually marked and compared with the evaluation results In Table 1. The evaluation results include the accuracy rate and mis-classification rate. The average accuracy rate is 95.1%. The proposed system performs perfectly (100% accuracy rate) for 5 types of ADL: standing, raising one hand, raising two hands, sitting plus drinking, and standing plus drinking. The proposed system also works effectively with an accuracy recognition rate greater than 95% for the ADL of sitting, eating, and falling. It is the industry health care standard that the proposed system detects falling with a high accuracy rate at 97%, as falling is especially dangerous for seniors. There are two types of ADL (bending and squatting) that are relatively easy for the proposed system to misclassify: bending can be misclassified as squatting or sitting, and squatting may be misclassified as sitting or bending. Compared with Figure 1, there was one case where eating was misclassified as bending perhaps due to the similarity of the bending of the arm(s) or leg(s) to the eating ADL while sitting. The reason for misclassification is mainly lies the similarity of skeletal positioning in certain postures, as shown in Table 1 and Figure 1. Our proposed methodology combines human behavior recognition, image processing, movement calculation, and DNN for smart care applications. The originality of our approach lies in the calculation of the limb joint angle, angle between the limb and the horizontal axis, changes in length for the wrist joint, and using the sliding click method to filter out video noise. We have demonstrated the originality of our approach and it feasibility for both practical and academic applications.

Table 1. Evaluation result for DNN-based system.

	Standing	Bending	Squatting	Sitting	Eating	Raising One Hand	Raising Two Hands	Sitting plus Drink-ing	Standing Plus Drink-ing	Falling	Accuracy
Standing	100	-	-	-	-	-	-	-	-	-	100
Bending	4	80	7	6	1	-	-	-	-	-	80
Squatting	1	6	82	11	-	-	-	-	-	-	82
Sitting	-	-	3	97	-	-	-	-	-	-	97
Eating	-	-	-	-	95	-	-	1	4	-	95
Raising one hand	-	-	-	-	-	100	-	-	-	-	100
Raising two hands	-	-	-	-	-	-	100	-	-	-	100
Sitting plus drink-ing	-	-	-	-	-	-	-	100	-	-	100
Standing plus drink-ing	-	-	-	-	-	-	-	-	100	-	100
Falling	-	2	-	-	1	-	-	-	-	97	97

6. Conclusions

A feasible detection system for ADL is beneficial for practitioners, especially for health care and safety applications designed to protect seniors from falling. This research develops a NN-based system to detect the ten most common types of ADL including standing, bending, squatting, sitting, eating, raising one hand, raising two hands, sitting plus drinking, standing plus drinking, and falling. The proposed system starts with ADL image collection and processing using the sliding window concept, followed by the skeletal recognition technique for identification of ADL. Four types of most common NN methods are compared to determine which one is optimal for ADL recognition. The results show the DNN-based system to have the optimal outcome of a 95% accuracy rate in comparison to the single layer BPNN, multi-layer BPNN, and CNN systems. The empirical evaluation using lengthier footage containing all types of ADL randomly mixed together yields a high average accuracy rate of 95.1%. The proposed system even performs perfectly with a 100% accuracy rate for five types of ADL: standing, raising one hand, raising two hands rising, sitting plus drinking, and standing plus drinking.

This study describes a novel mechanism suitable for both practical and academic applications. Integrating the easily accessible ADL images, data processing, and noise filtering concepts with DNN method, we produce a camera-ready system for practical use. It has a high successful identification rate >95% for the recognition of most common ADL, especially for the detection of falling at 97%. The system does not require high-end equipment to obtain footage for recognition and can easily process most common ADL. It is affordable and efficient enough to benefit the users. Some suggestions for follow-up studies could include in more efficient algorithms that yield higher accuracy rates and more detailed posture recognition. The evaluation was conducted using a 5-min footage containing all 10 types of the most common ADL. Although each type of ADL appeared randomly 3 to 5 times in the footage, a larger data set is needed for further evaluation of the method such as lengthier videos and numerous videos with more complex or mixed ADLs. Future studies may also focus on improving the relatively poor recognition rates for postures such as bending and squatting either by providing higher-resolution video or developing more advanced algorithms.

Author Contributions: Conceptualization M.S.; Methodology, M.S. and S.T.; Validation, D.W.H. and J.C.; Resources, M.S. and S.T.; Writing—original draft preparation, D.W.H. and J.C.; writing—review and editing, J.C. and H.W. All authors have read and agreed to the published version of the manuscript.

Funding: This paper was partly supported by the Ministry of Science and Technology (MOST), Taiwan, for promoting academic excellent of universities under grant numbers of [MOST 109-2622-E-008-018-CC2]; [MOST 108-2221-E-008-002-MY3]; [MOST 109-2221-E-008-059-MY3]; [MOST 107-2221-E-008-084-MY2]; [MOST 109-2634-F-008-007]; [MOST 108-2634-F-008-001].

Conflicts of Interest: The authors declare no conflict of interest.

References

1. Department of Economic and Social Affairs. *World Population Ageing 2019*; United Nations: New York, NY, USA, 2020.
2. Landi, F.; Tua, E.; Onder, G.; Carrara, B.; Sgadari, A.; Rinaldi, C.; Gambassi, G.; Lattanzio, F.; Bernabei, R. Minimum data set for home care: A valid instrument to assess frail older people living in the community. *Med. Care* **2000**, *38*, 1184–1190. [CrossRef] [PubMed]
3. Fortinsky, R.H.; Granger, C.V.; Seltzer, G.B. The use of functional assessment in understanding home care needs. *Med. Care* **1981**, *19*, 489–497. [CrossRef] [PubMed]
4. Sainsbury, A.; Seebass, G.; Bansal, A.; Young, J.B. Reliability of the Barthel Index when used with older people. *Age Ageing* **2005**, *34*, 228–232. [CrossRef] [PubMed]
5. Shah, S.; Vanclay, F.; Cooper, B. Improving the sensitivity of the Barthel Index for stroke rehabilitation. *J. Clin. Epidemiol.* **1989**, *42*, 703–709. [CrossRef]
6. Alamri, A.; Eid, M.; Iglesias, R.; Shirmohammadi, S.; El-Saddik, A. Haptic Virtual Rehabilitation Exercises for Poststroke Diagnosis. *IEEE Trans. Instrum. Meas.* **2008**, *57*, 1876–1884. [CrossRef]

7. Brennan, D.M.; Mawson, S.; Brownsell, S. Telerehabilitation: Enabling the remote delivery of healthcare, rehabilitation, and self management. *Stud. Health Technol. Inform.* **2009**, *145*, 48.
8. Gambi, E.; Temperini, G.; Galassi, R.; Senigagliesi, L.; De Santis, A. ADL Recognition Through Machine Learning Algorithms on IoT Air Quality Sensor Dataset. *IEEE Sens. J.* **2020**, *20*, 13562–13570. [CrossRef]
9. Viard, K.; Fanti, M.P.; Faraut, G.; Lesage, J.J. Human activity discovery and recognition using probabilistic finite-state automata. *IEEE Trans. Autom. Sci. Eng.* **2020**, *17*, 2085–2096. [CrossRef]
10. Howedi, A.; Lotfi, A.; Pourabdollah, A. An Entropy-Based Approach for Anomaly Detection in Activities of Daily Living in the Presence of a Visitor. *Entropy* **2020**, *22*, 845. [CrossRef]
11. Rawashdeh, M.; Al Zamil, M.G.; Samarah, S.; Hossain, M.; Muhammad, G. A knowledge-driven approach for activity recognition in smart homes based on activity profiling. *Future Gener. Comput. Syst.* **2020**, *107*, 924–941. [CrossRef]
12. Rafferty, J.; Nugent, C.; Liu, J.; Chen, L. An approach to provide dynamic, illustrative, video-based guidance within a goal-driven smart home. *J. Ambient. Intell. Hum. Comput.* **2016**, *11*, 3045–3056. [CrossRef]
13. Kim, K.; Jalal, A.; Mahmood, M. Vision-Based Human Activity Recognition System Using Depth Silhouettes: A Smart Home System for Monitoring the Residents. *J. Electr. Eng. Technol.* **2019**, *14*, 2567–2573. [CrossRef]
14. Jalal, A.; Kamal, S.; Kim, D. A Depth Video-based Human Detection and Activity Recognition using Multi-features and Embedded Hidden Markov Models for Health Care Monitoring Systems. *Int. J. Interact. Multimed. Artif. Intell.* **2017**, *4*, 54–62. [CrossRef]
15. Harikumar, R.; Vinothkumar, B. Performance analysis of neural networks for classification of medical images with wavelets as a feature extractor. *Int. J. Imaging Syst. Technol.* **2015**, *25*, 33–40. [CrossRef]
16. Gupta, A.; Shreevastava, M. Medical diagnosis using back propagation algorithm. *Int. J. Emerg. Technol. Adv. Eng.* **2011**, *1*, 55–58.
17. Arulmurugan, R.; Anandakumar, H. Early detection of lung cancer using wavelet feature descriptor and feed forward back propagation neural networks classifier. *VipIMAGE 2019* **2018**, 103–110.
18. Najafabadi, M.M.; Villanustre, F.; Khoshgoftaar, T.M.; Seliya, N.; Wald, R.; Muharemagic, E. Deep learning applications and challenges in big data analytics. *J. Big Data* **2015**, *2*, 1. [CrossRef]
19. Shen, D.; Wu, G.; Suk, H. Deep Learning in Medical Image Analysis. *Annu. Rev. Biomed. Eng.* **2017**, *19*, 221–248. [CrossRef]
20. Markoff, J. How many computers to identify a cat? 16,000. *New York Times*, 25 June 2002.
21. Jouppi, N.; Young, C.; Patil, N.; Patterson, D. Motivation for and Evaluation of the First Tensor Processing Unit. *IEEE Micro* **2018**, *38*, 10–19. [CrossRef]
22. Pandey, P.; Basu, P.; Chakraborty, K. Green TPU: Improving timing error resilience of a near-threshold tensor processing unit. In Proceedings of the 2019 56th ACM/IEEE Design Automation Conference (DAC), Las Vegas, NV, USA, 2–6 June 2019; pp. 1–6.
23. Dean, J.; Patterson, D.; Young, C. A new golden age in computer architecture: Empowering the machine-learning revolution. *IEEE Micro* **2018**, *38*, 21–29. [CrossRef]
24. Zhao, G.; Zhang, G.; Ge, Q.; Liu, X. Research advances in fault diagnosis and prognostic based on deep learning. In Proceedings of the 2016 Prognostics and System Health Management Conference (PHM-Chengdu), Chengdu, China, 19–25 October 2016; pp. 1–6.
25. Abu Ghosh, M.M.; Maghari, A.Y. A Comparative Study on Handwriting Digit Recognition Using Neural Networks. In Proceedings of the 2017 International Conference on Promising Electronic Technologies (ICPET), Deir El-Balah, Poland, 16–17 October 2017; pp. 77–81.
26. Jia, Y.; Shelhamer, E.; Donahue, J.; Karayev, S.; Long, J.; Girshick, R.; Guadarrama, L.; Darrell, T. Caffe: Convolutional architecture for fast feature embedding. In Proceedings of the 22nd ACM international conference on Multimedia, Orlando, FL, USA, 21–25 October 2015; pp. 675–678.
27. Je, S.; Nguyen, H.; Lee, J. Image Recognition Method Using Modular Systems. In Proceedings of the 2015 International Conference on Computational Science and Computational Intelligence (CSCI), Las Vegas, NV, USA, 7–9 December 2015; pp. 504–508.
28. Ignatov, A.; Timofte, R.; Chou, W.; Wang, K.; Wu, M.; Hartley, T.; Van Gool, L. AI Benchmark: Running Deep Neural Networks on Android Smartphones. In Proceedings of the Computer Vision, European Conference on Computer Vision, Munich, Germany, 8–14 September 2018.
29. Turchenko, V.; Luczak, A. Creation of a deep convolutional auto-encoder in caffe. In Proceedings of the 2017 9th IEEE International Conference on Intelligent Data Acquisition and Advanced Computing Systems: Technology and Applications (IDAACS), Bucharest, Romania, 21–23 September 2017; pp. 651–659.
30. Ikeda, M.; Oda, T.; Barolli, L. A vegetable category recognition system: A comparison study for caffe and Chainer DNN frameworks. *Soft Comput.* **2017**, *23*, 3129–3136. [CrossRef]
31. Hn, C.; Saito, T.; Kai, I. Functional disability in activities of daily living and instrumental activities of daily living among Nepalese Newar elderly. *Public Health* **2008**, *122*, 394–396.
32. Liu, Y.-H.; Chang, H.-J.; Huang, C.-C. The Unmet Activities of Daily Living (ADL) Needs of Dependent Elders and their Related Factors: An Approach from Both an Individual- and Area-Level Perspective. *Int. J. Gerontol.* **2012**, *6*, 163–168. [CrossRef]
33. Wang, Q.; Tapia, G.; Jose, A.G. Household heating associated with disability in activities of daily living among Chinese middle-aged and elderly: A longitudinal study. *Environ. Health Prev. Med.* **2020**, *25*, 49. [CrossRef] [PubMed]
34. Song, W.J.; Choi, S.G.; Lee, E.S. Prediction and Comparison of Electrochemical Machining on Shape Memory Alloy (SMA) using Deep Neural Network (DNN). *J. Electrochem. Sci. Technol.* **2018**, *10*, 276–283. [CrossRef]

35. Wang, R.; Jiang, Y.; Lou, J.; Cheng, H.K. TDR: Two-stage deep recommendation model based on mSDA and DNN. *Expert Syst. Appl.* **2020**, *145*, 113116. [CrossRef]
36. Zaki, A.U.M.; Hu, Y.; Jiang, X. Partial discharge localization in 3-D with a multi-DNN model based on a virtual measurement method. *IEEE Access* **2020**, *8*, 87434–87445. [CrossRef]

applied sciences

MDPI

Technical Note

Smart Project Management: Interactive Platform Using Natural Language Processing Technology

Jieh-Haur Chen [1,2,*], Mu-Chun Su [3], Vidya Trisandini Azzizi [2], Ting-Kwei Wang [4] and Wei-Jen Lin [3]

1 Research Center of Smart Construction, National Central University, Jhongli, Taoyuan 32001, Taiwan
2 Department of Civil Engineering, National Central University, Jhongli, Taoyuan 32001, Taiwan; ipidski@gmail.com
3 Department of Computer Science and Information Engineering, National Central University, Jhongli, Taoyuan 32001, Taiwan; muchun@csie.ncu.edu.tw (M.-C.S.); k946201@gmail.com (W.-J.L.)
4 School of Management Science and Real Estate, Chongqing University, Chongqing 400044, China; tingkwei@cqu.edu.cn
* Correspondence: jhchen@ncu.edu.tw; Tel.: +886-3-422-7151 (ext. 34112); Fax: +886-3-425-0675

Abstract: Technological developments have made the construction industry efficient. The aim of this research is to solve communication interaction problems to build a project management platform using the interactive concept of natural language processing technology. A comprehensive literature review and expert interviews associated with techniques dealing with natural languages suggests the proposed system containing the Progressive Scale Expansion Network (PSENet), Convolutional Recurrent Neural Network (CRNN), and Bi-directional Recurrent Neutral Networks Convolutional Recurrent Neural Network (BRNN-CNN) toolboxes to extract the key words for construction projects contracts. The results show that a fully automatic platform facilitating contract management is achieved. For academic domains, the Contract Keyword Detection (CKD) mechanism integrating PSENet, CRNN, and BRNN-CNN approaches to cope with real-time massive document flows is novel in the construction industry. For practice, the proposed approach brings significant reduction for manpower and human error, an alternative for settling down misunderstanding or disputes due to real-time and precise communication, and a solution for efficient documentary management. It connects all contract stakeholders proficiently.

Keywords: project management platform; natural language processing; interactive concept; construction contract; keyword detection

Citation: Chen, J.-H.; Su, M.-C.; Azzizi, V.-T.; Wang, T.-K.; Lin, W.-J. Smart Project Management: Interactive Platform Using Natural Language Processing Technology. *Appl. Sci.* **2021**, *11*, 1597. https://doi.org/10.3390/app11041597

Academic Editors: Marlene Amorim, Yuval Cohen and João Reis
Received: 24 December 2020
Accepted: 7 February 2021
Published: 10 February 2021

1. Introduction

Most of current construction industry management is mainly based on human rule management assisted by technology systems to implement automatic construction management [1–5]. However, the quality of construction management systems on the market is uneven, a common blind point for them is that they cannot effectively connect and interact with each party [6]. Data input and output for systems cannot be easily shared according to the needs of the work, which becomes obstacles among parties [7–10]. As a result, party cooperation within a construction project may not work smoothly among all phases, including planning, procurement, etc. Party members may need to face consequences by poor management, which may be as serious as litigation [11–14]. A need to facilitate management process and lower barriers among all contract parties is overwhelming. In summary, the construction and property industry are currently facing problems caused by the inability of the current management system to share and interact information [15–17]. The aim of this research is to solve communication interaction problems and to build a project management platform using an interactive concept of natural language processing technology. Through a comprehensive literature review, interviewing experts, developing the bridges (keyword detection) connecting parties, the interactive platform for construction contract stakeholders is developed for more in-depth management.

2. Project Management and Performance

The Project Management Body of Knowledge (PMBOK) issued by the Project Management Institute (PMI) defines project management as applying knowledge, skills, tools, and techniques to project activities to meet project needs [18]. The PMBOK also divides the project management process into five stages: Initializing, Planning, Executing, Control, and Closing. It also explains in detail the ten areas of knowledge required for project management in the process of project management, such as the knowledge, skills, tools, and techniques required by the project management team at each stage. For engineering, in order to improve the quality and efficiency of the project, it is necessary to complete the entire life cycle of the project. It can be used as a reference for the entire life cycle of a development project. It states that the entire life cycle of public works includes feasibility assessment, planning, design, tendering, construction, acceptance to takeover, and operation stages; it also states that important work items at each stage include planning and design stage, project bidding stage, project implementation phase, and takeover operation phase [19]. In addition, a handbook for the Management of the Life Cycle Performance suggested public building design plans as a perspective plan [20]. The whole life cycle of the plan is divided into five main phases: editing, review, pre-operation, project implementation, and term/operation phases. Project management success encompasses both the project's objectives and its completion within its normal time, cost, and scope, and its focus by including stakeholder requirements [21].

However, for construction projects, the life cycle scope does not refer to new construction or expansion work. The life cycle defined in this study focuses on the stages of project bidding and performance. Through the platform's progress management and quality management functions, it can be assured that the project can be carried out as expected. The questions in developing a platform to deal with construction project management are raised as: (1) system availability for project contracts, (2) system's impact to a company, (3) precise control for project's change orders, and (4) the company's willingness to promote a system that can facilitate project management albeit being costly.

3. Applications for Scene Text Detection

Scene text detection is intuitively understood. Given an image, all the positions where the text appears in this image are needed, that is, find the position of each object in the image, and mark the objects in the bounding box because images are divided into two categories, with and without text, which is a single-class detection task. Faster Region-based Convolutional Recurrent Neural Network (RCNN) can be used for text detection [22,23]. The Faster RCNN model is mainly composed of two modules: the Region Proposal Network (RPN) candidate frame extraction module and the Faster RCNN detection module, which can be subdivided into four parts: (1) Conv Layer, (2) RPN, (3) Roll Pooling, and (4) Classification and Regression. The steps of Faster RCNN are divided into [24]: (1) The basic network performs feature extraction, (2) features are sent to RPN for candidate frame extraction, (3) the classification layer classifies the objects in the candidate frame, and the regression layer fine-tunes the (x, y, w, h) of the candidate frame. However, the effect of Faster RCNN as text detection is not ideal due to the uniqueness of each text. For example, common objects have obvious closed edge contours, but the text does not. The text contains multiple texts, and there is text between the texts. If the interval between texts cannot be detected, each character is treated as a text line and it is framed instead of the entire line. Based on the said reasons, general networks such as Faster RCNN must be improved to design a new network framework suitable for text detection.

A work regarding detecting text in Natural Image was proposed [24]. This deep neural network is called Connectionist Text Proposal Network (CTPN), which can accurately locate lines of text in natural images. CTPN detects text lines directly in a series of fine-grained text proposals in convolutional feature correspondence. In this paper, a vertical anchor mechanism was developed to jointly predict the position and text/non-text score of each fixed-width proposal, greatly improving. For positioning accuracy, the sequence is proposed to be naturally connected through a loop neural network, which is integrated into the convolutional network to form an end-to-end trainable model. This allows CTPN to explore rich image context information and detect blurry text. CTPN works reliably on multiple scales and multiple languages without further follow-up processing. It departs from the previous method that required multiple steps of filtering from the bottom up.

However, CTPN has an obvious disadvantage. It is not good for non-horizontal text detection. In this paper, the text in the detection result picture is horizontal [25,26]. In order to solve the shortcomings of poor performance of CTPN in non-horizontal detection, a study introduced a detection approach that can detect text at any angle, which is generally called, in this approach, Segment Linking (SegLink) [24]. The main idea is to decompose the text into two locally detectable elements, that is, segments and links. For example, according to Figure 1, the first picture is a box of segments detected in the picture; the second picture is a line with links detected between adjacent segments; the third picture merges the whole words into segments connected by links [24].

Figure 1. Illustration for Segment Linking (SegLink) processes [24].

The characteristic of text detection is that the aspect ratio is particularly large or small, and there is usually a rotation angle. If four parameters (x, y, w, h) of target detection were used to specify a target position, the error obtained will obviously be too big, so, then, one lets the model learn another parameter θ, and this θ represents the rotation angle of the text box. The parameters returned from the original (x, y, w, h) to (x, y, w, h, θ), the error in solving the angle occurs. This approach incorporates both the idea of the CTPN small-scale candidate box and the idea of the Single Shot MultiBox Detector (SSD) approach, and achieves the effect of state-of-art of text detection in natural scenes. Then one analyzes the network architecture of SegLink to further understand how SegLink can achieve efficient multi-angle text detection. The SegLink architecture adopts the idea of SSD. First, Visual Geometry Group (VGG) 16 is used as the feature extraction for the backbone. The fully connected layers (fc6, fc7) of VGG are replaced by convolutional layers (conv6, conv7). One connects the conv layers conv8 to conv11. It is worth noting that the size between conv4–conv11 decreases in turn (each layer is one-half of the previous layer). This approach is for multiscale target detection, that is, large feature maps are good at detecting small objects. By using multiple feature maps of different scales and detecting segments and links from six feature layers, text lines of different sizes can be detected.

There is no mention of whether the approach can detect curved text [27]. The method of segmenting and integrating the complete text line first detects and then merges, which undoubtedly greatly increases the loss of text detection accuracy and time consumption. A study in 2017 proposed that efficient and accurate scene text can solve multi-angle text detection and is simple and powerful [25]. There are multiple stages of text detection; taking the region proposals detection approach as an example, it includes the stages of candidate box extraction, bounding box regression, and merging candidate box. There is (a) horizontal word detection and recognition pipeline proposed by [28], (b) multidirectional text detection pipeline [29], (c) horizontal text detection using CTPN, and (d) Efficient and

Accurate Scene Text (EAST) pipeline, which eliminates most of the intermediate steps, consists of only two stages, and is much simpler than previous solutions. The author of EAST believes that splitting a text detection approach into multiple phases does not actually have many benefits, and it is correct to implement a true end-to-end text detection network. Therefore, the EAST process is quite concise, and is only divided into the Fully Convolutional Network (FCN) generation text line parameter stage and the local perception Non-Maximum Suppression (NMS) stage [30], which has further improved the accuracy and speed of text detection. To understand the advantages of EAST for text detection from the network architecture, EAST's network architecture is divided into three parts: feature extraction layer, feature fusion layer, and output layer. Feature extraction layer: Backbone uses deep but lightweight neural networks (PVANet) for feature extraction [31], and then sends it to the convolution layer, and the size of the subsequent volume base layer decreases sequentially (the size is half of the previous layer), and the number of convolution kernels increases sequentially (for the previous layer double). Feature maps at different stages are extracted so that feature maps of different scales can be obtained. The purpose is to solve the problem of intense text line scale transformation. Large-size layers can be used to predict small text lines, and small-size layers can be used to predict large text. Feature merging layer: merge the extracted features. The merging rule adopts the U-net method [32]. The merging rule is to merge the top features from the feature extraction network downward according to the corresponding rules [27].

4. Expert Interview

Having a comprehensive understanding for the interactive concepts, the follow-up steps are to determine what and how to develop the platform. It starts from the suggestions by expert interviews, which are set to explore the feasibility and know-how in the construction industry. Scholars suggested any number between 6 and 20 of experts with experience greater than 10 years in the target industry [33–35]. Based on convenient sampling method, interviews with 10 experts in different professional fields were conducted. The first part for expert interviews is to fill in the basic information of name, company/origination, job title, and service years in the construction industry. The second part is the interview for 40–60 min individually based on the questions derivative from the summary of Section 2:

- Does your company currently have a management system related to project contracts?
- How do you think that a management system influences your company?
- If there were a change order occurring to anyone of your construction projects, would it make the contract stakeholder(s) not to precisely perform cost control?
- If an interactive platform for stakeholders of a construction contract can be established and carried out, coordination and communication between parties should be improved, benefiting the project. Would you be willing to introduce it? Any other concerns?

The summary from the expertise can be recapitulated as follows: a common problem in the construction industry today is the inequality of information and the lack of a platform to integrate information. It can be seen that interviews show that most of the respondents are willing to introduce interactive platform(s) for stakeholders to benefit engineering project contracts. In addition to ensure information sharing, their expertise also bring about the establishment of a complete resume for buildings, the realization of evidence preservation in combination with the documentary management, intellectual property rights, risk identification, early warnings for overdue progress, budget, and schedule. Therefore, they recommend a robust system that automatically processes documentary management by contract keyword detection.

5. Mechanism for Contract Keyword Detection Approach

Integrating the suggestions from the literature review and expert interviews, the proposed approach is to adopt natural language processing technology to build an interactive platform for engineering project contract stakeholders. To do so, based on pre-determined keywords by users and applications introduced in the literature review, we designed a mechanism that integrates Progressive Scale Expansion Network (PSENet), Convolutional Recurrent Neural Network (CRNN), and Bi-directional Recurrent Neutral Networks Convolutional Recurrent Neural Net-work (BRNN-CNN) toolboxes to extract the key words for contracts shown in Figure 2. The dotted box in Figure 2 is the proposed approach, Contract Keyword Detection (CKD), where there are three steps to accomplish keyword contract extraction inclusive of text detection, text recognition, and interpretation. Starting from the inputs that may be gathered in figure or photo format, PSENet detects all possible text location and then positions them in order to yield bounding boxes where PSENet is a built toolbox that contains Chinese text with a databank of ICDAR 2017 Reading Chinese Text In the Wild (RCTW) with a total of 12,263 images, of which 8034 were used as the training set and 4229 were used as the test set [24]. In this step, shape robust text detection was used as a method for scene text recognition [31]. This method is compared with other scene text detection methods and the quadrilateral bounding box is not required. It can accurately detect text instances with any shape, and its accuracy is higher than that of other methods. In this stage of the experiment, a real lease contract was prepared, and the PSENet method to detect the text part of the contract was run, shown in Appendix A. PSENet accurately determined the location of the text with a success rate of nearly 95%. Extracting crops, which comprise text information in the bounding boxes, CRNN converts them into texts in step 2. The final step is to finalize the text meanings using the BRNN-CNN tool and to determine the matching keywords by referring to the term-banks. The outputs (detected contract keywords) become the "bridges" connecting the interactive platforms among parties.

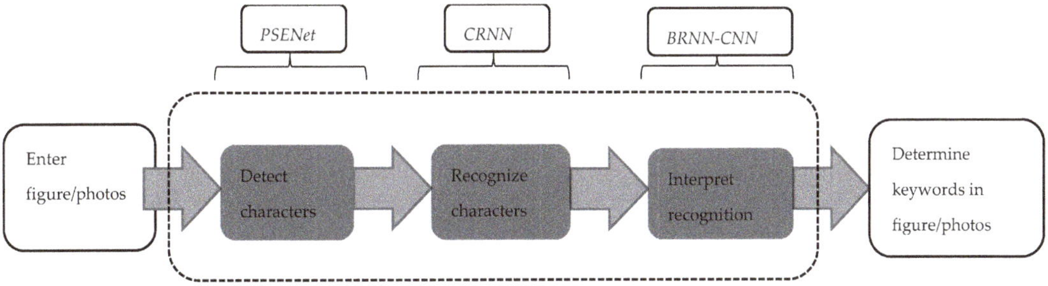

Figure 2. Mechanism for Contract Keyword Detection (CKD) approach.

6. Implementation and Discussion

Considering that the CKD approach is constructed using PSENet, CRNN, and BRNN-CNN toolboxes, the settings remain as suggested from the original work [24,31]. The implementation for the proposed approach also involves three phases: (1) the text position detected by PSENet in the first stage was taken, afterwards a screenshot was taken of the text in sections, and it was sent to the second stage for text recognition. The original contract is detected by the first stage as shown in Figure 3.

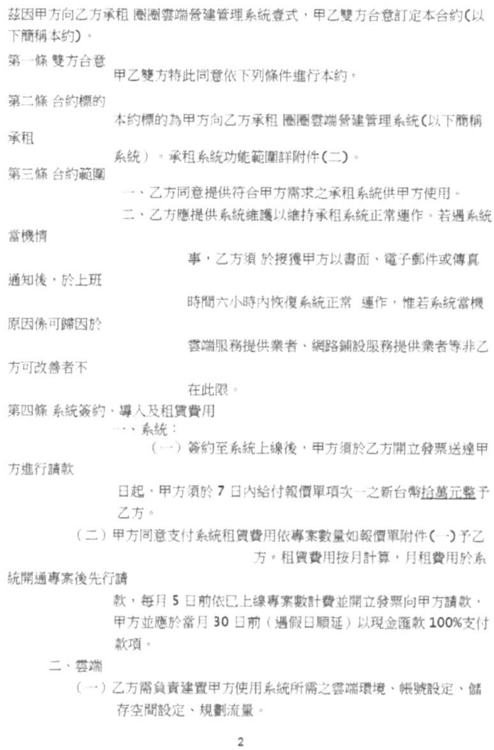

茲因甲方向乙方承租 團團雲端營建管理系統壹式，甲乙雙方合意訂定本合約(以
下簡稱本約)。
第一條 雙方合意
甲乙雙方特此同意依下列條件進行本約。
第二條 合約標的
本約標的為甲方向乙方承租 團團雲端營建管理系統(以下簡稱
承租
系統）。承租系統功能範圍詳附件(二)。
第三條 合約範圍
一、乙方同意提供符合甲方需求之承租系統供甲方使用。
二、乙方應提供系統維護以維持承租系統正常運作。若遇系統
當機情
事，乙方須 於接獲甲方以書面、電子郵件或傳真
通知後，於上班
時間六小時內恢復系統正常 運作，惟若系統當機
原因係可歸因於
雲端服務提供業者、網路鋪設服務提供業者等非乙
方可改善者不
在此限。
第四條 系統簽約、導入及租賃費用
一、系統：
（一）簽約至系統上線後，甲方須於乙方開立發票送達甲
方進行請款
日起，甲方須於 7 日內給付報價單項次一之新台幣拾萬元整予
乙方。
（二）甲方同意支付系統租賃費用依專案數量如報價單附件(一)予乙
方。租賃費用按月計算，月租費用於系
統開通專案後先行請
款，每月 5 日前依已上線專案數計費並開立發票向甲方請款，
甲方並應於當月 30 日前（遇假日順延）以現金匯款 100%支付
款項。
二、雲端
（一）乙方需負責建置甲方使用系統所需之雲端環境、帳號設定、儲
存空間設定、規劃流量。

2

Figure 3. Original text image (A contract stating purposes, scope, and payment methods for IoT platform system service).

Figure 4 shows the result, explaining how texts are segmented from Figure 3. The text lines are segmented and processed to generate multiple text image files.

Figure 4. Illustration for segmented text lines (The segmented text highlighting all possible Chinese text and terms for recognition).

(2) Having the results from Figure 4, the contract keyword detection approach converts the segmented text image file into the code and compile it. Then, the output text is presented as a txt file as shown in Figure 5. It can be seen in the output where errors may occur but the text can be roughly distinguished without affecting processing.

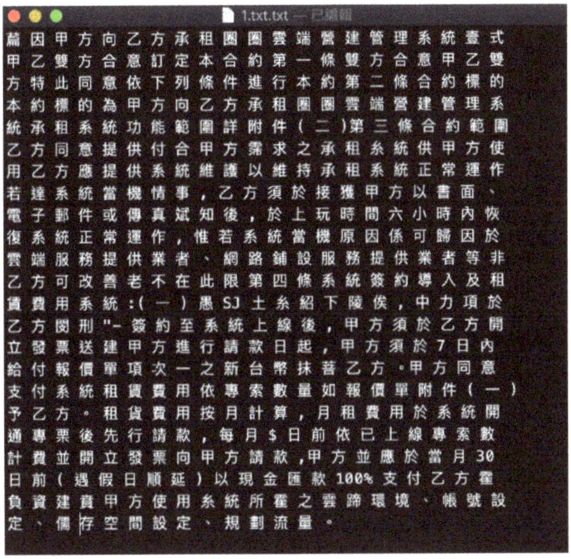

Figure 5. Illustration for text identification (The text identification listing all possible key Chinese characters from the recognition on Figure 4).

(3) Another environment, rather than the English spoken, is the final stage to test the proposed system. The CKD approach is designed to be carried out in different languages, as long as the databank supports it. USA is the first experimental environment where construction contract parties may have language usage different from what we have read in official documents. The process follows the above-mentioned steps to have the model established. Therefore, in this stage, CKD is to send the recognized text to the word segmentation and entity recognition system developed by the Central Academy of Sciences for part-of-speech analyses, BRNN-CNN [36]. The output result of word segmentation recognition is shown in Figure 6, and the part of speech represented by English speech tags is shown in Table 1.

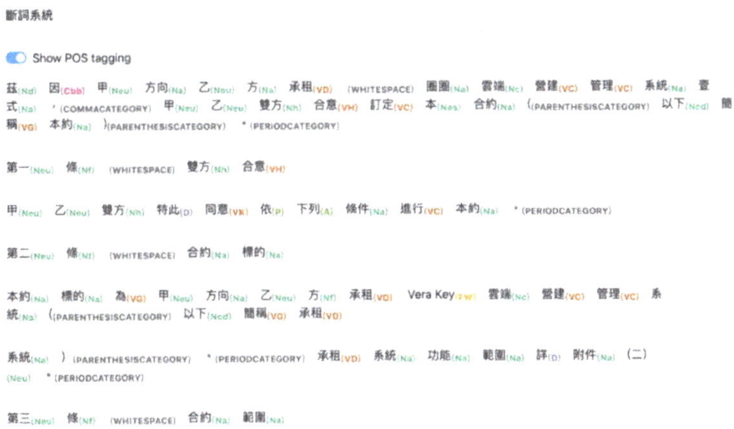

Figure 6. Illustration for word segmentation recognition (The result for word segmentation recognition converting all Chinese keywords to codes).

Table 1. English speech tags.

Speech Code	Explanation	Speech Code	Explanation
A	Non-predicative adjective	Caa	Peer conjunction
Cab	Conjunctions, such as: etc.	Cba	Conjunctions, such as: if
Cbb	Related connectives	D	Adverb
Da	Adverbs of quantity	Dfa	Pre-verb adverb
Dfb	Post-verb adverb	Di	Tense mark
Dk	Sentence adverbs	DM	Quantitative
I	Interjection	Na	Common noun
Nb	Proper noun	Nc	Local word
Ncd	Position word	Nd	Time word
Nep	Referent	Neqa	Quantifier
Neqb	Post-quantifier	Nes	Specific word
Neu	Numeral attributive	Nf	Quantifier
Ng	Postposition	Nh	Synonym
Nv	Nominalized verb	P	Preposition
T	Particle	VA	Intransitive verb
VAC	Action verb	VB	Action and transitive verbs
VC	Transitive verb action	VCL	Action-to-local object verb
VD	Double object verb	VF	Action predicate verb
VE	Object verb	VG	Categorical verb
VH	Intransitive verb	VHC	State-verb
VI	Transitive verb	VJ	Transitive verb
VK	Object verb	VL	State predicate verb
V_2	Have	DE	Place of gain
COLONCATEGORY	Colon	COMMACATEGORY	Comma
DASHCATEGORY	Dash	DOTCATEGORY	Dot
ETCCATEGORY	Truncation number	EXCLAMATIONCATEGORY	Exclamation point
PARENTHESISCATEGORY	Brackets	PAUSECATEGORY	Comma
PERIODCATEGORY	Period	QUESTIONCATEGORY	Question mark
SEMICOLONCATEGORY	Semicolon	SPCHANGECATEGORY	Dual straight line
WHITESPACE	Blank		

For example, in Figure 6, referring to the results from the first sentence: "Party A and Party B agree to conclude this contract hereinafter referred to as this contract since Party A and Party B lease a circle to build a cloud management system.", <Cause> Cbb is displayed in the system, and its meaning is a relational connective; <A> and <B> are displayed as Neu, representing numerals or definite words; <System> is displayed as Na, representing common nouns; VC stands for action and transitive verb. From the above results, it can be seen that the CKD approach can recognize the part of speech represented by the text and its accuracy rate is high.

The result of the second system output is entity identification, and the parts of speech represented by it are described in detail in Table 1. As shown in Figure 7 (the CKD output), from the output result, <first>, <second>, and <third> are expressed as ordinal, which represents the ordinal number; <AB> is expressed as person; <six hours> expressed as time, representative of the mean time. Using the technology of named entity identification, the part of speech it represents can be found and the required keywords can be identified by part of speech. Information can be found quickly, reducing search time in a large amount of data.

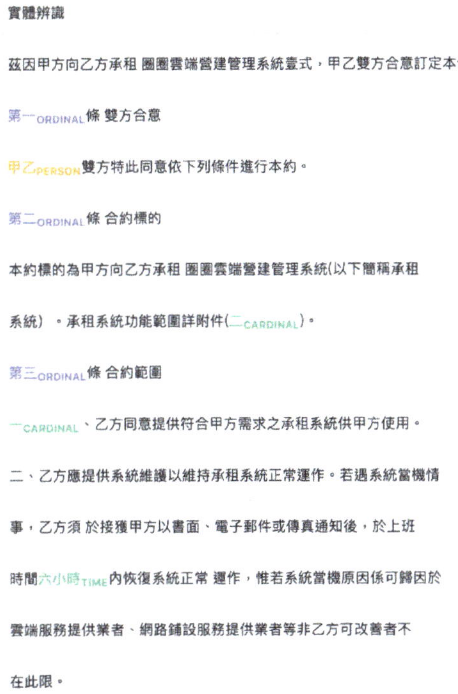

Figure 7. Outputs of CKD (Contract keyword in Chinese showing parties, duration, ordinal numbers, technologies used, and so on in the contract for easier and faster communication for project management).

The study presents notable implication for practicing engineering managers, which lie in the interactive platform for construction contract stakeholders, which is developed for more in-depth management, facilitates interactive communication, and, thus, reduces human errors, improves the accuracy in document processing, and enhances party relationships. Human errors can be viewed in personal and systematic ways. Although flaws or errors occur sometimes, the CKD approach is a countermeasure where it cuts the middleman, shaving work hours required to revise document processing, and allow errors to be rectified. To gain competitive advantage, it is important for engineering managers to utilize their resources efficiently and embrace innovation potential. Consequentially, the proposed approach has proven significant in project coordination between all parties by, for example, sharing real-time information, rapidly dealing with uncertainties and changes, automatically processing routine tasks, and saving manpower and costs.

7. Conclusions

The study integrates techniques associated with the natural language processing technology to develop the CKD approach that involves PSENet, CRNN, and BRNN-CNN toolboxes to deal with interactive connections among parties for construction projects. The CKD mechanism is original and effective in construction practice that facilitates contract management especially in documentary handling for mega projects. It serves not only as an interactive platform that automatically and real-time connects, tracks, and handles document tasks but also as a countermeasure to prevent personal or systematic human errors since what the contract document management CKD can provide is text extraction, recognition, and interpretation free of human interaction. It is efficient to handle massive document and tasks flows while a contraction project is ongoing. As a result, significant manpower is reduced. The research contributions lie on both academic and practical domains. For academic domains, the CKD mechanism integrating PSENet, CRNN, and BRNN-CNN approaches to cope with real-time massive document flows is novel in the construction industry. For practice, the proposed approach brings significant reduction for manpower and human error, an alternative for settling down misunderstanding or disputes due to real-time and precise communication, and a solution for efficient documentary management. It connects all contract stakeholders proficiently. The follow-up studies can focus on new toolboxes that may replace the current methods in an efficient way. Other languages than Chinese are recommended to test, to see if the mechanism works efficiently. Using the CKD mechanism as the core, practitioners may develop related applications to facilitate specific domains for construction projects such as financing, dispute management, quality control, and scheduling mapping.

Author Contributions: Conceptualization J.-H.C.; Methodology, J.-H.C., M.-C.S. and W.-J.L.; Expert Interview, V.-T.A.; Implementation, V.-T.A. and W.-J.L.; Writing—original draft preparation, V.-T.A. and J.-H.C.; writing—review and editing, J.-H.C. and T.-K.W. All authors have read and agreed to the published version of the manuscript.

Funding: This research is partly supported by the Ministry of Science and Technology (MOST), Taiwan, for promoting academic excellent of universities under grant numbers of MOST 109-2622-E-008-018-CC2 and MOST 108-2221-E-008-002-MY3.

Institutional Review Board Statement: Not applicable.

Informed Consent Statement: Not applicable.

Data Availability Statement: The data presented in this study are available on request from the corresponding author. The data are not publicly available due to the sponsored investigation.

Conflicts of Interest: The authors declare no conflict of interest.

Appendix A

Figure A1. PSENet Test Chart (Original Chinese contract segmented using PSENet method).

References

1. Chen, J.-H.; Nguyen, T.T.H.; Tai, H.W.; Chang, C.A. The willingness to adopt the Internet of Things (IoT) conception in Taiwan's construction industry. *J. Civ. Eng. Manag.* **2020**, *26*, 534–550. [CrossRef]
2. Shahhosseini, V.; Sebt, M.H. Competency-based selection and assignment of human resources to construction projects. *Sci. Iran.* **2011**, *18*, 163–180. [CrossRef]
3. Ibrahim, M.W.; Hanna, A.; Kievet, D. Quantitative comparison of project performance between project delivery systems. *Asce J. Manag. Eng.* **2020**, *36*, 04020082. [CrossRef]
4. Ji, T.; Chen, J.-H.; Wei, H.-H.; Su, Y.-C. Towards people-centric smart city development: Investigating the citizens' preferences and perceptions about smart-city services in Taiwan. *Sustain. Cities Soc.* **2021**, *67*, 102691. [CrossRef]
5. Chen, J.-H.; Hsu, S.-C.; Wang, R.; Chou, H.-A. Improving hedging decision for financial risks of construction material suppliers using grey system theory. *Asce J. Manag. Eng.* **2017**, *33*, 04017016. [CrossRef]

6. Yang, L.-R.; Chen, J.-H.; Wang, X.-L. Assessing the effect of requirements definition and management on performance outcomes: Role of interpersonal conflict, product advantage and project type. *Int. J. Proj. Manag.* **2015**, *33*, 67–80. [CrossRef]
7. Yeh, H.-H.; Hsieh, T.-Y.; Chen, J.-H.; Peng, H.-T. Preventive interface management for design-build wireless train control mass rapid transit projects. *ASCE J. Perform. Constr. Facil.* **2019**, *34*, 06019004. [CrossRef]
8. Lu, C.; Yu, Z.W.; Wang, X.T.; Hong, Y.M. Empirical study on the obstacles to the success of joint ventures in construction projects. *Adv. Civ. Eng.* **2020**, *2020*, 1748198. [CrossRef]
9. Khattak, M.S.; Mustafa, U. Management competencies, complexities and performance in engineering infrastructure projects of Pakistan. *Eng. Constr. Archit. Manag.* **2019**, *26*, 1321–1347. [CrossRef]
10. Wang, T.-K.; Gu, X.; Li, K.; Chen, J.-H. Competitive location selection of a commercial center based on the vitality of commercial districts and residential motion. *J. Urban Plan. Dev.* **2021**, *147*, 04021001. [CrossRef]
11. Wang, R.; Lee, C.-J.; Hsu, S.-C.; Chen, J.-H. Preventing or encouraging illegal activities by construction firms: The effects of top management team compensation and aspiration-performance discrepancies. *Eng. Constr. Archit. Manag.* **2021**. Accepted. [CrossRef]
12. Cheung, S.O.; Chow, P.T.; Tse, J.K.M. Performance of mediator tactics in building management disputes. *ASCE J. Manag. Eng.* **2015**, *31*, 04014033. [CrossRef]
13. Mahfouz, T.; Kandil, A. Litigation outcome prediction of differing site condition disputes through machine learning models. *ASCE J. Comput. Civ. Eng.* **2012**, *35*, 298–308. [CrossRef]
14. Hsu, K.-M.; Hsieh, T.-Y.; Chen, J.-H. Resolution toward the disputes caused by trial operation for construction projects. *Int. J. Organ. Innov.* **2019**, *12*, 375–388.
15. Li, H.; Lalla-Ruiz, E.; Vo, S. Modeling and solving cloud service purchasing in multi-cloud environments. *Expert Syst. Appl.* **2020**, *147*, 113165.
16. Wang, Y.; Hong, K.; Zou, J.; Peng, T.; Yang, H.A. CNN-based visual sorting system with cloud-edge computing for flexible manufacturing systems. *Ieee Trans. Ind. Inform.* **2019**, *16*, 4726–4735. [CrossRef]
17. Wu, I.; Liu, C.-C. A visual and persuasive energy conservation system based on BIM and IoT technology. *Sensors* **2020**, *20*, 139. [CrossRef]
18. Project Management Institution. *A Guide to the Project Management Body of Knowledge (PMBOK Guide)*; Project Management Institution: Newtown Square, PA, USA, 2017.
19. Papic, L. Special issue: Current research in life cycle engineering and management. *Int. J. Syst. Assur. Eng. Manag.* **2019**, *10*, 1–2. [CrossRef]
20. Fuller, S.K.; Petersen, S.R. *Life-Cycle Costing Manual for the Federal Energy Management Program*; Handbook: New York, NY, USA, 1996.
21. Anantatmula, V. Project manager leadership role in improving project performance. *Eng. Manag. J.* **2010**, *22*, 13–22. [CrossRef]
22. Tian, Z.; Huang, W.; He, T.; He, P.; Qiao, Y. Detecting text in natural image with connectionist text proposal network. In Proceedings of the European Conference on Computer Vision (ECCV), Amsterdam, The Netherlands, 8–16 October 2016.
23. Ren, S.; He, K.; Girshick, R.; Sun, J. Faster r-cnn: Towards real-time object detection with region proposal networks. *IEEE Trans. Pattern Anal. Mach. Intell.* **2016**, *39*, 1137–1149. [CrossRef] [PubMed]
24. Shi, B.; Bai, X.; Belongie, S. Detecting oriented text in natural images by linking segments. In Proceedings of the IEEE Conference on Computer Vision and Pattern Recognition (CVPR), Honolulu, HI, USA, 21–26 July 2017.
25. Zhou, X.; Yao, C.; Wen, H.; Wang, Y.; Zhou, S.; He, W. East: An efficient and accurate scene text detector. In Proceedings of the IEEE conference on Computer Vision and Pattern Recognition (CVPR), Honolulu, HI, USA, 21–26 July 2017.
26. Jaderberg, M.; Simonyan, K.; Vedaldi, A.; Zisserman, A. Reading text in the wild with convolutional neural networks. *Intern. J. Comput Vis.* **2016**, *116*, 1–20. [CrossRef]
27. Zhang, Z.; Zhang, C.; Shen, W.; Yao, C.; Liu, W.; Bai, X. Multi-oriented text detection with fully convolutional networks. In Proceedings of the IEEE Conference on Computer Vision and Pattern Recognition (CVPR), Las Vegas, NV, USA, 26 June–1 July 2016.
28. Long, J.; Shelhamer, E.; Darrell, T. Fully convolutional networks for semantic segmentation. In Proceedings of the IEEE Conference on Computer Vision and Pattern Recognition (CVPR), Boston, MA, USA, 7–12 June 2015.
29. Kim, K.-H.; Hong, S.; Roh, B.; Cheon, Y.; Park, M. PVANET: Deep but lightweight neural networks for real-time object detection. In Proceedings of the IEEE Conference on Computer Vision and Pattern Recognition (CVPR), Las Vegas, NV, USA, 26 June–1 July 2016.
30. Ronneberger, O.; Fischer, P.; Brox, T. U-net: Convolutional networks for biomedical image segmentation. In Proceedings of the International Conference on Medical Image Computing and Computer-Assisted Intervention, Munich, Germany, 4–8 October 2015.
31. Wang, W.; Xie, E.; Li, X.; Hou, W.; Lu, T.; Yu, G. Shape robust text detection with progressive scale expansion network. In Proceedings of the IEEE Conference on Computer Vision and Pattern Recognition (CVPR), Long Beach, NY, USA, 16–20 June 2019.
32. Lin, T.-Y.; Dollár, P.; Girshick, R.; He, K.; Hariharan, B.; Belongie, S. Feature pyramid networks for object detection. In Proceedings of the IEEE Conference on Computer Vision and Pattern Recognition (CVPR), Honolulu, HI, USA, 21–26 July 2017.

33. Baker, S.E.; Rosalind, E. *How Many Qualitative Interviews is Enough? Expert Voices and Early Career Reflections on Sampling and Cases in Qualitative Research*; University of Southampton Institutional Repository: Southampton, UK, 2012.
34. Guest, G.; Bunce, A.; Johnson, L. *How Many Interviews Are Enough? An Experiment with Data Saturation and Variability*; Sage Publications: Newbury Park, CA, USA, 2006.
35. Poleacovschi, C.; Javernick-Will, A. Who are the experts? Assessing expertise in construction and engineering organizations. *Asce J. Constr. Eng. Manag.* **2017**, *143*, 04017033. [CrossRef]
36. Nadeau, D.; Sekine, S. A survey of named entity recognition and classification. *Lingvisticae Investig.* **2007**, *30*, 3–26. [CrossRef]

applied sciences

MDPI

Article

Increasing the Reliability of an Electrical Power System in a Big European Hospital through the Petri Nets and Fuzzy Inference System Mamdani Modelling

Constâncio António Pinto [1], José Torres Farinha [1,2,*], Sarbjeet Singh [3] and Hugo Raposo [1,2]

[1] CEMMPRE, Department of Mechanical Engineering, University of Coimbra, 3030-788 Coimbra, Portugal; watumaubere@gmail.com (C.A.P.); hugo.raposo@isec.pt (H.R.)
[2] Instituto Superior de Engenharia de Coimbra/Instituto Politécnico de Coimbra (ISEC/IPC), 3030-199 Coimbra, Portugal
[3] Department of Civil, Environmental and Natural Resources Engineering, Lulea University of Technology, 97187 Luleå, Sweden; sarbjeet.singh@ltu.se
* Correspondence: torres.farinha@dem.uc.pt

Abstract: The big hospitals' electricity supply system's reliability is discussed in this article through Petri nets and Fuzzy Inference System (FIS). To simulate and analyse an electric power system, the FIS Mamdani in MATLAB is implemented. The advantage of FIS is that it uses human experience to provide a faster solution than conventional techniques. The elements involved are the Main Electrical Power, the Generator sets, the Automatic Transfer Switches (ATS), and the Uninterrupted Power Supply (UPS), which are analysed to characterize the system behaviour. To evaluate the system and identified the lower reliability modules being proposed, a new reliable design model through the Petri Nets and Fuzzy Inference System approach. The resulting approach contributes to increasing the reliability of complex electrical systems, aiming to reduce their faults and increase their availability.

Keywords: maintenance reliability; availability; Petri nets; fuzzy inference system; dynamic modelling

Citation: Pinto, C.A.; Farinha, J.T.; Singh, S.; Raposo, H. Increasing the Reliability of an Electrical Power System in a Big European Hospital through the Petri Nets and Fuzzy Inference System Mamdani Modelling. *Appl. Sci.* **2021**, *11*, 2604. https://doi.org/10.3390/app11062604

Academic Editor: Marlene Amorim

Received: 20 February 2021
Accepted: 9 March 2021
Published: 15 March 2021

1. Introduction

The electric power system plays a strategic function in a big European hospital. Therefore, the managers have an extreme interest in maintaining the electricity system working correctly. If a failure happens, it will cause dangerous problems for the hospital's activities and people in its operational context. Thus, the power source system must be designed to be very reliable to maintain the system working with maximum availability. Because of the specificity of this type of asset, its maintenance and reliability are strategic. This paper aims to improve this system's reliability by using the fuzzy inference system and Petri nets to simulate and improve the existing system with a new and more reliable design, using MATLAB as the simulation tool.

The structure of the paper is the following: Section 1 presents the introduction; Section 2 presents state of the art—the maintenance concepts, the maintenance activity in a hospital, the reliability and availability of maintenance systems, the Petri nets system, and the fuzzy Petri nets and fuzzy logic system; Section 3 describes the electrical power system of a big European hospital—the characterization of the hospital, the hospital electrical system modelling using block diagrams, the group of generators, the automatic transfer switch (ATS), and the uninterrupted power supply (UPS); Section 4 presents the modelling of the hospital's electrical system using the Petri nets software simulator HiPS description, the modelling of the hospital's electrical system using Petri nets, the explanation of the hospital electrical system, and the modelling and analysis using fuzzy logic; Section 5 presents the conclusions, including proposals for future developments.

2. State of the Art

2.1. The Maintenance Concept

Maintenance is an essential factor for the sustainability of the asset's operating functions and, by consequence, its availability and reliability. Maintenance is also a way to mitigate the damages that will occur in assets; therefore, the people in charge must be competent in their professional fields. This paper is based on existing norms and relevant research papers relating to maintenance aiming to support new ideas that may be relevant for further improvement, namely based on the following quotations. The American Hospital Association (1980) mentions that "proper maintenance of the power system is essential to its safety and reliability. The designer may incorporate certain features into the system to make maintenance safer and more comfortable and to make it possible to perform routine maintenance and inspection without dropping essential hospital load" [1]. Anderson and Neri (1990) reported that "support deals with the specific procedures, tasks, instructions, personnel qualification, equipment needed to satisfy the system maintainability requirement within an actual environment use" [2]. According to the Department of the Army, maintenance is defined as "those operations and actions that directly retain the appropriate activity of an item or renewing that operation when it is disturbed by failure or some other anomaly—within the context of RCM, the necessary process of an object means that it can perform its intended function" [3]. Farinha (2011) also referred to the norm EN 13306:2010 that defines maintenance as the "combination of all technical, administrative and managerial actions during the life cycle of an item intended to retain it in or restore it to, a state in which it can perform the required function" [4]. Gulati (2009) stated that "Maintenance is concerned with keeping an asset in right working conditions, so that the asset may be used to its full productive capacity. The maintenance function includes both upkeep and repairs" [5]. Moubray (1997) stated that "the role of Maintenance is to ensure that physical assets continue to do what their users want to do" [6]. Wang (2012) said that "Maintenance is a function that operates in parallel to production and can have a significant impact on the capacity of the production and quality of the products produced, and therefore, it deserves continuous improvement" [7]. It can be considered that maintenance is a management tool to prevent failures in the physical assets, using both planned and non-planned interventions to maintain their useful lives, in charge of the maintenance engineers.

2.2. The Electrical Maintenance Activity in Hospitals

This paper discusses the maintenance and modelling of the electricity system that supplies electricity to a big European hospital, as shown in Figures 7 and 8. To analyse the maintenance of the electricity system, the norms and papers of other researchers relating to hospitals were used to support new ideas that are relevant for further improvement based on the following quotations. AHA (1980) states that "the engineering and maintenance department charged with the responsibility for ensuring the safe, cost-effective operation and maintenance of hospital facilities and expensive equipment" [1]. Farinha (2001) mentioned that "another way of analysing the useful life was proposed by (AHA, 1996), based on the knowledge of type parameters of most hospital equipment, which allows establishing the maximum limit of maintenance expenses from the ones it is more economical to replace the equipment than to repair it" [4]. Mwanza and Mbohwa (2015) concluded that "the maintenance practices in three hospitals are not effective. The conclusion based on the lack of work order system to capture all work to manage labour, no skill training programs and poor spare inventory and purchasing system" [8]. The IEEE C2: National Electrical Safety Code (2007) mentions that "the purpose of this standard covers basic provisions for safeguarding of people from hazards arising from the installation, action, or maintenance of (1) conductors and equipment in electric supply stations, and (2) overhead and underground electric supply and communication lines" [9]. Christiansen (2015) mentioned that "this paper presents a model approach based on over 33,500 h of measurements within a modern University Medical Centre of Hamburg/Germany to assess the time-dependent course as well as the weekly sum of the demand for electrical energy due to medical laboratory plug loads" [10]. According to AHA (1980), "safety requires adequate provision for the protection of life, property, and continuity of hospital services. The protection of human life is paramount" [1]. BenSaleh et al. (2010) mentioned that "as there are more and more automated hospitals, the greater protection against the lack of energy. Hospital systems are increasingly dependent on technology, well-designed emergency energy systems, and the ability to adapt to the changing environments" [11]. Jamshidi (2014) mentioned that "Risk-Based Maintenance (RBM) is composed of two main components: (1) A comprehensive framework for prioritization of the critical medical devices; (2) A method for selecting the best maintenance strategy for each device. Risk-based prioritization of medical devices is valuable to health organizations in the sequencing of maintenance activities and budget allocation for maintenance activities" [12]. The World Health Organization (WHO) and Pan American Health Organization (2015) mention that "promoting 'the aims of 'hospitals safe from disasters' by ensuring that all new hospitals aware about the safety that will provide them to function in disaster situations and implement mitigation measures to reinforce existing health facilities, particularly those providing primary health care" [13]. Abdul et al. (2015) presented a "study on equipment inspection and shutdown at optimized, risk-based maintenance intervals for a processing facility unit, considering the human errors that introduced during these activities" [14].

2.3. Maintenance, Reliability, and Availability

Maintenance, reliability, and availability are essential tools to prevent failures, damages, and delays in the production processes and services in terms of time, costs, and systems' performance. The quality management effort for internal and external customer's satisfaction, guided by the international norms and world conventions, takes advantage of the research relating to hospital physical assets to support new ideas relevant to further improvement like the following authors described. Ali et al. (2019) stated that "to develop a safety and profitable process, uncertainty quantification is necessary for a reliability, availability, and maintainability (RAM) analysis. The uncertainties of 3% in each key decision variable are propagated, bringing the system into an unreliable/risk region. This approach reduces about 90% of the total computational time when compared with the conventional simulation approaches required for a complex first principle-based model" [15]. Arias et al. (2019) stated that the "reliability model is based on the information available in the maintenance system—driven framework using both classical and Bayesian methodologies. It illustrates the ageing process and the necessary data for the creation of the model. This model can be demonstrated and analysed with an important factor; it represents the flexibility to build the reliability expected during the maintenance strategy-making and the knowledge of the equipment" [16]. Calixto (2016) stated that "RAM analysis is the basis for complex system performance analysis. To demonstrate such a methodology, the RAM analysis steps, such as scope definition, lifetime data analysis, modelling, simulation, critical analysis, sensitivity analysis, and conclusions, will be discussed" [17]. Çekyay and Özekici (2015) stated that "system reliability, mean time to failure, and steady-state availability, are functions of the component failure rates. The primary objective is providing explicit expressions for these performance measures and obtaining various characterizations on their mathematical structures" [18]. Corvaro et al. (2017) stated that "the complex of RAM factors constitutes a strategic approach for integrating reliability, availability, and maintainability, by using methods, tools and engineering techniques (Mean Time to Failure, Equipment Down Time and System Availability values) to identify and quantify equipment and system failures that prevent the achievement of productive objectives" [19]. Ebeling (2010) suggested that "Reliability is defined to be the probability that a component or system will perform a required function for a given period when used under state operating conditions" and that "Maintainability is defined to be a probability that a failed component or system will be restored or repaired to a specified condition within a period when maintenance is performed following prescribed procedures and Availability is defined as the probability that a component or system is performing its required function at a given point in time when used under state operation condition" [20]. Feng et al. (2011) stated that "many problems have existed in synthesis of design of Reliability, Maintainability, Supportability (RMS) and performance; such as RMS design activities are numerous and optional, variable feedback branches can satisfy same RMS requirement, some iteration among RMS and Performance activities is necessary, and many uncertainties exist in the design process" [21]. Hameed et al. (2011) stated that "the need, method, benefits, and possible areas of application for the proposed RAM database have been identified. Both the technical and managerial challenges were outlined, which could be encountered during this database's realisation. The structure for the database is suggested keeping in view the implementation of RAM concepts quickly and efficiently" [22]. Sikos and Klemeš (2010) stated that "the proposed methodology focuses on HEN maintenance through the influence of availability and reliability rather than the optimization of cleaning schedules only. It has been shown that the failure analysis is capable of predicting heat exchanger bundle replacement times, leading to significant savings" [23]. Song and Wang (2013) presented "a comprehensive review of reliability assessment and improvement of power electronic systems from three levels: (1) metrics and methodologies of reliability assessment of existing system; (2) reliability improvement of an existing system using algorithmic solutions without change of the hardware; and (3) reliability-oriented design solutions that are based on the fault-tolerant operation of the overall systems" [24]. Sutton (2015) stated that "Reliability, Availability, and Maintainability (RAM) programs are an integral part of any risk management system. RAM techniques possess many similarities to those that are used for safety" [25]. Wang et al. (2013) stated that "failure of a component in Building Cooling, Heating and Power (BCHP) system may fail a sub-system or the whole system. The reliability and availability analysis of the BCHP system is helpful to the designer to decide the redundancy in case of equipment failure" [26]. Zio et al. (2019) considered "reliability engineering in the modern civil aviation industry, and the related engineering activities and methods. They consider reliability in a broad sense, referring to other system characteristics that are related to it, like availability, maintainability, safety and durability" [27]. Shen et al. (2019) mentioned that "to describe the system performance, system availabilities including instantaneous availability and limiting average availability, and some time distributions of interest are important indexes. Then, the problem of optimal maintenance policy is formulated by considering constraints of availability and operating times" [28]. Do et al. (2015) proposed and showed "how to optimize a dynamic maintenance decision rule on a rolling horizon? The heuristic optimization scheme for the maintenance decision is developed by implementing two optimization algorithms (genetic algorithm and MULTI FIT) to find optimal maintenance planning under both availability and limited repairmen constraints" [29].

From the dynamics of various opinions regarding reliability, availability, and maintenance, it is essential to pay close attention to these variables to ensure the production industry's successor service satisfies customers.

2.4. Petri Nets Systems

This paper corresponds to the evolution of the authors' research. Because of this, some of the next sections are strongly supported in Reference [30].

A Petri net may be defined by 5-tuples N = (P, T, 1, 0, Mo), where

(1) P = {P1, P2, . . . , Pm} is a limited set of *places;*
(2) T = {t1, t2, . . . , tn} is a limited set of *transitions*, $P \cup T \neq \emptyset$, and $P \cap T = \emptyset$;
(3) I (P, T) → N is an *Input function* that defines an arc directed from a Place to a Transition, where N is a set of negative integers;
(4) (T, P) → N is the *Output function* that defines the arc directed from Transition to Place; and
(5) Mo: P → N is the *initial marking.*

Marking is the assignment of *tokens* to places of the Petri net. The number and position of tokens may change during the implementation of the Petri network.

The simulation example refers to Figure 1, where we have in the Petri net:
P = {p1, p2, . . . , p7};
T = {t1, t2, . . . , t5};
I (t1, p1) = 2, I(t1, pi) = 0 for i = 2, 3, . . . , 7;
I (t2, p2) = 1, I(t2, p7) = 1, I(t2, pi) = 0 for i = 1, 3, 4, 5, 6;
O (t1, p2) = 1, O(t1, p3) = 2, O(t1, pi) = 0 for i = 1, 4, 5, 6, 7;
O (t2, p4) = 1, O(t2, pi) = 0 for i = 1, 2, 3, 5, 6, 7;
Mo = (2 0 0 0 0 0 1).

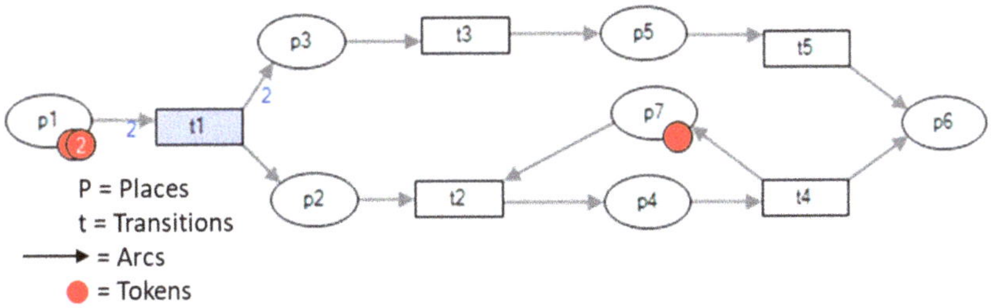

Figure 1. The Petri nets simulation circuit as an example, using HiPS software [30].

According to Wang (1998), "Petri nets were named after Carl A. Petri, who defined a general-purpose mathematical tool for describing relations existing between conditions and events. This work was done in the years 1960–1962. Since then, Petri nets have resulted in considerable research because they can be used to model properties such as process synchronization, asynchronous events, sequential operations, concurrent operations, and conflicts, or resource sharing. These properties characterize Discrete Event Dynamic Systems (DEDS). This, and other factors, makes Petri nets a promising tool and technology for applying to various types of DEDS. Petri nets provide a powerful communication medium between the user, typically requirements engineer, and the customer as a graphical tool. Instead of using ambiguous textual descriptions or mathematical notation difficult to understand by the customer, complex requirements specifications can be represented graphically using Petri nets. This, combined with computer tools, allows interactive graphical simulation of Petri nets and puts the development engineers a powerful tool to assist in complex engineering systems' development process. The graphical representation also makes Petri nets intuitively very appealing. They are straightforward to understand and grasp—even for people who are not very familiar with Petri nets' details. This is because Petri net diagrams resemble many of the drawings that designers and engineers make while constructing and analysing a system" [31]. Volovoi (2003) dealt with "the dynamic modelling of degrading and repairable complex systems as modularity allows a focus on the needs of a system reliability modelling and tailoring of the modelling formalism accordingly" [32]. Chew et al. (2007) mentioned that "Petri Nets provide a logical, easily understood, and compelling way of predicting the reliability of a system or platform" [33]. Garg (2012) mentions that "Petri Nets tool is applied to represent the asynchronous and concurrent processing of the order instead of the fault tree analysis" [34]. Leigh and Dunnett (2016) mentioned that "the study has aimed to develop a model using Petri Nets to determine the feasibility of adopting this technique to model the maintenance processes efficiently" [35]. Ren et al. (2014) mentioned that "if a Petri Nets are required to model processes that have a random (or pseudorandom) nature to them, and this randomness follows a specific pattern such as a statistical distribution, the transitions can sample their switching times from this distribution" [36]. Sadou et al. (2009) mentioned that "this new representation of the Petri net with formulae of linear logic allows us to define the notion of scenario formally. To obtain a minimal situation, we have considered three elements: (i) the order of events governed by a useful relation of cause and effect in the system, (ii) the list of activities of the scenario must be minimal (i.e., without loop events), and (iii) the final marking corresponding to the feared state must be minimal" [37]. Eisenberger and Fink (2017) stated that "Petri nets are such a mathematical tool that has been applied for maintenance modelling and simulations of different applications. Several types of Petri nets with different properties have been introduced" [38]. Pinto et al. (2021) stated that "the importance of Petri Nets as a powerful tool in maintenance management, providing analysis and simulation of the systems to increase the reliability and availability of the individual assets and their operations" [30]. Farinha (2018) showed the example using Petri nets on the electrical circuit through "an Emergency Generator that, as is known, starts operating when the external mains voltage from below a certain value about the nominal voltage. In the example, the value assumed for starting the Emergency Generator is 350 V. When the value of the voltage of the external electrical network from below this value, the Generator starts, turning off when the electrical network's value is above that. For this purpose, the following situations are assumed for the Emergency Generator: The Generator can be in two possible operational states: in standby and operation (generating electricity); two situations give rise to those states: mains voltage above 350 V (> 350 V) and below this value (<350 V); Other possible states, such as malfunction, are not considered. Figure 2 illustrates the state diagram and the Petri Net for the preceding situations, respectively" [39].

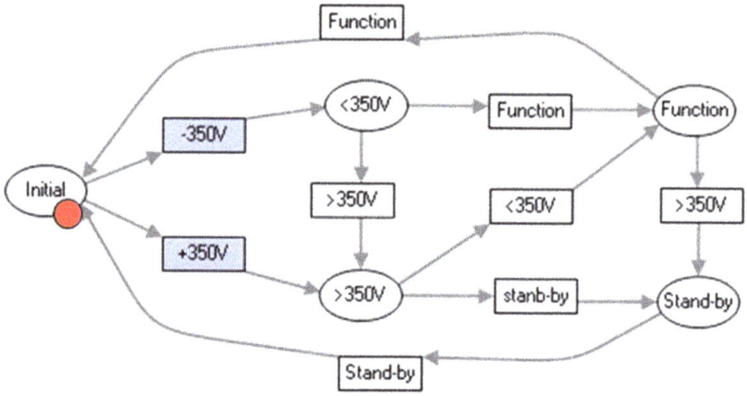

Figure 2. Example of a Petri net on standby (red dot = token = energy of electrical power) [39].

2.5. Fuzzy Inference System (FIS) and Fuzzy Petri Nets

Fuzzy Petri Nets is a combination of two different sciences—the set of fuzzy logic and Petri nets theory—which are held to provide answers to vague or unclear problems in a system that is about to be examined. Therefore, we use fuzzy Petri nets to see and provide solutions to problems that are not clear, such as an asset or system that does not have historical data but wants to get a definite answer regarding the reliability and reliability of maintenance to improve the performance of these assets. Also, several previous researchers put forward their ideas in articles they wrote as follows. Cannarile et al. (2017) "propose a method based on the Fuzzy Expectation-Maximization (FEM) algorithm, which integrates the evidence of the field inspection outcomes with information taken from the maintenance operators about the transition times from one state to another. Possibility distributions are used to describe the imprecision in the expert statements" [40]. Ladj et al. (2017) proposed "a new interpretation of PHM outputs to define machine degradations that are corresponding to each job. Moreover, to consider several sources of uncertainty in the prognosis process, the authors choose to model PHM outputs using fuzzy logic. Motivated by the computational complexity of the problem, Variable Neighbourhood Search (VNS) methods are developed, including well-designed local search procedures" [41]. Touat et al. (2017) mentioned that "to solve the problem, we developed two fuzzy genetic algorithms that are based on respectively the sequential and total scheduling strategies. The one respecting the sequential approach consists of two phases. In the first phase, the integrated production and maintenance schedules are generated. In the second one, the human resources are assigned to maintenance activities. The second algorithm respecting a total strategy consists of developing the integrated production and maintenance schedules that explicitly satisfy the human resource constraints" [42]. Jabari et al. (2019) mentioned that "Based on the results obtained in the case study, it can conclude that the fuzzy set for calculation is more rigorous than the qualitative results. The calculated unified qualitative and fuzzy risk number shows that the plant was classified as semi-critical. It obtained the highest fuzzy risk number of 99.1452 for both blowers (BW 20 21 and BW 20 23 A) assets failure" [43]. Ratnayake and Antosz (2017) mentioned that, "also, a fuzzy logic-based risk rank calculation approach has been presented. The suggested RBM approach, together with the fuzzy inferencing process, enables us to minimize suboptimal calculations when the input values are at the boundaries of the particular ranges. Fuzzy membership functioned together with the rule base. It enabled to insert numbers with the least uncertainty" [44]. Seiti et al. (2017) mentioned that, "for this purpose, a model based on Fuzzy Axiomatic Design (FAD) is presented, wherein each evaluation has both optimistic and pessimistic fuzzy scores, as the fuzzy evaluations themselves have risks. To improve the accuracy of the presented method, a new concept called "acceptable risk" has been suggested" [45]. Babashamsi et al. (2016) stated that "to determine the weights of the indices, the fuzzy AHP is used. Subsequently, the alternatives' priorities are ranked according to the indices weighted with the VIKOR model" [46]. According to Cordón (2011), "The current contribution constitutes a review on the most representative genetic fuzzy systems relying on Mamdani-type fuzzy rule-based systems to obtain interpretable linguistic fuzzy models with a good accuracy" [47]. Zahabi and Kaber (2019) mentioned that "use the Mamdani max-min inference method to calculate a 'risk reliability (R-R) score based on a fuzzy definition of frequency of hazard occurrence, the severity of hazard outcomes, and system reliability. The application of the proposed model is presented in the context of a complex-human-in-the-loop system using the MATLAB fuzzy logic toolbox" [48]. According to Akgun et al. (2012), "For this purpose, an easy-to-use program, 'MamLand,' was developed for the construction of a Mamdani fuzzy inference system and employed in MATLAB. Using this newly developed program, it is possible to construct a landslide susceptibility map based on expert opinion" [49]. According to Kacimi et al. (2020), "The Mamdani fuzzy system is known as a linguistic model where the semantic meaning of the fuzzy rules is an intrinsic characteristic that must be retained during the learning process while seeking for high accuracy" [50]. Lu and Sy (2009) mentioned that "A fuzzy logic approach is adopted to handle the uncertainty conditions. To meet the requirement of real-time decision-making, the fuzzy project programs were coded and compiled into DLL files" [51]. Dhimish et al. (2018) stated that "Mamdani fuzzy logic system interface and Sugeno type fuzzy system. Both examined fuzzy logic systems show approximately the same output during the experiments. However, there are slight differences in developing each type of the fuzzy system such as the output membership functions and the rules applied for detecting the type of the fault occurring in the PV plant" [52]. Kraidi et al. (2020) stated that "A Computer-Based Risk Analysis Model (CBRAM) was designed to analyse the risk influencing factors using a fuzzy logic theory to consider any uncertainty that is associated with stakeholders' judgments and data scarcity. The CBRAM has confirmed the most critical risk influencing factors, in which this study has explained the effective methods to manage them" [53]. Khosravanian et al. (2016) stated that "The Mamdani-type FIS requires defuzzification, whereas the Sugeno-type FIS applies a constant weighted-average technique avoiding defuzzification. The results for the two field cases evaluated convincingly demonstrate that the Sugeno-type FIS is superior to the Mamdani-type FIS for WOB prediction using the same input data and membership functions" [54].

About this type of approach, the research developed by Teo et al. [55–57] must be considered as very relevant, regardless of to be focused on mainly in energy management, namely for a grid-connected microgrid with renewable energy sources and energy storage system, including the design of fuzzy logic-based controllers to be embedded in a grid-connected microgrid with renewable and energy storage capability.

From the many approaches done by many researchers and the authors' research, it can consider that fuzzy Petri nets have a very high potential to help solve complex reliability problems inside the systems.

2.6. The HiPS Software Simulator Description

According to the HiPS (Hierarchical Petri net Simulator), the "tool was developed by the Department of Computer Science and Engineering, Shinshu University, being a tool for Petri nets design and analysis; it was developed using Microsoft Visual C # and C++. HiPS tool has a very intuitive GUI, which enables hierarchical and/or timed-net design. HiPS tool has also functioned of static/dynamic analysis: T-invariant detection, Reachability path analysis, deadlock state detection, and k-boundedness analysis. Also, it is possible to perform a random walk simulation with each firing step" [58]. The definition of the Petri net model using the HiPS software can be seen in Figure 3.

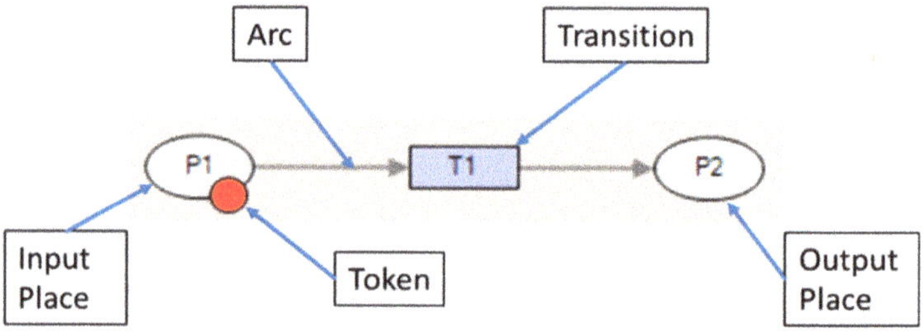

Figure 3. The definitions tools in HiPS.

3. Electrical Power System of a Big European Hospital

3.1. Characterization of the Hospital

The big European hospital is a medical care building that has a total construction area of 90,000 m^2.

This paper focuses on the emergency power supply system (EPSS) of the hospital, which has the following equipment: three units of 1000 KVA generators; two units of UPS (uninterrupted power supply) with 300 KVA; one unit of UPS of 8 KVA; 20 units of UPS of 20 KVA; one unit of ATS (automatic transfer switch); three transformer units; two PT (power transfer); three LVDB (low-voltage distribution board) input units; six LVDB central output units and other peripheral instruments (correction battery, LV distribution network, indoor lighting (normal/emergency), output and obstruction signalling, normal/emergency outlets); and ground network. The paper uses Petri net time methods and fuzzy logic to analyse and diagnose the power system's operation and reliability and propose a new design to improve its availability [30].

3.2. Modelling of the Hospital's Electrical System Using Block Diagrams

The main contribution of the Petri nets system is based on their ability to simulate the process and to analyse complex structures. Figure 4 shows the process block flow diagram of the electrical power system of the hospital under study.

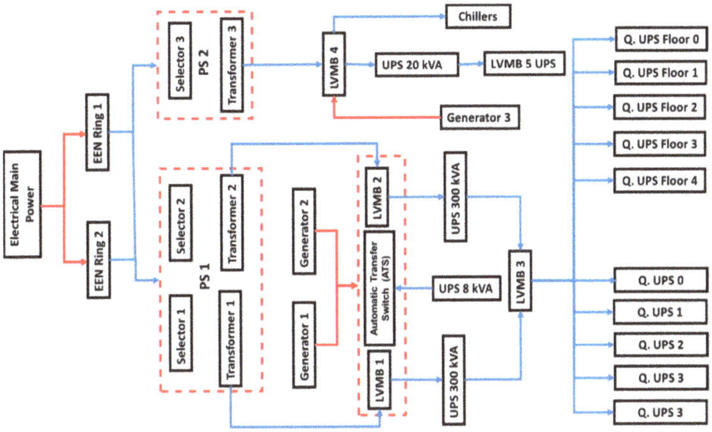

Figure 4. Asset process flow diagram (APFD) [30].

3.3. The Group of Generators, Automatic Transfer Switch, and UPS

In case of power failure of the external electrical energy supplier, the hospital is equipped with three generators, two of 1000 kVA and one of 500 kVA, powered by diesel engines. The command and transfer board of the most potent power groups have also an installed synchronization system between the two groups that can operate in parallel after synchronization between both groups (Figure 5) [30].

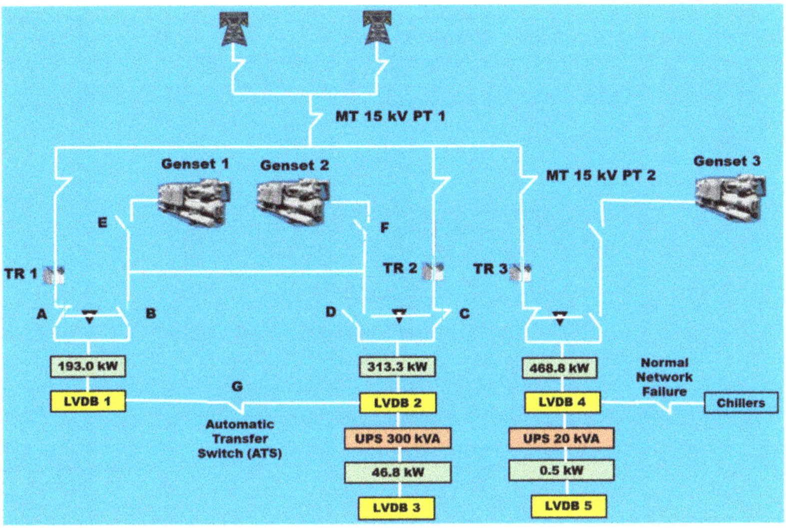

Figure 5. Diagram of the electric power system in the hospital [30].

4. Modelling the Hospital's Electrical System Using Petri Nets

4.1. Modelling the Hospital's Electrical System by Petri Nets

In the present case, the physical assets under study have maintenance procedures to guarantee their adequate reliability and availability conditions and mitigate failures (Figure 6).

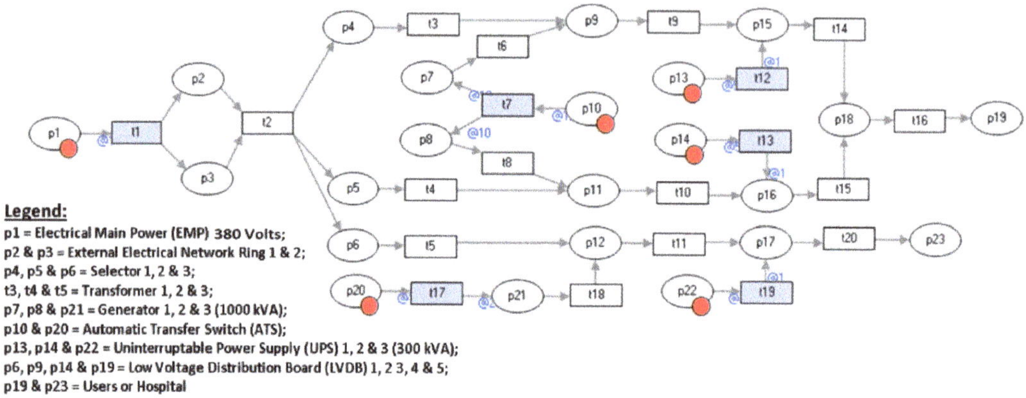

Figure 6. Modelling and simulation in the Petri net of the electrical power system [30].

4.2. The Hospital Electrical System Block Diagrams

As can be seen in Figure 7, the ATS manages the generators—if it does not work, then the generators must be activated manually, which hurts the system. Additionally, it can be emphasized that only one ATS is installed. Thus, the question arises: how do the above circuit behaviours answer to the expected security system? To respond to this question, the present situation was simulated and a solution to solve the identified handicap with block diagrams, as shown in Figures 8 and 9, is proposed [30].

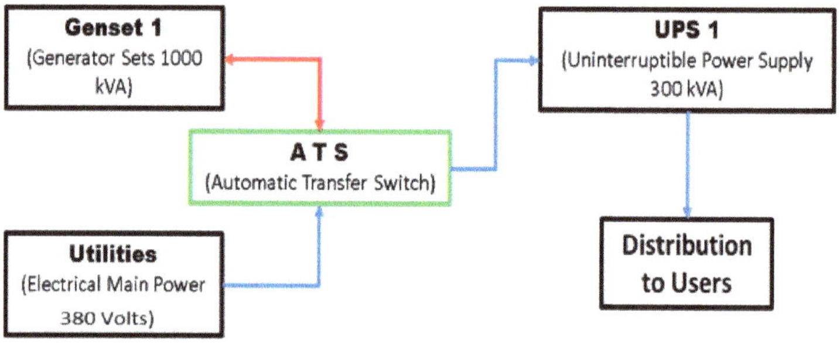

Figure 7. Design with an evident weakness, with one ATS, one UPS, and one Genset [30].

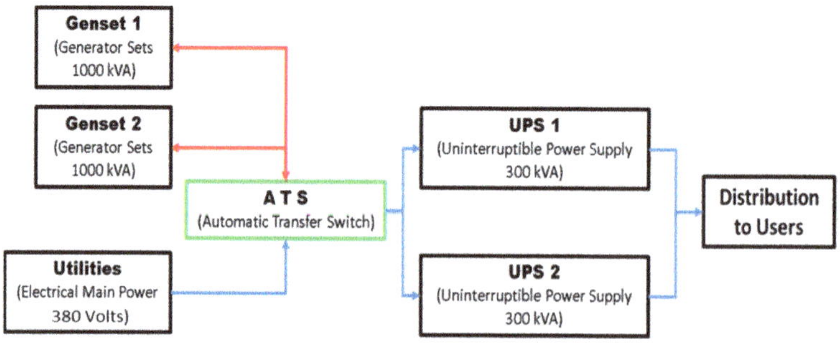

Figure 8. Weakness module with increased reliability, through 1 ATS, 2 UPSs, and 2 Gensets [30].

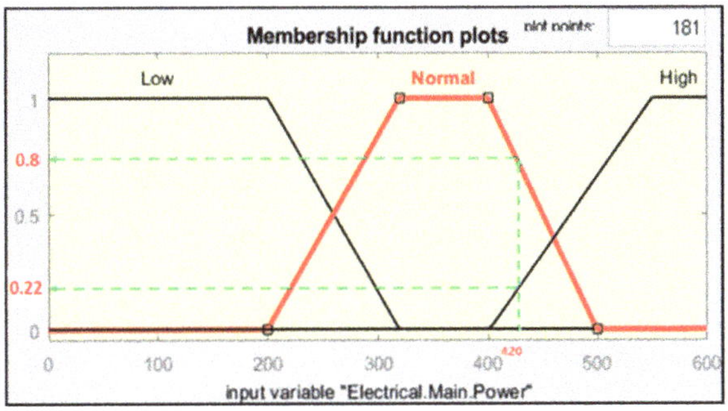

Figure 9. Electrical main power.

In the block diagram of Figure 7, the hypothesis of a fault in the main electrical power is emphasized when the UPS takes over the primary function. In this situation, the ATSs activate the generator that replaces the UPS while waiting until the main electrical power is on again; unfortunately, if one of the ATS, UPS, and generator fails, then a fatal accident occurs, which permits to infer that this is a fragile module.

In the block diagram of Figure 8, if there is a current fault from the main power, UPS 1, 2, and 3 will turn on the main power's functions. Then, ATS activates Genset 1, 2, and 3, replacing the UPS function, while waiting for an intervention from the maintenance team; if one of the UPS, Genset, or ATS fails, then it will be replaced by the other UPS (Genset and ATS) because there is a redundancy of three units; thus, the probability of fatality accidents is extremely low. This design can be considered a good design because it is deemed very reliable; however, its cost and maintenance are more expensive because it needs more equipment to be installed. It can be concluded that the components of the system are critical to the electrical hospital functioning, and the ATS is the most critical item.

Because of the preceding, the electrical sequences that must be carefully targeted for research to identify the main functions and failures of each module for the installed load are discussed and analysed. However, because the hospital does not provide historical data, Petri nets are used to analyse this case study.

4.3. Modelling and Analysing with a Fuzzy Inference System

For computing, the authors use the MATLAB fuzzy tool and the fuzzy Mamdani method.

4.3.1. Fuzzification Data Processing

After analysing the electricity system of the hospital, using Petri nets and the block diagrams design to find the most critical instruments or items in the asset, now we use fuzzy MATLAB to determine how reliable and available the system is according to their several states to determine the input and output functions of the system by the specified setpoint; it will use information and conditions, such as electric main power worth 420, Genset 1 and 2700, ATS 140, and UPS 1 and 2220. The removal of all inputs and outputs is presented in Figures 9–12.

$$\mu Normal(420) = \frac{(500-420)}{(500-400)} = 0.8$$

$$\mu High(420) = \frac{(420-400)}{(550-400)} = \frac{20}{150} = 0.215$$

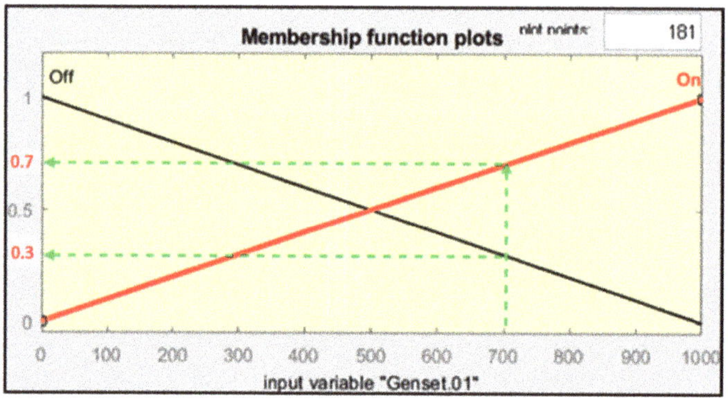

Figure 10. Genset 1 and 2.

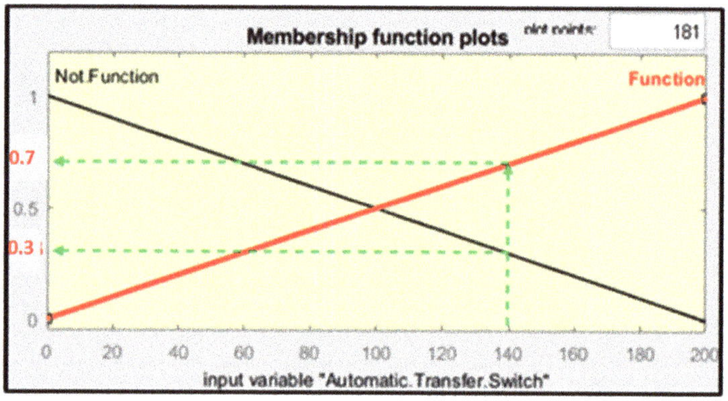

Figure 11. ATS.

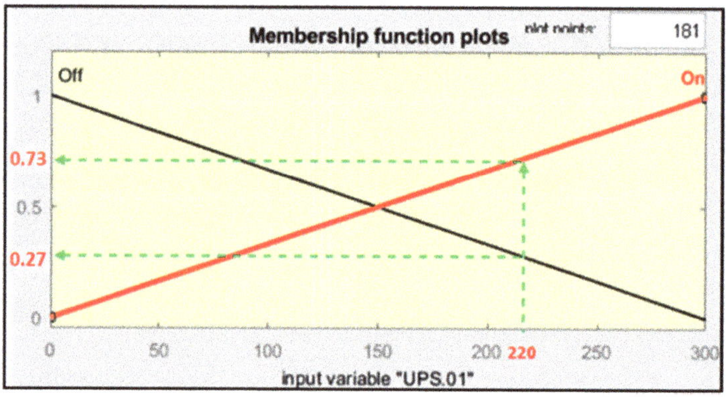

Figure 12. UPS 1 and 2.

Thus, we can conclude that the fuzzy set for input "Electrical Main Power" is as follows:

Fuzzy Low set: μLow (420) = 0
Fuzzy Normal set: μNormal (420) = 0.8
Fuzzy High set: μHigh (420) = 0.215

$$\mu On(700) = \frac{700-0}{1000-0} = \frac{700}{1000} = \frac{7}{10} = 0.7$$

$$\mu Off(700) = \frac{1000-700}{1000-0} = \frac{300}{1000} = \frac{3}{10} = 0.3$$

Thus, we can conclude that the fuzzy set for input "Genset 01 = Genset 02" is as follows:

Fuzzy set On: μOn (700) = 0.7
Fuzzy set Off: μOff (700) = 0.3

$$\mu Function(140) = \frac{140-0}{200-0} = 0.7$$

$$\mu Not\ Function(140) = \frac{200-140}{200-0} = 0.3$$

Thus, we can conclude that the fuzzy set for input "Automatic Transfer Switch" is as follows:

Fuzzy Function set: $\mu Function$ (140) = 0.7
Fuzzy Not Function set: μOff (700) = 0.3

$$\mu On(220) = \frac{220-0}{300-0} = 0.73$$

$$\mu Off(220) = \frac{300-220}{300-0} = 0.27$$

Thus, we can conclude that the fuzzy set for input "UPS 01 = UPS 02" is as follows:

Fuzzy On set: μOn (220) = 0.73
Fuzzy Off set: μOff (220) = 0.27

If we collect all input variables: Electrical Main Power = 420, Genset 01 and 02 = (700 $\times$ 2), Automatic Transfer Switch = 140, and UPS 01 and UPS 02 = (220 x 2). Then we get the following values:

Fuzzy Low set: μLow (420) = 0
Fuzzy Normal set: $\mu Normal$ (420) = 0.8
Fuzzy High set: $\mu High$ (420) = 0.215
Fuzzy set On: μOn (700) = 0.7
Fuzzy set Off: μOff (700) = 0.3 $\times$ 2 (the value of two Genset)
Fuzzy Function set: $\mu Function$ (140) = 0.7
Fuzzy Not Function set: μOff (700) = 0.3
Fuzzy set On: μOn (220) = 0.73
Fuzzy set Off: μOff (220) = 0.27 $\times$ 2 (the value of two UPS)

So, the Maximum and Minimum Values of the above calculation are as follows (Figure 13):

Maximum Value: $\mu 1 = 0$; $\mu 2 = 0.8$; $\mu 3 = 0.7$; $\mu 4 = 0.7$; $\mu 5 = 0.7$; $\mu 6 = 0.73$ and $\mu 7 = 0.73$
Minimum Value: $\mu 1 = 0$; $\mu 2 = 0.215$; $\mu 3 = 0.3$; $\mu 4 = 0.3$; $\mu 5 = 0.3$; $\mu 6 = 0.27$ and $\mu 7 = 0.27$.

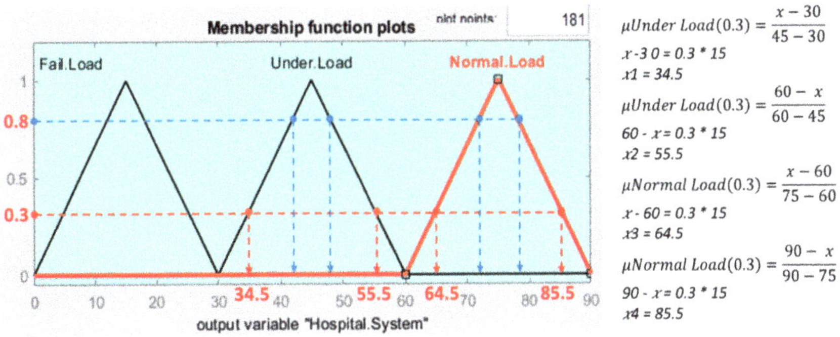

Figure 13. Output maximum and minimum point in fuzzification.

Using the fuzzy set operator "AND", the value taken is the lowest, and thus: $\{0.215 + (0.3 * 2) + 0.3 + 0.27 * 2)\}/6 = 0.28 \approx 0.3$ (minimum total value of input variable) (Figure 14).

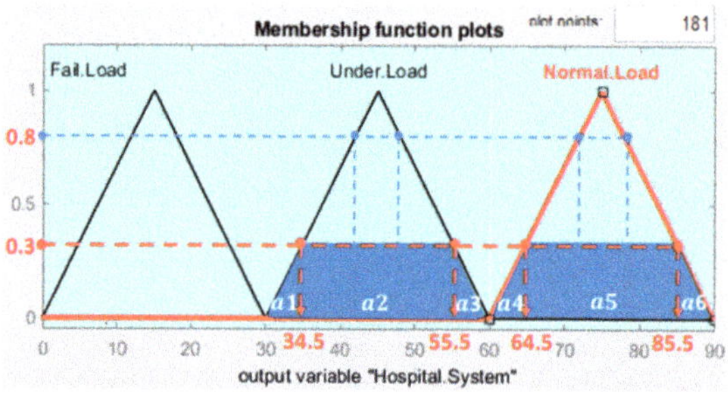

$$a1 = \frac{(34.5 - 30) * 0.3}{2} = 0.68$$

$$a2 = (55.5 - 34.5) * 0.3 = 6.3$$

$$a3 = \frac{(60 - 55.5) * 0.3}{2} = 0.68$$

$$a4 = \frac{(64.5 - 60) * 0.3}{2} = 0.68$$

$$a5 = (85.5 - 64.5) * 0.3 = 6.3$$

$$a6 = \frac{(64.5 - 60) * 0.3}{2} = 0.68$$

Figure 14. Output area of fuzzification.

The defuzzification method used is the centroid of gravity (COG).

In this case, we used the minimum value of μ because the rules "AND" follow fuzzy logic requirements.

Minimum Value: $\mu1 = 0$; $\mu2 = 0.215$; $\mu3 = 0.3$; $\mu4 = 0.3$; $\mu5 = 0.3$; $\mu6 = 0.27$ and $\mu7 = 0.27$.

$$Z^* = \frac{(0.215 * 34.5) + (0.3 * 55.5) + (0.3 * 64.5) + (0.27 * 85.5)}{(0.215 + 0.3 + 0.3 + 0.27)} = 61.3$$

The other way to solve the Centroid of Gravity method is using calculus mathematics as follows:

$$\mu(z) = \begin{cases} 0, & x \leq or\ x \geq 90 \\ \frac{x-30}{45-30}, & 30 \leq x \leq 34.5 \\ 0.3, & 34.5 \leq x \leq 55.5 \\ \frac{60-x}{60-45}, & 55.5 \leq x \leq 60 \\ \frac{x-60}{75-45}, & 60 \leq x \leq 75 \\ 0.3, & 64.5 \leq x \leq 85.5 \\ \frac{90-x}{90-75}, & 85.5 \leq x \leq 90 \end{cases} \quad \Rightarrow \quad \mu(z) = \begin{cases} 0, & x \leq or\ x \geq 90 \\ 0.067x - 2, & 30 \leq x \leq 34.5 \\ 0.3, & 34.5 \leq x \leq 55.5 \\ 4 - 0.067x, & 5.5 \leq x \leq 60 \\ 0.067x - 4, & 60 \leq x \leq 75 \\ 0.3, & 64.5 \leq x \leq 85.5 \\ 6 - 0.067, & 85.5 \leq x \leq 90 \end{cases}$$

The defuzzification method uses the centroid of gravity (COG):

$$M1 = \int_{30}^{34.5} (0.0666z - 2)z\,dz = \int_{30}^{34.5} \left(0.00666z^2 - 2z\right)dz = 0.0222z^3 - z^2|_{30}^{34.5} = 21.9625$$

$$M2 = \int_{34.5}^{55.5} (0.3)z\,dz = \int_{34.5}^{55.5} (0.3z)dz = 0.15z^2 - z^2|_{34.5}^{55.5} = 283.5$$

$$M3 = \int_{55.5}^{60} (4 - 0.0666z)z\,dz = \int_{55.5}^{60} \left(4z - 0.00666z^2\right)dz = 2z^2 - 0.0222z^3|_{55.5}^{60} = 39.4761$$

$$M4 = \int_{60}^{64.5} (0.0666z - 4)z\,dz = \int_{60}^{64.5} \left(0.00666z^2 - 4z\right)dz = 0.0222\,z^3 - z^2|_{60}^{64.5} = 41.362$$

$$M5 = \int_{64.5}^{85.5} (0.3)z\,dz = \int_{64.5}^{85.5} (0.3z)dz = 0.3z^2|_{64.5}^{85.5} = 472.5$$

$$M6 = \int_{85.5}^{90} (6 - 0.0666z)z\,dz = \int_{85.5}^{90} \left(6z - 0.00666z^2\right)dz = 3z^2 - 0.0222z^3|_{85.5}^{90} = 61.0356$$

Calculation of the centre point (centroid of gravity):

$$Z^* = \frac{(M1 + M2 + M3 + M4 + M5 + M6)}{(a1 + a2 + a3 + a4 + a5 + a6)}$$

$$Z^* = \frac{(21.9625 + 283.5 + 39.4761 + 41.362 + 472.5 + 61.0356)}{(0.68 + 6.3 + 0.68 + 0.68 + 6.3 + 0.68)} = 60$$

Therefore, the centre of gravity of the calculated drawing area is at point x = 60 and point y = 0 as a balance of the average electrical current in the said hospital system (Figure 15).

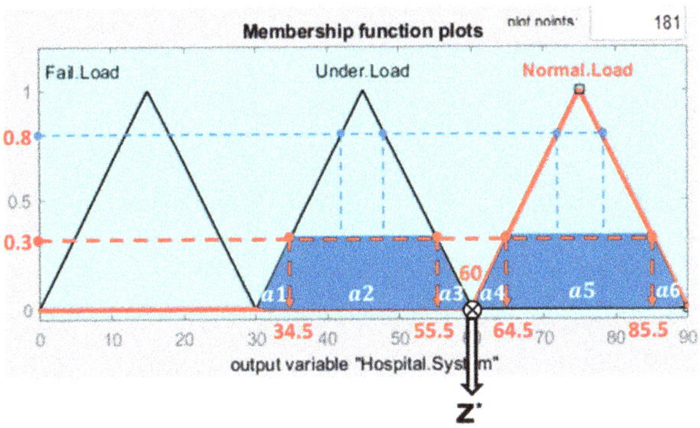

Figure 15. Representing the centre of gravity at coordinates x = 60 and μ = 0 of the drawing.

4.3.2. Fuzzy Logic Designer

Fuzzy logic designer in this study involves parameters including six "inputs": (a) electrical main power (350 MVA); (b) two Gensets 1 and Gensets 2 (1000 KVA); (c) one automatic transfer switch (ATS); and (d) two UPS 1 and UPS 2 (300 KVA). The input is shown in Figure 16.

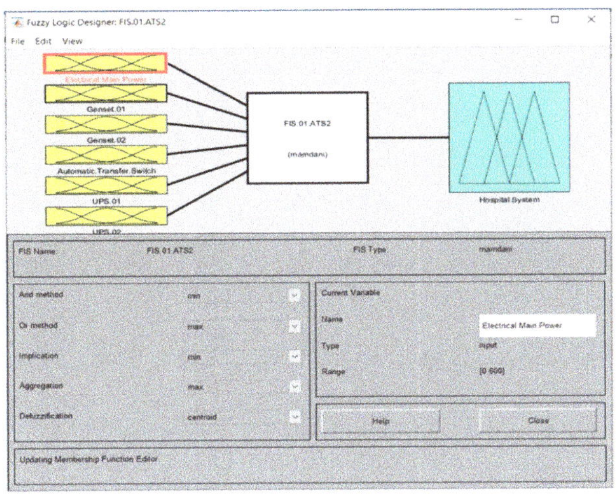

Figure 16. Fuzzy logic design variable inputs and output.

4.3.3. Membership Function Editor

The Membership Function Editors of the fuzzy logic design input variables are shown in Figure 17a–f.

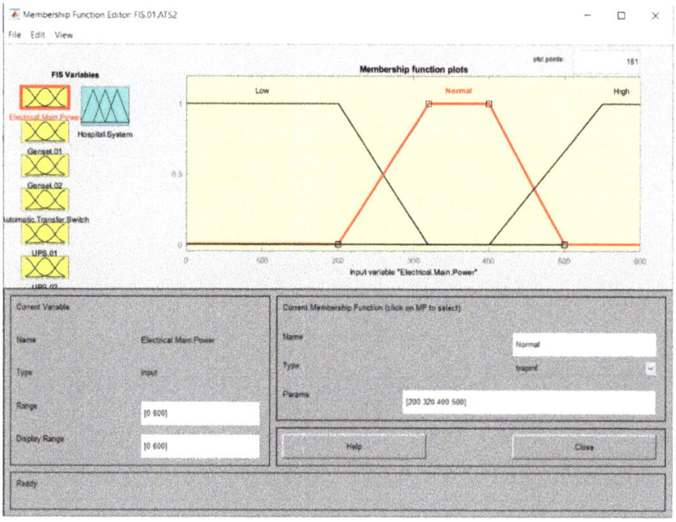

(**a**)

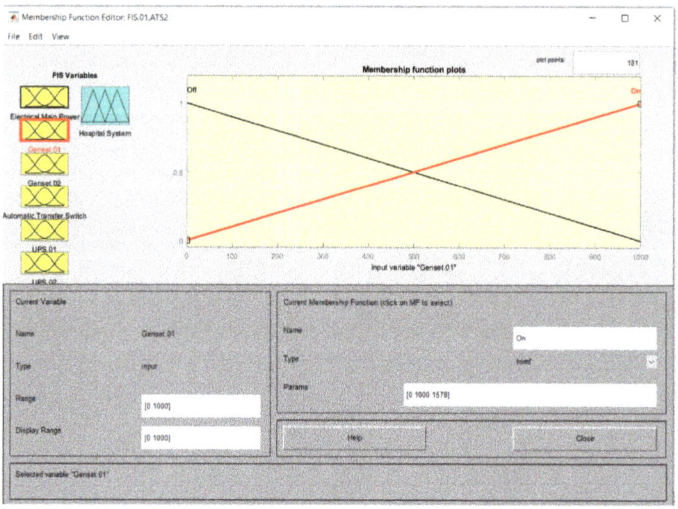

(**b**)

Figure 17. *Cont.*

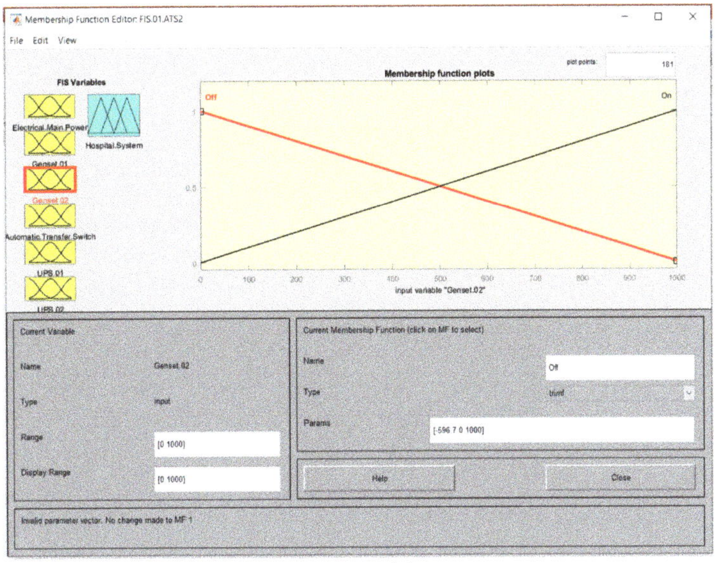

(c)

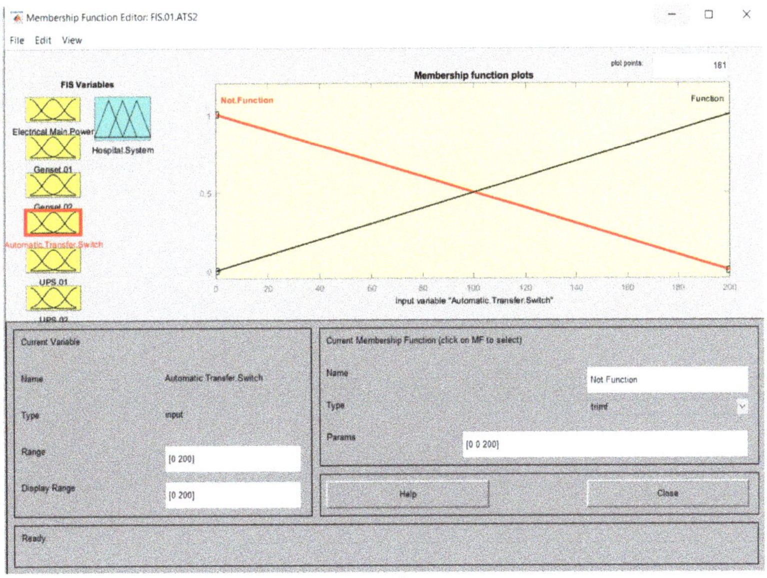

(d)

Figure 17. *Cont.*

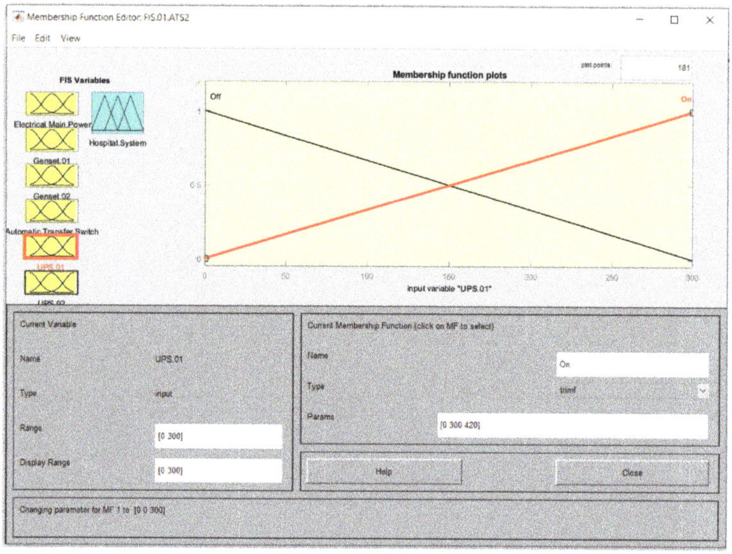

(e)

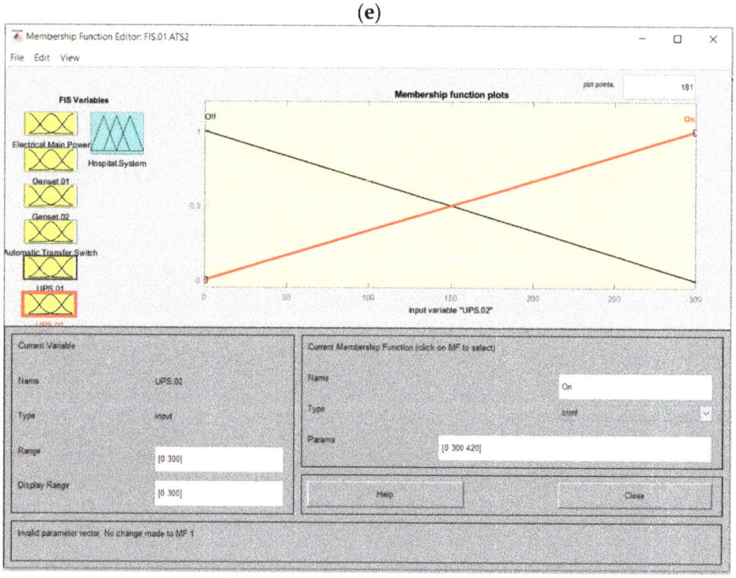

(f)

Figure 17. Membership Function Editor input variable: (**a**) electrical main power; (**b**) Genset 1; (**c**) Genset 2; (**d**) automatic transfer switch; (**e**) UPS 1; and (**f**) UPS 2.

In Figure 17, from (a) to (f), it is clear that the elements contained therein are intervals and parameters; however, the approach can be completed with Table 1, from (a) to (f), which corresponds to each corresponding item of Figure 17, from (a) to (f), respectively.

The Membership Function Editor of the fuzzy logic design for "output" variables is designed based on the input voltage variation: if the voltage received on the system for Under load is 34.5% up to 55.5% and at Normal load is 64.5% up to 85.5%, then the output that appears in the fuzzy MATLAB simulation is shown in Figure 18.

In Figure 18, it is clear that the elements enclosed in it are the intervals and parameters; however, they can be supported by Table 2.

Table 1. Membership Function Editor corresponding to Figure 17, respectively.

	Imput Fuction "EMP"		
Situation	**Low**	**Normal**	**High**
Range	(0 600)	(0 600)	(0 600)
Parameters	(−300 0 200 319)	(200 320 400 500)	(401 550 699 799)
	(a)		
	Imput Fuction "Genset 1 = Genset 2"		
Situation	**Off**		**On**
Range	(0 1000)		(0 1000)
Parameters	(−512 0 1000)		(0 1000 1578)
	(b–c)		
	Imput Fuction "ATS"		
Situation	**Not Function**		**Function**
Range	(0 200)		(0 200)
Parameters	(−80 0 200)		(0 200 280)
	(d)		
	Imput Fuction "UPS 1 = UPS 2"		
Situation	**Off**		**On**
Range	(0 300)		(0 300)
Parameters	(−120 0 300)		(0 300 420)
	(e–f)		

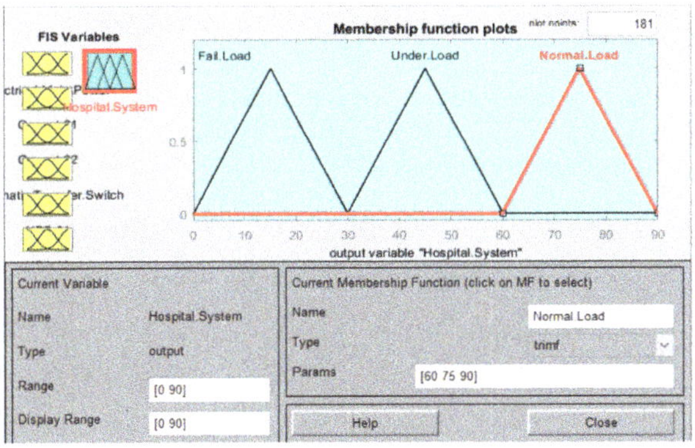

Figure 18. Membership Function Editor output variable "Hospital System".

Table 2. Output function "Hospital System".

	Output Function "EMP"		
Situation	**Fail Load**	**Under Load**	**Normal Load**
Range	(0 90)	(0 90)	(0 90)
Parameters	(0 15 30)	(30 45 60)	(60 75 90)

4.3.4. Rules of Editor

The next step is to apply the fuzzy operator "AND & THEN" in fuzzy rules, and the fuzzy rules that are by data collected and processed according to fuzzy logic with the following 17 rules: (1) If (Electrical Main Power is Low) and (Genset1 is Off) and (Genset2 is Off) and (Automatic Transfer Switch is Not Function) and (UPS1 is Off) and (UPS2 is Off) then (Hospital System is Failing Load); (2) If (Electrical Main Power is Low) and (Genset1 is On) and (Genset2 is Off) and (Automatic Transfer Switch is Function) and (UPS1 is On) and (UPS2 is On) then (Hospital System is Under Load); (3) If (Electrical Main Power is Low) and (Genset1 is Off) and (Genset2 is On) and (Automatic Transfer Switch is Function) and (UPS1 is On) and (UPS2 is On) then (Hospital System is Under Load); (4) If (Electrical Main Power is Low) and (Genset1 is On) and (Genset2 is On) and (Automatic Transfer Switch is Function) and (UPS1 is On) and (UPS2 is Off) then (Hospital System is Under Load); (5) If (Electrical Main Power is Low) and (Genset1 is On) and (Genset2 is On) and (Automatic Transfer Switch is Function) and (UPS1 is Off) and (UPS2 is On) then (Hospital System is Under Load); (6) If (Electrical Main Power is Low) and (Genset1 is On) and (Genset2 is On) and (Automatic Transfer Switch is Not Function) and (UPS1 is On) and (UPS2 is On) then (Hospital System is Under Load); (7) If (Electrical Main Power is Low) and (Genset1 is On) and (Genset2 is On) and (Automatic Transfer Switch is Function) and (UPS1 is On) and (UPS2 is On) then (Hospital System is Normal Load); (8) If (Electrical Main Power is Normal) & (Genset1 is Off) and (Genset2 is Off) and (Automat-ic Transfer Switch is Not Function) and (UPS1 is Off) and (UPS2 is Off) then (Hospital System is Failing Load); (9) If (Electrical Main Power is Normal) and (Genset1 is Off) and (Genset2 is Off) and (Automatic Transfer Switch is Not Function) and (UPS1 is On) and (UPS2 is On) then (Hospital System is Under Load); (10) If (Electrical Main Power is Normal) and (Genset1 is Off) and (Genset2 is Off) and (Automatic Transfer Switch is Function) and (UPS1 is On) and (UPS2 is On) then (Hospital System is Normal Load); (11) If (Electrical Main Power is High) and (Genset1 is Off) and (Genset2 is Off) and (Automatic Transfer Switch is Not Function) and (UPS1 is Off) and (UPS2 is Off) then (Hospital System is Failing Load); (12) If (Electrical Main Power is High) and (Genset1 is On) and (Genset2 is Off) and (Automatic Transfer Switch is Function) and (UPS1 is On) and (UPS2 is On) then (Hospital System is Under Load); (13) If (Electrical Main Power is High) and (Genset1 is Off) and (Genset2 is On) and (Automatic Transfer Switch is Function) and (UPS1 is On) and (UPS2 is On) then (Hospital System is Under Load); (14) If (Electrical Main Power is High) and (Genset1 is On) and (Genset2 is On) and (Automatic Transfer Switch is Function) and (UPS1 is On) and (UPS2 is Off) then (Hospital System is Under Load); (15) If (Electrical Main Power is High) and (Genset1 is On) and (Genset2 is On) and (Automatic Transfer Switch is Function) and (UPS1 is Off) and (UPS2 is On) then (Hospital System is Under Load); (16) If (Electrical Main Power is High) and (Genset1 is On) and (Genset2 is On) and (Automatic Transfer Switch is Not Function) and (UPS1 is On) and (UPS2 is On) then (Hospital System is Under Load); (17) If (Electrical Main Power is High) and (Genset1 is On) and (Genset2 is On) and (Automatic Transfer Switch is Function) and (UPS1 is On) and (UPS2 is On) then (Hospital System is Normal Load).

To support the fuzzy rules above, it is necessary to sort out the working orders of some important equipment of the electrical power system of the hospital that are being analysed. Based on MATLAB software, the fuzzy inference system was used to simulate how reliable and available their functions are in order to prevent any failure. The support of the fuzzy rules that show the simulation of the referred electrical circuits functioning is shown in Table 3.

Table 3. Rules editor with numerical values for the fuzzy inference system of electrical systems.

Rules Editor in Terms of Numerical in the Fuzzy Inference System								
	FIS Membership Fuctions Inputs						FIS Membership Outputs	
No.	EMP	Genset 1	Genset 2	ATS	UPS 1	UPS 2	Hospital System	
1	0	0	0	0	0	0	15	Fail
2	0	1000	0	200	300	300	45	Under Load
3	0	0	1000	200	300	300	45	Under Load
4	0	1000	1000	200	300	0	45	Under Load
5	0	1000	1000	200	0	300	45	Under Load
6	0	1000	1000	0	300	300	45	Under Load
7	0	1000	1000	200	300	300	75	Normal Load
8	360	0	0	0	0	0	15	Fail
9	360	0	0	0	300	300	45	Under Load
10	360	0	0	200	300	300	75	Normal Load
11	600	0	0	0	0	0	15	Fail
12	600	1000	1000	200	300	300	45	Under Load
13	600	0	1000	200	300	300	45	Under Load
14	600	1000	1000	200	300	0	45	Under Load
15	600	1000	1000	200	0	300	45	Under Load
16	600	1000	1000	0	300	300	45	Under Load
17	600	1000	1000	200	300	300	75	Normal Load

4.3.5. Rules Viewer

If (Electrical Main Power is Low) and (Genset1 is off) and (Genset2 is out) and (Automatic Transfer Switch is not function) and (UPS1 is off) and (UPS2 is off) then (Hospital System is failing load)—Figure 19.

Figure 19. Rules viewer of the fuzzy logic system for Failing Load.

If (Electrical Main Power is Normal) and (Genset1 is off) and (Genset2 is off) and (Automatic Transfer Switch is not function) and (UPS1 is on) and (UPS2 is on) then (Hospital System is under load)—Figure 20.

If (Electrical Main Power is Low) and (Genset1 is On) and (Genset2 is On) and (Automatic Transfer Switch is function) and (UPS1 is On) and (UPS2 is On) then (Hospital System is Normal load)—Figure 21.

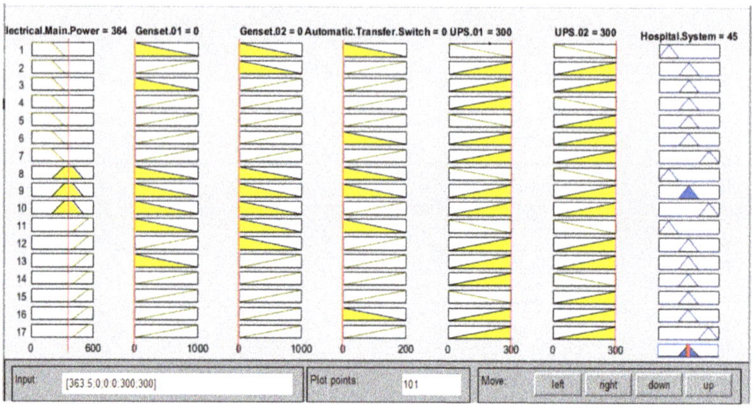

Figure 20. Rules viewer of the fuzzy logic system for Under Load.

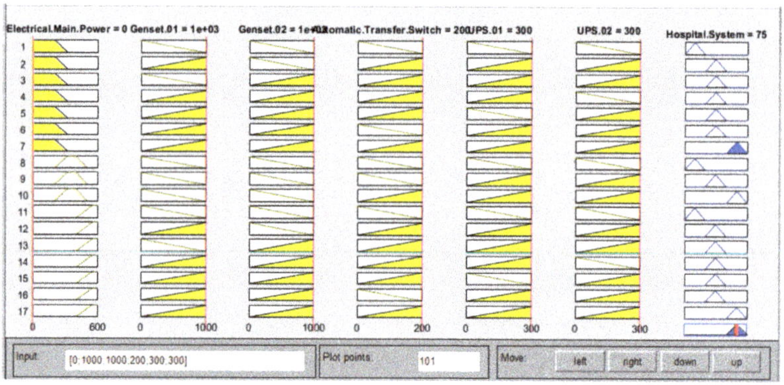

Figure 21. Rules viewer of the fuzzy logic system for Normal Load.

4.3.6. Surface Viewer

Fuzzy inference system (FIS) surface viewer for Electrical Main Power (EMP), Genset1 and Genset2, Auto Transfer Switch (ATS), UPS1, and UPS2 is shown in Figure 22a–c.

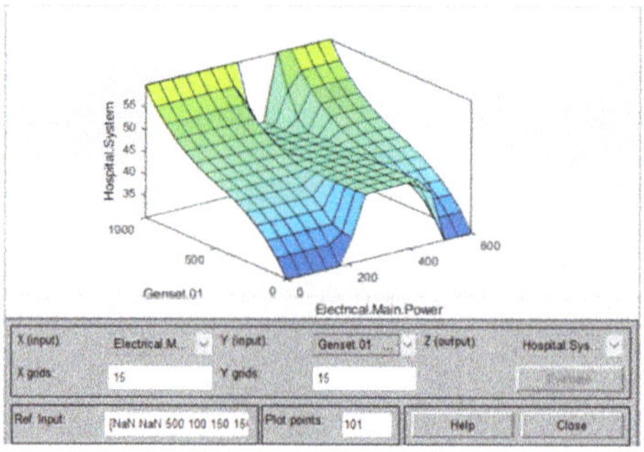

(**a**)

Figure 22. *Cont.*

Table 3. Rules editor with numerical values for the fuzzy inference system of electrical systems.

Rules Editor in Terms of Numerical in the Fuzzy Inference System								
	FIS Membership Fuctions Inputs						FIS Membership Outputs	
No.	EMP	Genset 1	Genset 2	ATS	UPS 1	UPS 2	Hospital System	
1	0	0	0	0	0	0	15	Fail
2	0	1000	0	200	300	300	45	Under Load
3	0	0	1000	200	300	300	45	Under Load
4	0	1000	1000	200	300	0	45	Under Load
5	0	1000	1000	200	0	300	45	Under Load
6	0	1000	1000	0	300	300	45	Under Load
7	0	1000	1000	200	300	300	75	Normal Load
8	360	0	0	0	0	0	15	Fail
9	360	0	0	0	300	300	45	Under Load
10	360	0	0	200	300	300	75	Normal Load
11	600	0	0	0	0	0	15	Fail
12	600	1000	1000	200	300	300	45	Under Load
13	600	0	1000	200	300	300	45	Under Load
14	600	1000	1000	200	300	0	45	Under Load
15	600	1000	1000	200	0	300	45	Under Load
16	600	1000	1000	0	300	300	45	Under Load
17	600	1000	1000	200	300	300	75	Normal Load

4.3.5. Rules Viewer

If (Electrical Main Power is Low) and (Genset1 is off) and (Genset2 is out) and (Automatic Transfer Switch is not function) and (UPS1 is off) and (UPS2 is off) then (Hospital System is failing load)—Figure 19.

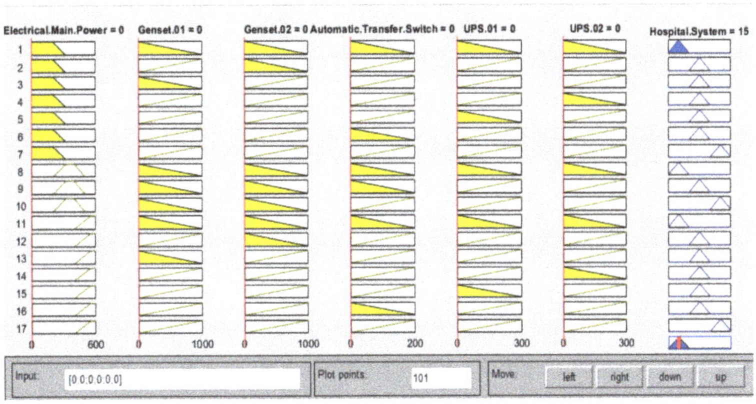

Figure 19. Rules viewer of the fuzzy logic system for Failing Load.

If (Electrical Main Power is Normal) and (Genset1 is off) and (Genset2 is off) and (Automatic Transfer Switch is not function) and (UPS1 is on) and (UPS2 is on) then (Hospital System is under load)—Figure 20.

If (Electrical Main Power is Low) and (Genset1 is On) and (Genset2 is On) and (Automatic Transfer Switch is function) and (UPS1 is On) and (UPS2 is On) then (Hospital System is Normal load)—Figure 21.

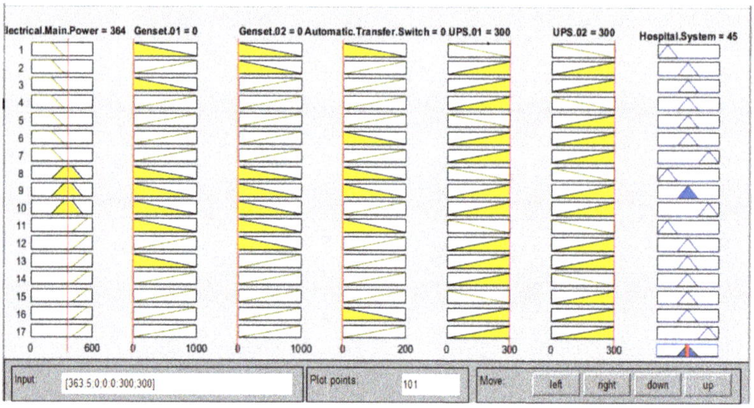

Figure 20. Rules viewer of the fuzzy logic system for Under Load.

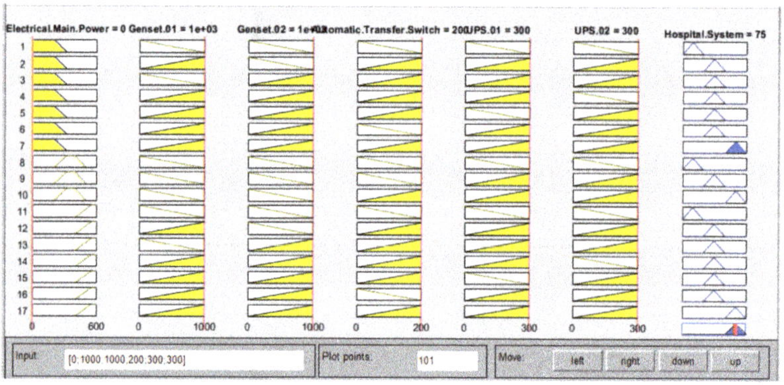

Figure 21. Rules viewer of the fuzzy logic system for Normal Load.

4.3.6. Surface Viewer

Fuzzy inference system (FIS) surface viewer for Electrical Main Power (EMP), Genset1 and Genset2, Auto Transfer Switch (ATS), UPS1, and UPS2 is shown in Figure 22a–c.

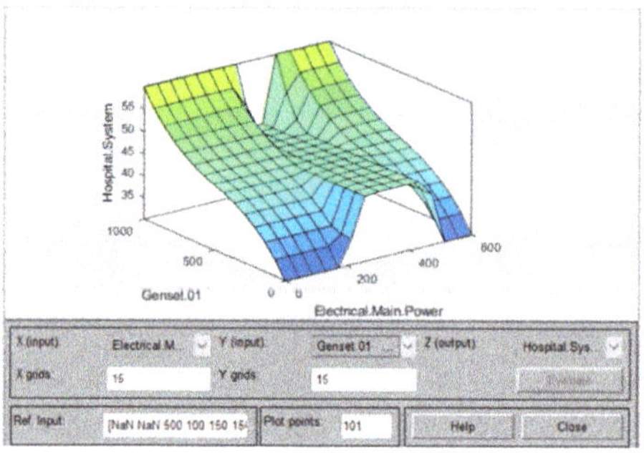

(**a**)

Figure 22. *Cont.*

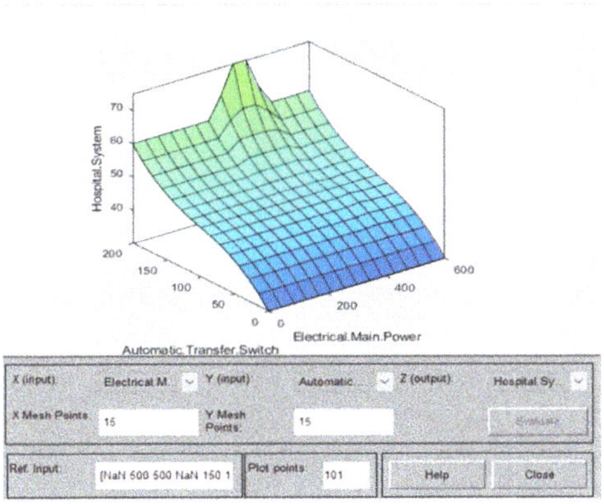

(**b**)

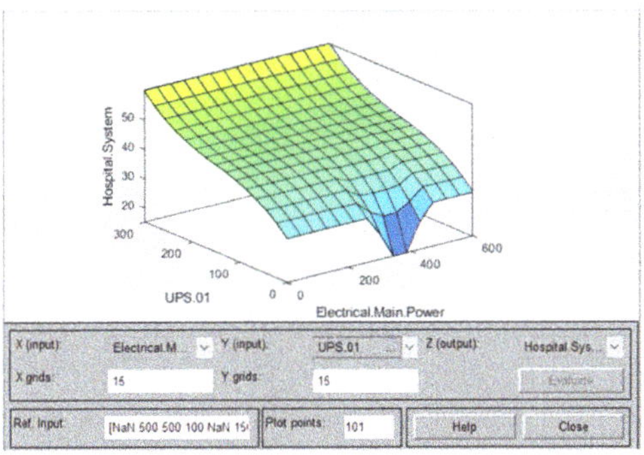

(**c**)

Figure 22. (**a**) The surface viewer of the FIS for Electrical Main Power and Genset 01 = Genset 02; (**b**) Electrical Main Power with ATS; (**c**) Electrical Main Power with UPS 01 = UPS 02.

4.4. *Synthesis*

The synthesis of the steps shown in previous sections is shown in Figure 23, representing the inference process corresponding to five inputs, 17 rules system, and one output plot.

Based on the description above, the analysis of the electrical power system of a large hospital can be described using Petri nets and a fuzzy inference system based on the following steps: (1) Creating an asset register and numbering system hierarchically; (2) Creating a functional block diagram; (3) Creating a process flow chart; (4) Establishing the system boundary definitions; (5) Creating a Petri net modelling and a fuzzy inference system; and (6) Describing the work function and the operational potential failures.

Based on the steps above, the following results can be obtained that support the actual operational documents in the field: (1) To identify the reliability and the weak points of the system; (2) To redesign the system aiming to remove the weakest points of the system to guarantee the asset reliability; (3) To simulate the most important solutions to improve the system reliability; and (4) To choose the best solution for the desired system reliability.

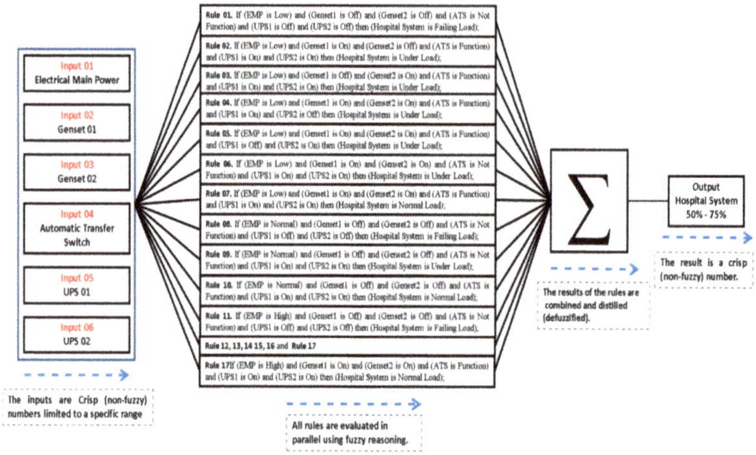

Figure 23. The surface viewer of the fuzzy logic system for the cycle of the process.

5. Conclusions

The paper demonstrates the usefulness and relevance of Petri nets in the dynamic modelling and analysing of the hospital's electrical power supply systems. The paper demonstrates how Petri nets can help to identify the weaknesses in a complex electrical system, to simulate more reliable solutions, and to validate them. With Petri nets, it is possible to identify the most critical components of the electrical system in a hospital. As there is no historical maintenance available, the authors used the fuzzy inference system to analyse the system with excellent results, as shown in the paper. The paper emphasizes the Petri nets and fuzzy inference system as a powerful tool to support maintenance management, providing the analysis and simulation approach for this type of system aiming to increase their reliability and availability. Based on the simulations of Petri nets, it is possible to identify the most critical devices in the electrical energy system of a large European hospital. The case study used a fuzzy inference system that demonstrates that the function of the assets, on average, reaches only 45% of reliability and availability since the function of the assets in their usefulness is only between 50% to 75%. To solve this weakness, the authors propose to install redundant automatic transfer switches (ATSs) to increase the asset's reliability and availability. Based on the preceding, it can be stated the contribution of the approach carried out along the paper, based on Petri nets and fuzzy logic to identify the reliability weak points in electrical power systems and to evaluate the new performance after the improvements are done in order to reach the desired availability. Still, the approach done can be generalized to any other organization, regardless of its nature.

The future developments to be carried on will be based on the comparison between the approach done in the present paper and a stochastic one, namely when it is used as a Reliability Centred Maintenance policy.

Author Contributions: Main research was done by C.A.P.; J.T.F. is the Supervisor; S.S. and H.R. contributed through their critical analysis about the methodology and results. All authors have read and agreed to the published version of the manuscript.

Funding: This research is sponsored by FEDER funds through the program COMPETE—Programa Operacional Factores de Competitividade—and by national funds through FCT—Fundação para a Ciência e a Tecnologia—under the project UIDB/00285/2020.

Institutional Review Board Statement: Not applicable.

Informed Consent Statement: Not applicable.

Data Availability Statement: Data is contained within the article.

Conflicts of Interest: The authors declare no conflict of interest.

References

1. American Hospital Association (AHA). *Hospital Engineering Handbook*; American Hospital Association: Chicago, IL, USA, 1980; ISBN 0-939450-74-7.
2. Anderson Ronald, T.; Lewis, N. *Reliability Centred Maintenance Management and Engineering Methods*; Elsevier Science Publishing Co., Inc: New York, NY, USA, 1990; ISBN 1-85166-470-X.
3. Department of the Army. *TM 5-698-2 Reliability-Centred Maintenance (RCM) for Command, Control, Communications, Computer, Intelligence, Surveillance, and Reconnaissance (C4ISR) Facilities*; Headquarters Department of the Army: Washington, DC, USA, 2003; Available online: https://www.wbdg.org/FFC/ARMYCOE/COETM/tm_5_698_2.pdf (accessed on 27 December 2015).
4. Farinha, J. *Manutenção A Terologia e as Novas Ferramentas de Gestão*; Edição, Monitor, Lda: Lisboa, Portugal, 2011; ISBN 9789729413827.
5. Gulati, R.; Smith, R. *Maintenance and Reliability Best Practices*; Industrial Press: New York, NY, USA, 2009; ISBN 978-0-8311-3311-5.
6. Moubray, J. *Reliability-Centred Maintenance*; Industrial Press: New York, NY, USA, 1997; ISBN 0-8311-3078-4.
7. Wang, W. An overview of the recent advances in delay-time-based maintenance modelling. *Reliab. Eng. Syst. Saf.* **2012**, *106*, 165–178. [CrossRef]
8. Mwanza, B.G.; Mbohwa, C. An Assessment of the Effectiveness of Equipment Maintenance Practices in Public Hospitals. *Procedia Manuf.* **2015**, *4*, 307–314. [CrossRef]
9. *The "IEEE C2: National Electrical Safety Code, 2007"*; The Instituto of Electrical and Electronics Engineering: New York, NY, USA, 2007; ISBN 0-7381-4893-8.
10. Christiansen, N.; Kaltschmitt, M.; Dzukowski, F.; Isensee, F. Electricity consumption of medical plug loads in hospital laboratories: Identification, evaluation, prediction and verification. *Energy Build.* **2015**, *107*, 392–406. [CrossRef]
11. BenSaleh, M.S.; Hermache, A.S. Planning, optimizing and analyzing of safety and maintenance for the critical role of emergency power plant in saudi healthcare facilities. In Proceedings of the 2010 IEEE Region 8 International Conference on Computational Technologies in Electrical and Electronics Engineering (SIBIRCON), Irkutsk, Russia, 11–15 July 2010. [CrossRef]
12. Jamshidi, A.; Rahimi, S.A.; Ait-Kadi, D.; Ruiz, A. A comprehensive fuzzy risk-based maintenance framework for prioritization of medical devices. *Appl. Soft Comput.* **2015**, *32*, 322–334. [CrossRef]
13. *The WHO (World Health Organization and Pan American Health Organization)*; World Health Organization: Geneva, Switzerland, 2015; ISBN 978-92-4-154898-4.
14. Hameed, A.; Khan, F.; Ahmed, S. A risk-based shutdown inspection and maintenance interval estimation considering human error. *Process. Saf. Environ. Prot.* **2016**, *100*, 9–21. [CrossRef]
15. Ali, W.; Qyyum, M.A.; Khan, M.S.; Duong, P.L.T.; Lee, M. Knowledge-inspired operational reliability for optimal LNG production at the offshore site. *Appl. Therm. Eng.* **2019**, *150*, 19–29. [CrossRef]
16. Velásquez, R.M.A.; Lara, J.V.M.; Melgar, A. Reliability model for switchgear failure analysis applied to ageing. *Eng. Fail. Anal.* **2019**, *101*, 36–60. [CrossRef]
17. Calixto, E. Reliability, Availability, and Maintainability (RAM Analysis). In *Gas and Oil Reliability Engineering*; Elsevier: Amsterdam, The Netherlands, 2016; pp. 269–470. [CrossRef]
18. Çekyay, B.; Özekici, S. Reliability, MTTF and steady-state availability analysis of systems with exponential lifetimes. *Appl. Math. Model.* **2015**, *39*, 284–296. [CrossRef]
19. Corvaro, F.; Giacchetta, G.; Marchetti, B.; Recanati, M. Reliability, Availability, Maintainability (RAM) study, on reciprocating compressors API 618. *Petroleum* **2017**, *3*, 266–272. [CrossRef]
20. Ebeling, C. *An Introduction to Reliability and Maintainability Engineering*; Waveland Press: Long Grove, IL, USA, 2010.
21. Feng, Q.; Zhu, C.; Sun, B.; Liu, L. Process reengineering method for synthesis design of reliability maintainability supportability and performance. In Proceedings of the 2011 9th International Conference on Reliability, Maintainability, and Safety, Guiyang, China, 12–15 June 2011. [CrossRef]
22. Hameed, Z.; Vatn, J.; Heggset, J. Challenges in the reliability and maintainability data collection for offshore wind turbines. *Renew. Energy* **2011**, *36*, 2154–2165. [CrossRef]
23. Sikos, L.; Klemeš, J. Reliability, availability and maintenance optimisation of heat exchanger networks. *Appl. Therm. Eng.* **2010**, *30*, 63–69. [CrossRef]
24. Song, Y.; Wang, B. Survey on Reliability of Power Electronic Systems. *IEEE Trans. Power Electron.* **2013**, *28*, 591–604. [CrossRef]
25. Sutton, I. Reliability, Availability, and Maintainability. In *Process Risk and Reliability Management*; Elsevier: Amsterdam, The Netherlands, 2015; pp. 667–688. [CrossRef]
26. Wang, J.-J.; Fu, C.; Yang, K.; Zhang, X.-T.; Shi, G.-H.; Zhai, J. Reliability and availability analysis of redundant BCHP (building cooling, heating and power) system. *Energy* **2013**, *61*, 531–540. [CrossRef]
27. Zio, E.; Fan, M.; Zeng, Z.; Kang, R. Application of reliability technologies in civil aviation: Lessons learnt and perspectives. *Chin. J. Aeronaut.* **2019**, *32*, 143–158. [CrossRef]
28. Shen, J.; Cui, L.; Ma, Y. Availability and optimal maintenance policy for systems degrading in dynamic environments. *Eur. J. Oper. Res.* **2019**, *276*, 133–143. [CrossRef]
29. Do, P.; Vu, H.C.; Barros, A.; Bérenguer, C. Maintenance grouping for multi-component systems with availability constraints and limited maintenance teams. *Reliab. Eng. Syst. Saf.* **2015**, *142*, 56–67. [CrossRef]

30. Pinto, C.A.; Farinha, J.T.; Singh, S. Contributions of Petri Nets to the Reliability and Availability of an Electrical Power System in a Big European Hospital-A Case Study. *WSEAS Trans. Syst. Control.* **2021**, *16*, 21–42. [CrossRef]
31. Wang, J. *Timed Petri Nets: Theory and Application*; Springer US: Boston, MA, USA, 1998; ISBN 978-1-4615-5537-7.
32. Volovoi, V. Modeling of system reliability Petri nets with aging tokens. *Reliab. Eng. Syst. Saf.* **2004**, *84*, 149–161. [CrossRef]
33. Chew, S.; Dunnett, S.; Andrews, J. Phased mission modelling of systems with maintenance-free operating periods using simulated Petri nets. *Reliab. Eng. Syst. Saf.* **2008**, *93*, 980–994. [CrossRef]
34. Garg, H. Reliability analysis of repairable systems using Petri nets and vague Lambda-Tau methodology. *ISA Trans.* **2013**, *52*, 6–18. [CrossRef] [PubMed]
35. Leigh, J.M.; Dunnett, S.J. Use of Petri Nets to Model the Maintenance of Wind Turbines. *Qual. Reliab. Eng. Int.* **2014**, *32*, 167–180. [CrossRef]
36. Ren, Z.; Wu, Y. Modeling the Performance of Aircraft Utilizing Maintenance Free Operating Periods. *Procedia Eng.* **2015**, *99*, 214–218. [CrossRef]
37. Sadou, N.; Demmou, H. Reliability analysis of discrete event dynamic systems with Petri nets. *Reliab. Eng. Syst. Saf.* **2009**, *94*, 1848–1861. [CrossRef]
38. Eisenberger, D.; Fink, O. Assessment of maintenance strategies for railway vehicles using Petri-nets. *Transp. Res. Procedia* **2017**, *27*, 205–214. [CrossRef]
39. Farinha, J. *Asset Maintenance Engineering Methodologies*; CRC Press/Taylor & Francis Group: Boca Raton, FL, USA, 2018.
40. Cannarile, F.; Compare, M.; Rossi, E.; Zio, E. A fuzzy expectation maximization based method for estimating the parameters of a multi-state degradation model from imprecise maintenance outcomes. *Ann. Nucl. Energy* **2017**, *110*, 739–752. [CrossRef]
41. Ladj, A.; Tayeb, F.B.-S.; Varnier, C.; Dridi, A.A.; Selmane, N. A Hybrid of Variable Neighbor Search and Fuzzy Logic for the permutation flowshop scheduling problem with predictive maintenance. *Procedia Comput. Sci.* **2017**, *112*, 663–672. [CrossRef]
42. Touat, M.; Bouzidi-Hassini, S.; Benbouzid-Sitayeb, F.; Benhamou, B. A hybridization of genetic algorithms and fuzzy logic for the single-machine scheduling with flexible maintenance problem under human resource constraints. *Appl. Soft Comput.* **2017**, *59*, 556–573. [CrossRef]
43. Jaderi, F.; Ibrahim, Z.Z.; Zahiri, M.R. Criticality analysis of petrochemical assets using risk based maintenance and the fuzzy inference system. *Process. Saf. Environ. Prot.* **2019**, *121*, 312–325. [CrossRef]
44. Ratnayake, R.C.; Antosz, K. Development of a Risk Matrix and Extending the Risk-based Maintenance Analysis with Fuzzy Logic. *Procedia Eng.* **2017**, *182*, 602–610. [CrossRef]
45. Seiti, H.; Hafezalkotob, A.; Fattahi, R. Extending a pessimistic–optimistic fuzzy information axiom based approach considering acceptable risk: Application in the selection of maintenance strategy. *Appl. Soft Comput.* **2018**, *67*, 895–909. [CrossRef]
46. Babashamsi, P.; Golzadfar, A.; Yusoff, N.I.M.; Ceylan, H.; Nor, N.G.M. Integrated fuzzy analytic hierarchy process and VIKOR method in the prioritization of pavement maintenance activities. *Int. J. Pavement Res. Technol.* **2016**, *9*, 112–120. [CrossRef]
47. Cordón, O. A historical review of evolutionary learning methods for Mamdani-type fuzzy rule-based systems: Designing interpretable genetic fuzzy systems. *Int. J. Approx. Reason.* **2011**, *52*, 894–913. [CrossRef]
48. Zahabi, M.; Kaber, D. A fuzzy system hazard analysis approach for human-in-the-loop systems. *Saf. Sci.* **2019**, *120*, 922–931. [CrossRef]
49. Akgun, A.; Sezer, E.; Nefeslioglu, H.; Gokceoglu, C.; Pradhan, B. An easy-to-use MATLAB program (MamLand) for the assessment of landslide susceptibility using a Mamdani fuzzy algorithm. *Comput. Geosci.* **2012**, *38*, 23–34. [CrossRef]
50. Kacimi, M.A.; Guenounou, O.; Brikh, L.; Yahiaoui, F.; Hadid, N. New mixed-coding PSO algorithm for a self-adaptive and automatic learning of Mamdani fuzzy rules. *Eng. Appl. Artif. Intell.* **2020**, *89*, 103417. [CrossRef]
51. Lu, K.-Y.; Sy, C.-C. A real-time decision-making of maintenance using fuzzy agent. *Expert Syst. Appl.* **2009**, *36*, 2691–2698. [CrossRef]
52. Dhimish, M.; Holmes, V.; Mehrdadi, B.; Dales, M. Comparing Mamdani Sugeno fuzzy logic and RBF ANN network for PV fault detection. *Renew. Energy* **2018**, *117*, 257–274. [CrossRef]
53. Kraidi, L.; Shah, R.; Matipa, W.; Borthwick, F. Using stakeholders' judgement and fuzzy logic theory to analyze the risk influencing factors in oil and gas pipeline projects: Case study in Iraq, Stage II. *Int. J. Crit. Infrastruct. Prot.* **2020**, *28*, 100337. [CrossRef]
54. Khosravanian, R.; Sabah, M.; Wood, D.A.; Shahryari, A. Weight on drill bit prediction models: Sugeno-type and Mamdani-type fuzzy inference systems compared. *J. Nat. Gas Sci. Eng.* **2016**, *36*, 280–297. [CrossRef]
55. Teo, T.T.; Logenthiran, T.; Woo, W.L.; Abidi, K.; John, T.; Wade, N.S.; Greenwood, D.M.; Patsios, C.; Taylor, P.C. Optimization of Fuzzy Energy-Management System for Grid-Connected Microgrid Using NSGA-II. *IEEE Trans. Cybern.* **2020**, 1–12. [CrossRef]
56. Teo, T.T.; Thillainathan, L.; Woo, W.L.; Abidi, K. Intelligent Controller for Energy Storage System in Grid-Connected Microgrid. *IEEE Trans. Syst. Man Cybern. Syst.* **2021**, *51*, 650–658. [CrossRef]
57. Teo, T.T.; Logenthiran, T.; Woo, W.L.; Abidi, K. Fuzzy logic control of energy storage system in microgrid operation. In Proceedings of the 2016 IEEE Innovative Smart Grid Technologies-Asia (ISGT-Asia), Melbourne, VIC, Australia, 28 November–1 December 2016; pp. 65–70.
58. HiPS: Hierarchical Petri Net Simulator. Available online: http://sourceforge.net/projects/hips-tools/ (accessed on 27 December 2015).

applied sciences

MDPI

Article

The Role of Industry 4.0 and BPMN in the Arise of Condition-Based and Predictive Maintenance: A Case Study in the Automotive Industry

Jorge Fernandes [1], João Reis [1,2,*], Nuno Melão [3], Leonor Teixeira [4] and Marlene Amorim [1]

1 Department of Economics, Management, Industrial Engineering and Tourism, GOVCOPP, Campus Universitário de Santiago, Aveiro University, 3810-193 Aveiro, Portugal; jorge.fernandes27@live.ua.pt (J.F.); mamorim@ua.pt (M.A.)
2 Industrial Engineering and Management, EIGeS, Lusófona University, 1749-024 Lisbon, Portugal
3 Research Center in Digital Services, CISeD, Polytechnic Institute of Viseu, Campus Politécnico, 3504-510 Viseu, Portugal; nmelao@estgv.ipv.pt
4 Department of Economics, Management, Industrial Engineering and Tourism, IEETA, Campus Universitário de Santiago, Aveiro University, 3810-193 Aveiro, Portugal; lteixeira@ua.pt
* Correspondence: reis.joao@ua.pt

Abstract: This article addresses the evolution of Industry 4.0 (I4.0) in the automotive industry, exploring its contribution to a shift in the maintenance paradigm. To this end, we firstly present the concepts of predictive maintenance (PdM), condition-based maintenance (CBM), and their applications to increase awareness of why and how these concepts are revolutionizing the automotive industry. Then, we introduce the business process management (BPM) and business process model and notation (BPMN) methodologies, as well as their relationship with maintenance. Finally, we present the case study of the Renault Cacia, which is developing and implementing the concepts mentioned above.

Keywords: Industry 4.0; condition-based maintenance; predictive maintenance; business process model and notation; business process management

Citation: Fernandes, J.; Reis, J.; Melão, N.; Teixeira, L.; Amorim, M. The Role of Industry 4.0 and BPMN in the Arise of Condition-Based and Predictive Maintenance: A Case Study in the Automotive Industry. *Appl. Sci.* **2021**, *11*, 3438. https://doi.org/10.3390/app11083438

Academic Editors: Federico Divina, Piera Centobelli and Stephanos Theodossiades

Received: 3 February 2021
Accepted: 8 April 2021
Published: 12 April 2021

1. Introduction

With the continuous development of Industry 4.0 (I4.0) and its applications, business models have been adapted to keep up with the incorporation of new technologies. Since industrial companies are operating in an increasingly competitive environment, with very short cycles of technological innovation, where process optimization and automation are pivotal to the company's survival [1], researchers and managers are called to contribute to the understanding and description of the phenomenon. While the concept of the intelligent factory has evolved over time, today it is highly digitalized and interconnected [2,3], supported by emerging information and communication technologies (ICT), and involves the operation of the so-called cyber-physical systems (CPS). In this environment, the main components are usually robotized and connected through complementary technologies, such as the Internet of Things (IoT), which enables measurement, sensing, control, and communication in all the manufacturing processes. As a result, it is expected that facilities can be managed in real-time and with the necessary flexibility to meet continuous changes.

The vision of an intelligent factory will only be possible if machines work properly, with the desired precision and efficiency. Herein lies the crucial role of maintenance, which must fulfill the delicate task of keeping machines and their components operational [4]. With the arrival of predictive maintenance (PdM) and condition-based maintenance (CBM) in the context of I4.0, the whole process changed, creating new challenges and opportunities. At the same time, it is expected that productivity will continue to grow through the prediction of failures and consequent maximization of the machines' life cycle [5]. However, these new forms of maintenance represent a very complex process and involve an indeterminate number of variables. Here, the use of artificial intelligence (AI) techniques and advanced algorithms are crucial to gather and interpret the data acquired from the physical world, namely, from machines. The acquired knowledge, often resulting from the analysis of large volumes of data, is instrumental in supporting the decision-making process. In fact, the objective is that the machines reach a self-decision capacity [4] to directly identify which problems occur and when components need to be replaced. I4.0 can, thus, improve maintenance decision-making through the employment of industrial sensors and big data technology, which can lead to a more responsive information system [6]. However, we need viable solutions to assist the maintenance decision-making process. Its application to the automotive industry is of paramount importance, as this industry has to comply with key performance indicators [7] to control the overall manufacturing performance (e.g., IATF 16949:2016) [8]. Indeed, the automotive industry invests significant amounts in new technologies and automation to achieve short lead times, high-quality standards, and high levels of competitiveness [9].

Similar research has been carried out in the context of intelligent, condition-based, and predictive maintenance systems, mainly in the context of I4.0 [10–12] and in the automotive industry [13,14]. However, none of those articles used business process management (BPM) and business process model and notation (BPMN) to improve the maintenance systems. The literature shows that BPM and BPMN have gained greater significance, as they promote better communication and transparency in the decision-making process [15], especially with regard to the integration of new concepts that need to be understood and accepted by all the companies' stakeholders. That said, we developed two research questions (RQ), as follows:

Research Questions 1 (RQ1). *How does BPMN contribute to predictive and condition-based maintenance?*

Research Questions 2 (RQ2). *What contributions are identified from the use of predictive and condition-based maintenance in the automotive industry?*

The next section focuses on the literature review, where the most relevant concepts are presented; following, we make some considerations about the methodological process and focus on the results of the case study; in the last section, we present the conclusions, where the practical and theoretical contributions of the work are evidenced.

2. Literature Review

This section presents the most relevant concepts, namely the I4.0 principles and technologies, as well as how these technologies trigger changes to the maintenance paradigm. It also discusses the theoretical framework, which includes the concepts of CBM, PdM, BPM, and BPMN.

2.1. Brief Considerations of I4.0

Industries are the part of the economy that produces typically highly mechanized and automated material goods [16]. However, the concept of an industry can be traced back to the end of the eighteenth century, with the first industrial revolution (Industry 1.0), characterized by the introduction of mechanical manufacturing systems utilizing water and steam power [17,18]. Almost one century later, in 1870, the electrification and labor division led to a second industrial revolution (Industry 2.0), evidenced by mass production and assembly lines that used electric power [17]. Following, the need to increase the efficiency of the production process led to the third industrial revolution (Industry 3.0) that was shaped by the introduction of electronic and ICT systems for automation [17], which represents the basis of all changes in the production paradigm. The continuous developments of ICT also led to the introduction of CPS, the core of the latest and current industrial revolution (Industry 4.0) (Figure 1).

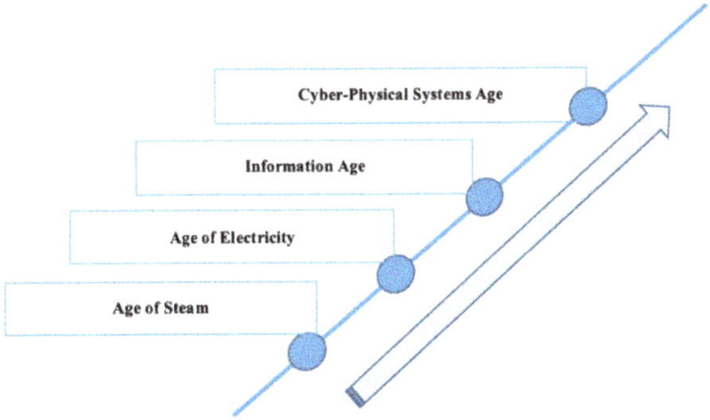

Figure 1. From Industry 1.0 to Industry 4.0 (Adapted from Xu et al. [17]).

Ultimately, I4.0 aims to achieve process automation, digitalization [3], and computerization using instantaneous data. I4.0 can then be identified as a new industrial vision [19] focused on increasing productivity, high product customization capabilities [20], real-time alerts and interventions [21], innovative service models [22], dynamic product improvement, and, ultimately, new business models [17]. The integration of all these factors translates into an intelligent factory, the central object of this new industrial age [23]. In general terms, I4.0 follows six principles, which help to identify potential uses and provide a guide for implementing this concept in, for example, facilities. Following Hermann et al. [18], we present the following principles: interoperability, which is the capacity of two systems to communicate reciprocally; virtualization identified as the dematerialization of physical procedures and processes (e.g., sensors); decentralization that aims to enable machines with decision-making capabilities based on the interpretation of the collected data; real-time capacity, which is the ability to solve production errors in real-time through the development of advanced technologies and new processes; service orientation, where software is directed to deliver solutions as services that meet the needs and expectations of the customer; and modularity stands by the ease of coupling and decoupling production modules, following current demand and orders. Not surprisingly, not all authors agree with such principles. However, the most crucial aspect to retain is that I4.0 is an integrative value creation system [24] that brings disruptive changes to supply chains, business models, and business processes [25,26]. The automotive industry, being one of the most critical industries globally, has also undergone a major transformation [27]. At the same time, the automotive industry integrates several automated, innovative, and technological systems (I4.0) [28], which contribute to cost reduction [29], as well as to increase quality, production, and customer satisfaction [30]. Therefore, the automotive industry influences a wide range of partner industries worldwide, as it plays a key role in the upstream and downstream supply chain [31], being itself a promoter of I4.0-oriented technologies.

2.2. *Industry 4.0 Technologies That Changed the Maintenance Paradigm*

As we mentioned earlier, the objective behind I4.0 is networking, as if it were a collaborative community, to collect, exchange and analyze data through embedded computer-controlled feedback circuits looking for optimal solutions and predict future behaviors. In that regard, ICT has allowed people, machines, and other objects to connect, and it has been possible to build a highly flexible production model, called the Cyber-Physical Production System (CPPS), which consists of transforming production supported in physical processes into production sustained by the use of CPS [19,23]. On the other hand, sensors play a fundamental role in collecting data from the physical world to cyberspace, functioning as actuators that transmit feedback information generated from the cyber level to the physical space again, the latter feedback being obtained through computational skills and data analysis and management [32]. Naturally, these systems are complemented with other features, such as IoT that enable data transmission or other short-range communication technologies, such as near field communication (NFC) or radio frequency identification (RFID). It is, therefore, possible for physical devices to be connected to each other (e.g., NCF) and/or by networks (e.g., IoT), so that it is feasible to obtain information from sensors or processes throughout the plant and store it in cloud-based data centers [33]. In addition, data production has reached unprecedented levels in many domains and has not been restricted to industry [34]. In the industry domain, though, the development of Big Data analysis techniques and technologies aims to promote the interpretation of data (i.e., that the data makes sense) that is usually collected from a wide variety of heterogeneous sources (e.g., sensors, temperature, voltages), increasing its complexity. The concept of the Internet of Services (IoS), sometimes identified as an extension of the IoT, is also involved in the exchange of information, adding a service-focused view to production [10]. Therefore, it is evident that the technologies mentioned are not only changing the paradigm of the production process but are also impacting the entire supply chain [35], from transportation to logistics, through health, and even maintenance and diagnosis [36].

After the 2nd industrial revolution, engineers and industrialists started working on developing methods to optimize production in the search for a balance between cost reduction and quality increase [37]. As a result of mass production, machines and their components began to experience greater wear and tear and, consequently, higher degradation, making its mitigation a growing concern in order to ensure continuous and flawless production [5]. Thereat, the concept of maintenance finds its centrality in the industrial world. Perhaps, the best-known typology is the run-to-failure (R2F) or, also known as, corrective maintenance (CM) [38]. This type of maintenance essentially consists of repairing a machine only when a particular failure is detected, which typically implies that this equipment will stop producing when it is being repaired. Its underlying advantage is that the machine or component will exceed the maximum period of use that the supplier has stipulated. However, there is no way to avoid the unplanned shutdown of the machine and the consequent interruption of production [4]. To avoid breakage due to maintenance stops, the time-based (TM) or preventive maintenance (PM) was introduced. In PM, time planning or process iterations are foreseen for carrying out inspections and maintenance according to a schedule [38]. PM is commonly identified as the best form of preventing failures [38], but there is no learning about the machine's degradation profile for future actions [33], as well as a long suspension time and high operating costs [4]. Recently, with the emergence of I4.0, companies were able to start breaking the scenario of compensation between maintenance cost and performance with the use of condition-based maintenance (CBM) and predictive maintenance (PdM) [5].

Figure 2 summarizes the characterization of the three basic types of maintenance. As can be seen, the actions taken by the industrial engineer in the corrective maintenance take place after the failure occurrence; on the other hand, there are also preventive maintenance activities that can be applied in the pre- and post-failure periods; finally, predictive maintenance deals with errors in advance. Disruptive maintenance technologies are transforming all types of industries, in particular the automotive industry. Therefore, these technologies are changing traditional business models into more competitive models [30].

2.3. Condition-Based and Predictive Maintenance

Advances in the automation and integration of mechatronics in industrial machines have enabled real-time information about their status and functioning, namely through sensors [39]. CBM is a maintenance program that recommends maintenance decisions based on the information collected through condition monitoring. It consists of three main steps: data acquisition, data processing, and maintenance decision-making [40]. Thus, sensors have promoted predictive maintenance typologies, since CBM involves a prior assessment of the asset's condition, monitoring significant parameters for its operation. According to the Portuguese standard NP EN 13306:2007—Maintenance terminology, this monitoring can be made according to a predefined calendar or according to a certain number of units of use of the equipment, serving as a reference for future actions.

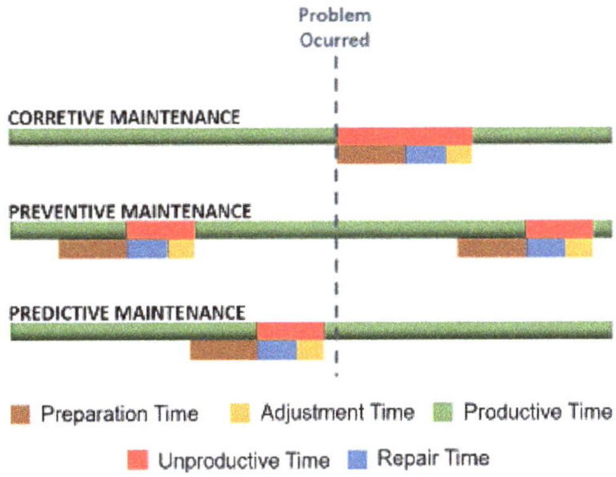

Figure 2. Types of maintenance.

In recent years, several techniques have been developed to monitor and control the desired parameters of the equipment, such as analysis of vibrations, temperatures, pressures, ultrasounds, currents, and voltages [41–45]. Predictive maintenance can be based on the continuous monitoring of certain parameters of a machine or the entire process so that its current condition is monitored in real-time and its future operational state can be predicted [4]. Ruiz-Sarmiento et al. [33] consider that PdM aims to monitor and analyze the evolution of the degradation state of a machine, being possible to identify, in advance, the need for maintenance interventions before the occurrence of malfunctions. Thus, maintenance actions are performed only when necessary in order to maintain the operational status of the equipment. Susto et al. [46] state that this process is aided by predictive tools based on historical data and integrity factors. Lee et al. [4] further point out that the introduction of this maintenance practice optimizes a compensation scenario, maximizing the life cycle of the machine's components while maximizing its uptime (Figure 3a).

We also highlight the fact that there is no universal agreement for the definitions of CBM and PdM. In some cases, there are authors who identify the concepts as synonyms [47], although many others make a clear distinction between the two practices [39,48], and most of them observe CBM as a short-term measure, while PdM allows taking into account the future conditions of the asset, in order to maximize its life cycle and its components (Figure 3b). Lee et al. [4] also stress that a proper integration of predictive maintenance can lead to a significant reduction of operational costs, which is one of the main objectives of I4.0, including, for example: schedule of maintenance actions; reduction of unexpected stoppage; reduction of unavailability by stopping when it is really necessary (i.e., when the degradation state requires it); development of data history for each equipment; elimination of unnecessary replacement of components if the machine is operating satisfactorily, and so on. Although CBM and PdM have been studied in the context of I4.0 in recent years, few researchers have paid attention to this type of maintenance techniques in the automotive industry [49]. Nevertheless, a major issue in production planning of the automotive industry is related to the unexpected downtime, which is associated with aging equipment [50]. The adoption of CMB and PdM is fundamental in this industry because it allows detecting defects, to predict failures, thus increasing performance [51]. It is in this regard that the application of modeling and management tools, such as BPMN in the maintenance process becomes useful, as is its use in other industries [52].

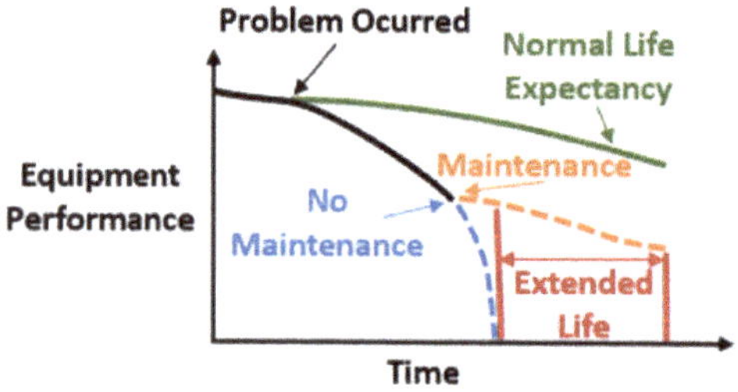

(a)

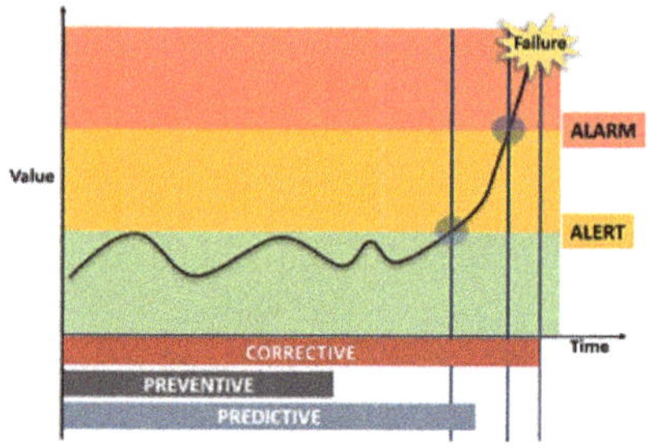

(b)

Figure 3. Factory maintenance: (**a**) Predictive maintenance (example); (**b**) Condition-based maintenance (example).

2.4. BPM and BPMN Concepts and Their Role in Maintenance

BPM has become a reference in the last decade, bringing together various techniques and tools that combine information, management, and engineering technologies to improve business processes [53,54]. Therefore, BPM can be relevant to evaluate the strategic processes of organizations so that there is a continuous improvement in the effectiveness and efficiency of business processes [55], and, ultimately, an increase in the productivity and competitiveness of a company [56]. Inter-organizational sharing of business processes has also become a difficult task due to the lack of a single semantics and the use of various standards in the modeling and execution of business processes [57]. To overcome this problem, many organizations have chosen to model their processes using BPMN, a standard language that graphically represents business processes [58]. In automotive production, processes are often complex and difficult to describe and, therefore, are more susceptible to errors. Companies have tried to describe their processes through diagrams, which allow them to transmit the information associated with the processes more easily, as well as to discover inconsistencies and/or possible bad practices. By using BPMN notation, it is possible to represent a process, validating it and guaranteeing its consistency, with the same meaning as the textual/documentary description of the existing organizational processes [57]. As a result, BPMN can be an asset and an interesting practice for all employees to understand a particular business process [57,58].

In sum, the BPM can be a valuable approach to model processes in the I4.0 and, in particular, in condition-based predictive maintenance [17]. In this regard, it will be essential to standardize processes, enabling different parties to describe and communicate their needs, problems, and relationships [59,60], albeit it requires a communication effort between stakeholders. In the case of PdM, the raised issues are generally related to the lack of information (e.g., difficulty in collecting data) or excess of information (e.g., difficulties in data processing), conflict of existing evidence, the ambiguity of information, and measurement of certain parameters. The BPMN can then be a beneficial approach in the I4.0 domain, as well-defined processes will help to limit uncertainty in the decision-making process, eliminate redundant activities, and also manage resources in a rational way. In addition, the modularization of the process also facilitates communication and promotes transparency [61].

3. The Case Study of Renault Cacia Factory

This article follows qualitative, exploratory, and descriptive case study research. Specifically, it investigates the maintenance projects at a well-known Renault factory (also known as Renault Cacia) that has been operating in Portugal for over 40 years [62]. Given that case studies typically aim to understand and describe a particular real-life phenomenon [63], the choice of Renault Cacia as the unit of analysis seemed appropriate. First, it is a reference in the international segment of the automotive industry, producing large volumes of gearboxes and other mechanical engine components. Further, it carries out several successful maintenance projects that end up justifying the relevance of this research.

Through the use of several data collection techniques, ranging from semi-structured interviews to participant observation and analysis of organizational documents, we sought to understand how the latest maintenance projects were carried out at the factory. Thus, this study reports on the: (1) contributions of the project leaders, operators, maintenance group, and elements of the engineering department; (2) analysis of the operators' behavior and reactions to the implementation of new maintenance projects at the factory; (3) analysis of the technical documents of the test bench, notably the component maintenance plan, the technical recommendations of the factory suppliers and the Failure Mode and Effect Analysis (FMEA) reports.

The group of interviewees included informants with high technical knowledge and who could observe the phenomenon from different angles. As such, they were chosen from different areas, i.e., project leader, maintenance group, and engineering department. We used an interview protocol that served to establish a consistent standard to compare participants' responses, assisting in identifying and mitigating inconsistencies [64]. The interviews were transcribed and discussed with all informants so that there were no errors in interpretation and to understand all contextual details, a procedure that allowed to increase the research validity [65]. It is worth highlighting the valuable contribution of Renault engineers, who actively participated in the validation of the article results.

The participant observation and documental analysis were very relevant as secondary sources in that they allowed corroborating the information collected through the interviews [66]. The participant observation was useful because it allowed seeing the phenomenon first hand, but also because it allowed close interaction with operators. To corroborate the data collected from the interviews, we photographed a series of maintenance activities [67]. A diary was used [68] to record all observations in loco (i.e., description of the photographs) and informal conversations that occurred throughout the research. This data collection source allowed to clarify issues that were raised during the interview phase. Lastly, the official documents (e.g., FMEA reports) associated with the project enabled a better understanding of the overall process and associated technologies. The secondary sources allowed to increase the research's reliability, as they contributed to triangulate and corroborate the data obtained during the interviews phase [66].

The studied process includes a part of the JT4 gearbox project, namely, one of its components—the JT4 mechanism crankcase (MC). This structure is a metallic container of a single reference that protects and fits into other gearbox components, as can be observed in Figure 4.

The initial step of the research was to understand the manufacturing process of the crankcase mechanism, whose line is called module 1 (M1). Renault Cacia buys the raw parts abroad, which logistics providers transport to the storage area of the production line using automated guided vehicles (AGV). The operator responsible for starting the M1 must order parts to supply the line through the Renault Order Management System (RSGP) and validate the containers' arrival by zipping the accompanying label called GALIA. Then, the parts are sent to operation, where vertical and horizontal machining of the workpiece is performed. The parts pass through the washing machine to remove impurities and residues from machining operations. There are two control posts at the end of the line to check the product's quality, measuring seal and quality. If it complies, the operator zips the finished product containers, which are then transported again via AGV to the corresponding finished product warehouse. Otherwise, the MC is sent to nonconforming products' screening mat, where it is later analyzed. The process described above is relevant to contextualize and understand the sequence of module 1 and bridge with the next section (i.e., Results and Discussion).

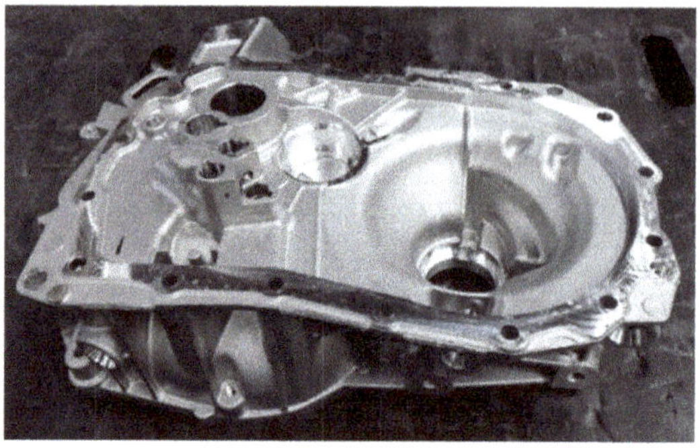

Figure 4. Crankcase mechanism.

The data collected has a twofold purpose. First, it helped the researchers draw BPMN diagrams and, thus, gain a visual understanding of the process and compare different maintenance programs (Annex A). The diagrams also had a pedagogical purpose, as they permitted to define a standard of action for maintenance, which all operators should follow. Second, it enabled an understanding of maintenance projects at the factory. To structure data analysis, we used the content analysis technique, following three steps [69,70]: (1) reading all the data to identify key phrases and ideas; (2) codification of words and phrases; (3) identification of categories and patterns in the codes to find relevant topics; (4) generation of an overview of the phenomenon. Overall, the content analysis allowed us to integrate, code, and analyze a significant volume of data by building a hierarchy of categories and subcategories and identifying emerging patterns and ideas [34].

4. Results and Discussion

At the factory, there are 12 machining centers for the manufacture of crankcases, of which six are GROB equipment, and the remaining six are DMG 63H equipment (Figure 5) (see also Silva et al. [71]). They all perform the same vertical and horizontal machining of the MC.

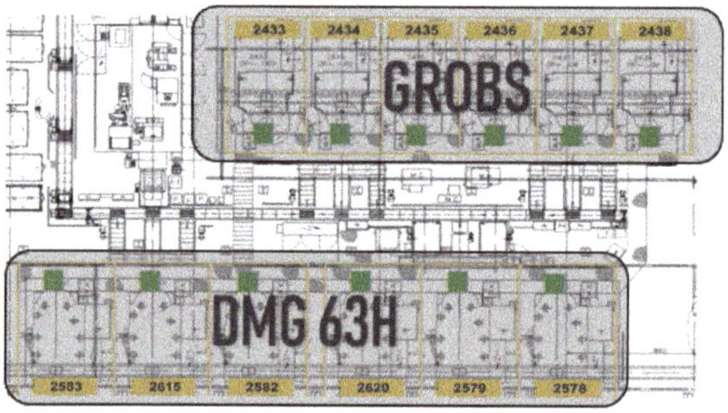

Figure 5. Module 1—Manufacturing machines.

These machines have an installed capacity of 500,000 MC per year. However, with the arrival of the JT4 gearbox project, production is expected to increase up to 650,000 MC per year. Such expansion is an essential and delicate step for Renault Cacia, as it is the only company in the Renault Group that produces this new gearbox.

- Changing the maintenance paradigm to improve productivity and reduce costs

Renault has long known that achieving high productivity levels is crucial, and, thus, failures in product quality and delivery times cannot be tolerated. In this context, equipment maintenance plays an increasingly important role because if machines are optimized and working at approximately 100%, Renault is closer to meeting its manufacturing objectives and its commitment to customers and suppliers.

However, this is a challenging assignment to achieve, in particular, when using the concepts of corrective and preventive maintenance. Given the excessive number of periodic inspections, emergency stops, and equipment downtime, which compromise performance, Renault decided, with the help of technologies from I4.0, to introduce the concepts of PdM and CBM in its facilities.

To better understand the subject area, the first step was to carry out extensive scientific research with the help of an external company. It was easy to conclude that this new maintenance paradigm has unequivocal advantages, as long as it is well applied and integrated into the organization, which is in line with the arguments by Lee et al. [4]. Thus, Renault went on to an experimentation phase, using, among others, the MC JT4 line, namely the machines already mentioned previously, as a test pilot.

As this research was carried out in light of the maintenance concepts and practices used at Renault Cacia, the need to create a standard operating procedure was identified, referring to the activities inherent to each maintenance process. In this regard, we sought to develop a more intuitive comparison between preventive and conditioned/predictive maintenance and promote better communication of the maintenance process so that all stakeholders could have shared knowledge. Thus, the proposed challenge was to introduce the BPMN notation that mainly helped to visually compare the differences between the preventive and CBM/PhM maintenance process (see Appendix A). The changes were evident to the extent that it was possible to verify that the actors used practices of continuous verification of the production equipment, namely through systematic inspections, which involved long hours of work. Most of these actions were unnecessary and involved high operating costs. That is, while in preventive maintenance, industrial operators and engineers played a role in collecting and analyzing data on-site (and the consequent equipment shutdown), the predictive and condition-based maintenance automated the process through the action of a monitoring system and an information system called "Smart Observer".

To illustrate the advantages of CBM/PhM, we will present two cases at the end of this section. In the first case, Module 1 required an initial financial investment in sensors and a corporate network, motivated by the incorporation of predictive technologies. The latter allowed for timely intervention in Module 1 and, therefore, prevented an unexpected stoppage of the machines for 24 h, which resulted in a return of approximately 70% of the initial investment. Thus, it was possible to recognize that the use of CBM/PhM practices in the automotive industry, in addition to reducing lead times, improving quality standards, and increasing competitiveness, as mentioned by Voisin et al. [9], also drastically reduces operating costs. The second case is very similar to the first one; however, the percentage of savings is much higher, which was about 200% of the initial investment.

- Condition-Based Maintenance Techniques in Renault Cacia

In the CBM concept, several parameters can be controlled through monitoring. That is, CBM involves making decisions about maintenance or repair based on the actual deteriorating conditions of the components [72]. The most advanced and impactful predictive techniques in the industrial sector to date are vibration analysis [45], ultrasound [42], thermography [44], voltage [43], dynamic pressure, and visual inspection.

In the case of Renault Cacia, namely in M1, it started by implementing pressure and temperature measurement techniques. In particular, the pressure technique was implemented in the hydraulic system of all 12 manufacturing machines to detect irregular parameters in the exchanger, the oil pump, or the hydraulic material. As for the temperature analysis, it was implemented in three different areas: refrigeration, where malfunctions can be caused by leaks, poor ventilation, and low temperatures; hydraulic, where anomalies detected can be associated with several hydraulic materials; electrical panel, where the detected problems may be related to the door not being closed, poor ventilation, and inadequate power modules. The implementation of these techniques in Renault Cacia reinforces what has been described in the literature that CBM is practical to implement [57,58], notably in the automotive industry. Nevertheless, it increasingly requires greater use of various disciplines in the maintenance field, such as AI [73].

- Condition-based maintenance and predictive maintenance practices in Renault Cacia

PdM essentially aims to complement the CBM purpose by assisting in decision-making regarding equipment repair actions. The monitoring of parameters above gives rise to a large set of data, which is then collected by the Renault server (i.e., Smart Observer). The monitoring system is composed of sensors, which continuously collects data of critical parameters of each machine. Subsequently, this data is sent via corporate networks to the central server. The Smart Observer then automatically collects the data in real-time, analyzing and presenting it via dashboards, which allow a graphical depiction of the values collected by the sensors. Thus, it is expected to eliminate most of the periodic inspections, a characteristic of the preventive practices, maximizing the life cycle of the machine components. With this system, it is also possible to promptly detect failures by early identifying anomalies in the equipment, resulting in financial and operational benefits. In short, it is possible to infer that this practice (i.e., monitoring systems and Smart Observer) automates and digitalizes maintenance activities, resulting in greater speed and operational efficiency with regard to maintenance actions. It also eliminated mentioned periodic inspections and manual troubleshooting operations of the machines in Module 1, as maintenance is now performed only when a particular component reaches a state that will lead to its failure.

The CBM consists of defining limits that the measured values must not exceed so that machines work in optimal operating conditions. This was Renault Cacia's main challenge in the server operationalization process since each asset (machine) is particular and must operate within a specific range of values, which means that its functional limits will also be different. Indeed, this may be similarly true to most automotive industry companies, as they have machines with different production specifications, which increases the degree of complexity of the analysis.

Following Sakib and Wuest [5], the Renault Cacia team defined two upper limits, the alert, and the alarm. The first, when exceeded, will give rise to an alert notification, meaning that certain equipment started to operate at values higher than those allowed under normal conditions. If this anomaly is not resolved and continues to evolve, it triggers a more severe notification, an alarm. As soon as the first notification occurs, the maintenance group employees must begin to identify which problem has arisen and whether it can be solved without replacing a component of the machine, then acting on the conclusion that they reached. These limits, together with the values of the collected data, are represented using time-based graphs, which help to detect anomalies in the machines in an intuitive way and without the need for contact with the physical world.

- Case 1: Problem-solving in Module 1

Bearing in mind that Renault machinery is subject to high wear and tear, machines will have to undergo several maintenance operations. An example of this case study is related to the occurrence of an anomaly in the electrical panel during the month of November of 2019. The maintenance group first received an alert notification on all six DMG machines of M1, where they could see that they had higher temperature values than those accepted, which should be below 40 °C. After an investigation in the shop floor, where the condition of one of the DMG machines was first analyzed, it was found that its ventilation was inadequate, resulting in higher temperature values (Figure 6). This problem was confirmed on the remaining machines, which led to the replacement of the external fans on all six DMG machines.

The previous graphs (Figure 6a,b) show the condition of machines before and after the maintenance operation. In Figure 6a, it can be observed that some of the lines, which represent the temperature, are above 40 °C. From this moment, the engineering team realized that something was wrong with the six DMG machines of M1. In Figure 6b, it is evident that the measures implemented allowed to make corrections on time (i.e., fan replacement) and before it caused significant damage to the Renault industrial machines (i.e., before reaching breaking temperatures).

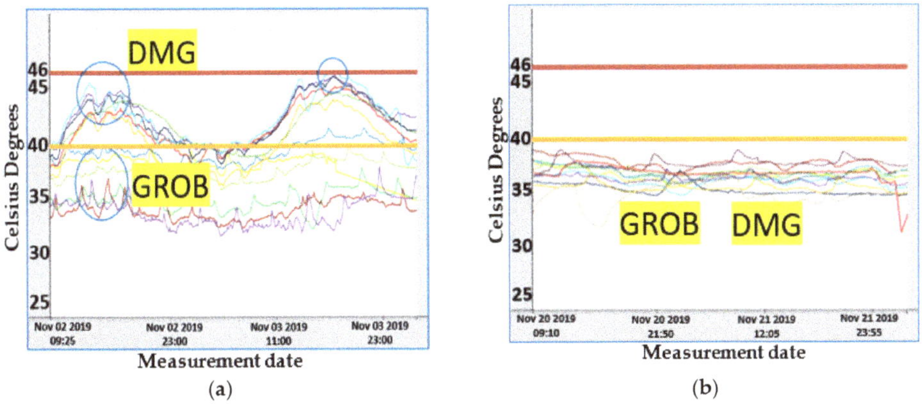

Figure 6. Machine state: (**a**) before maintenance; (**b**) after maintenance.

- Case 2: Problem-solving in the Differential Box Production Line

The second case that we present refers to an anomaly detected in the machining line of the differential box (Figure 7), which is also one of the components of the JT4 gearbox (Figure 7a). The production line where the JT4 gearbox is located comprises a total of six machines, of which four are from HESSAP, one MARPOSS, and the other LIEBHERSS brands. Renault Cacia decided to install vibration and temperature sensors on the 4th HESSAP asset, which had a long history of malfunctions.

After installing the sensors, an anomaly was detected in one of the HESSAP machines (Figure 7b), caused by unwanted collisions with the boxes produced. Initially, the maintenance group received an alert notification, and it was possible to observe that the equipment was operating at values above the established alert limit of 7.5 mm/s. After the alarm was activated, the maintenance team went to the site to analyze the vibration values. Based on similar cases previously solved at Renault Cacia, the team estimated that the probability of failure due to the machines' breakage was unlikely, despite having reached vibration values above the alarm limit of 17.5 mm/s. According to the team's estimation, the machine could operate for about six months until the end of its life cycle without compromising the quality of the equipment´s operation. The advantage of early identification of non-conformities allowed Renault to have the opportunity to purchase the replacement material on time and select the best day to carry out the intervention on the equipment. So, the mechanism was replaced during a period of reduced activity. The result is twofold, while there was no loss of productivity and the use of the mechanism was maximized, Renault reduced its operational costs. This maintenance action allowed a return of approximately 200% of the initial investment.

After these promising results, Renault Cacia projected a considerable expansion in the use of CBM/PhM practices in its equipment, taking into account the success evidenced to date. Additionally, Renault Cacia requested the selection of critical equipment that produced unsatisfactory results and high operational costs in the medium and long term. The selection of these assets was based on a proposal from the project leader, later approved by the maintenance committee. The approval of this project highlights the relevance that each asset has to Renault Cacia's production system and that consequently may have for other similar industries.

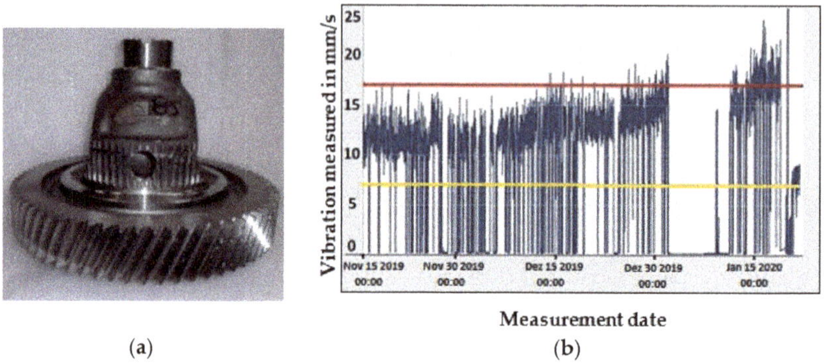

Figure 7. Renault Cacia differential box asset: (**a**) Differential box; (**b**) HESSAP machine status before the intervention.

5. Concluding Remarks

The conclusion section focuses on the contributions to practice and theory and perspectives for future research. Overall, with this article, it was possible to ascertain that the expenses incurred in the M1 monitoring system were profitable in a very short period of time. If errors were not previously detected, it would most likely cause the full failure of those industrial machines, which would lead to more extended downtime and, consequently, loss of production. Thus, the consequences of an unexpected failure were minimized.

5.1. Practical and Theoretical Contributions

To compare the differences between the preventive process and the CBM/PdM process, two diagrams were drawn in the BPMN format (Appendix A). When analyzing the two different approaches, it was possible to verify that their actors were different. Unlike preventive maintenance, where operators and industrial engineers play a role in collecting and analyzing data in the physical space, predictive and condition-based maintenance has replaced their actions with a monitoring system and an information system, the "Smart Observer". These changes led to the automation of the data collection process. Thus, the question that arises is no longer "What has failed or what can fail?", but "What will fail and when?". Renault can now better anticipate the breakdown of its machines before failures occur and also schedule the replacement of components in the most convenient way. This, in turn, has allowed the company to minimize periodic inspections, emergency stops, and shutdowns. Ultimately, this led to the fulfillment of the company's goal, which was to increase productivity and, at the same time, successfully test this concept in Renault facilities.

Although the integration of this concept has already been a success in M1 and other Renault Cacia manufacturing lines, the complexity of this new approach cannot be overlooked. Therefore, before thinking about moving towards a global application of this maintenance program, the entire team of the maintenance group and the other actors in the company's production processes must follow the same path and contribute to the advancement of the project.

The elaborated BPMNs, as well as others that may arise in the process, can play an essential role in this journey, helping to integrate all employees without having to attend a large number of training and meetings. In addition, these diagrams are intended to assist in the definition of a standard of action for maintenance, which every worker related to the subject must know and follow. In the future, it is also expected that a process model cannot only illustrate the links between different activities but can also assist in the execution of experiments that cannot be performed on a real object, namely through long-term simulations and analyzes.

5.2. Future Research

It can be interesting to develop new dynamics in the automotive industry by applying AI technologies (i.e., machine learning) to enable machines to learn from the collected data and to predict what will happen next, instead of having actions fully programmed and controlled by humans. Another alternative may be the inclusion of a hybrid system, where AI-based machines perform analytical-cognitive tasks based on the collection of a large volume of data. While, in the first stage, industrial engineers can be in charge of the decision-making process, machines can develop the ability to learn and act in the subsequent phases.

Author Contributions: Conceptualization, J.F.; methodology, J.F. and J.R.; software, J.F.; validation, J.R.; formal analysis, J.F. and J.R.; investigation, J.F.; resources, J.F.; data curation, J.F.; writing—original draft preparation, J.F.; writing—review and editing, J.R.; visualization, J.F.; supervision, J.R.; project administration, J.F., J.R., N.M., L.T. and M.A.; funding acquisition, N.M. All authors have read and agreed to the published version of the manuscript.

Funding: This work is funded by National Funds through the FCT—Foundation for Science and Technology, I.P., within the scope of the project Ref. UIDB/05583/2020. We would like to thank the Research Center in Digital Services (CISeD) and the Polytechnic of Viseu for their support.

Institutional Review Board Statement: Not applicable.

Informed Consent Statement: The research was carried out under the cooperation protocol UA.RC/02/09/2019, which was established between the University of Aveiro (UA) and Renault Cacia.

Data Availability Statement: The data used in this study was collected by the authors, any questions or clarifications can be addressed to: reis.joao@ua.pt.

Conflicts of Interest: The authors declare no conflict of interest.

Appendix A

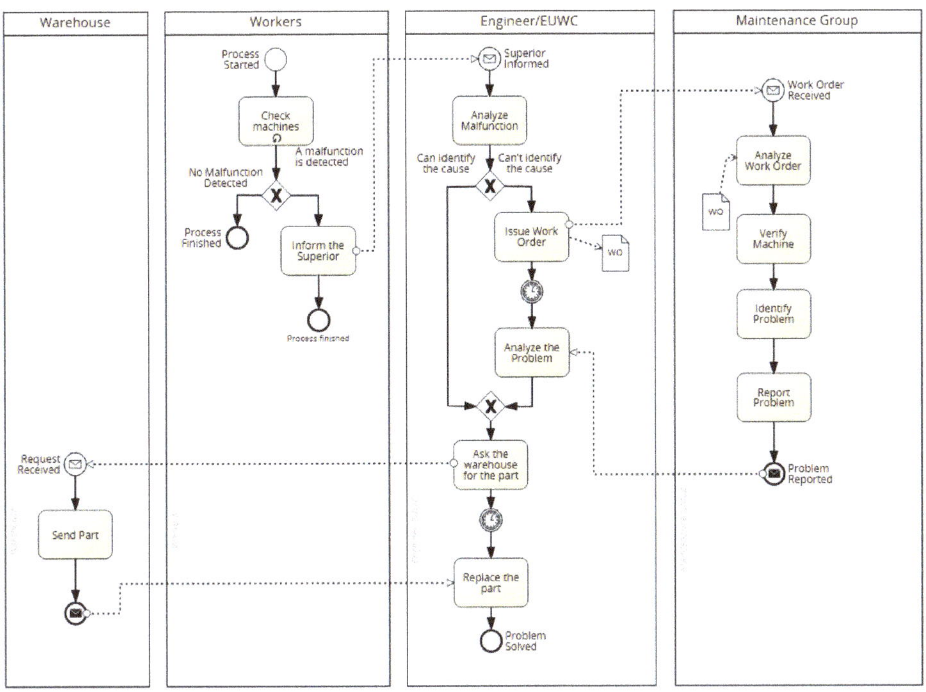

Figure A1. Preventive maintenance action plan.

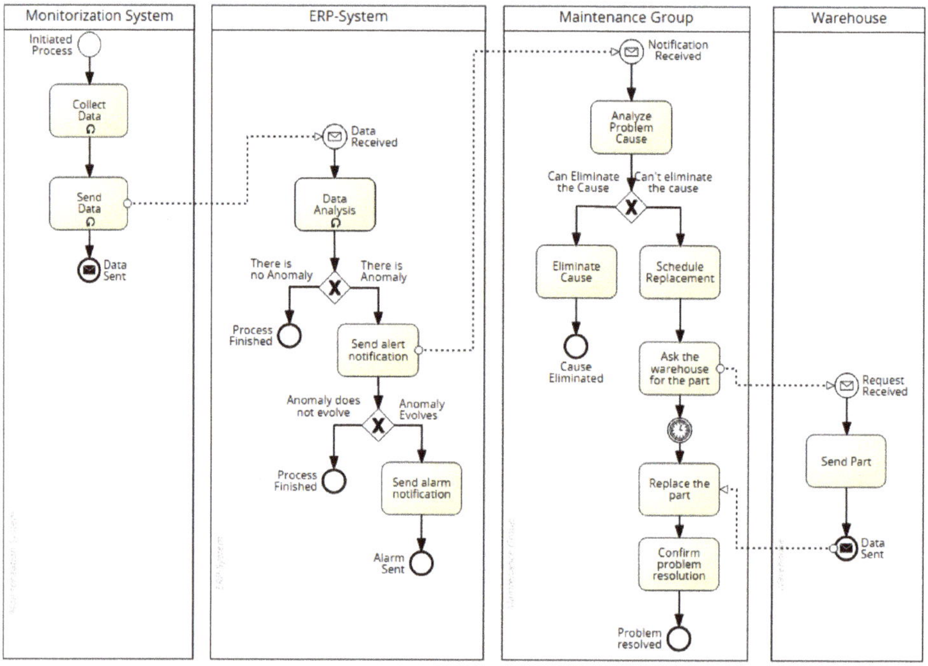

Figure A2. Predictive and condition-based maintenance action plans.

References

1. Mrugalska, B.; Wyrwicka, M. Towards lean production in Industry 4.0. *Procedia Eng.* **2017**, *182*, 466–473. [CrossRef]
2. Reis, J.; Amorim, M.; Melão, N.; Matos, P. Digital transformation: A literature review and guidelines for future research. In *World Conference on Information Systems and Technologies*; Springer: Cham, Switzerland, 2018; pp. 411–421.
3. Reis, J.; Amorim, M.; Melão, N.; Cohen, Y.; Rodrigues, M. Digitalization: A literature review and research agenda. In *International Joint Conference on Industrial Engineering and Operations Management*; Springer: Cham, Switzerland, 2019; pp. 443–456.
4. Lee, W.; Wu, H.; Yun, H.; Kim, H.; Jun, M.; Sutherland, J. Predictive maintenance of machine tool systems using artificial intelligence techniques applied to machine condition data. *Procedia Cirp.* **2019**, *80*, 506–511. [CrossRef]
5. Sakib, N.; Wuest, T. Challenges and opportunities of condition-based predictive maintenance: A review. *Procedia Cirp* **2018**, *78*, 267–272. [CrossRef]
6. Bousdekis, A.; Lepenioti, K.; Apostolou, D.; Mentzas, G. Decision Making in Predictive Maintenance: Literature Review and Research Agenda for Industry 4.0. *IFAC-PapersOnLine* **2019**, *52*, 607–612. [CrossRef]
7. Laloix, T.; Iung, B.; Voisin, A.; Romagne, E. Towards the control of product quality from the process deviation monitoring: Overview and investigation in automotive sector. *IFAC-PapersOnLine* **2016**, *49*, 79–84. [CrossRef]
8. Pinto, G.; Silva, F.; Campilho, R.; Casais, R.; Fernandes, A.; Baptista, A. Continuous improvement in maintenance: A case study in the automotive industry involving Lean tools. *Procedia Manuf.* **2019**, *38*, 1582–1591. [CrossRef]
9. Voisin, A.; Laloix, T.; Iung, B.; Romagne, E. Predictive Maintenance and part quality control from joint product-process-machine requirements: Application to a machine tool. *Procedia Manuf.* **2018**, *16*, 147–154. [CrossRef]
10. Cachada, A.; Barbosa, J.; Leitño, P.; Gcraldcs, C.; Deusdado, L.; Costa, J.; Teixeira, C.; Teixeira, J.; Moreira, A.; Moreira, P.; et al. Maintenance 4.0: Intelligent and predictive maintenance system architecture. In Proceedings of the 2018 IEEE 23rd International Conference on Emerging Technologies and Factory Automation (ETFA), Torino, Italy, 4–7 September 2018; pp. 139–146.
11. Wang, K. Intelligent predictive maintenance (IPdM) system–Industry 4.0 scenario. *Wit Trans. Eng. Sci.* **2016**, *113*, 259–268.
12. Souza, M.; da Costa, C.; de Oliveira Ramos, G.; da Rosa Righi, R. A survey on decision-making based on system reliability in the context of Industry 4.0. *J. Manuf. Syst.* **2020**, *56*, 133–156. [CrossRef]
13. Bodensohn, A.; Haueis, M.; Mäckel, R.; Pulvermüller, M.; Schreiber, T. System monitoring for lifetime prediction in automotive industry. In *Advanced Microsystems for Automotive Applications*; Springer: Berlin, Heidelberg, 2005; pp. 149–158. [CrossRef]
14. Ambani, S.; Li, L.; Ni, J. Condition-based maintenance decision-making for multiple machine systems. *J. Manuf. Sci. Eng.* **2009**, *131*, 031009. [CrossRef]
15. Polančič, G.; Orban, B. A BPMN-based language for modeling corporate communications. *Comput. Stand. Interfaces* **2019**, *65*, 45–60. [CrossRef]

16. Lasi, H.; Fettke, P.; Kemper, H.; Feld, T.; Hoffmann, M. Industry 4.0. *Bus. Inf. Syst. Eng.* **2014**, *6*, 239–242. [CrossRef]
17. Xu, L.; Xu, E.; Li, L. Industry 4.0: State of the art and future trends. *Int. J. Prod. Res.* **2018**, *56*, 2941–2962. [CrossRef]
18. Hermann, M.; Pentek, T.; Otto, B. Design principles for industry 4.0 scenarios. In Proceedings of the 2016 49th Hawaii International Conference on System Sciences (HICSS), Koloa, HI, USA, 5–8 January 2016; pp. 3928–3937.
19. Wagner, T.; Herrmann, C.; Thiede, S. Industry 4.0 impacts on lean production systems. *Procedia Cirp* **2017**, *63*, 125–131. [CrossRef]
20. Yin, Y.; Stecker, K.; Li, D. The evolution of production systems from Industry 2.0 through Industry 4.0. *Int. J. Prod. Res.* **2018**, *56*, 848–861. [CrossRef]
21. Powell, D.; Romero, D.; Gaiardelli, P.; Cimini, C.; Cavalieri, S. Towards digital lean cyber-physical production systems: Industry 4.0 technologies as enablers of leaner production. In *IFIP International Conference on Advances in Production Management Systems*; Springer: Cham, Switzerland, 2018; pp. 353–362.
22. Lee, J.; Kao, H.; Yang, S. Service innovation and smart analytics for Industry 4.0 and big data environment. *Procedia Cirp* **2014**, *16*, 3–8. [CrossRef]
23. Pîrvu, B.; Zamfirescu, C. Smart factory in the context of 4th industrial revolution: Challenges and opportunities for Romania. *IOP Conf. Ser. Mater. Sci. Eng.* **2017**, *227*, 012094. [CrossRef]
24. Ghobakhloo, M. The future of manufacturing industry: A strategic roadmap toward Industry 4.0. *J. Manuf. Technol. Manag.* **2018**, *29*, 910–936. [CrossRef]
25. Schmidt, R.; Möhring, M.; Härting, R.; Reichstein, C.; Neumaier, P.; Jozinović, P. Industry 4.0-potentials for creating smart products: Empirical research results. In *International Conference on Business Information Systems*; Springer: Cham, Switzerland, 2015; pp. 16–27.
26. Lu, Y. Industry 4.0: A survey on technologies, applications and open research issues. *J. Ind. Inf. Integr.* **2017**, *6*, 1–10. [CrossRef]
27. Wagner, R. The Role of Projects in the Process of Transforming Automotive Industry. In *Research on Project, Programme and Portfolio Management. Lecture Notes in Management and Industrial Engineering*; Cuevas, R., Bodea, C.N., Torres-Lima, P., Eds.; Springer: Cham, Switzerland, 2021. [CrossRef]
28. Sága, M.; Bulej, V.; Čuboňova, N.; Kuric, I.; Virgala, I.; Eberth, M. Case study: Performance analysis and development of robotized screwing application with integrated vision sensing system for automotive industry. *Int. J. Adv. Robot. Syst.* **2020**, *17*, 1729881420923997. [CrossRef]
29. Neal, A.; Sharpe, R.; van Lopik, K.; Tribe, J.; Goodall, P.; Lugo, H.; Segura-Velandia, D.; Conway, P.; Jackson, L.; Jackson, T.; et al. The potential of industry 4.0 Cyber Physical System to improve quality assurance: An automotive case study for wash monitoring of returnable transit items. *Cirp J. Manuf. Sci. Technol.* **2021**, *32*, 461–475. [CrossRef]
30. Llopis-Albert, C.; Rubio, F.; Valero, F. Impact of digital transformation on the automotive industry. *Technol. Forecast. Soc. Chang.* **2021**, *162*, 120343. [CrossRef]
31. Lin, D.; Lee, C.K.M.; Lau, H.; Yang, Y. Strategic response to Industry 4.0: An empirical investigation on the Chinese automotive industry. *Ind. Manag. Data Syst.* **2018**, *118*, 589–605. [CrossRef]
32. Tsvetkova, R. What does Industry 4.0 mean for sustainable development? *Industry 4.0* **2017**, *2*, 294–297.
33. Ruiz-Sarmiento, J.; Monroy, J.; Moreno, F.; Galindo, C.; Bonelo, J.; Gonzalez-Jimenez, J. A predictive model for the maintenance of industrial machinery in the context of industry 4.0. *Eng. Appl. Artif. Intell.* **2020**, *87*, 103289. [CrossRef]
34. Reis, J.; Santo, P.; Melão, N. Impact of Artificial Intelligence Research on Politics of the European Union Member States: The Case Study of Portugal. *Sustainability* **2020**, *12*, 6708. [CrossRef]
35. Tjahjono, B.; Esplugues, C.; Ares, E.; Pelaez, G. What does industry 4.0 mean to supply chain. *Procedia Manuf.* **2017**, *13*, 1175–1182. [CrossRef]
36. Masoni, R.; Ferrise, F.; Bordegoni, M.; Gattullo, M.; Uva, A.; Fiorentino, M.; Carrabba, E.; Di Donato, M. Supporting remote maintenance in industry 4.0 through augmented reality. *Procedia Manuf.* **2017**, *11*, 1296–1302. [CrossRef]
37. Sommer, L. Industrial revolution-industry 4.0: Are German manufacturing SMEs the first victims of this revolution? *J. Ind. Eng. Manag.* **2015**, *8*, 1512–1532. [CrossRef]
38. Carvalho, T.; Soares, F.; Vita, R.; Francisco, R.; Basto, J.; Alcalá, S. A systematic literature review of machine learning methods applied to predictive maintenance. *Comput. Ind. Eng.* **2019**, *137*, 106024. [CrossRef]
39. Chebel-Morello, B.; Nicod, J.; Varnier, C. *From Prognostics and Health Systems Management to Predictive Maintenance 2: Knowledge, Reliability and Decision*; John Wiley & Sons: Hoboken, NJ, USA, 2017.
40. Jardine, A.; Lin, D.; Banjevic, D. A review on machinery diagnostics and prognostics implementing condition-based maintenance. *Mech. Syst. Signal Process.* **2006**, *20*, 1483–1510. [CrossRef]
41. Edwards, D.; Holt, G.; Harris, F. Predictive maintenance techniques and their relevance to construction plant. *J. Qual. Maint. Eng.* **1998**, *4*, 25–37. [CrossRef]
42. Coandă, P.; Avram, M.; Constantin, V. A state of the art of predictive maintenance techniques. In *IOP Conference Series: Materials Science and Engineering*; IOP Publishing: Bristol, UK, 2020; Volume 997, p. 012039.
43. Hoffmann, M.; Wildermuth, S.; Gitzel, R.; Boyaci, A.; Gebhardt, J.; Kaul, H.; Amihai, I.; Frog, B.; Suriyah, M.; Leibfried, T.; et al. Integration of novel sensors and machine learning for predictive maintenance in medium voltage switchgear to enable the energy and mobility revolutions. *Sensors* **2020**, *20*, 2099. [CrossRef]

44. Soliman, M. *Industrial Applications of Infrared Thermography: How Infrared Analysis Can Be Used to Improve Equipment Inspection*; Lulu Press: Morrisville, NC, USA, 2020. ISBN-13: 979-8696181073/ISBN: 9781393551355. Available online: https://ssrn.com/abstract=3743671 (accessed on 23 February 2021).
45. Schwendemann, S.; Amjad, Z.; Sikora, A. A survey of machine-learning techniques for condition monitoring and predictive maintenance of bearings in grinding machines. *Comput. Ind.* **2021**, *125*, 103380. [CrossRef]
46. Susto, G.; Schirru, A.; Pampuri, S.; McLoone, S.; Beghi, A. Machine learning for predictive maintenance: A multiple classifier approach. *IEEE Trans. Ind. Inform.* **2014**, *11*, 812–820. [CrossRef]
47. Duffuaa, S.; Raouf, A.; Campbell, J. *Planning and Control of Maintenance Systems*; Springer: Cham, Switzerland, 2000. [CrossRef]
48. Levitt, J. *Complete Guide to Preventive and Predictive Maintenance*; Industrial Press Inc.: New York, NY, USA, 2003.
49. Ciancio, V.; Homri, L.; Dantan, J.; Siadat, A. Towards prediction of machine failures: Overview and first attempt on specific automotive industry application. *IFAC-PapersOnLine* **2020**, *53*, 289–294. [CrossRef]
50. Ramere, M.; Laseinde, O. Optimization of condition-based maintenance strategy prediction for aging automotive industrial equipment using FMEA. *Procedia Comput. Sci.* **2021**, *180*, 229–238. [CrossRef]
51. Aksa, K.; Aitouche, S.; Bentoumi, H.; Sersa, I. Developing a Web Platform for the Management of the Predictive Maintenance in Smart Factories. *Wirel. Pers. Commun.* **2021**, 1–29. [CrossRef]
52. Jasiulewicz-Kaczmarek, M.; Waszkowski, R.; Piechowski, M.; Wyczółkowski, R. Implementing BPMN in Maintenance Process Modeling. In *Information Systems Architecture and Technology: Proceedings of 38th International Conference on Information Systems Architecture and Technology-ISAT 2017. ISAT 2017. Advances in Intelligent Systems and Computing, 656*; Świątek, J., Borzemski, L., Wilimowska, Z., Eds.; Springer: Cham, Switzerland, 2018. [CrossRef]
53. Van Der Aalst, W.; Ter Hofstede, A.; Weske, M. Business process management: A survey. In *International Conference on Business Process Management*; Springer: Berlin/Heidelberg, Germany, 2003; pp. 1–12.
54. Hammer, M. What is business process management? In *Handbook on Business Process Management*; Springer: Berlin/Heidelberg, Germany, 2015; pp. 3–16.
55. Melão, N.; Pidd, M. A Conceptual Framework for Understanding Business Processes and Business Process Modelling. *Inf. Syst. J.* **2000**, *10*, 105–129. [CrossRef]
56. Meidan, A.; García-García, J.; Escalona, M.; Ramos, I. A survey on business processes management suites. *Comput. Stand. Interfaces* **2017**, *51*, 71–86. [CrossRef]
57. Chinosi, M.; Trombetta, A. BPMN: An introduction to the standard. *Comput. Stand. Interfaces* **2012**, *34*, 124–134. [CrossRef]
58. Van Der Aalst, W.; La Rosa, M.; Santoro, F. Don't forget to improve the process! *Bus. Process Manag.* **2016**, *58*, 1–6.
59. Suri, K.; Cadavid, J.; Alferez, M.; Dhouib, S.; Tucci-Piergiovanni, S. Modeling business motivation and underlying processes for RAMI 4.0-aligned cyber-physical production systems. In Proceedings of the 2017 22nd IEEE International Conference on Emerging Technologies and Factory Automation (ETFA), Limassol, Cyprus, 12–15 September 2017; pp. 1–6.
60. Kannengiesser, U.; Müller, H. Industry 4.0 Standardisation: Where Does S-BPM Fit? In Proceedings of the 10th International Conference on Subject-Oriented Business Process Management, Linz, Austria, 5–6 April 2018; pp. 1–8. [CrossRef]
61. Jasiulewicz-Kaczmarek, M.; Waszkowski, R.; Piechowski, M.; Wyczółkowski, R. Implementing BPMN in maintenance process modeling. In *International Conference on Information Systems Architecture and Technology*; Springer: Cham, Switzerland, 2017; pp. 300–309.
62. Savary, J. Competitive Strategies in the World Market: The Case of Renault and the Emergence of a European Group? In *Towards a New Map of Automobile Manufacturing in Europe?* Springer: Berlin/Heidelberg, Germany, 1995; pp. 147–172.
63. Yin, R. *Case Study Research and Applications: Design and Methods*; Sage Publications: Los Angeles, CA, USA, 2017.
64. Mills, A.; Durepos, G.; Wiebe, E. *Encyclopedia of Case Study Research*; Sage Publications: London, UK, 2010.
65. Blaxter, L. *How to Research*; McGraw-Hill Education: New York, NY, USA, 2010.
66. Given, L. *The SAGE Encyclopedia of Qualitative Research Methods*; Sage Publications: London, UK, 2008.
67. Savin-Baden, M.; Major, C. *New Approaches to Qualitative Research: Wisdom and Uncertainty*; Routledge, Taylor & Francis Group: New York, NY, USA, 2010.
68. Taylor, S.; Bogdan, R.; DeVault, M. *Introduction to Qualitative Research Methods: A Guidebook and Resources*; Wiley & Sons: Hoboken, NJ, USA, 2016.
69. Hsieh, F.; Shannon, S. Three approaches to qualitative content analysis. *Qual. Health Res.* **2005**, *15*, 1277–1288. [CrossRef]
70. Neuendorf, K. *The Content Analysis Guidebook*; Sage Publications: Los Angeles, CA, USA, 2017.
71. Silva, A.; Mateus, C.; Węgrzyn, T.; Miros, M. High speed machining of aluminium gear box without temperature stabilization. *Transp. Probl.* **2010**, *5*, 57–66.
72. Adsule, A.; Kulkarni, M.; Tewari, A. Reinforcement learning for optimal policy learning in condition-based maintenance. *IET Collab. Intell. Manuf.* **2020**, *2*, 182–188. [CrossRef]
73. Prajapati, A.; Bechtel, J.; Ganesan, S. Condition based maintenance: A survey. *J. Qual. Maint. Eng.* **2012**, *18*, 384–400. [CrossRef]

applied sciences

MDPI

Article

Augmented Reality Maintenance Assistant Using YOLOv5

Ana Malta [1,*], Mateus Mendes [1,2,*] and Torres Farinha [1,3]

1 Polytechnic of Coimbra, ISEC, 3045-093 Coimbra, Portugal; tfarinha@isec.pt
2 ISR, University of Coimbra, 3004-531 Coimbra, Portugal
3 Centre for Mechanical Engineering, Materials and Processes—CEMMPRE, 3030-788 Coimbra, Portugal
* Correspondence: a21230211@isec.pt (A.M.); mmendes@isr.uc.pt (M.M.)

Abstract: Maintenance professionals and other technical staff regularly need to learn to identify new parts in car engines and other equipment. The present work proposes a model of a task assistant based on a deep learning neural network. A YOLOv5 network is used for recognizing some of the constituent parts of an automobile. A dataset of car engine images was created and eight car parts were marked in the images. Then, the neural network was trained to detect each part. The results show that YOLOv5s is able to successfully detect the parts in real time video streams, with high accuracy, thus being useful as an aid to train professionals learning to deal with new equipment using augmented reality. The architecture of an object recognition system using augmented reality glasses is also designed.

Keywords: task assistant; YOLOv5; car engine dataset; car part detection; augmented reality

Citation: Malta, R.; Farinha, T.; Mendes, M. Augmented Reality Maintenance Assistant Using YOLOv5. *Appl. Sci.* **2021**, *11*, 4758. https://doi.org/10.3390/app11114758

Academic Editors: João Reis, Marlene Amorim and Yuval Cohen

Received: 28 April 2021
Accepted: 20 May 2021
Published: 22 May 2021

1. Introduction

Maintenance technicians often have to perform a large number of different jobs, involving numerous parts, manufactured by numerous different companies. The main objective of the present work is to build a system to recognize mechanical parts in car engines, and give directions, which come from a work order, to the technician. The technician wears augmented reality glasses during the procedure. Through the glasses, he sees the car parts and also the instructions on how to proceed, which are added in real time.

The field of object detection has garnered new attention with recent developments in deep neural network architectures, and it is constantly growing. More and more research is proposed, aiming to solve various problems to make people's lives easier. Many neural network architectures can detect a large number of objects, with high accuracy, in real time. The detection of engine parts of an automobile can bring major developments in the scope of manufacturing and maintenance, especially facilitating correct maintenance tasks, with the objective of maximizing the quality of maintenance procedures, aiming to increase engines' life and reliability.

To be able to build a good task assistant system, it is necessary to implement a good detection method. The present work relies on a YOLOv5 deep neural network, which is one of the fastest and most reliable detectors available nowadays. The YOLOv5 receives images in real time from the technician's augmented reality glasses and detects the parts. The task assistant suggests actions to perform, based on the sequence of actions of the work order and on which objects are detected in the technician's field of view.

To properly train the YOLOv5 neural network, it is essential to have a good dataset. The larger the dataset, the higher the chances of training the network to have good performance. For this first step, the dataset created consisted of 582 images taken from three videos with similar lighting conditions, where it was possible to identify a total of eight different types of parts: oil dipstick; battery; engine oil reservoir; wiper water tank; air filter; brakes fluid reservoir; coolant reservoir; and power steering reservoir. The images taken from each frame are converted to a 416 × 416 format, which is the format that the chosen architecture needs to use as input.

Two versions of YOLOv5 were tried, namely YOLOv5s and YOLOv5m. They are available at https://pytorch.org/hub/ultralytics_yolov5/ (accessed on 21 May 2021). The data were split into training, validation and testing sets and converted to YOLOv5 PyTorch format. Then, data were saved into a data.yaml file, which describes the classes to be used for training, validating and testing the model. This process was done using Roboflow, which is available online at http://www.roboflow.com (accessed on 21 May 2021). Then, using a Google Colab virtual machine, which is available at http://colab.research.google.com (accessed on 21 May 2021), the models were trained, with a total of 250 epochs. Different evaluation metrics were used, to evaluate the quality and reliability of the system. In a second experiment, the dataset size was increased to a total of 900 images with different lighting conditions, in order to optimize object recognition and test the system under more challenging situations.

Section 2 presents a brief review of the state of the art in the context of neural networks, mentioning some examples of the use of YOLOv5 architecture from other studies. Section 3 describes the proposed architecture for the augmented reality system. Sections 4 and 5 describe the materials used and the development of datasets for the intended work. Section 6 describes the YOLOv5 network and the models. The tests and results are described in Section 7 and discussed in Section 8. The conclusions and future work are presented in Section 9.

2. Related Work

2.1. Object Detection with YOLO

Deep learning-based object detection has been a research hotspot in recent years. For better image understanding methods, it is necessary not only to concentrate on classifying different images, but also to try to precisely estimate which objects are present in the images and their locations. This task is referred to as object detection [1], and the state of the art detectors are deep neural networks, namely convolution neural networks (CNN).

ImageNet is a dataset of more than 15 million high-resolution labeled images, which belong to about 22,000 categories. In the article "ImageNet classification with deep convolutional neural networks." [2], two error rates need to be analyzed: top-1 and top-5. The error rate of top-5 is the fraction of test images, where the caption is not one of the five captions considered most likely by the model. In the test data, error rates of 37.5% and 17% were achieved for top-1 and top-5, respectively, which is significantly better than the state of the art. In this context, a convolutional-based network appeared for the first time, which drastically reduced the error rates of the previous state-of-the-art methods. That new network is the now famous AlexNet.

Many modern detectors are usually pre-trained on ImageNet or on COCO datasets. Although the CNN architectures are still recent models, other works on object detection have already been developed using the pre-trained YOLOv5 architecture in the COCO dataset. In the article "Face Mask Detection using YOLOv5 for COVID -19" [3], the model correctly classified both people wearing a mask and people not wearing a mask. The model was tested using both YOLOv5s and YOLOv5x. The training process was completed by running the model through Google Colab. YOLOv5s is significantly better than YOLOv5x in terms of performance and speed. The mean average precision (mAP) is quite similar for both the processes, but when the processing speed is considered, YOLOv5s is slightly superior to YOLOv5x.

Another article purports to train the YOLOv5 architecture to recognize handguns in images. This project uses the pre-trained YOLOv5x model to determine the initial weights from which it started the training. The rest of the configuration settings are mostly preset: 50 epochs, 640 px image size for training including test set and stack size of 64. The model can successfully detect the presence of a handgun in an image, even if the handgun is not ideally oriented, does not have the traditional shape, or contains multiple handguns in the image. The results show 0.80 for precision, 0.89 for recognition, and 0.905 for mAP [4].

2.2. *Augmented Reality Applications*

Most of the existing augmented reality systems are able to understand the 3D geometry of the surroundings but lack the ability to detect and classify complex objects in the real world. Such capabilities can be enabled with deep convolutional neural networks [5]. The proposed architecture for these works combines deep learning-based object detection with AR technology to provide user-centered task assistance. In the paper [6], proposes two studies, matching a virtual object to a real object. in a real environment, and performing a realistic task, that is, the maintenance and inspection of a 3D printer. These tests are performed using HoloLens from Microsoft and combine object detection and instance segmentation and the results show the advantage, effectiveness, and extensibility to various real applications.

Augmented reality is being used in different industrial fields. Another example is the use of AR in conceptual prototyping processes in product design by overlaying different car interior mock-ups, which are usually only available as 3D models in the initial phases of development [7].

2.3. *Task Assistance in Industrial Augmented Reality*

Task assistance is one of the main areas of application of AR in the industry. Siam and Tonggoed [8] proposed a human–robot collaboration with augmented reality for virtual assembly task and conclude that the use of augmented reality in the assembly task can save cost and training time.

Augmented reality (AR) is considered to provide user-centric information easily in different environments, thus being able to reduce a worker's cognitive load and increase work efficiency [9]. Augmented reality is slowly gaining ground in industry by embedding visual information onto the real objects directly. In particular, the AR-based visualization of manufacturing information, called industrial AR, can provide more effective task assistance [10,11]. In some areas, industrial workers use AR glasses as an auxiliary tool or as a training simulator to be prepared for specific situations. Bosch's Common Augmented Reality Platform (CAP) is now also available for the new Microsoft HoloLens 2. The interactive training provides holographic step-by-step instructions that help workshop trainees understand new products and technologies and enable service technicians to conduct repair and maintenance tasks more efficiently and with fewer errors [12,13].

Kim et al. [9] propose an approach to industrial AR, which can complement existing AR methods and provide manufacturing information more effectively through the deep learning-based instance segmentation and depth prediction of physical objects in the AR scene. The proposed approach can provide consistent AR visualization regardless of the movement of the physical object. Therefore, manufacturing information can be provided to the worker more intuitively and situation-dependently based on the estimated 3D spatial relation and depth perception.

3. Proposed Architecture

The system proposed manages and processes work orders, which are sequences of procedures that need to be done by the maintenance technicians.

3.1. *Workflow*

Figure 1 represents, in a flowchart, the sequence of actions that are necessary to perform to go through a typical work order, to perform a planned maintenance task. The use of intelligent task assistants can facilitate the technician's job to go through the procedures, while reducing execution time and the risk of human errors.

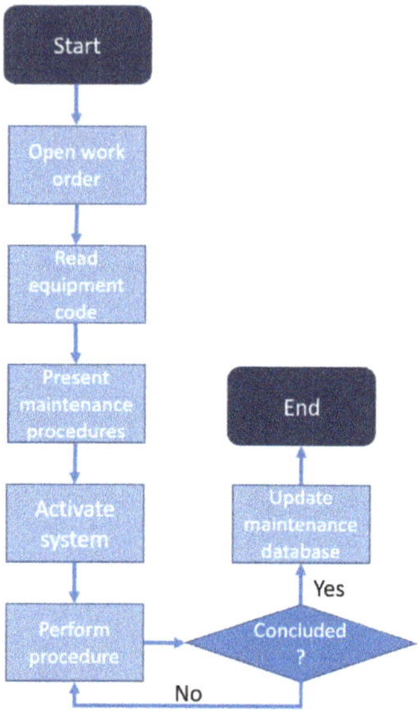

Figure 1. Flowchart showing the sequence of actions necessary to process a given work order, to perform maintenance tasks. The task assistant guides the maintenance technician through the steps shown.

The system proposed aims to guide the technician through all the steps, showing information and directions in the virtual reality glasses and audio messages. The steps illustrated in the flowchart are:

1. Open work order—This is the first step, where the technician opens the work order which was previously assigned to him by a manager. The work order is specific for an equipment, such as a given car or industrial machine.
2. Read equipment code—After opening the work order, the technician must read the equipment code. Each equipment has a unique code, and this step ensures that the technician is at the right equipment. The code can be a barcode, QR code, RF-id or other type of code used in the factory.
3. Present maintenance procedures—Once the equipment code is validated, the technician sees the sequence of procedures required for that particular work order. This gives an overview of the work that needs to be done. The technician can then choose to start working or cancel for some reason.
4. Activate system—After seeing the procedures, the technician must then activate the system to start working and going through each procedure.
5. Perform procedure—Once the system is activated, the task assistant guides the technician through all the procedures in a valid order. The technician is told to search for a particular part, and once that part is in his field of view, the assistant gives directions on how to correctly perform each task necessary. This is repeated for all procedures of the work order.
6. Once the work order is completed, the maintenance database is updated. This step may be done at the end for offline assistants, or in near real time for online assistants.

3.2. System Architecture

Figure 2 shows the architecture proposed for the system. The work orders (WO) are created and managed in a Computerized Maintenance Management System (CMMS), by a team manager. CMMS systems are special applications used to manage maintenance operations. It helps optimize the reliability and availability of physical assets [14]. The present system adds new potential to execute maintenance interventions, both planned and non-planned. The final result will correspond to the reduction of the maintenance time of each intervention and, globally, to optimize the mean time to repair (MTTR).

For each intervention, the maintenance technician has an interface to the CMMS, where he picks the WO and downloads them to the augmented reality (AR) glasses, which can work offline or online with the CMMS. If they work online, the maintenance WO can be updated at the end of each procedure. If they work offline, the technician is only required to connect them again to the CMMS at the end of the task, to update the WO and send it back to the maintenance manager.

The picture also shows another user, who is the administrator, who has special privileges to manage the CMMS teams and tasks.

Farinha (2018) presents a holistic approach for the maintenance of physical assets, including technological solutions like AR [15].

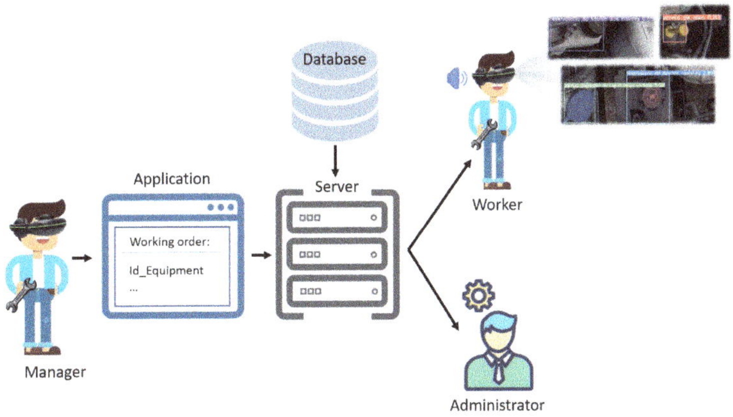

Figure 2. System architecture, showing the main components and interactions. The technician wears Augmented Reality glasses, where he receives directions to go through the procedures of the Working Order, that is created and managed through a CMMS application.

4. Materials and Methods

The complete system requires different types of software and hardware, for development and then for use when it is deployed.

4.1. Hardware Using for Development

The hardware used during development included computers, for running software, and cell phones, for capturing videos and pictures. The object detection model was trained using, laptop computer with access to a Google Colab virtual machine, which offers free GPU cloud service that allows one to obtain 0.007 second inference time. That is, 140 FPS on a TESLA P100 GPU.

To obtain the videos to construct the dataset, two mobile devices were used. The first mobile device was a Samsung Galaxy S10 and the second an IPhone 11. Both are devices with high quality 4K video recording. Table 1 summarizes the characteristics of the mobile devices' cameras.

Table 1. Mobile Devices Camera Characteristics.

Mobile Device	Camera Characteristics
Samsung Galaxy S10	Triple lens camera on the back with a 12 MP regular lens, 12 MP optical zoomed telephoto lens, and a brand new 16 MP ultra wide angle lens.
IPhone 11	Dual 12 MP Ultra Wide and Wide cameras.

4.2. Software Used for Development

The object detection model runs in Python and therefore requires a python interpreter. However, other applications were required for creating the dataset. The list of applications and libraries is as follows.

- **PyTorch**—An open source machine learning library for deep learning, used for applications such as computer vision and natural language processing. This framework was developed by Facebook and it was created to provide models that are easier to write than other frameworks such as TensorFlow [16]. The YOLOv5 architecture is available only for PyTorch at this point.
- **VoTT**—Visual Object Tagging Tool (VoTT) is an open source annotation and labeling tool for image and video assets. It is possible to import data from local or cloud storage providers and to export labeled data to local or cloud storage providers. There is an online version available at https://vott.z22.web.core.windows.net/#/ (accessed on 21 May 2021). VoTT was used to manually tag the images, marking the bounding boxes of each object for the training and testing sets.
- **Roboflow**—Hosts free public computer vision datasets in many popular formats. In the present project, Roboflow was used after VoTT, to tag the images, apply data augmentation and convert the dataset to YOLOv5 PyTorch format.
- **FFmpeg**—Platform to record, convert and stream audio and video. It was necessary to use it to convert the videos recorded through the mobile device to a format that VoTT would recognize. This framework is available at https://www.ffmpeg.org/ (accessed on 21 May 2021).

4.3. Software and Hardware Used for AR System

The proposed augmented reality system requires augmented reality glasses and a server to run the CMMS.

There are currently many augmented reality glasses, but none have been tested at this point. Microsoft HoloLens is a popular platform, which could serve for the proposed task assistant [17]. Another example is Vuzix smart glasses [18].

As for the server, it needs to run the CMMS software to manage the different equipment, maintenance procedures and work orders. The server and the augmented reality glasses can communicate in real time, via wireless network, or they can synchronize periodically according to the technician's needs.

5. Datasets

5.1. Dataset Search

For the present research, a dataset of the mechanical components of an automobile was necessary. However, publicly available datasets that were found were not compatible with the goals intended for the present research. Due to the increasing development of technology in the field of autonomous driving, there are a variety of datasets related to public roads for detecting pedestrians, traffic signs, pedestrian crossings, etc. One dataset widely used in this field is the "KITTI" [19]. KITTI was created mostly for autonomous driving platforms and contains a set of object detection data, including monocular images and object bounding boxes. However, KITTI is not useful for the development of the present project, which aims to detect car motor parts. Datasets of car components were also found, but again, those were not the most relevant components, for they were just non-mechanical components such as the steering wheel or lighting [20]. After an exhaustive search, it was not possible to find a dataset which would be appropriate for the present research. Therefore, it was deemed necessary to build a custom dataset to proceed with the project.

5.2. Dataset Created

To create a custom dataset, the first step was to shoot three videos of the engine components of a car. The car model chosen was a Peugeot 206, built in 1998. The first videos were recorded with a Samsung Galaxy S10 cell phone. The quality was 4 K at 60 fps. It was necessary to produce multiple videos with different angles and distances, so that the algorithm could more easily identify the desired components. More videos were shot, using another cell phone, namely an iPhone 11. The video characteristics were maintained, to facilitate comparing the results. After the videos were produced using the mobile devices, the videos shot with the Samsung device were in "mp4" format. The videos shot with the iPhone were in "mov" format. This format is not well recognized by VoTT tool, which was used for the part tagging process. So, it was necessary to convert the video through a conversion application, which was "FFmpeg".

Once the videos were ready, they were tagged in VoTT. Eight car parts were chosen as targets for the present project. They are: 1—battery; 2—air filter; 3—power steering reservoir; 4—engine oil reservoir; 5—coolant reservoir; 6—brakes fluid reservoir; 7—water tank of the wiper; 8—oil dipstick. The first dataset had a total of 582 images. The second dataset had additional 318 images, for a total of 900 images, as shown in Table 2. As the table shows, there are a total of 510 targets in the first dataset, 335 targets in the second dataset and a total of 845 targets in the combined dataset.

The part class names were written in Portuguese, which is the official language of the application being developed. Table 3 shows the correspondence of each class name from English to Portuguese, so that in the test images, it is possible to perceive which classes are identified.

Table 2. Characteristics of the Datasets created for training and testing the object detector.

	Mobile Device	Videos	Total Images	Total Labels	Targets
	Samsung Galaxy S10	3	582	8	510
	IPhone 11	3	318	8	335
Total		6	900	8	845

Table 3. Target classes labels translation.

Labels in English	Labels in Portuguese
Battery	Bateria
Air filter	Filtro de ar
Power steering reservoir	Reservatório da direção assistida
Engine oil reservoir	Reservatório de óleo do motor
Coolant reservoir	Reservatório do líquido de arrefecimento
Brakes fluid reservoir	Reservatório do líquido dos travões
Wiper water tank	Reservatório de água dos limpa-vidros
Oil dipstick	Vareta de óleo

6. Object Detection with Deep Learning

6.1. YOLO Deep Neural Network

YOLO (You Only Look Once) is one of the most popular deep convolution neural models for object detection, due to its good performance and short time requirements.

The first model was proposed in 2016, and it is known as YOLOv1. Several updates were made since then, and the latest model is now YOLOv5, released by Glenn Jocher in 2020. To the best of the authors' knowledge, there is no peer-reviewed research paper proposing the YOLOv5 architecture. Nonetheless, there are already more than 240 research papers referring to the architecture. YOLOv5 is based on the PyTorch framework. It is the latest version of the YOLO object recognition model, developed with the continuous efforts of 58 open source contributors [21]. There are a few model configuration files and different versions of the object detector. The present implementation uses YOLOv5s, which is the smallest model, and YOLOv5m, which is the next model in size. The other models available are YOLOv5l and YOLOv5x, the latter being the largest of all. As the network size increases, its performance may also increase, at the cost of additional processing times [22]. Therefore, the larger models may only be useful for complex problems where large datasets are available.

There are many other deep neural networks that can be used to detect objects. One of them is the mask-RCNN, which aims to solve the instance segmentation problem in machine learning or computer vision. The mask-RCNN is therefore, in theory, more precise, at the cost of additional processing time. In a comparison study, for the task of detecting a sports ball, both YOLO and Mask R-CNN with pre-trained weights show good precision and recall [23].

Because it is a good and faster detector, with high levels of performance [24], it was decided to choose the YOLOv5 network for the present project. Other architectures, such as the mask-RCNN, could provide similar detection performance and more precise location of the objects. However, the YOLO speed is a great advantage for real time operation of the task assistant. Moreover, in the present case, a bounding box is enough to give good directions to the technician.

6.2. Performance Evaluation

To evaluate the performance of an object detector, it is crucial to use appropriate metrics for each problem. Object detection is a very challenging problem because it is necessary to draw a bounding box around each detected object in the image. To evaluate the detection performance, some of the most common metrics are shown in Equations (1)–(3): precision, recall, and mAP.

$$\text{precision} = \frac{\text{TP}}{\text{TP} + \text{FP}} \tag{1}$$

$$\text{recall} = \frac{\text{TP}}{\text{TP} + \text{FN}} \tag{2}$$

$$\text{mAP} = \frac{1}{N}\sum_{N}^{i=1} \text{AP}i \tag{3}$$

True positive (TP) is a correct detection of an object that actually exists in the picture. False positive (FP) is an incorrect detection of an object, i.e., the network marks an object that is not there in the picture. False negative (FN) is an object that actually exists in the picture but is not detected by the network. In object detection, the intersection over union (IoU) measures the overlap area between the predicted bounding box and the ground truth bounding box of the actual object. Comparing the IoU with a given threshold, detection can be classified as correct or incorrect. Each value of the IoU threshold provides a different average precision (AP) metric, so it is necessary to specify this value.

7. Experiments and Results

The model was trained and tested with the datasets described in Section 5.

7.1. Train the Model

For the first experiment of the proposed system, the smallest and fastest YOLOv5 model was chosen (YOLOv5s). A notebook was adapted for the first tests [25], with all the necessary steps for training and validating the performance of the model recognizing the desired objects. The training procedure consisted of 250 epochs, which took 55 min 12 s for the dataset. Moreover, 466 of the 582 images were used for training, and 116 were used for validation. The second test used 571 of the 900 images for training and 159 for validation. The training was completed with 250 epochs in 1 h 15 min 7 s.

For the second experiment of the system, the YOLOv5m was used. The test with YOLOv5m and the first dataset was completed with 250 epochs in 55 min 1 s. The test with the second dataset was completed with 250 epochs in 1 h 15 min 39 s.

7.2. Performance for Real Time Operation

Table 4 shows the results of those metrics for all classes, obtained on the first dataset with model YOLOv5s. Table 5 shows the same results for the same dataset but for the second model, YOLOv5m.

The tables show the performance for each of the eight classes and for the whole validation set. The third column shows the number of known targets to be detected. The fourth and fifth columns show the precision and recall of the detector. The sixth and seventh columns show the mean average precision for the IoU specified. As the tables show, YOLOv5s performs about the same as the larger network. So, for the volume of data and complexity of the problem, it is adequate and bigger models are not justified.

Table 4. Performance of the model YOLOv5s for first dataset (582 images).

Class	Images	Targets	Precision	Recall	mAP 0.5	mAP 0.5:0.95
All	116	510	0.98	0.987	0.992	0.813
1	116	81	0.987	0.967	0.993	0.892
2	116	72	0.972	0.977	0.982	0.873
3	116	46	0.968	1	0.995	0.801
4	116	68	0.985	0.956	0.993	0.826
5	116	56	1	1	0.995	0.883
6	116	79	0.986	1	0.99	0.792
7	116	43	0.976	1	0.994	0.777
8	116	65	0.963	1	0.994	0.656

Table 5. Performance of the model YOLOv5m for first dataset (582 images).

Class	Images	Targets	Precision	Recall	mAP 0.5	mAP 0.5:0.95
All	116	510	0.806	0.981	0.993	0.806
1	116	81	0.987	0.966	0.993	0.882
2	116	72	0.971	0.972	0.986	0.867
3	116	46	0.978	0.987	0.995	0.771
4	116	68	0.981	0.956	0.993	0.806
5	116	56	1	0.987	0.995	0.886
6	116	79	0.987	1	0.99	0.811
7	116	43	0.985	1	0.995	0.875
8	116	65	0.985	1	0.995	0.775

7.3. Prediction Examples

After the models were trained and tested, they were also tested against images that had not been used during training and some example results are shown in Figures 3 and 4. The figures show bounding boxes around objects detected. Each bounding box has a label identifying which object is detected inside the bounding box. Each bounding box is also pointed out by a red arrow, where instructions will be added for the technicians. In the figures, all the instructions are just "open here", for that part of the software is left as future work.

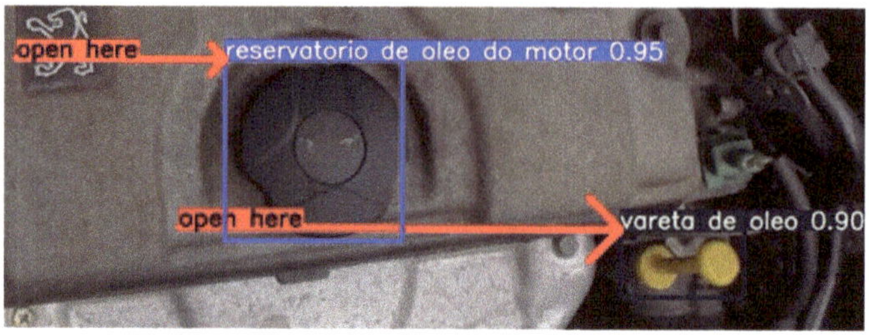

Figure 3. Example of object detection on a test image, where the engine oil reservoir and oil dipstick are detected.

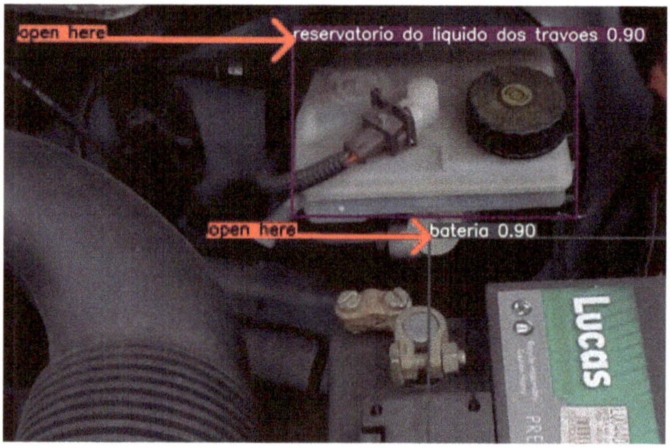

Figure 4. Example of object detection on a test image, where brakes fluid reservoir and battery are detected.

In test mode, the IoU parameter was lowered to 0.3. This means that a detection box is considered valid for $IoU \geq 30\%$. This was decided because to the human eye, it becomes difficult to distinguish between correct predictions considering a threshold of 0.5 and 0.3, according to [26–28]. When considering a lower IoU threshold, it will be possible to view a more significant number of valid detections, avoiding false negatives in the analysis of each image.

7.4. Comparison of Model YOLOv5s with Model YOLOv5m

In terms of speed, the two models are very similar. In terms of accuracy, the YOLOv5m model turned out to be slightly superior.

The two models were tested on both datasets. For the dataset with 900 images, the differences between the models in terms of mAP@0.5, mAP@0.5:0.9, precision and recall are shown in Figure 5. The color blue corresponds to model YOLOv5s and the color orange corresponds to the model YOLOv5m. As the graphs show, YOLOv5m is a bit more stable during the train. Nonetheless, both models converge to the same point.

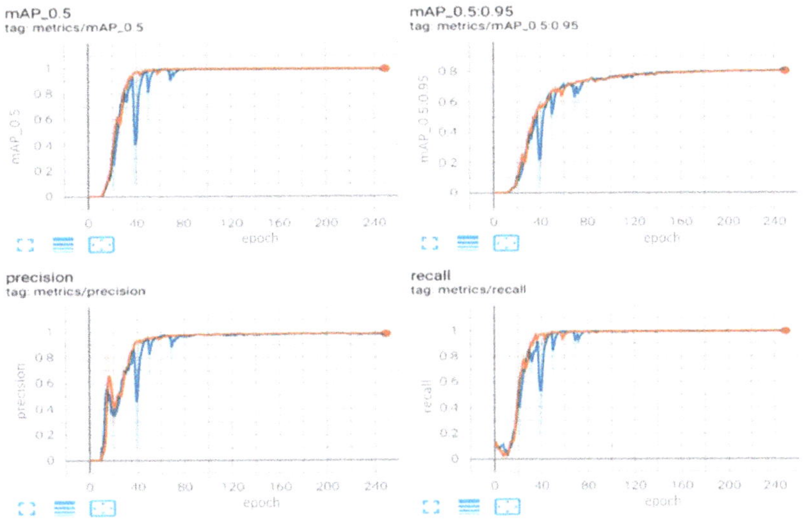

Figure 5. Comparison of performance metrics, during training, for YOLOv5s and YOLOv5m. The performance of YOLOv5s is shown in blue and YOLOv5m is shown in orange.

The plots show that the models are progressively learning through every epoch because the performance is increasing and 250 epochs are enough training, considering that the curves are stable at that point.

The loss function shows the performance of a given predictor in classifying the input data points in a dataset. The smaller the loss, the better the classifier is at modeling the relationship between the input data and the output targets. There are two different types of loss shown in Figure 6. The loss represented at the top is related to both the predicted bounding box and the loss related to the given cell containing an object during the training. The graphs of val Box and val Objectness represent their validation scores. Training loss is measured during each epoch while validation loss is measured after each epoch.

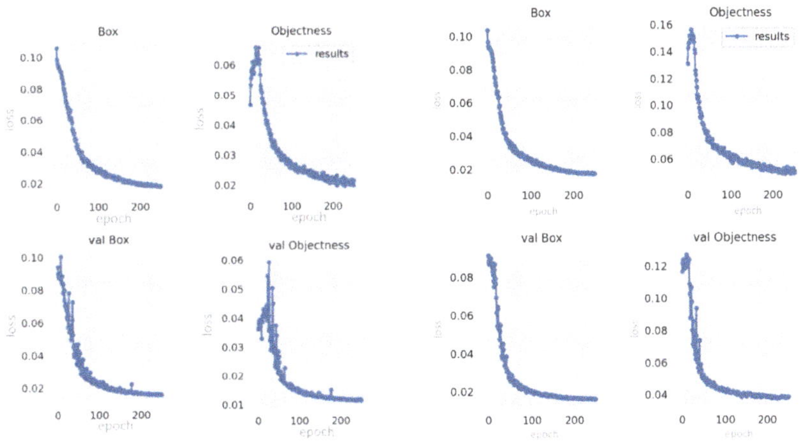

Figure 6. Loss during training, related to both the predicted bounding box and the loss related to the given cell containing an object, as well as their validation scores displayed as Box and Objectness. Results for the YOLOv5s are on the left hand side, for the YOLOv5m at the right hand side.

On the left-hand side, there are those values for the dataset with 582 images with the model YOLOv5s, and on the right are the same values for the model YOLOv5m. The charts show that both models are very similar. The YOLOv5m is faster stabilizing the learning process, but the model YOLOv5s seems to be enough.

Figure 7 shows the loss related to the predicted bounding box, a cell containing an object and the class loss for the two models YOLOv5s and YOLOv5m on the dataset with 900 images. YOLOv5m results are represented in orange and YOLOv5s results are in blue. Again, the results show that the evolution of loss for both models are very similar. Actually, the lines are practically overlapping.

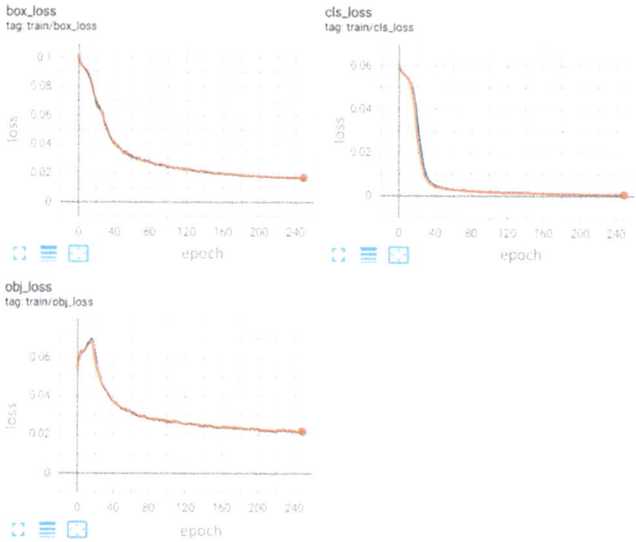

Figure 7. Loss functions for both the models YOLOv5s (blue) and YOLOv5m (orange).

8. Discussion

A task assistant was proposed, using a YOLO deep network for object detection and augmented reality glasses. The model of object detection trained learns quickly and gives a prediction in a fraction of a second, making it suitable for use in real time.

The precision obtained for the two models is in line with that obtained by other authors for similar problems, namely the "Artificial Intelligence for Real Time Threat Detection and Monitoring" [4] that has a precision of 0.803, 0.89 for recall and 0.905 for mAP 0.5. Prediction time is approximately 0.007 seconds, which allows up to 140 FPS on a TESLA P100 GPU. This shows that the system of detection can be integrated with the architecture proposed, to be used in real time, as intended, by maintenance professionals.

Table 6 compares the results for detection for all classes for both models, YOLOv5s and YOLOv5m, on both datasets. The first two lines show the results of training and testing the models with the largest dataset. A total of 571 images were used for training, 159 used for validation and 170 images were used for testing. The last two lines are the results obtained with the smaller dataset, as described in Section 7.1.

Table 6. Tests with YOLOv5s YOLOv5m for both datasets.

Model	Class	Test Dataset	Precision	Recall	mAP 0.5	mAP 0.5:0.95
YOLOv5s	All	dataset 2	0.975	0.992	0.994	0.797
YOLOv5m	All	dataset 2	0.985	0.994	0.994	0.8
YOLOv5s	All	dataset 1	0.969	1	0.992	0.818
YOLOv5m	All	dataset 1	0.974	0.997	0.994	0.829

9. Conclusions and Future Work

The goal of the present work was to train a neural network for deep learning that can serve as a basis for integrating into an augmented reality system that helps professionals in the field of maintenance.

To train the model, two different datasets were created, using two different devices in different illumination conditions. Two versions of YOLOv5 were also tested, and it was determined that YOLOv5s can be sufficient for the intended detection problem.

YOLOv5s demonstrated to be capable of identifying eight different mechanical parts in a car engine with high precision and recall always above 96.8% in the test sets, which, compared to the larger model, has almost the same results. All tests and results prove that the network is good and fast enough to be applied to the proposed system.

Future work includes the integration of the trained model in the CMMS, with the main objective of communicating with the virtual reality glasses, so that the technician is guided through the procedures of the working order in real time.

Author Contributions: Conceptualization, T.F. and M.M.; Methodology, A.M., T.F. and M.M.; software, A.M.; validation, T.F. and M.M.; formal analysis, T.F. and M.M.; investigation, A.M.; writing—original draft preparation, A.M.; writing—review and editing, T.F. and M.M.; visualization, A.M. and M.M.; supervision, T.F. and M.M. All authors have read and agreed to the published version of the manuscript.

Funding: The authors acknowledge Fundação para a Ciência e a Tecnologia (FCT) for the financial support to the project UIDB/00048/2020. FCT had no interference in the development of the research.

Institutional Review Board Statement: Not applicable

Conflicts of Interest: The authors declare no conflict of interest.

Abbreviations

The following abbreviations are used in this manuscript:

Ap	Average Precision
AR	Augmented Reality
CAP	Common Augmented Reality Platform
CMMS	Computerized Maintenance Management System
CNN	Convolutional Neural Network
COCO	Common Objects in Context
FFmpeg	Fast Forward MPEG
FN	False Negative
FP	False Positive
FPS	Frames per Second
GPU	Graphics Processing Unit
IoU	Intersection over Union
mAP	Mean Average Precision
MP	Megapixel
MTTP	Mean Time To Repair
RCNN	Region Based Convolutional Neural Networks
TP	True Positive
VoTT	Visual Object Tagging Tool
WO	Worker Order
YOLO	You Only Look Once

References

1. Zhao, Z.Q.; Zheng, P.; Xu, S.T.; Wu, X. Object detection with deep learning: A review. *IEEE Trans. Neural Netw. Learn. Syst.* **2019**, *30*, 3212–3232. [CrossRef] [PubMed]
2. Krizhevsky, A.; Sutskever, I.; Hinton, G.E. Imagenet classification with deep convolutional neural networks. *Adv. Neural Inf. Process. Syst.* **2012**, *25*, 1097–1105. [CrossRef]

3. Sharma, V. Face Mask Detection Using YOLOv5 for COVID-19. Mater's Thesis, Master of Science in Computer Science, California State University San Marcos, San Marcos, CA, USA, 2020.
4. Tolbert, S.W. Artificial Intelligence for Real Time Threat Detection and Monitoring. Available online: https://stevenwtolbert.com/pdf/threat_detection.pdf (accessed on 15 March 2021)
5. Liu, L.; Li, H.; Gruteser, M. Edge assisted real-time object detection for mobile augmented reality. In Proceedings of the 25th Annual International Conference on Mobile Computing and Networking, Los Cabos, Mexico, 21–25 October 2019; pp. 1–16.
6. Park, K.B.; Kim, M.; Choi, S.H.; Lee, J.Y. Deep learning-based smart task assistance in wearable augmented reality. *Robot. Comput. Integr. Manuf.* **2020**, *63*, 101887. [CrossRef]
7. Nee, A.Y.; Ong, S.K. Virtual and augmented reality applications in manufacturing. *IFAC Proc. Vol.* **2013**, *46*, 15–26. [CrossRef]
8. Charoenseang, S.; Tonggoed, T. Human–robot collaboration with augmented reality. In *International Conference on Human-Computer Interaction*; Springer: Berlin/Heidelberg, Germany, 2011; pp. 93–97.
9. Kim, M.; Choi, S.H.; Park, K.B.; Lee, J.Y. A Hybrid Approach to Industrial Augmented Reality Using Deep Learning-Based Facility Segmentation and Depth Prediction. *Sensors* **2021**, *21*, 307. [CrossRef]
10. Kim, M.; Choi, S.H.; Park, K.B.; Lee, J.Y. User Interactions for Augmented Reality Smart Glasses: A comparative evaluation of visual contexts and interaction gestures. *Appl. Sci.* **2019**, *9*, 3171. [CrossRef]
11. Choi, S.H.; Kim, M.; Lee, J.Y. Situation-dependent remote AR collaborations: Image-based collaboration using a 3D perspective map and live video-based collaboration with a synchronized VR mode. *Comput. Ind.* **2018**, *101*, 51–66. [CrossRef]
12. Bosh. Bosch Connected Devices and Solutions GmbH—Interplay of Augmented Reality and IoT. Available online: https://www.bosch-connectivity.com/newsroom/blog/interplay-of-augmented-reality-and-iot/. (accessed on 15 April 2021).
13. Microsoft. Mixed Reality in der Automobilindustrie Oder Wie Bosch Mobilität Digitaler Gestaltet. 2019. Available online: https://news.microsoft.com/de-de/mixed-reality-in-der-automobilindustrie-oder-wie-bosch-mobilitaet-digitaler-gestaltet/ (accessed on 15 April 2021).
14. IBM. What Is a CMMS? Available online: https://www.ibm.com/topics/what-is-a-cmms (accessed on 23 April 2021).
15. Farinha, J.M.T. *Asset Maintenance Engineering Methodologies*, 1st ed.; CRC Press: Boca Raton, FL, USA, 2018; ISBN-10 1138035890, ISBN-13 978-1138035898.
16. Johns, R. Real Python—PyTorch vs. Tensorflow For Your Python Deep Learning Project. 2020. Available online: https://realpython.com/pytorch-vs-tensorflow (accessed on 10 February 2021).
17. Microsoft. Micrisoft-HoloLens2. Available online: https://www.microsoft.com/en-us/hololens/hardware (accessed on 21 April 2021).
18. Vuzix. Vuzix—Manufacturing Solutions. Available online: https://www.vuzix.com/solutions/manufacturing (accessed on 21 April 2021).
19. Andreas Geiger. Welcome to the KITTI Vision Benchmark Suite! Available online: http://www.cvlibs.net/datasets/kitti/ (accessed on 10 April 2021).
20. The Comprehensive Cars (CompCars) Dataset. Available online: http://mmlab.ie.cuhk.edu.hk/datasets/comp_cars/index.html (accessed on 10 April 2021).
21. Analytics India Magazine. Analytics India Magazine—Guide to Yolov5 for Real-Time—Object Detection. 2020. Available online: https://analyticsindiamag.com/yolov5/ (accessed on 10 February 2021).
22. Glenn Jocher. 2020. Available online: https://github.com/ultralytics/yolov5 (accessed on 21 April 2021).
23. Buric, M.; Pobar, M.; Ivasic-Kos, M. Ball detection using YOLO and Mask R-CNN. In Proceedings of the 2018 International Conference on Computational Science and Computational Intelligence (CSCI), Las Vegas, NV, USA, 12–14 December 2018; pp. 319–323.
24. Simon, M.; Amende, K.; Kraus, A.; Honer, J.; Samann, T.; Kaulbersch, H.; Milz, S.; Michael Gross, H. Complexer-yolo: Real-time 3d object detection and tracking on semantic point clouds. In Proceedings of the IEEE/CVF Conference on Computer Vision and Pattern Recognition Workshops, Long Beach, CA, USA, 16–17 June 2019.
25. Jacob, S.; Nelson, J. How to Train YOLOv5 on a Custom Dataset. 2020. Available online: https://blog.roboflow.com/how-to-train-yolov5-on-a-custom-dataset/ (accessed on 21 April 2021).
26. Bochkovskiy, A.; Wang, C.Y.; Liao, H.Y.M. Yolov4: Optimal speed and accuracy of object detection. *arXiv* **2020**, arXiv:2004.10934.
27. Redmon, J.; Farhadi, A. Yolov3: An incremental improvement. *arXiv* **2018**, arXiv:1804.02767.
28. Redmon, J.; Farhadi, A. YOLO9000: Better, faster, stronger. In Proceedings of the IEEE Conference on Computer Vision and Pattern Recognition, Las Vegas, NV, USA, 12–14 December 2018; pp. 7263–7271.

applied sciences

MDPI

Review

High-Tech Defense Industries: Developing Autonomous Intelligent Systems

João Reis [1,2,*], Yuval Cohen [3], Nuno Melão [4], Joana Costa [5] and Diana Jorge [1]

1 Industrial Engineering and Management, Faculty of Engineering, Lusófona University and EIGeS, Campo Grande, 1749-024 Lisbon, Portugal; diana.jorge@ulusofona.pt
2 Research and Development Center, Military University Institute, Rua de Pedrouços, 1449-027 Lisbon, Portugal
3 Department of Industrial Engineering, Afeka Tel-Aviv College of Engineering, Tel Aviv 69988, Israel; yuvalc@afeka.ac.il
4 CISeD–Research Center in Digital Services, Polytechnic Institute of Viseu, Campus Politécnico, 3504-510 Viseu, Portugal; nmelao@estgv.ipv.pt
5 Department of Economics, Management, Industrial Engineering and Tourism, GOVCOPP, Aveiro University, Campus Universitário de Santiago, 3810-193 Aveiro, Portugal; joanacosta@ua.pt
* Correspondence: p40500@ulusofona.pt

Abstract: After the Cold War, the defense industries found themselves at a crossroads. However, it seems that they are gaining new momentum, as new technologies such as robotics and artificial intelligence are enabling the development of autonomous, highly innovative and disruptive intelligent systems. Despite this new impetus, there are still doubts about where to invest limited financial resources to boost high-tech defense industries. In order to shed some light on the topic, we decided to conduct a systematic literature review by using the PRISMA protocol and content analysis. The results indicate that autonomous intelligent systems are being developed by the defense industry and categorized into three different modes—fully autonomous operations, partially autonomous operations, and smart autonomous decision-making. In addition, it is also important to note that, at a strategic level of war, there is limited room for automation given the need for human intervention. However, at the tactical level of war, there is a high probability of growth in industrial defense, since, at this level, structured decisions and complex analytical-cognitive tasks are carried out. In the light of carrying out those decisions and tasks, robotics and artificial intelligence can make a contribution far superior to that of human beings.

Keywords: artificial intelligence; defense industry; high technology; intelligent systems; level of war; robotics

Citation: Reis, J.; Cohen, Y.; Melão, N.; Costa, J.; Jorge, D. High-Tech Defense Industries: Developing Autonomous Intelligent Systems. *Appl. Sci.* **2021**, *11*, 4920. https://doi.org/10.3390/app11114920

Academic Editor: Andrea Prati

Received: 12 May 2021
Accepted: 26 May 2021
Published: 27 May 2021

1. Introduction

Advances in intelligent defense systems are growing and paving the way for high technological defense industries. Technologies such as robotics [1,2], artificial intelligence [3], and the internet of things [4] are driving considerable changes and impacts on defense industries [5]. These technologies are known to be capable of developing autonomous intelligent systems, increasingly designed for military applications and capable of operating efficiently in conflict areas and war zones. Thus, technology is often considered to be the key to many military revolutions in history, the so-called major military innovations or, as others have named, radical change in military affairs [6]. Three main factors are driving the latest revolution in military affairs: (1) rapid technological advancements that moved the Industrial Age into the Information Age; (2) the end of the Cold War; and (3) the decline in United States defense budgets [7].

In recent years, we have identified several studies on the development of autonomous defense systems in the industry sector. Some examples are presented in Zhang et al. [8], who focus on studying autonomous defense systems and relevant technological applications (e.g., X47-B, Predator, Global Hawk). However, apart from the division of warfare applications, to the best of our knowledge, no article has so far made a characterization of the autonomous defense systems literature in modes. That said, our intention is to explore and understand the following two research questions:

Research Question 1. How can the several modes of autonomous defense systems in the defense industry be categorized?

Research Question 2. How does the characterization of the autonomous defense systems modes contribute to making the defense industry highly technological?

Considering these research questions, it is quite evident that this research aims to understand and describe a real-life phenomenon, as suggested by Yin [9]. Although the research is of a qualitative and descriptive nature, it falls within the domain of applied sciences since it aims to identify the existing gaps and fill these gaps by initiating new scientific research in robotics and artificial intelligence applications at the various levels of war. It would seem, thus, inappropriate to carry out a more in-depth study to improve the high-tech defense industry without first knowing the holistic view of the use of autonomous defense systems.

This topic is important since there has been an exponential investment in autonomous intelligent systems in the military sector [5]. However, to the best of our knowledge, there has been no prior characterization of the modes of operations of these systems. In that regard, our article provides a comprehensive characterization of autonomous intelligent systems according to the various levels of war and different types of decisions and artificial intelligence. In addition to presenting a characterization of the various modes of autonomous intelligent systems in the defense industry, this article also characterizes how these modes contribute to making the defense industry highly technological. The novelty of this article is associated with the need to increase the degree of intelligent automation at the lowest levels of war. The need for automation is justified by the argument that, at the tactical/operational level, the military follows clear orders and makes structured decisions. Therefore, if structured decisions are made at the tactical level, which requires the performance of tasks of an analytical-cognitive nature, the type of intelligence needed is mechanical, thus, justifying the replacement of military personnel by machines, creating an excellent opportunity for the technological defense industries. On the other hand, at the strategic level of war, there is limited scope for the use of lethal autonomous weapon systems, given the need for human intervention, so as not to run into the current United Nations ethical, moral, and legal guidelines. Thus, this article's specific strengths are also associated with the managerial contribution, insofar as it provides the due knowledge on where to invest innovation and development resources of intelligent autonomous technologies, where they have a more significant growth perspective (i.e., in field operations—tactical level).

The remaining of the paper is organized as follows: the next section presents a conceptualization of the most relevant terms and applications; this is followed by an explanation of the methodological process; the results of this study are presented in Section 4, where the answers to the research questions can be found; in the last section, the conclusions are withdrawn, focusing on theoretical and managerial contributions, research gaps and suggestions for future work.

2. Conceptual Background

This section presents a brief conceptualization of the most relevant terms for this research. It also discusses the challenges for the defense industry and analyses the applications of autonomous intelligent systems in war.

2.1. Concepts and Definitions

In recent years, one of the most profound changes in the defense sector has been the use of robots, aiming to replace human beings in tasks of high precision and analytical-cognitive complexity [10], tasks of high risk for human life [11] and/or physically and physiologically strenuous [12,13]. To that end, the defense industry developed various sophisticated warfare applications that can operate in multiple domains (i.e., space, cyberspace, air, sea, and land). Due to a wide range of defense technologies, it is currently difficult, if virtually impossible, to describe consensual warfare applications among all defense researchers and academics. In addition to the growing demand for autonomous defense systems, a relevant argument that justifies the writing of this article is the degree of maturity that some military technologies have achieved [14]. The degree of maturity is somewhat related to the high learning curve of autonomous defense systems, due to the increased connectivity of these systems, via remote and network connection (e.g., fifth-generation technology standard for broadband cellular networks—5G) [15,16] and easy access to big data. Those characteristics allow autonomous defense systems to make decisions quickly, without empathetic or emotional impasses, which is an important distinctive characteristic when compared to human beings [17,18]. Thus, autonomous defense systems work without human interference, boosted by the latest advances in intelligence, cognition, computing, and system sciences [19]. When referring to autonomous defense systems, most are robots that detect, identify, understand, and interact autonomously with the external environment. Their capacity is based essentially on three functionalities: (1) sensors, which detect the environment characteristics [20]; (2) artificial intelligence, which identifies and understands the surrounding reality [21]; and (3) mechanisms, which allow real interaction [22].

Several articles in the literature carried out an analysis of automation, autonomy, and intelligence, which allows us to understand the most relevant terms. For instance, Insaurralde and Lane [23] define automation as the ability of a system to automatically carry out a certain process by following a code. They define autonomy as the ability of a system to carry out an automatic process by making decisions, implementing the choices made, and checking the evolution of such actions, i.e., make choices on its own. On the other hand, the human intelligence literature usually defines intelligence as the human ability to learn over time and adapt to the external environment [24,25]. Moreover, the artificial intelligence literature refers that intelligence is the capacity of mimicking human intelligence [26], such as the ability of knowledge and reasoning [27], problem-solving [28], communicating, interacting, and learning [29]. Huang and Rust [26] and Huang et al. [30] also proposed three artificial intelligences—mechanical, thinking, and feeling (Figure 1).

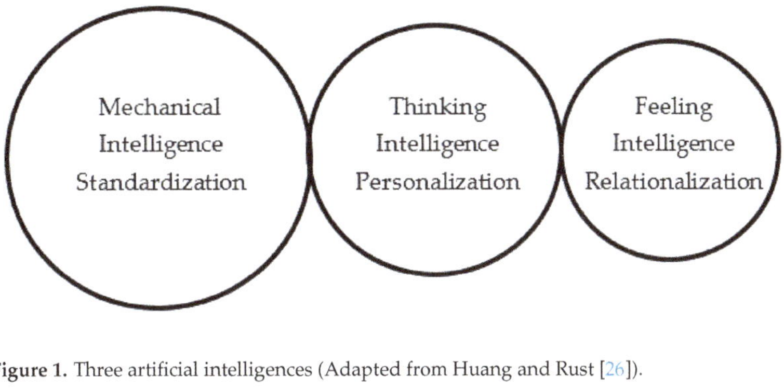

Figure 1. Three artificial intelligences (Adapted from Huang and Rust [26]).

Mechanical artificial intelligence is used for simple, standardized, repetitive, and routine tasks. An example of a civil application of mechanical intelligence is the use of service robots to clean hotel rooms, replacing humans in routine and standardized tasks [18]. Thinking artificial intelligence is used for complex, systematic, rule-based, and well-defined tasks. An example of this is Boston Dynamics' quadrupedal robots, highly adaptable, versatile, and capable of capturing the mobility, autonomy, and speed of living creatures [31,32]. Feeling artificial intelligence is used for social, emotional, communicative, and interactive tasks ([33], p. 32). Due to limited empathic and socioemotional capacity of machines, we believe that feeling artificial intelligence in the military domain should be performed by human beings. This argument is justified by the current state of social and emotional evolution of intelligent machines, which has not yet reached the desirable stage. For instance, it is difficult to imagine a lethal autonomous weapon system [34] in a combat situation with socioemotional ability capable of deciding whether to kill a child with a weapon in his possession. Such complex and socioemotional tasks require skills that are currently at the limit of the human being; some activities can eventually be shared with intelligent machines, but in the context of the decision-making process. We will hardly see a robot crying for a human in its current stage of evolution, whereas the opposite is already true. For example, when Boomer "died" in Iraq, the American soldiers offer him an impromptu military funeral—in this case Boomer was not a human being, but a robot whose job was to search for and defuse bombs [35]. Perhaps due to examples such as this one, robots have been increasingly integrated and accepted into military teams [36].

It is likely that the types of intelligence are also related to the types of decisions, as we will see in the Results section. Laudon and Laudon [37] classified decisions as structured, semi-structured, and unstructured. According to these authors, unstructured decisions are those in which decision-makers must evaluate and decide about something that is new, not routine, and for which there is no previously defined procedure. These decisions are made at the strategic level of the organization. In contrast, structured decisions are repetitive and routine, where established rules and accepted procedures are previously defined. Decisions of this type are taken at the operational management level. Intermediate decisions are semi-structured, where only part of the problem has a clear answer defined by a well-accepted procedure.

2.2. Type and Levels of Autonomy

The type and levels of autonomy are also well described in the literature, although the measurement scales are not always consensual, making it difficult to select a model. In that regard, Vagia et al. [38] presented a literature review of the evolution of the levels of autonomy since the end of 1950s (Table 1).

Table 1. A taxonomy for the levels of autonomy (Adapted from Vagia et al. [38]).

Levels of Automation	Description
Level 1—Manual control.	The computer offers no assistance.
Level 2—Decision proposal stage.	The computer offers some decision to the operator. The operator is responsible for deciding and executing.
Level 3—Human decision select stage.	The human selects one decision, and the computer executes.
Level 4—Computer decision stage.	The computer selects one decision and executes with human approval.
Level 5—Computer execution and on human information stage.	The computer executes the selected decision and informs the human.
Level 6—Computer execution and on-call human information stage.	The computer executes the selected decision and informs the human only if asked.
Level 7—Computer execution and voluntary information stage.	The computer executes the selected decision and informs the human only if it decides to.
Level 8—Autonomous control stage.	The computer does everything without human notification, except if an error that is not into the specifications occurs. In that case, the computer needs to inform the operator.

One of the most interesting aspects we highlight in Table 1 is the introduction of the failure mode at the fully autonomous control stage (level 8), which means the computer operates completely autonomously unless an unexpected error occurs. If the error does not appear in the program specifications, the computer must seek human support. This human support is relevant to the subject of this paper since, at the limit of the use of military technologies, there may be a need to attack human beings without any margin of error in selecting those who live or die. The intervention of human beings was not frequently considered at this level, as observed in one of the most relevant studies about levels of autonomy, published by Endsley and Kaber [39]. The taxonomy of Vagia et al. [38] intends to combine a series of levels from other articles that seem to have no significant differences between them, presenting the reader with a simpler and easier-to-understand model. The authors also intended to present a taxonomy that could be widely used, and, in this regard, the authors stated that it is up to the user to decide how to create their own taxonomy at the automation level and prioritize their needs and requirements. The modes of autonomous intelligent systems that we further developed show some similarities with the model of Vagia et al. [38], although it is not as comprehensive as it focuses on a specific domain (i.e., military field).

2.3. Military Applications of Autonomous Intelligent Systems

The defense industry is increasingly conducting autonomous defense systems research and development in several domains: space, cyberspace, air, sea, and land. It is in that regard that we present an overview of military application of autonomous defense systems in each of the aforementioned domains:

- Space robotics and autonomous intelligent systems;
- Autonomous intelligent cyber-defense agents;
- Intelligent unmanned autonomous systems—in the air, at sea, and on land.

Space robotics autonomous intelligent systems are presented as machines capable of operating in space and carrying out exploration in adverse environments that may not be found in the natural conditions of earth. In general, space robots are divided into two types: (1) orbital robots [40], which are characterized by robotics in low earth orbit or robotics in geostationary orbit; and (2) planetary robots [41], which are capable of closely examining extraterrestrial surfaces. As mentioned by Gao et al. [42], depending on the applications (orbital or planetary), space robots are often designed to be mobile, manipulate, grab, drill and/or collect samples, such as the National Aeronautics and Space Administration's recent Mars 2021 Perseverance Rover [43]. These robots are expected to have several levels of autonomy, from tele-operation by humans to fully autonomous operations. Depending on the level of autonomy, a space robot can act as [42]: (1) a robotic agent (or human proxy) that can perform tele-operation up to semi-autonomous operations; (2) a robotic assistant, who can help human astronauts that range from semi- to fully-autonomous operations; or (3) a robotic explorer capable of exploring unknown territory in space using fully autonomous operations. As an exemplary method, Giordano et al. [40] is presented as a validating benchmark. They reported an efficient fuel control strategy for a spacecraft equipped with a manipulator. Their key findings are associated with the strategy of using the thrusters, the reaction wheels, and the arm drives in a coordinated way to limit the use of the thrusters and achieve the ideal zero fuel consumption in non-contact maneuvers. The authors were able to validate the method via a hardware-in-the-loop simulator composed of a seven degrees of freedom arm mounted on a simulated six degrees of freedom spacecraft. Some military space robotics autonomous intelligent systems are related to spy satellites of some military powers and space-based missile defense systems.

Autonomous cyber defense is an area that has been driven by the defense sector in anticipation of threats to military infrastructures, systems, and operations [44]. These systems will be implemented through autonomous and intelligent cyber-defense agents that will fight against intelligent autonomous malware [44] and are likely to become primary cyber fighters on the future battlefield [45].

The popularity of advanced applications in the domains of air, land, and sea has also been steadily increasing [46] with the intelligent unmanned autonomous systems, which can perform operations without human intervention with the help of artificial intelligence [8]. In that regard, intelligent unmanned aircraft systems have aimed at autonomous flight, navigation, sensory, and decision-making capabilities [47] above conventional unmanned aircraft systems or unmanned aerial vehicles. Currently, unmanned aircraft systems and unmanned aerial vehicles systems have often been used for intelligence, surveillance, and reconnaissance activities or to carry out attack missions against high-value targets [48]. In addition, several methodologies have been targeted to these systems, such as Jourdan et al. [49], who designed an approach to mitigate common unmanned aerial vehicle failures, including primary control surface damage, airframe damage, and complete engine failure. Intelligent unmanned aircraft systems are beginning to be developed mainly in the civil context, such as package delivery [50], agriculture, and agroindustry [51], to name a few. The intelligent unmanned maritime and underwater systems have pushed the technology beyond imaginable limits in order to deal with complex ocean and sea missions [23]. These systems present new opportunities for naval use, in particular for dangerous missions, such as highly efficient mine sweeping. Recognizing the potential of autonomous underwater vehicles for both science and the military, in 1997 the Massachusetts Institute of Technology and the North Atlantic Treaty Organization joined efforts to develop robotic technologies applicable to mine countermeasures [52]. These systems have evolved with the use of disruptive technologies until today [53]. For example, Sands [54] developed very relevant methodologies in this regard. He studied deterministic artificial intelligence for unmanned underwater vehicles, proposing an automated control and learning methodology that requires simple user inputs. Noteworthy is also the attention that has been given to unmanned ground vehicles. Of these, an interesting example is the BigDog, developed by Boston Dynamics, which is a four-legged robot for transporting loads in difficult terrain [46] and has been adapted with autonomous navigation [55]. Moreover, mathematical structures and expectation-maximization and Gaussian mixture models algorithms have been developed [53]. Besides its applications in robotics and unmanned ground vehicles, these algorithms can also be used in various domains such as cybersecurity, object detection, and military logistics. The practical application of these algorithms has resulted in modern technology that can be applied on the battlefield, as presented by Bistron and Piotrowski [53], who give us examples of solutions such as Spot and Atlas (also developed by Boston Dynamics). In addition to the potential for civil society, much is speculated about the use of these autonomous robots in the revolution of military ground operations [6].

3. Methodology

This study was carried out as a systematic literature review, based on the original guidelines proposed by Moher et al. [56]. This research strategy is well justified by Fink [57], who argues that it is: systematic, since it embraces a methodological approach; explicit, as all data collection procedures are described in it; and comprehensive, as it brings together a wide range of scientific knowledge. The search process was undertaken in Elsevier´s Scopus, one of the world´s largest abstract and citation databases of peer-reviewed literature. By choosing Scopus over other scientific databases (e.g., Web of Science, EBSCO Host, ScienceDirect) and/or academic search engines (e.g., Google Scholar), this article takes advantage of (1) greater transparency and easy replicability of results [58], (2) superior coverage of journals in the fields of applied and technological sciences [59], (3) peer-reviewed articles, which increases the quality of the results and the credibility of the research, (4) wider application of filters, and (5) immediate generation of search results in graphs and tables. Thus, based on the previous advantages, the use of a single scientific database has been accepted by the academic community [59]. By following the assumptions of Moher et al. [56], this research uses the PRISMA Statement (also known as Preferred Reporting Item for Systematic Reviews and Meta-Analysis), which consists of a 27-item checklist and a four-phase flow diagram. The checklist includes items considered essential for the transparent reporting of a systematic review [60]. As Page [61] points out, each item on the checklist was accompanied by an "explanation and elaboration", providing additional pedagogical justifications and guidance for each item, along with examples to demonstrate complete reports. The adoption of the guideline has been extensive, as indicated by its citation in tens of thousands of systematic reviews and frequent use as a tool to assess the integrity of published systematic review reports [62]. To do so, the search was initially conducted on 14 April 2021, by identifying documents with the terms "Defense Industry" and "Intelligent Systems" in all fields of search.

Following the typical application of filters during the screening phase of the PRISMA protocol, manuscripts were selected by source type, document type, and language (Table 2). The screening phase allowed more accurate results to be obtained. The selection of the source and type of document is closely related to the quality of the publication, as there seems to be a consensus among the academic community that journal articles are those that generally have superior scientific quality. Moreover, the option of selecting articles in English seemed to be an adequate option in order to avoid misinterpretations of the articles; on the other hand, as English is used worldwide, it involved a greater article coverage when compared to any other language. Following, the eligibility phase allowed to exclude articles that were not strictly related to the topic; and the inclusion criteria, which allowed to add manuscripts that were relevant to corroborate some information retrieved from Scopus. The final sample consisted of 62 articles from peer-reviewed journals (Table 2). The data analysis followed the technique known as content analysis [63,64] in order to highlight new concepts and ideas [65]. The first phase started with the reading of all articles so as to identify similar words and terms [66]. After grouping the text, we identified the most relevant categories and subcategories [67]. In a next phase, we hierarchized the categories and subcategories to identify the patterns and ideas [68]. To assist in the analysis, we used a qualitative data analysis software—NVivo 11 [69], whose process allowed to obtain a holistic view of the existing literature, which is presented in the next chapter.

Table 2. Scopus search with PRISMA statement.

Elsevier's Scopus® Database	*n*
Identification	
"Defense Industry" AND "Intelligent Systems" (All fields)	153
Screening	
Source type (Journals)	67
Document type (Articles)	61
Language (English)	57
Eligibility	
Full-text articles assessed for eligibility	51
Included	
Included studies (+11 articles)	62

4. Results

Since early, Hetrick [70] defined the high-tech defense in four manufacturing industries. The first two manufacturing industries are known as the aerospace industry—aircrafts, guided missiles, and space vehicles; the third is the ordinance and accessories, and the fourth corresponds to navigation systems and equipment manufacturing. All of these industries can operate in the development of autonomous defense systems. One example is the research on ammunitions in future intelligent combat, which is a timely topic [71]. After carefully evaluating the applications of autonomous defense systems, it is safe to argue that three generic modes can be identified in the defense industry.

Three Modes of Autonomous Intelligent Systems in the Defense Industry

We identified high-technological autonomous defense systems that are being developed by the defense industry, and that can be categorized in three different modes (Table 3). The proposal to categorize autonomous defense systems modes is due to the scarcity of scientific production that favors a taxonomy for this type of systems, both autonomous and intelligent. Given the above, we continue by answering both research questions through real-life examples, taking into account the challenges and opportunities of each modality.

Table 3. Modes of autonomous intelligent systems in the defense industry.

Modes of Autonomous Intelligent Systems	Description	Levels of War	Decisions Type	Types of Artificial Intelligence
Mode 1–Fully autonomous operation	The human has no control over the operation	Military tactical	Structured decision	Mechanical intelligence
Mode 2–Partially autonomous operation	The human has some kind of control over the operation, or the system assists humans and vice-versa	Military operational	Semi-structured decisions	Thinking intelligence
Mode 3– Smart autonomous decision-making	The intelligent system supports humans in case of need	Military strategic	Unstructured decisions	Feeling intelligence

- Mode 1. Fully autonomous operation (the human has no control over the operation).

The doctrine of war is normally divided into three levels—strategic, operational, and tactical [72,73]. The first mode of autonomous defense systems usually operates at the tactical level, as it requires structured decisions in the field of operations. While the Mode 1 has greater efficiency when compared to humans, humans are expected to be replaced by machines in the middle and long term. Taking into account the previous argument, Mode 1 is expected to strongly contribute to make the defense industry highly technological. At lower levels of war (i.e., tactical level), structured decisions are made since soldiers are limited to following well-defined orders on the battlefield. In these situations, the performance of tasks is of an analytical-cognitive nature, where mechanical intelligence is the most recommended; that is, machines must take control of military operations. One example of Mode 1 from the data collected from Scopus is given by Rossiter [6], who recently published an article on the use of unmanned ground vehicles and how they are revolutionizing ground military operations. Rossiter [6] corroborates our previous arguments in the extant that unmanned ground vehicles' use has been intensified in recent years due to artificial intelligence, advanced computing, sensors, vision systems, and propulsion technologies. Rossiter [6] also refers that the United States Autonomous Systems Strategy (published in 2017) defined as a medium-term priority (2021–2030) the need to have fully autonomous unmanned combat vehicle operations. However, when it comes to the use of unmanned ground vehicles, recent history has shown that technological developments are promising but, so far, are unsatisfactory due to the created expectations. Thus, expectations have been made that there will be machines that will completely replace humans on the battlefield, but the defense industry is far from achieving that goal. In short, as can be seen in Table 3, fully autonomous operations (Mode 1) operate at the level of tactical warfare where structured decisions are made and which, in turn, refer to a type of mechanical intelligence. As far as mechanical intelligence is concerned, humans are likely to start losing control of these military operations to machines. Building upon the previous arguments, the next natural step is to define the construction elements of different types of weapons, as suggested by Božanić et al. [74], in order to produce autonomous systems suitable for users.

- Mode 2. Partially autonomous operation (the human has some kind of control over the operation, or the system assists humans and vice-versa).

Mode 2 is suitable for the operational level of warfare, as humans generally need to make semi-structured decisions with a medium level of responsibility. In this case, machines are recommended to take control over military operations, albeit with some kind of human control. An example of Mode 2 was also obtained from Scopus. In a first stage, it was possible to ascertain that in the context of the naval defense situation, awareness of the battle space is mission-critical. According to Dalkiran et al. [75], in platform-centered warfare, each combat unit keeps an individual situational awareness that is limited by a geographical area due to the limited range of the sensors (e.g., radar, optical and infrared sensors, sonar). The authors also refer that it is possible to achieve a shared battlefield awareness by connecting combat management systems on warships with command and control systems. Therefore, they proposed a communication mechanism for integrating data distribution service systems in real-time, where a combat management system could support military personnel on a warship with two main functions: (1) creating awareness of the battle space in real-time; (2) eliminating enemy forces using onboard weapon systems. According to Dalkiran et al.'s [75] research, a combat management system generates a tactical image with tracking data from various sensors and using data fusion algorithms. Subsequently, the collected information is sent to the weapon systems at high frequencies to engage enemy forces. These systems are generally used at an operational and strategic level, helping commanders to accomplish the security mission. Briefly, and as can be seen in Table 3, military operations are partially autonomous. These are carried out at the operational level of war and where semi-structured decisions are made. These levels/decisions result in the domain of thinking intelligence, as mentioned by Huang and Rust [25,32]. This type of intelligence applies to complex tasks based on well-defined rules. Therefore, it is likely that humans will also lose some control of these military operations to the machines or to models which support decision making [76–78]. Typically, artificial intelligence algorithms are used to simulate the human analytical, cognitive, and intuitive components.

- Mode 3. Smart autonomous decision-making (the intelligent system supports human decision).

Mode 3 is suitable for strategic military operations, as humans are usually required to take complex and unstructured decisions with a high level of responsibility. In that regard, autonomous defense systems advise and support the human decision-making process, but do not replace humans in their decision. As these advanced systems are intelligent and autonomous, the upper limit of their military use can result in serious injury or loss of human life's, which means that, at a strategic level of war, it may be advisable to maintain some degree of human intervention and decision-making, preventing machines from killing humans indiscriminately in case of error. Furthermore, whereas in the manufacturing and services industry some degree of automation may be acceptable at high levels of decision, in the military and defense industry this is highly discouraged. So, it is necessary to find ways that allow the development of intelligent machines without coming up against the current ethical, moral, and legal guidelines of the United Nations (UN) [79,80]. These guidelines emphasize responsibility in deciding by humans over machines to safeguard interest in preserving human life. Given the above, it is likely that there will be little room for automation in Mode 3, which will not contribute to the same extent as Mode 1 to make the defense industry highly technological. From the content analysis, we can verify a relevant finding associated with the diversity of the degree of performance of the autonomous defense systems at the strategic level. That is, the autonomous defense systems that operate at the strategic level, mostly also operate at the lowest levels of the war. An example of the previous argument is unmanned aerial vehicles, which, due to their exponential growth and wide variety, can be used at all levels of war. The range of performance of unmanned aerial vehicles is discussed by Hamurcu and Eren [81] when they argue that they can be piloted remotely or fly autonomously or semi-autonomously. Their variety is mainly due to technological advances in robotics, which can imply widespread use, ranging from surveillance, tactical reconnaissance, and combat operations. If within the scope of surveillance and reconnaissance it can be acceptable for unmanned aerial vehicles to be autonomous and intelligent, with regard to combat operations, there has been much resistance in automating their decision.

Table 3 summarizes all the information regarding the autonomous defense systems Modes in the defense industry. Below we present the section of conclusions that focus on the main contributions of this research.

5. Conclusions

The purpose of this article was twofold. It first presented a characterization of the various modes of autonomous intelligent systems in the defense industry. Then, it characterized how those modes contribute to making the defense industry highly technological.

The results indicate that the autonomous intelligent systems can be categorized in three different modes—fully autonomous operations, partially autonomous operations, and intelligent autonomous decision-making. With regard to Mode 1, since autonomous defense systems perform complex analytical-cognitive operations more efficiently than humans, it is likely that the latter will be replaced by machines in the medium and long term. Mode 2 is recommended to be run by autonomous defense systems, while humans can assume some kind of control. At this level, operational missions are developed, where human beings are called upon to make semi-structured decisions. Finally, at a strategic level, autonomous defense systems support humans in case of need. Therefore, in this specific case, autonomous defense systems only support but do not replace humans in its decision. Each mode contributes differently to making the defense industry highly technological. In other words, from our analysis, we conclude that it is likely that automation in Mode 3 will be much more limited when compared to Mode 1. This is because in Mode 3 there must be a higher degree of decision and human intervention, which surpasses the previous modes that should have a higher degree of automation. These results provide guidance on the levels of automation where defense managers must invest their time and resources in research and development. So, scientific research in military technologies is recommended to focus on the first two levels of war (i.e., Tactical and Operational). As for the strategic level, the technological application is still very limited in the domain of empathic capacity in decision making, so it will likely continue to be operated in the hands of humans.

As this article follows a systematic literature review, some limitations are worth mentioning. First, the research presents a snapshot of the reality. Indeed, the Scopus database is constantly being updated, and, thus, it is likely that some relevant research has been left out of the analysis. Second, it is possible that other articles are left out of the analysis due to the application of filters. However, the PRISMA protocol allows the inclusion of relevant articles, mitigating the effects of that exclusion. Third, if different keywords are selected on Scopus, the search may also yield different results. However, after having performed several simulations with synonymous words, we found that the keywords chosen were those with the largest number of search results. Finally, the results have not been empirically tested and validated. Despite the aforementioned limitations, the analysis of the existing literature allowed the presentation of a holistic view of the phenomenon, which is focused on the autonomous defense systems in the context of defense, but also to provide managerial guidelines on where to invest the resources. Following this article, we suggest to empirically test and validate the findings to analyze if the research and development in the defense industry is moving in the right way. A second study can be focused on the technological transfer to the production industry and its commercialization, given that many of the existing theoretical studies end up not being carried out in practice. Finally, it may be interesting to study complementary fields of research for intelligent autonomous systems. This is the case of notable researchers such as Kwon et al. [82,83] who bring us neural network applications and adversarial examples. These military applications allow to deceive enemy classifiers and to safeguard the tactical use of intelligent autonomous systems.

Author Contributions: Conceptualization, J.R.; methodology, J.R.; software, J.R.; validation, Y.C., N.M., J.C. and D.J.; formal analysis, J.R.; investigation, J.R.; resources, J.R.; data curation, J.R.; writing—original draft preparation, J.R.; writing—review and editing, J.R., N.M. and D.J.; visualization, J.R.; supervision, N.M.; project administration, J.R.; funding acquisition, J.R. and Y.C. All authors have read and agreed to the published version of the manuscript.

Funding: This research received no external funding.

Institutional Review Board Statement: Not applicable.

Informed Consent Statement: Not applicable.

Data Availability Statement: The data used in this study was collected by the authors, any questions or clarifications can be addressed to the first author (p40500@ulusofona.pt).

Acknowledgments: We would like to thank the contribution of the anonymous reviewers.

Conflicts of Interest: The authors declare no conflict of interest.

References

1. Lin, P.; Bekey, G.; Abney, K. Autonomous Military Robotics: Risk, Ethics, and Design. California Polytechnic State University of San Luis Obispo. 2008. Available online: https://apps.dtic.mil/sti/pdfs/ADA534697.pdf (accessed on 14 April 2021).
2. Ha, Q.; Yen, L.; Balaguer, C. Robotic autonomous systems for earthmoving in military applications. *Autom. Constr.* **2019**, *107*, 102934. [CrossRef]
3. Mori, S. US defense innovation and artificial intelligence. *Asia-Pac. Rev.* **2018**, *25*, 16–44. [CrossRef]
4. Mariani, J.; Williams, B.; Loubert, B. Continuing the March: The Past, Present, and Future of the IoT in the Military. The Internet of Things in Defense. Technical Report. 2015. Available online: https://www2.deloitte.com/us/en/insights/focus/internet-of-things/iot-in-military-defense-industry.html (accessed on 14 April 2021).
5. Payal, M.; Dixit, P.; Sairam, T.; Goyal, N. Robotics, AI, and the IoT in Defense Systems. In *AI and IoT-Based Intelligent Automation in Robotics*; Wiley-Scrivener: Hoboken, NJ, USA, 2021.
6. Rossiter, A. Bots on the ground: An impending UGV revolution in military affairs? *Small Wars Insur.* **2020**, *31*, 851–873. [CrossRef]
7. Tilford, E. The Revolution in Military Affairs: Prospects and Cautions. US Army War College. 1995. Available online: https://www.jstor.org/stable/pdf/resrep11803.pdf (accessed on 14 April 2021).
8. Zhang, T.; Li, Q.; Zhang, C.; Liang, H.; Li, P.; Wang, T.; Li, S.; Zhu, Y.; Wu, C. Current trends in the development of intelligent unmanned autonomous systems. *Front. Inf. Technol. Electron. Eng.* **2017**, *18*, 68–85. [CrossRef]
9. Yin, R. *Case Study Research and Applications: Design and Methods*; SAGE Publications: Thousand Oaks, CA, USA, 2018.
10. Chamola, V.; Kotesh, P.; Agarwal, A.; Gupta, N.; Guizani, M. A Comprehensive Review of Unmanned Aerial Vehicle Attacks and Neutralization Techniques. *Ad. Hoc. Netw.* **2020**, *111*, 102324. [CrossRef] [PubMed]
11. Šipoš, D.; Gleich, D. A lightweight and low-power UAV-borne ground penetrating radar design for landmine detection. *Sensors* **2020**, *20*, 2234. [CrossRef] [PubMed]
12. Sapaty, P. Military robotics: Latest trends and spatial grasp solutions. *Int. J. Adv. Res. Artif. Intell.* **2015**, *4*, 9–18.
13. Walsh, G.; Low, D. Military load carriage effects on the gait of military personnel: A systematic review. *Appl. Ergon.* **2021**, *93*, 103376. [CrossRef]
14. Rossiter, A. The impact of robotics and autonomous systems (RAS) across the conflict spectrum. *Small Wars Insur.* **2020**, *31*, 691–700. [CrossRef]
15. Garg, S.; Aujla, G.; Erbad, A.; Rodrigues, J.; Chen, M.; Wang, X. Guest Editorial: Blockchain Envisioned Drones: Realizing 5G-Enabled Flying Automation. *IEEE Netw.* **2021**, *35*, 16–19. [CrossRef]
16. Rathje, J.; Katila, R. Enabling technologies and the role of private firms: A machine learning matching analysis. *Strategy Sci.* **2021**, *6*, 5–21. [CrossRef]
17. Reis, J.; Melão, N.; Salvadorinho, J.; Soares, B.; Rosete, A. Service robots in the hospitality industry: The case of Hennna hotel, Japan. *Technol. Soc.* **2020**, *63*, 101423. [CrossRef]
18. Rosete, A.; Soares, B.; Salvadorinho, J.; Reis, J.; Amorim, M. Service robots in the hospitality industry: An exploratory literature review. In *International Conference on Exploring Services Science*; Springer: Cham, Switzerland; Porto, Portugal, 2020; pp. 174–186.
19. Wang, Y.; Hou, M.; Plataniotis, K.; Kwong, S.; Leung, H.; Tunstel, E.; Rudas, I.; Trajkovic, L. Towards a theoretical framework of autonomous systems underpinned by intelligence and systems sciences. *IEEE/Caa J. Autom. Sin.* **2020**, *8*, 52–63.
20. Campbell, S.; O'Mahony, N.; Krpalcova, L.; Riordan, D.; Walsh, J.; Murphy, A.; Ryan, C. Sensor technology in autonomous vehicles: A review. In Proceedings of the 2018 29th Irish Signals and Systems Conference (ISSC), Belfast, UK, 21–22 June 2018; pp. 1–4.
21. Horowitz, M.C.; Scharre, P.; Velez-Green, A. A Stable Nuclear Future? The Impact of Autonomous Systems and Artificial Intelligence. *arXiv* **2019**, arXiv:1912.05291. Available online: https://arxiv.org/abs/1912.05291 (accessed on 20 April 2021).
22. Sandin, P. *Robot Mechanisms and Mechanical Devices Illustrated*; McGraw Hill Professional: New York, NY, USA, 2003.
23. Insaurralde, C.; Lane, D. Metric assessment of autonomous capabilities in unmanned maritime vehicles. *Eng. Appl. Artif. Intell.* **2014**, *30*, 41–48. [CrossRef]
24. Schlinger, H. The Myth of Intelligence. *Psychol. Rec.* **2003**, *53*, 15–32.
25. Sternberg, R. The Theory of Successful Intelligence. *Interam. J. Psychol.* **2005**, *39*, 189–202.
26. Huang, M.; Rust, R. Artificial intelligence in service. *J. Serv. Res.* **2018**, *21*, 155–172. [CrossRef]
27. Leidner, D. *Cognitive Reasoning for Compliant Robot Manipulation*; Springer International Publishing: Cham, Switzerland, 2019.
28. Ibarz, J.; Tan, J.; Finn, C.; Kalakrishnan, M.; Pastor, P.; Levine, S. How to train your robot with deep reinforcement learning: Lessons we have learned. *Int. J. Robot. Res.* **2021**, *40*, 0278364920987859. [CrossRef]
29. Richards, L.; Matuszek, C. Learning to Understand Non-Categorical Physical Language for Human Robot Interactions. *UMBC Student Collection* 2016. Available online: http://hdl.handle.net/11603/21316 (accessed on 30 April 2021).
30. Huang, M.; Rust, R.; Maksimovic, V. The feeling economy: Managing in the next generation of artificial intelligence (AI). *Calif. Manag. Rev.* **2019**, *61*, 43–65. [CrossRef]
31. Raibert, M.; Blankespoor, K.; Nelson, G.; Playter, R. Bigdog, the rough-terrain quadruped robot. *IFAC Proc. Vol.* **2008**, *41*, 10822–10825. [CrossRef]

32. Murphy, M.; Saunders, A.; Moreira, C.; Rizzi, A.; Raibert, M. The littledog robot. *Int. J. Robot. Res.* **2011**, *30*, 145–149. [CrossRef]
33. Huang, M.; Rust, R. Engaged to a robot? The role of AI in service. *J. Serv. Res.* **2021**, *24*, 30–41. [CrossRef]
34. Taylor, I. Who Is Responsible for Killer Robots? Autonomous Weapons, Group Agency, and the Military-Industrial Complex. *J. Appl. Philos.* **2020**, *38*, 320–334. [CrossRef]
35. Nyholm, S.; Smids, J. Can a robot be a good colleague? *Sci. Eng. Ethics* **2020**, *26*, 2169–2188. [CrossRef] [PubMed]
36. Bellas, A.; Perrin, S.; Malone, B.; Rogers, K.; Lucas, G.; Phillips, E.; Tossel, C.; Visser, E. Rapport building with social robots as a method for improving mission debriefing in human-robot teams. In Proceedings of the 2020 Systems and Information Engineering Design Symposium (SIEDS), Charlottesville, VA, USA, 24 April 2020; pp. 160–163.
37. Laudon, K.; Laudon, J. *Management Information Systems*; Pearson: Upper Saddle River, NJ, USA, 2015.
38. Vagia, M.; Transeth, A.; Fjerdingen, S. A literature review on the levels of automation during the years. What are the different taxonomies that have been proposed? *Appl. Ergon.* **2016**, *53*, 190–202. [CrossRef] [PubMed]
39. Endsley, M.; Kaber, D. Level of automation effects on performance, situation awareness and workload in a dynamic control task. *Ergonomics* **1999**, *42*, 462–492. [CrossRef]
40. Giordano, A.; Dietrich, A.; Ott, C.; Albu-Schäffer, A. Coordination of thrusters, reaction wheels, and arm in orbital robots. *Robot. Auton. Syst.* **2020**, *131*, 103564. [CrossRef]
41. Sancho-Pradel, D.; Gao, Y. A survey on terrain assessment techniques for autonomous operation of planetary robots. *JBIS-J. Br. Interplanet. Soc.* **2010**, *63*, 206–217.
42. Gao, Y.; Jones, D.; Ward, R.; Allouis, E.; Kisdi, A. Space Robotics and Autonomous Systems: Widening the Horizon of Space Exploration. *UK-RAS White Paper*, 2016. Available online: https://www.surrey.ac.uk/sites/default/files/UK_RAS_wp_print_single_pages.pdf (accessed on 23 April 2021).
43. Voosen, P. Perseverance will explore history of ancient lake. *Science* **2021**, *371*, 870–871. [CrossRef]
44. Théron, P.; Kott, A. When Autonomous Intelligent Goodware Will Fight Autonomous Intelligent Malware: A Possible Future of Cyber Defense. In Proceedings of the MILCOM 2019-2019 IEEE Military Communications Conference (MILCOM), Norfolk, VA, USA, 12–14 November 2019; pp. 1–7.
45. Kott, A. Intelligent autonomous agents are key to cyber defense of the future army networks. *Cyber Def. Rev.* **2018**, *3*, 57–70.
46. Campbell, S.; Naeem, W.; Irwin, G. A review on improving the autonomy of unmanned surface vehicles through intelligent collision avoidance manoeuvres. *Annu. Rev. Control* **2012**, *36*, 267–283. [CrossRef]
47. Santoso, F.; Garratt, M.A.; Anavatti, S. State-of-the-art intelligent flight control systems in unmanned aerial vehicles. *IEEE Trans. Autom. Sci. Eng.* **2017**, *15*, 613–627. [CrossRef]
48. Udeanu, G.; Dobrescu, A.; Oltean, M. Unmanned aerial vehicle in military operations. *Sci. Res. Educ. Air Force* **2016**, *18*, 199–206. [CrossRef]
49. Jourdan, D.; Piedmonte, M.; Gavrilets, V.; Vos, D.; McCormick, J. Enhancing UAV survivability through damage tolerant control. In Proceedings of the AIAA Guidance, Navigation, and Control Conference, Toronto, ON, Canada, 2–5 August 2010; p. 7548.
50. Stolaroff, J.; Samaras, C.; O'Neill, E.; Lubers, A.; Mitchell, A.; Ceperley, D. Energy use and life cycle greenhouse gas emissions of drones for commercial package delivery. *Nat. Commun.* **2018**, *9*, 1–13.
51. Hartanto, R.; Arkeman, Y.; Hermadi, I.; Sjaf, S.; Kleinke, M. Intelligent Unmanned Aerial Vehicle for Agriculture and Agroindustry. In *IOP Conference Series: Earth and Environmental Science*; IOP Publishing: Bristol, UK, 2019; Volume 335, p. 012001.
52. Bovio, E.; Cecchi, D.; Baralli, F. Autonomous underwater vehicles for scientific and naval operations. *Annu. Rev. Control* **2006**, *30*, 117–130. [CrossRef]
53. Bistron, M.; Piotrowski, Z. Artificial Intelligence Applications in Military Systems and Their Influence on Sense of Security of Citizens. *Electronics* **2021**, *10*, 871. [CrossRef]
54. Sands, T. Development of Deterministic Artificial Intelligence for Unmanned Underwater Vehicles (UUV). *J. Mar. Sci. Eng.* **2020**, *8*, 578. [CrossRef]
55. Wooden, D.; Malchano, M.; Blankespoor, K.; Howardy, A.; Rizzi, A.; Raibert, M. Autonomous navigation for BigDog. In Proceedings of the 2010 IEEE International Conference on Robotics and Automation (ICRA), Anchorage, AK, USA, 3–7 May 2010; pp. 4736–4741.
56. Moher, D.; Liberati, A.; Tetzlaff, J.; Altman, D.; Prisma Group. Preferred reporting items for systematic reviews and meta-analyses: The PRISMA statement. *PLoS Med.* **2009**, *6*, e1000097. [CrossRef] [PubMed]
57. Fink, A. *Conducting Research Literature Reviews: From the Internet to Paper*, 2nd ed.; Sage Publications: Thousand Oaks, CA, USA, 2005.
58. Tranfield, D.; Denyer, D.; Smart, P. Towards a methodology for developing Evidence-Informed Management Knowledge by Means of Systematic Review. *Br. J. Manag.* **2003**, *14*, 207–222. [CrossRef]
59. Reis, J.; Santo, P.; Melão, N. Influence of artificial intelligence on public employment and its impact on politics: A systematic literature review. *Braz. J. Oper. Prod. Manag.* **2021**, *18*, 1–22. [CrossRef]
60. Liberati, A.; Altman, D.; Tetzlaff, J.; Mulrow, C.; Gøtzsche, P.; Ioannidis, J.; Clarke, M.; Devereaux, P.; Kleijnen, J.; Moher, D. The PRISMA statement for reporting systematic reviews and meta-analyses of studies that evaluate health care interventions: Explanation and elaboration. *J. Clin. Epidemiol.* **2009**, *62*, e1–e34. [CrossRef] [PubMed]
61. Page, M.; McKenzie, J.; Bossuyt, P.; Boutron, I.; Hoffmann, T.; Mulrow, C.; Shamseer, L.; Telzlaff, J.; Moher, D. Updating guidance for reporting systematic reviews: Development of the PRISMA 2020 statement. *J. Clin. Epidemiol.* **2021**, *134*, 103–112. [CrossRef]

62. Page, M.J.; Moher, D. Evaluations of the uptake and impact of the Preferred Reporting Items for Systematic reviews and Meta-Analyses (PRISMA) Statement and extensions: A scoping review. *Syst. Rev.* **2017**, *6*, 1–14. [CrossRef]
63. Flick, U.; Kardorff, E.; Steinke, I. *A Companion to Qualitative Research*; Sage Publications: Thousand Oaks, CA, USA, 2004.
64. Neuendorf, K.; Kumar, A. Content analysis: An Introduction to Its Methodology. In *The International Encyclopedia of Political Communication*; Wiley Online Library: Cleveland, OH, USA, 2015; pp. 1–10. [CrossRef]
65. Krippendorff, K. *Content Analysis: An Introduction to Its Methodology*; Sage Publications: Thousand Oaks, CA, USA, 2018.
66. Stemler, S. An overview of content analysis. *Pract. Assess. Res. Eval.* **2000**, *7*, 17.
67. Elo, S.; Kyngäs, H. The qualitative content analysis process. *J. Adv. Nurs.* **2008**, *62*, 107–115. [CrossRef]
68. Hsieh, H.; Shannon, S. Three approaches to qualitative content analysis. *Qual. Health Res.* **2005**, *15*, 1277–1288. [CrossRef]
69. Bazeley, P.; Jackson, K. *Qualitative Data Analysis with NVivo*; Sage Publications: Thousand Oaks, CA, USA, 2013.
70. Hetrick, R. Employment in high-tech defense industries in a post-cold war era. *Mon. Labor Rev.* **1996**, *119*, 57.
71. Liu, D.; Sun, J.; Huang, D.; Wang, X.; Cheng, K.; Yang, W.; Ding, J. Research on development status and technology trend of intelligent autonomous ammunition. In *Journal of Physics: Conference Series*; IOP Publishing: Bristol, UK, 2021; Volume 1721, p. 012032.
72. MacGregor, D. *Future Battle: The Merging Levels of War*; Army War Coll Carlisle Barracks PA. 1992. Available online: https://apps.dtic.mil/sti/pdfs/ADA528099.pdf (accessed on 1 May 2021).
73. Kiszely, J. Thinking about the operational level. *RUSI J.* **2005**, *150*, 38–43. [CrossRef]
74. Božanić, D.; Ranđelović, A.; Radovanović, M.; Tešić, D. a hybrid lbwa-ir-mairca multi-criteria decision-making model for determination of constructive elements of weapons. *Facta Univ. Ser. Mech. Eng.* **2020**, *18*, 399–418.
75. Dalkıran, E.; Önel, T.; Topçu, O.; Demir, K. Automated integration of real-time and non-real-time defense systems. *Def. Technol.* **2021**, *17*, 657–670. [CrossRef]
76. Božanić, D.; Tešić, D.; Kočić, J. Multi-criteria FUCOM–Fuzzy MABAC model for the selection of location for construction of single-span bailey bridge. *Decis. Mak. Appl. Manag. Eng.* **2019**, *2*, 132–146. [CrossRef]
77. Malbašić, S.; Đurić, S. Risk assessment framework: Application of Bayesian Belief Networks in an ammunition delaboration project. *Vojnoteh. Glas.* **2019**, *67*, 614–641. [CrossRef]
78. Božanić, D.; Tešić, D.; Milić, A. Multicriteria decision making model with Z-numbers based on FUCOM and MABAC model. *Decis. Mak. Appl. Manag. Eng.* **2020**, *3*, 19–36. [CrossRef]
79. Arkin, R. Lethal autonomous systems and the plight of the non-combatant. In *The Political Economy of Robots*; Palgrave Macmillan: Cham, Switzerland, 2018; pp. 317–326.
80. Righetti, L.; Pham, Q.; Madhavan, R.; Chatila, R. Lethal autonomous weapon systems [ethical, legal, and societal issues]. *IEEE Robot. Autom. Mag.* **2018**, *25*, 123–126. [CrossRef]
81. Hamurcu, M.; Eren, T. Selection of Unmanned Aerial Vehicles by Using Multicriteria Decision-Making for Defence. *J. Math.* **2020**. [CrossRef]
82. Kwon, H.; Yoon, H.; Choi, D. Restricted evasion attack: Generation of restricted-area adversarial example. *IEEE Access* **2019**, *7*, 60908–60919. [CrossRef]
83. Kwon, H.; Yoon, H.; Park, K. Acoustic-decoy: Detection of adversarial examples through audio modification on speech recognition system. *Neurocomputing* **2020**, *417*, 357–370. [CrossRef]

applied sciences

Article

SemDaServ: A Systematic Approach for Semantic Data Specification of AI-Based Smart Service Systems

Maurice Preidel [1,*] **and Rainer Stark** [1,2]

1 Department of Industrial Information Technology, Institute for Machine Tools and Factory Management, Technische Universität Berlin, Pascalstr. 8-9, 10587 Berlin, Germany; rainer.stark@ipk.fraunhofer.de
2 Division of Virtual Product Creation, Fraunhofer Institute for Production Systems and Design Technology IPK, Pascalstr. 8-9, 10587 Berlin, Germany
* Correspondence: maurice.preidel@tu-berlin.de

Abstract: To develop smart services to successfully operate as a component of smart service systems (SSS), they need qualitatively and quantitatively sufficient data. This is especially true when using statistical methods from the field of artificial intelligence (AI): training data quality directly determines the quality of resulting AI models. However, AI model quality is only known when AI training can take place. Additionally, the creation of not yet available data sources (e.g., sensors) takes time. Therefore, systematic specification is needed alongside SSS development. Today, there is a lack of systematic support for specifying data relevant to smart services. This gap can be closed by realizing the systematic approach SemDaServ presented in this article. The research approach is based on Blessing's Design Research Methodology (literature study, derivation of key factors, success criteria, solution functions, solution development, applicability evaluation). SemDaServ provides a three-step process and five accompanying artifacts. Using domain knowledge for data specification is critical and creates additional challenges. Therefore, the SemDaServ approach systematically captures and semantically formalizes domain knowledge in SysML-based models for information and data. The applicability evaluation in expert interviews and expert workshops has confirmed the suitability of SemDaServ for data specification in the context of SSS development. SemDaServ thus offers a systematic approach to specify the data requirements of smart services early on to aid development to continuous integration and continuous delivery scenarios.

Keywords: smart services; data specification; domain knowledge; information needs; data needs; knowledge needs; data quality; smart service systems engineering

Citation: Preidel, M.; Stark, R. SemDaServ: A Systematic Approach for Semantic Data Specification of AI-Based Smart Service Systems. *Appl. Sci.* **2021**, *11*, 5148. https://doi.org/10.3390/app11115148

Academic Editors: Marlene Amorim, Yuval Cohen and João Reis

Received: 1 May 2021
Accepted: 27 May 2021
Published: 1 June 2021

1. Introduction

For smart services to be developed and successfully operated as a component of smart service system (SSS), a qualitatively and quantitatively sufficient amount of data is required. This is especially true when data-driven software components are implemented by using statistical methods from the field of artificial intelligence: the quality of the training data directly determines the quality of the trained AI model. However, the quality of the training data can only be evaluated at a late stage using existing methods in the context of smart service development, since the training success is only known when the artificial intelligence (AI) training takes place. Furthermore, automated machine learning (AutoML) approaches are rising [1–9]. AutoML is aiming for the automation of machine learning (ML) model development. This means that SSS development projects using AutoML will need to rely even more on sufficient data carrying the relevant information because the ML model created with AutoML relies completely on statistics on the raw data and ignores causality only available from domain experts. Therefore, the availability of sufficient data and especially data engineering [10,11] will stay a major bottle-neck of AI applications. If the information in the training data or the data to be analyzed in operations is missing, a statistical AI model will be of poor quality. If irrelevant data is fed into AutoML pipelines, spurious correlations could result in unpredictable and dangerous product behavior occurring during the operation of the SSS.

The purpose of the presented Semantic Data Specification for AI-Based Smart Services (SemDaServ) approach is to specify the data needs of an AI-based smart service as part of a SSS as early as possible using expert domain knowledge. This allows the identification of insufficient data quality and quantity without the need to train AI models. This is often necessary for practice if the data for a smart service in development is not yet available and therefore needs to be acquired. To acquire relevant data while omitting irrelevant data (and therefore saving time and cost) data specification describing the data needs of smart service's AI and other software components is required. Furthermore, it is crucial to identify all areas of smart service's data needs; an unidentified data need may require changing the physical product (e.g., integrating new sensors into the main bearings of an aircraft turbine)—which could result in high costs and delays. To make the domain knowledge of experts available to smart service and AI engineers, the domain knowledge is formalized in a way that preserves the semantic meaning of the data specified.

Take, for example, the service-oriented Power-by-the-Hour business model for aerospace engines, where the customers pay for hours using the engine while not owning the engine. The engine provider (SSS provider) needs to make sure that the customers always got an operational engine at the wing. If a critical component like a bearing is going to fail soon, this must be immediately known to the engine provider to trigger actions for maintenance or exchange of the engine. Therefore, the remaining life prediction for the bearing is a critical component of the SSS offering. Within this article, this kind of remaining life prediction is understood as a smart service being part of a SSS.

The structure of the article is presented in Figure 1: (A) Based on the state of the research field and resulting research gaps described in Section 1, research questions, working hypotheses, and research methods are described in Section 2. (B) Additionally, the purpose of the SemDaServ approach described in Section 1 and (C) the research questions described in Section 2 are setting the scope for Section 3. Section 3 is the main section of this article containing a detailed description of the SemDaServ approach in four sub-sections: (D) Section 3.1 describes the business roles required to conduct the guided process for semantic data specification described in Section 3.2. (E) The artifacts used in this process are described in Section 3.3. (F) The IT systems and tools described in Section 3.4 are helpful to support the realization of the process described in Section 3.2. (G) Additionally, IT Systems and tools described in Section 3.4 can be used for the creation and storage of the artifacts described in Section 3.3. The coloring of the boxes in Figure 1 that represent Sections 3.2–3.4 is used throughout the article: Blue represents processes, yellow represents artifacts, and green represents IT systems and tools. (H) Section 4 presents the evaluation of the SemDaServ approach. (I) The study design of the evaluation (Section 4) is described in Section 2. (I, J) The working hypotheses described in Section 2 are discussed in Section 5 while taking the results of the evaluation (Section 4) into account. (K) Section 5.1 describes the limitations of the presented SemDaServ approach, especially regarding the evaluation scope. These limitations will be addressed in future research, described in Section 5.2. (L) Section 6 summarizes the article. Appendix A presents details linked to the descriptive study I (cf. Section 2). As the focus of this article is on the SemDaServ approach, the descriptive study I—which mainly focuses on the state of the art and research gaps—is necessary to understand the research approach but is not part of the SemDaServ approach.

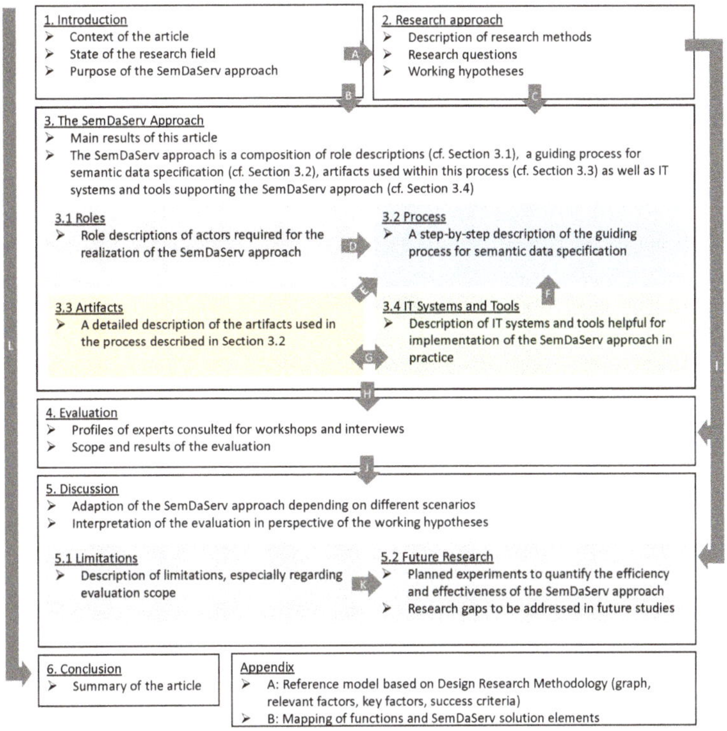

Figure 1. The structure of the article.

Reviewing the state of the art, new service engineering methods are required to systematically develop AI components of smart services. Ref. [12] While there are many methods, tools, and processes for SSS development (cf. [13] giving an overview), there is a lack of approaches that systematically make use of expert domain knowledge—which is highly relevant in industrial AI applications [14]—to specify the data needed for AI components of these services. This is especially the case if the data needed for AI training is not available at the stage of development. Anke [15] found that determining the required data and its quality is an important challenge. Rosa et al. [16] identify the major problem in the high probability of system designers ignoring the creation of relevant information in early product service system (PSS) design phases. They linked this problem to four main challenges: "[a] lack of completeness and structure on service-related information due to the intangibility and heterogeneity of services; [a] lack of integration among the PSS elements due to not considering its information requirements; dealing with a significant quantity and variety of knowledge; and ensuring completeness without limiting the flexibility of designers to select the methods and artifacts they intend to use" [16]. The SemDaServ approach addresses all four challenges within the scope of smart service data specification.

Data science perspectives have also contributed, well established, generic approaches to developing AI models (e.g., CRISP-DM [17], KDD [18], or SEMMA [19]). Azevedo and Santos [20] concluded that SEMMA and CRISP-DM were both implementations of the KDD process, though CRISP-DM is more complete than SEMMA. While these data-driven approaches perform well in situations where sufficient data is already available, their aim and scope limit their applicability in cases where relevant data needs to first be identified and acquired. This is especially true for SSS in development, where the data needs also define requirements for the physical components (e.g., the quality of sensors). As Wang et al. [21] pointed out, expert domain knowledge is crucial for clarifying data needs. In addition, expert knowledge is crucial in feature engineering (e.g., [22]).

Marx et al. [12] examined data science and smart service systems engineering (SSSE) together in a systematic literature review, finding that there was a lack of smart service engineering methods that dealt with the data perspective: Of 36 methods, only six mainly considered the data perspective.

2. Research Approach

The results were obtained using the Design Research Methodology described in [23] and presented in Figure 2.

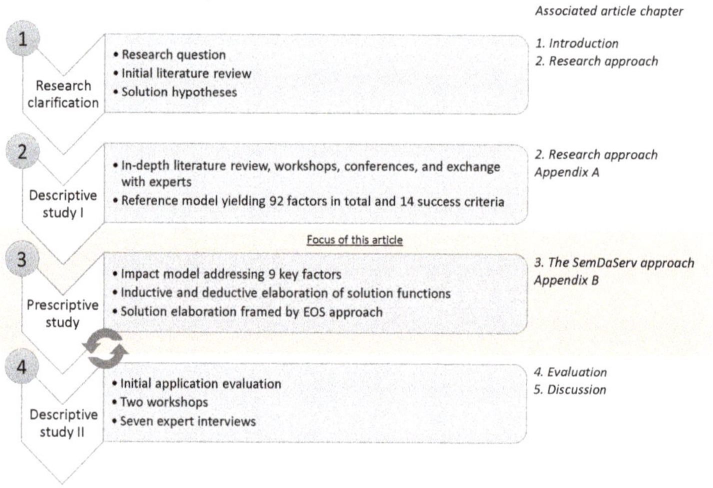

Figure 2. The research approach and focus of this article.

Research clarification (1): First, we formulated the following research questions (RQ):

RQ1 How can the probability of AI development with quality of results being in line with smart service requirements be increased?

RQ2 How can a clear understanding of relevant data for the development and operation of a smart service be systematically generated?

RQ3 How can domain knowledge relevant to AI training be formalized?

In light of these research questions, we initially reviewed the literature on the topics of SSSE, data science, data engineering, and semantic data modeling, as well as the use of domain knowledge in AI development. We used the Web of Science (webofknowledge.com accessed on 6 April 2021) , Google Scholar (scholar.google.de accessed on 7 April 2021), and Google Search (google.com accessed on 8 April 2021) to identify sources. After the initial literature review, we formulated the following working hypotheses (WH):

WH1 The probability of AI development with quality of results in line with smart service requirements can be increased by a domain knowledge-driven data specification approach.

WH2 A clear understanding of relevant data for the development and operation of a smart service can be systematically generated by using domain knowledge to clarify information needs and derive data needs from information needs.

WH3 Domain knowledge relevant for AI training can be formalized using the Systems Modeling Language (SysML).

WH4 Domain knowledge relevant for AI training can be formalized using a guided process.

Descriptive study (2): To get a deeper understanding of the current state-of-the-art as well as existing challenges in practice, we conducted an in-depth literature review, using the same database, search engines, and research areas as in Step 1. The insights gained were modeled in a graph-based reference model according to [23] and presented in Figure A1. The following sources from the literature yielded factors and links for the reference model: Refs. [10,14,15,21,24–32]. The first author of the research team also attended relevant conferences and workshops, resulting in an exchange with experts over a period of more than five years. This yielded additional factors and links, which were added to the reference model. In the last step, the reference model was analyzed regarding missing links and nodes from a logical point of view. Overall, 92 factors were identified within the descriptive study and 43 factors were declared outside the scope of the study (cf. Table A1), too far away from the core of the research questions and working hypotheses. This left 49 factors (cf. Table A2). From these factors, we identified 14 factors as success criteria (The research goal is to improve these factors as they are the most relevant factors to define success for the contribution to practice. ([23] p. 26) (cf. Table A3)).

Prescriptive study (3): The reference model was used to formulate the desired situation of positively impacting the success criteria. For this purpose, we first identified nine key factors (the most promising factors for improving on the existing situation ([23] p. 21), cf. Table A4). Then, we used an inductive approach to define solution functions in the context of the key factors. To do so, we abstracted sub-functions to more general main functions. After that, we applied a deductive approach to close gaps in the resulting functions architecture, detailing the main functions. The resulting functions architecture, as well as a mapping connecting it to the solution elements of the SemDaServ approach, are presented in Table A5. After designing the functions architecture, we systematically designed SemDaServ by addressing these functions according to the Engineering Operating System (EOS) [33] shown in Figure 3.

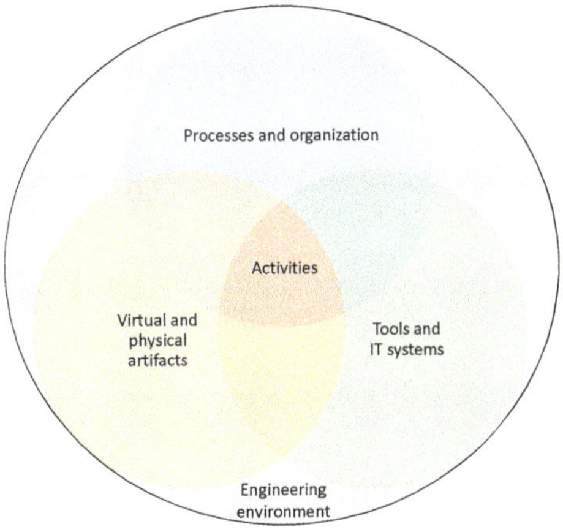

Figure 3. Engineering operating system, adapted from ([33] p. 319) with permission from IEEE.

Descriptive study II (4): This part of the research approach focuses on validation SemDaServ regarding logical correctness, applicability, and usefulness for real-world applications. The applicability of the SemDaServ approach was validated in two workshops lasting about 90 min each. Within the workshops, the SemDaServ approach was presented by the first author of this article for open discussion. The research questions RQ1, RQ2, and RQ3 guided the discussion. The second workshop was focused on the industrial point of view. In addition, the first author interviewed seven experts from academia and industry. The interviews were related to the specialization of the interviewed experts and therefore focused on specific aspects of the SemDaServ approach. The workshops and expert interviews took place over a period of five months. During this time, the SemDaServ approach was continuously improved based on the results of the workshops and expert interviews. Therefore, there were iterations between prescriptive study and descriptive study II. The profiles of the workshop participants and the interviewed experts as well as the outcomes of descriptive study II are presented in Section 4.

3. The SemDaServ Approach

The activity of semantic data specification of smart services is at the center of the proposed SemDaServ approach presented in Figure 4. The guidance to successfully conduct this activity is primarily provided by the SemDaServ process dimension: The three-step data specification process (Clarify domain knowledge needs, Clarify information needs, Specify data needs) systematically guides the actors involved through the individual steps of data specification and ensures that the knowledge pyramid is systematically traversed starting from domain knowledge (definition: information plus context, experience and cross-linking [34]), to information (definition: data plus meaning [34]) needs, and then to data (definition: symbols plus syntax [34]) needs (cf. [21]). As the SemDaServ approach is generally based on traversing the knowledge pyramid, the SemDaServ is applicable from new development of a smart service to continuous integration (CI) and continuous delivery (CD) scenarios. Realizing SemDaServ is expected to result in (1) a clear understanding of relevant data for the development and operation of the smart service, (2) formalized domain knowledge relevant for AI training, and (3) increased probability of AI development with quality of results in line with smart service requirements.

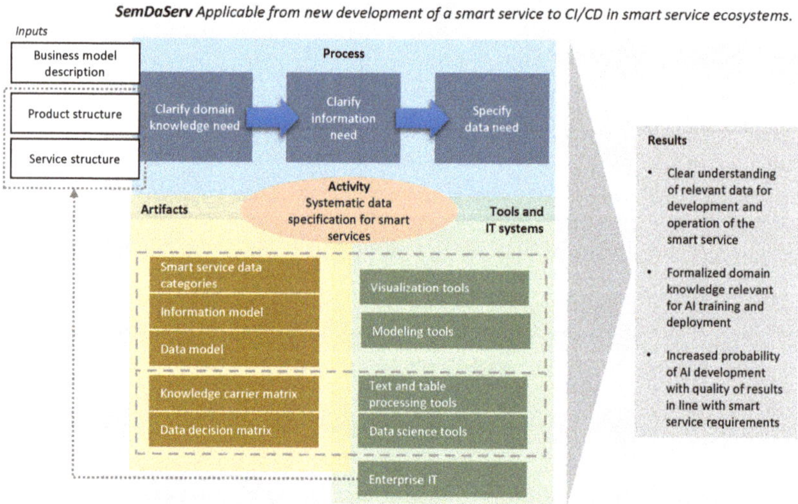

Figure 4. Overview of the SemDaServ approach.

The Clarify information needs process step is the most important step here, since the information level is where knowledge and data come together. Without the information level, it is difficult to infer concrete data needs (e.g., vibration sensor signal sampled at 200 Hz at the uppermost point of the outer ring) from general domain knowledge (e.g., damage in the bearing causes vibrations in the system). Here, the information layer serves to formalize the relevant domain knowledge in the context of the system (e.g., increasing vibration at the outer ring implies increasing wear of the ball bearings).

Various artifacts are used and created as part of the data specification process. On the one hand, these artifacts serve to facilitate individual process steps by specifying the result formats in a structured manner. On the other hand, the artifacts also document the process results. The artifacts can be divided into two groups: (1) artifacts for describing data and information and (2) artifacts for supporting neural points during process execution. Group 1 artifacts use SysML for three following reasons. Frist, computer scientists and data scientists benefit from semantic data specification due to the formalized domain knowledge, and SysML's proximity to Unified Modeling Language (UML), which is commonly used in SSSE [15], is useful here. Next, SysML is a powerful modeling language that can represent arbitrary technical systems and software components. This makes it possible to describe the connection between the smart service and the physical holistically. Third, the increasing diffusion of model-based systems engineering (MBSE) makes it likely that the diffusion of SysML will further grow as well, and will be increasingly supported by IT tools. Thus, in an MBSE environment, semantic data specification for smart services can be carried out without media discontinuity in the context of system specifications, and can be seamlessly integrated into the model-based engineering of the future.

Tools and IT systems increase the efficiency and quality of artifact creation. For example, visualization and modeling tools support the creation of SysML models. Text and spreadsheet tools enable the digital creation of documentation, such as tables and checklists. Theoretically, the creation of SysML models, checklists, and tables is also possible in a paper-based manner. However, using software tools for these activities is much more convenient, avoids errors, and increases process efficiency. Software tools from the field of data science (e.g., Python development environments) are another crucial element allowing insights from existing data to become part of the data specification process. This is necessary because domain experts may be unaware of correlations carrying causal links already present in the existing data. However, these previously unknown correlations may be of interest to the smart service but must be checked by domain experts, because these correlations may simply be spurious. The enterprise IT domain supports data specification as a data provider for important inputs (especially product and service structure) as well as Internet-of-Things (IoT) data and their context.

3.1. Roles

To design the responsibilities within the data specification process, we linked roles from (Hildebrand et al. [34] p. 240) (hereafter: "data-oriented roles") with roles of SSSE according to Anke et al. [35] (hereafter: "SSSE roles"). However, it is necessary to first analyze the intersection of the data-oriented and the SSSE roles. The analysis result and the associated role descriptions are shown in Table 1. It turns out that the primary SSSE roles largely overlap with the data-oriented roles. The data-oriented roles located in each row of Table 1 are mapped to the SSSE roles. This results in multiple assignments for the Service Operator role: The Service Operator acts simultaneously in the roles of Data Provider, Data Consumer, and Data Owner. This is caused by SSS data sources (e.g., sensors to monitor bearings) and sinks (e.g., ML model predicting the remaining life of a bearing) are equally present within the data specification process. Since the Service Provider is responsible for the technical operation of the SSS as a whole, the Data Provider and Data Consumer roles both fall to the Service Provider. Since the Service Provider is also responsible for service compliance in addition to the operational operation of the SSS, the Service Provider thus also has the role of Data Owner. The primary role of Digital Innovator is not assigned to a data-oriented role because the Digital Innovator is focused on idea generation and the business model. These aspects are upstream of the data specification process. Nevertheless, the Digital Innovator is an essential actor in the data specification process, whose role is particularly important in the first step of data specification (Clarify domain knowledge needs). The roles of Project Sponsor, System Integrator, and Service Provider are thus the main actors of the data specification process and are referred to as the Core Team below.

Table 1. Mapping of data-oriented roles to the SSSE roles that make up the Core Team for realizing the SemDaServ approach.

Data-Oriented Roles Described in ([34] p. 240) Role	Description		Core Team: Assigned SSSE Roles Described in [35] Role	Description
Process Owner	Responsible for the overall process including process definition, documentation, improvement, and timelines.	⟹	Project Sponsor	Responsible for SSS development project from initiation to completion including time and cost management.
Data Definition Owner	Responsible for data specification, including data quality, granularity, and format as well as storage media, if applicable. Usually shares the role of Data Consumer. Coordinates Data Consumers, should there be more than one.	⟹	System Integrator	Responsible for development and implementation of technical system elements including system architecture, technical conceptualization, and integration with existing systems.
Data Consumer	Beneficiaries of the data.	⟹	Service Operator	Responsible for the technical operation of the SSS, including software management, service availability, and compliance with existing policies.
Data Provider	Responsible for the timely acquisition and delivery of data as defined by the Data Definition Owner.			
Data Owner	Owner of the data, who is therefore responsible for its use, including data acquisition, and security as well as measurement ranges and methods.			

3.2. Process

The data specification process is described in the following on the first sublevel of the process using Business Process Modeling Language (BPMN). It is based on three process steps Clarify domain knowledge needs, Clarify information needs and Specify data needs (cf. Figure 4). These are based on the clarify needs section of the reference model described in [21].

3.2.1. Clarify Domain Knowledge Needs

The goal of the process step Clarify domain knowledge needs is the documented identification of the knowledge required for the data specification as well as the associated knowledge carriers from the domain of the SSS. This involves all roles of the Core Team as well as the Digital Innovator. To perform this process step, the following inputs must be available: The business model description (e.g., in the form of the Smart Service Canvas [36] or the framework for data-driven business models described in Exner et al. [37]), the product structure (derived from the product data management (PDM) system, see Section 3.4) and the service structure (e.g., created according to the MESSIAH [38] or PSS-layer method [39]). The results of this process should be an understanding of the smart service from within the application domain as well as the roles and the names of the knowledge carriers required for the data specification. The whole Clarify domain knowledge needs process step can be performed in a single kick-off meeting. Depending on the complexity of the smart service as well as the number of domain knowledge carriers in question, a short meeting (about one hour) is sufficient. If necessary, up to two full-day workshops are required, but this represents an extreme case. The sub-processes explained below are shown in Figure 5.

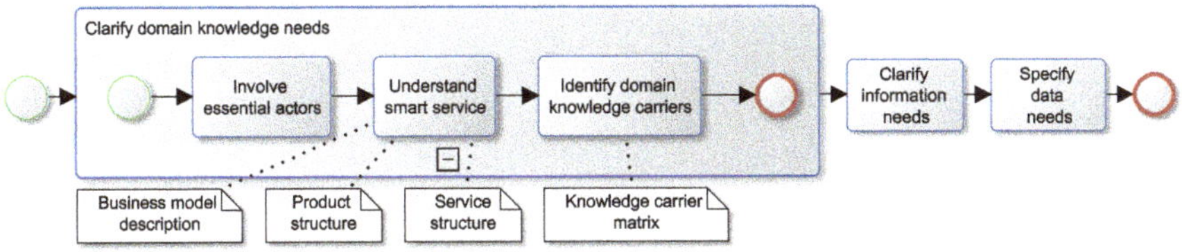

Figure 5. Process steps to clarify domain knowledge needs.

The goal of the Involve essential actors sub-process step is to onboard the Core Team to initially start the data specification process. Only the Core Team (cf. Table 1) is involved. This process step is completed when the Core Team has an understanding (tasks, areas of responsibility, own role in the data specification process) of how to execute the data specification process (as well as initiating contact among team members). For this purpose, the Project Sponsor explains the data specification process and general conditions (time, costs, quality). The Core Team discusses questions concerning the understanding of the process as well as the necessary process adjustments in light of given conditions, and they decide on the first process adjustments (e.g., the definition of the required level of detail of the results or the maximum number of domain experts to be involved).

The goal of the Understand smart service sub-process step is to give the Core Team as a whole a thorough understanding of the smart service at the outset so that they can competently guide the data specification process and identify what domain knowledge is required and who holds that in the next step. In addition to the Core Team, the Digital Innovator is also involved: This person carries knowledge regarding the business model and the innovative core of the smart service, which is fundamental to the holistic understanding of the smart service. The result of this sub-process step is therefore the Core Team's holistic understanding of the smart service. To achieve this, the Digital Innovator first explains the business model. Then the System Integrator guides the team through the service structure and explains the relevant parts of the product structure. In the process, questions of understanding are clarified so that at the end of this sub-process step all actors have an agreed level of knowledge on the smart service. Since the smart service is the focus (business model, product, and service structure) and the System Integrator, who has a close relationship to the knowledge domain of the SSS, is involved, an initial exchange of domain knowledge takes place at this point. This ensures that the Core Team has a basic understanding of the relevant domain knowledge. This is the basic prerequisite for starting the next process step.

The goal of the Identify domain knowledge carriers sub-process step is to determine the domain knowledge carriers to be involved downstream from the data specification process. At a minimum, the Core Team is involved. Optionally, other people can be involved as needed (e.g., ball bearing monitoring specialists if the smart service includes ball bearing failure prediction as an essential component). However, the group of people involved should be kept to a minimum in this step, because the data specification process is a framework allowing the integration of domain knowledge carriers as needed in any process step. At this point, however, the focus is on establishing a good starting point that takes into account the essential domain knowledge areas. The result of the process step is therefore to designate which knowledge carriers are to be involved in the data specification process. To do so, the Core Team fills in the knowledge carrier matrix described in Section 3.3.1, and, if necessary, adds additional knowledge areas. The Core Team should also keep the business model description and the product and service structure in mind: Valuable information on relevant domain knowledge areas (e.g., components or assemblies of the SSS concerned) can be found here.

3.2.2. Clarify Information Needs

The goal of the Clarify information needs process step is to use the domain knowledge of the previously identified knowledge carriers to describe what information needs the smart service will have. All sub-process steps in this section involve the Core Team and the identified knowledge carriers. The result is the description of the required information flow as an information model (including a description of the information quality) for the development and operation of the smart service under consideration. The entire process step Clarify information needs can be done synchronously (in the form of workshops) or asynchronously (by modeling using a shared SysML information model)(see Section 3.3.4). The sub-processes explained in the following are shown in Figure 6.

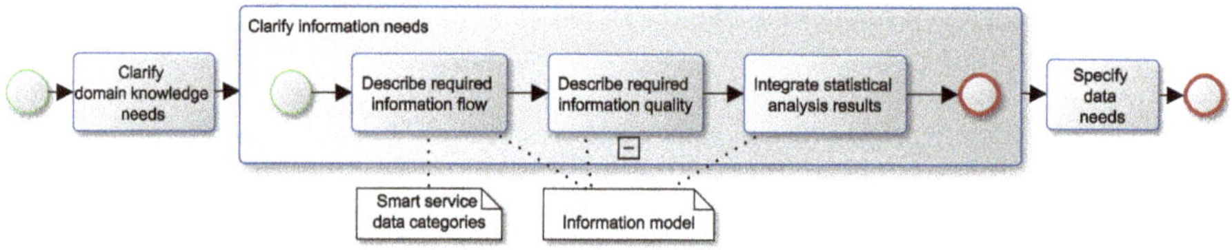

Figure 6. Process steps to clarify information needs.

The goal of the Describe required information flow sub-process step is to formalize the information flow required for the development and operation of the smart service. The result of the process step is the information flow of the information model described in Section 3.3.4. Guided by the System Integrator, the knowledge carriers answer the question: What information from which sources must flow into the components of the service structure so that the smart service can be developed and operated? The answers to this question can be described in the form of a graph: The target nodes are elements of the service structure, the source nodes are elements of the service or product structure, and possibly external data sources (e.g., weather data from an external information provider). The information content is represented by SysML Information Items in free text.

The goal of the Describe required information quality sub-process step is to detail the information flow concerning information quality. The result of this process step should be an information model that describes information flow as well as information quality. Guided by the System Integrator, this time, the knowledge carriers answer the question: What quality level must the information described within the information model have for the smart service to be developed and operated? The answers to this question are documented in the information model of the previous process step Describe required information flow by textual annotation of the Information Items. Consideration of the quality dimension is fundamental, because not only can costs increase exponentially with quality requirements, but also the probability of success in developing the desired quality of service (e.g., measurement every day versus every second for thousands of bearings) depends critically on the quality of information available in the data.

The goal of the Integrate statistical analysis results sub-process step is to account for any correlations that may occur in existing data that could be useful for the operation and development of the smart service. This is necessary because the data specification process has so far been designed to be purely knowledge driven. However, data relevant for the smart service is often already available in the company. Targeted statistical analyses of the available data can unearth previously undiscovered or even largely unknown relationships in a data-driven manner. The members involved include the Core Team, domain experts brought in as needed, and Data Analytics Specialists (Data analytics specialist and ML expert. Responsible for development and implementation of big data solutions [35]). The data analysis conducted by the Data Analytics Specialists is presented to the Core Team and relevant domain experts so that they can check whether there are spurious correlations or trustworthy causal relationships. This review is necessary because otherwise there is a risk of training AI models with spurious correlations, which in turn would lead to unpredictable misbehavior of the SSS in the operation of the smart service once the spurious correlation no longer holds. The knowledge gained from the statistical analyses is added to the information model. This describes the information requirements. In the next step, the information level (e.g., vibrations along the outer ring of the Ball Bearing 2 must be measured hourly) is broken down to the data level (e.g., vibrations at the Ball Bearing 2 are measured hourly with a sampling rate of 200 Hz and stored under the variable name vibration_mainBearing2_200).

3.2.3. Specify Data Needs

The goal of the Specify data needs process step is the final specification of the data requirements of the smart service. This involves all roles of the Core Team as well as the Data Analytics Specialist. If necessary, domain experts can be involved upon request of the Data Analytics Specialist. The sub-processes explained below and shown in Figure 7 are carried out.

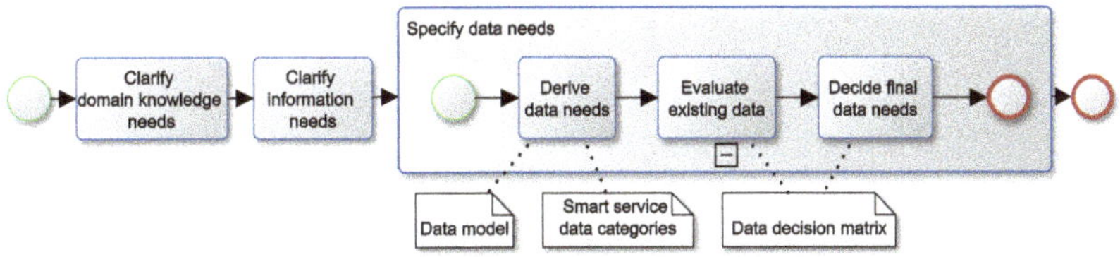

Figure 7. Process steps to specify data needs.

The goal of the Derive data needs sub-process step is to convert the information model into a data model. The data model describes which data are needed to meet the information requirements described in the information model. For this purpose, variables are defined (or documented in the case of existing data) and the information quality described is supplemented by figures, data, and facts from the field of data quality management. The data types are also defined in the process.

The goal of the Evaluate existing data sub-process step is to complete a technical fit-gap analysis comparing the data requirements described in the data model and the existing data. This involves assessing the extent to which the existing data meets the data needs. In addition to searching for relevant data, this also requires a technical assessment of the data quality. Here, the Data Analytics Specialist can be supported by the Information Service Provider (Provides supplementary data from external sources [35]), the Data Center Operator (Operates the IT infrastructure [35]), the Cloud Platform Provider (Operator of application-independent (external) cloud components [35]), and the Connectivity Provider (Responsible for technical interface (e.g., mobile network) between (smart) product and IT infrastructure [35]) are supported. The result of this process step is a qualitative assessment of the gap between data requirements from the domain expert's perspective and the existing data. Nevertheless, the economic perspective is still not yet included in this final definition of the data requirements but is taken into account in the next step of the data specification process.

The goal of the Decide final data needs sub-process step is the final specification of data requirements. However, after the domain experts finish specifying the data and information needs, maybe the costs for data acquisition exceed the expected revenue of the smart service. In this case, the smart service would be a loss-making business. Therefore, at this point, the profitability of the smart service is reviewed and optimized–if necessary by reducing the data requirements or removing variables. This process step is guided by the Project Sponsor. It involves the Core Team, the Data Analytics Specialist, and domain experts, as needed. This process step relies heavily on the data decision matrix (see Section 3.3.3). The final determination of data requirements concludes the data specification process. The artifacts described below add up to the semantic data specification.

3.3. Artifacts

The artifacts used within the data specification process are described below.

3.3.1. Knowledge Carrier Matrix

For the systematic documentation of relevant knowledge areas and the associated knowledge carriers, we developed a Knowledge carrier matrix, presented in Table 2. To do so, we took the matrix-like representation of knowledge requirements described in [40] and adapted it for data specification.

The Knowledge carrier matrix organizes knowledge into four knowledge area: service (e.g., predicting the remaining lifetime of the main ball bearing), physical product (e.g., main ball bearing wear behavior), data science and data engineering (e.g., the training of ML models), and other (e.g., legal requirements of aircraft maintenance).

Table 2. Knowledge carrier matrix.

	Knowledge Carrier		
Field of Knowledge	**Role (Name/Organization)**	**Role (Name/Organization)**	...
Service			
Sub-field 1	X		
...			
Physical product			
Sub-field 1	X		
...			
Data science and data engineering			
Sub-field 1		X	
...			
Other			
Sub-field 1		X	X
...			

The knowledge areas are noted in the first column and—depending on the project requirements (level of detail, relevant areas)—supplemented by additional knowledge areas in the rows. To fill this matrix, the following guiding question needs to be answered: Which areas from the categories of "service", "physical product", and "data science and data engineering" are directly or indirectly affected by this smart service development project? In answering this question, there will also be areas that do not fit into any of these three categories. Such knowledge areas can be noted in the Other category.

The column headers are filled in with the name of the person who has the most knowledge in the knowledge area of the corresponding row. If the role is carried out outside the company, the corresponding organizational name is entered. For filling the column headers, the following question needs to be answered: Which role carries the broadest knowledge in area A? The A is replaced by the knowledge area of the respective line. An X in a cell means that the person represented by this column has the broadest knowledge in the knowledge domain of the corresponding row. The formulation of this question ensures that the most relevant roles are documented as knowledge carriers. In this context, it is also possible that a single knowledge carrier will carry knowledge in many knowledge areas. This is justifiable and even helpful: a reduced number of knowledge carriers means a leaner data specification process (see Section 5). By focusing this question on the knowledge carriers that have the broadest knowledge, the process minimizes the number of people involved, while still maintaining comprehensive coverage of the knowledge domain. The wording of the question means that mainly technical leadership roles are documented in the first iteration of the knowledge carrier matrix. This is legitimate since the data specification process first takes place at the system-architect level and the technical leadership roles can easily involve additional subject matter experts for details if needed.

3.3.2. Data Categories

SemDaServ offers a hierarchical model of smart service data categories to create the most complete possible specification of the data required for a given smart service. The data category model presented in Figure 8 helps actors during the data specification to check if all data categories have been considered. The data category model is described hierarchically to tailor the abstraction level of the data specification appropriately to the smart service under consideration as well as to the particular requirements of the project (Particularly concerning the level of detail of the data specification (see Section 5)). We derived the data category model from the literature by combining data categorization systems from multiple domains. These domains included engineering, statistics, and computer science. The "data science" domain itself uses categorizations from statistics and computer science, so this domain was not considered separately.

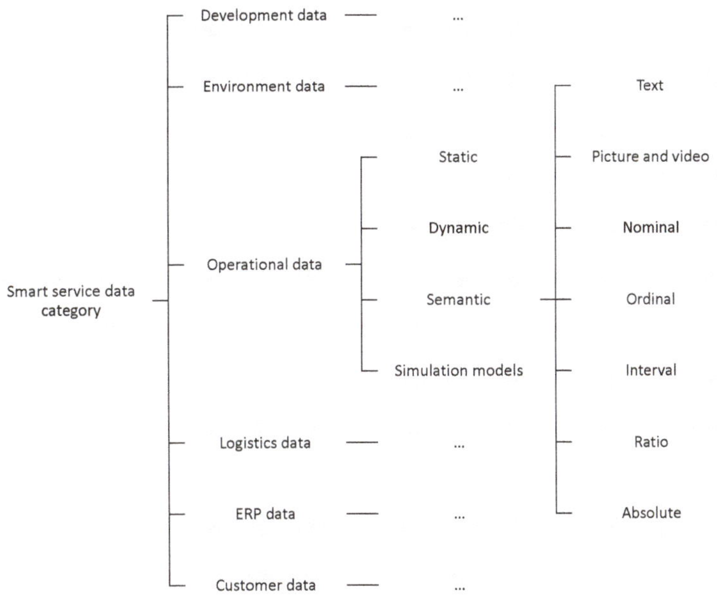

Figure 8. Data categories for the specification of smart service data.

After analyzing the presented data categorization systems, it turned out that the categorization system presented in ([41] p. 79) was the closest to the application domain of smart services and the most intuitive for actors with heterogeneous professional backgrounds to understand. For this reason, we adopted it as the top level of the data category model. There were two exceptions made: One exception was Exner et al. [41]'s category of expert knowledge, which SemDaServ does not conceptualize as a data category but as a type of knowledge, and therefore is not considered in the data category model. The second exception is in Exner et al. [41]'s data category machine data which we think is too narrow. Therefore, we reframed this data category as operational data (e.g., to cover data acquired from humans). A detailing of the data categories according to ([41] p. 79) is achieved by the data categories from ([42] pp. 40–41): This categorization classifies data according to various properties and can therefore be applied downstream to the domain-oriented data categories from ([41] p. 79). One level downstream, the categories from statistics can be found, as they are domain-independent and applicable to all other data categories from engineering, thus generating a deeper level of detail. Furthermore, the scale system of statistics is close to the methods from data science, which is why a description of the data in the categories of statistics is helpful for AI training in the context of smart service development bridging the gap between the application domain and statistical AI models. Text, image and video data categories as defined by (Runkler [43] pp. 1–2) are also included at the most detailed level because these categories cover important data domains that are not represented in the statistics scale system. The remaining data categories in Runkler's [43] text are were already included in the categories outlined in ([41] p. 79) and ([42] pp. 40–41), and do not need to be repeated.

3.3.3. Data Decision Matrix

The data decision matrix supports and documents the decision as to which data from which sources should ultimately be consumed by the smart service. To do so, the system takes technical (data quality) and economic (cost-benefit) aspects of the data collection requirements into account. Filling out the data decision matrix requires an upstream assessment of the gap between the defined data needs and the quality of existing data, as well as an estimation of what costs will be incurred to sufficiently cover the data needs.

For the smart service development project to be successful, the resulting smart service must be profitable. For this reason, the data decision matrix includes information about the cost–benefit ratio of data collection. Methodologically, this is done through the cost-benefit analysis presented in Figure 9. The goal is to maximize the cost-benefit ratio. The economic benefit of the smart service is usually already determined and thus known before the start of the data specification process in the context of business model development and analysis through appropriate SSS requirements. The costs of developing and operating the smart service result from data requirements, IT infrastructure, the required quality of the AI models, and data quality. Data requirements result in costs for adapting or redeveloping physical product components for product development, manufacturing and operation. Furthermore, the IT infrastructure must be adapted due to additional data streams: Again, this includes development, initial deployment, and operating costs. The data requirements of the smart service can be partly covered by synthetic data from simulation models. This reduces costs in the area of physical product components but generates modeling costs if the existing simulation models have to be adapted, created, or expanded.

Once the technical and economic assessment of the data requirements is available, the data decision matrix shown in Table 3 can be filled in by the actors involved in the decision-making process based on the results of earlier steps in the data specification process. To do this, the variables specified in the data model are entered in the first column. This is followed by the decision of the Project Sponsor whether the variable located in the respective row should be measured in real terms or generated synthetically by simulation models. Data requirements and the existing data quality are entered in the following columns. This is done by first assessing the relevance of the information content (RI) on a scale from 0 (information content of the variable is irrelevant) to 6 (the smart service cannot be developed according to the requirements without this variable). The Data Quality Score (DQS) is determined by assessing the existing data quality using the data quality dimensions based on [34,44] and shown in Figure 10. To do this, each major criterion is qualitatively estimated on a scale from 0 to 2. The meaning of the scale is defined as follows:

0 Existing data does not satisfy the data requirement of this data quality factor.

1 Existing data probably satisfy the data needs of this data quality factor.

2 Existing data satisfy the data needs of this data quality factor.

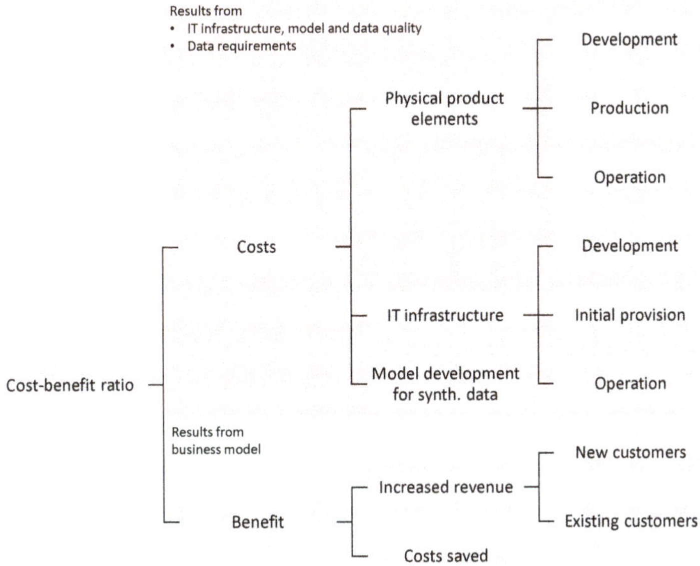

Figure 9. Cost–benefit analysis.

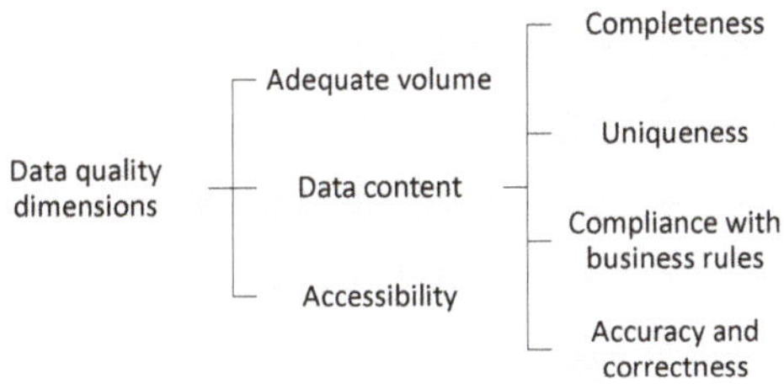

Figure 10. Data quality dimensions based on [34,44].

The rating for the main criterion of content data quality is the arithmetic average of the four sub-criteria but can be determined directly for efficiency reasons. The data quality value results from the sum of the ratings of the three main criteria and is thus at most six (existing data quality fulfills the data needs in all factors) and, at least zero (existing data quality fulfills the data needs in no factors). Thus, the Relevance to Quality Score (RQS) can be calculated according to Formula (1):

$$RQS = \frac{RI}{1 + \Delta DQS} = \frac{RI}{1 + 6 - DQS} = \frac{RI}{7 - DQS}. \quad (1)$$

The RQS is thus a means of focusing on the most relevant variables, which are already present in the highest quality. The maximum value of the RQS is 6 ($RI = DQS = 6$), meaning that the variable has the highest possible relevance for the smart service while already having sufficient data quality available. The cost of collecting this variable, in this case, is zero because the variable is already provided with existing simulation models, IT systems, and physical product components. If this were not the case, the DQS would be less than six, since at least one data quality factor would not fully satisfy the data requirement, resulting in costs for data collection. An RQS value of 0, on the other hand, would mean that a variable has no relevance to the smart service ($RI = 0; 0 \leq DQS \leq 6$). If the data decision matrix is now sorted in descending order by the RQS, the most relevant variables with the highest pre-existing data quality will be at the top. This allows the Core Team to prioritize which final data to collect.

To prioritize data needs, it is also important to consider the costs of data collection: For this purpose, the costs required to adequately collect a variable are filled in the rows physical product components, IT infrastructure, as well as modeling for synthetic data and totaled.

After all these elements have been entered, it is possible to make a final decision for each variable, whether it shall be collected or not. This decision can now be documented in the last column for each variable. The entry of yes or no in the last column indicates whether the data on the variable located in the row should be collected. The sum of the variables with a yes entry in this column represents the final set of data to be collected.

Table 3. Data decision matrix.

		Data Need and Existing Data Quality			Costs				
Variable Name	**Data Source**	**Relevance of Information *RI***	**Data Quality Score *DQS***	***Relevance to Quality Score RQS***	**Physical Product**	**IT Infrastructure**	**Modeling for Synthetic Data**	*Sum*	**Collect Data?**
Variable 1	real/synthetic	0–6	0–6	*0–6*	X $	X $	X $	*X $*	yes/no
...	...	...	...	...	...	...	...	...	...
Variable n	real/synthetic	0–6	0–6	*0–6*	X $	X $	X $	*X $*	yes/no

3.3.4. Data and Information Models

SemDaServ uses diagrams and modeling elements of the SysML language to model the information and data requirements. The data model is based on the information model and therefore uses the same SysML diagrams. The difference between information models and data models is in the object of study. However, the representation and modeling approach is identical—except for minor differences outlined below.

The central element of the data specification is the block definition diagram: This is used to build both the information model and data model. The basic elements of the information model are shown in Figure 11: The SysML element entitled Information Item is at the center of the information flow of the Producing element block (e.g., a sensor) and the Consuming element block (usually a software component of the smart service). These two blocks are linked to the Information Item by the SysML element of Information flow. The information contained in the information flow is modeled by a textual description of the Information Item. The quality requirements for the information are stored as free text by the SysML note element Description. This results in an information flow from the Producing element (source) to the Consuming element (target). This can be a one-to-n-relationship, which can be represented by additional information flows of an Information Item additional Consuming elements.

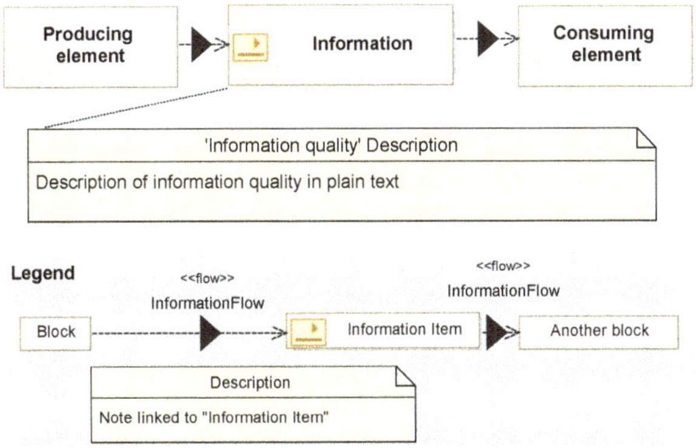

Figure 11. Information model.

The data model results from resolving the Information Items of the information model. The Information Item is replaced by a direct information flow linked to the data variable of the producing and the consuming elements. The variables are modeled as attributes of the blocks. If the information described in the Information Item can be completely covered by one variable, the information flow is modeled at the variable level (by direct linking of the variable using the SysML element Information flow). If several variables are required to realize the information flow, an Information Flow is modeled between the Producing element and Consuming element blocks. The basic elements of the data model are shown in Figure 12. The placeholder <no type> represents arbitrary data types. To resolve the Information Item, the information quality must also be broken down to the data quality. For this purpose, SemDaServ uses the SysML note element Description similarly as in the information model, but in this case, this element is directly linked with the variables. Thus, the data quality is described for each variable. The description of the data quality follows the scheme described in Figure 10. To increase the clarity of all information models and data models, the Note elements can be modeled outside the diagram by using a model-oriented tool.

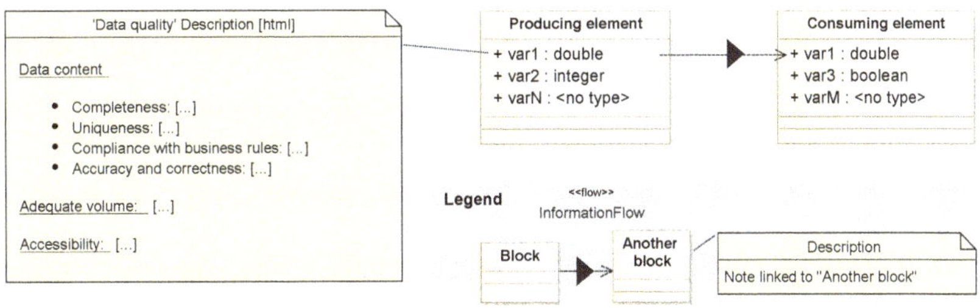

Figure 12. Data model.

If these initial modeling possibilities are not sufficient in a particular use case, the information model and the data model can be supplemented by additional UML and SysML diagrams: sequence diagrams, for example, can be used to model time-dependent relationships. The use of use case diagrams can help in understanding the use case when the business model description, as well as the product and service structure, are too complex, too complicated, or too superficial from the perspective of the actors involved. The use case diagram can then be used to focus on the essentials—especially from the user perspective. If a large number of detailed quality descriptions arise and/or exhibit a large number of mutual dependencies, the information and data quality descriptions can be combined in a requirement diagram, linked to the associated blocks, and modeled to take these dependencies into account. If it turns out during the data specification process that a block (e.g., an assembly of the SSS, represented as a block in the data model) needs to be considered in more detail, the corresponding block can be linked to an internal block diagram and described in detail. If the description of the generation of synthetic data by simulation models is particularly important or specific, the relevant correlations and calculation rules can be described in the parametric diagram and subsequently linked to the corresponding variables.

3.4. IT Systems and Tools

The SemDaServ approach benefits from the application of software tools and IT systems used in product creation. The following section gives an overview of how SemDaServ does so, based on typical tools and IT systems from three categories: System description tools, data science tools, and enterprise IT systems.

Model-based and document-oriented tools for system description support the creation of information and data models. A distinction must be made between model-based and document-based tools. Both model-oriented and document-oriented tools can be usefully employed for data specification. Therefore, we recommend users to rely on the approaches already established in their respective companies, to optimize the training effort, and thus the cost-benefit ratio of the data specification is optimized. Document-oriented tools include text and table processing tools (e.g., Microsoft Office, Libre Office, etc.)—programs generally used for office work. The advantage of this is that many people are familiar with them and they are widely distributed, meaning companies can easily access them. One disadvantage in the context of data specification is the poorly developed support for modeling with UML and SysML. Specialized visualization tools such as Microsoft Visio, yED, or DIA provide better support. The advantage here is again the comparatively high distribution and easy accessibility of visualization tools in contrast to specialized modeling tools. However, since these visualization tools take a document-based approach, there is a significant disadvantage that changes to the information or data models (e.g., renaming a block) may not be propagated throughout the model. In contrast, the use of model-based tools enables the creation of an information and data model that can be validated, is machine-readable, and maintains links among its elements. This provides higher compliance with modeling language specifications (e.g., model-based tools can alert users to model errors and can prevent elements from being used out-of-specification) and higher model quality (e.g., name changes of variables or blocks propagate themselves throughout the model).

Data science tools primarily support the role of the Data Analytics Specialist by providing ways to evaluate existing data (e.g., from older generations of products already in use). The tools presented in this section exemplify the range of data science tools that can be used to analyze and evaluate existing data as part of the data specification process. It is also possible to use these tools to train the AI models required for the smart service with AutoML methods on existing data to obtain a sound evaluation of the quality of this data.

A large number of IT systems are used in companies, and advancing digitalization means that the amount of data and information stored in these systems will only increase further (cf. [45]). This makes the enterprise IT of a company an important supplier of data and information in the context of data specification. In practice, the characteristics and operational use of a company's IT landscape are very heterogeneous. In principle, data specification can be performed with any type of enterprise IT landscape. However, a well-developed enterprise IT infrastructure in the areas of PDM and IoT is especially helpful: PDM systems provide a good source of structured, contextualized data (e.g., product structure), while IoT systems can manage the operational data of SSS being in the use phase of the product lifecycle.

4. Evaluation

The evaluation is based on two workshops and seven expert interviews described below. The profiles of experts consulted for evaluation are outlined in Table 4. The experts for interviews and workshops were chosen in a way that a broad range of professional backgrounds of actors relevant for SSSE as well as different company sizes are represented. The resulting group of chosen experts, therefore, ranges from academic to small and big companies. The sectors are focused on mobility, but the experts from academia have a history of researching a broad range of engineering-focused sectors. Overall, the majority of experts come from industry (7 out of 12). The following experts share the same employer: Experts 1, 6, and 10; experts 2 and 8; experts 3, 4, and 5; experts 7 and 9. The specialization of the experts covers all professional backgrounds relevant to the SemDaServ approach, ranging from the business perspective (expert IDs 5, 7, 11), to the SSSE perspective (expert IDs 1, 2, 8), the MBSE perspective (expert ID 6) a highly specialized knowledge carrier perspective (expert ID 12), the data science and data engineering perspective (expert IDs 3, 4, 7, 9), and the knowledge management in engineering perspective (expert ID 10). The professional experience of the experts also spans a wide range from more than two years up to more than 40 years of professional experience.

Table 4. Profiles of experts consulted for evaluation of the SemDaServ approach.

ID	Job Title	Specialization	Professional Experience	Company Type	Sector
1	Research assistant	Smart service platforms, Internet-of-Things, cloud computing	>2 years	Technical university (>7.500 employees)	Academia
2	Research engineer	Smart service systems engineering, Internet-of-Things	>3 years	Research institute for applied science (>25.000 employees)	Academia
3	Data scientist	Smart services, natural language processing, condition monitoring	>3 years	Big company (>30.000 employees)	Rail
4	Data scientist	Artificial intelligence, operations research, data engineering	>6 years	Big company (>30.000 employees)	Rail
5	Principal key expert	Project management, business strategy	>20 years	Big company (>30.000 employees)	Rail
6	Research assistant	Model-based systems engineering	>3 years	Technical university (>7.500 employees)	Academia
7	IT project manager	Artificial intelligence, production planning, six sigma	>4 years	Big company (>150.000 employees)	Automotive
8	Researcher and managing director	Smart service systems engineering, product lifecycle management	>7 years	Research institute for applied science (>25.000 employees)	Academia
9	Doctoral candidate	Artificial intelligence and digital twins	>6 years	Big company (>150.000 employees)	Automotive
10	Research assistant	Knowledge management in engineering	>8 years	Technical university (>7.500 employees)	Academia
11	CEO	Innovation, management and technology consulting	>30 years	Small company (<20 employees)	Consulting
12	System architect	Predictive maintenance, engine health monitoring, system architecture	>40 years	Big company (>50.000 employees)	Aerospace

The first workshop (participating experts: IDs 1 and 2; cf. Table 4) confirmed, that the SemDaServ approach is logically correct, consistent, and fills a research gap in the field of SSSE. Regarding the success criteria (cf. Table A3), it was pointed out that more experiments are needed to measure the impact of the SemDaServ regarding success criteria 20 (efficiency of smart service development methods) and 22 (efficiency of the application of domain knowledge). This is caused by the fact that the SemDaServ approach itself generates efforts that need to be compared to approaches not using the SemDaServ approach (e.g., trial and error mixed with explorative data analysis using established data science tools and methods). For all other success criteria, it could be validated from a logical perspective that they are well addressed by the SemDaServ approach.

The second workshop (participating experts: IDs 3, 4, and 5; cf. Table 4) confirmed, that the SemDaServ approach is logically correct, applicable, and useful for real-world applications. The comprehensibility and low access barrier of the artifacts used and the process steps were rated as very good. It was pointed out that scaling SemDaServ according to real-world project scenarios (budget, time, quality as well as the availability of experts) is an important aspect. Therefore, guidelines on tailoring SemDaServ to different project scenarios will be developed in future research. It was confirmed that the relevant stakeholders in the workshop participants' company can understand the artifacts resulting from SemDaServ and therefore a benefit is generated for the collaboration of product and service development. From a data scientist perspective, it was confirmed that the resulting semantic data specification provides great added value, as SemDaServ systematically describes relevant data and domain knowledge relevant for data understanding. Thus, iterations during smart service development can be prevented by developing a suitable data basis at an early stage.

The interview with expert 6 (cf. Table 4) was focused on the topic of MBSE and the related use of SysML. In this interview, it was confirmed that the SemDaServ approach is compatible with the MBSE procedures and that the chosen representation type in the block definition diagram, as well as the use of the diagrams optionally mentioned in Section 3.3.4, is reasonable and logically correct.

The interview with experts 7 and 9 (cf. Table 4) focused on current best practices established in the industry regarding the collaboration of product and service development related to data specification for AI applications. It turned out that in practice relevant data is mainly searched for according to a data-driven trial and error approach. For this purpose, the data scientists ask domain experts known to them from the past in an unstructured way which data is relevant for the application. Since the data scientists have little knowledge of the application domain, the questioning about relevant data usually remains at too general a level, as a result of which important details are lost. This process is time-consuming and causes many smart service projects to fail due to insufficient data. The systematic approach SemDaServ was evaluated as a suitable solution for reducing try and error iteration loops and thus increasing the efficiency in smart service development resulting from an improvement of the cooperation between product and service development.

The interview with expert 8 (cf. Table 4) focused on the connection between product and service structure, the compatibility of the SemDaServ approach with other methods of SSSE, and the trade-off between document-oriented and model-oriented approaches. As a result, it was determined that there are methods such as MESSIAH [38] that should be used to develop an initial service structure. The resulting elements of the service structure can then be related to the product structure via the information items and information flows described in SemDaServ. It was confirmed that SemDaServ is equally suitable for document-based and model-based approaches and thus fits well into the current state of the art (mostly document-based approach) and at the same time is fit for the future (model-based approach).

The interview with expert 10 (cf. Table 4) focused on the formalization of domain knowledge. The discussion mainly focused on the right degree of formal specifications regarding the modeling language for explicating domain knowledge. A higher degree of detail in the specifications and language constructs of the modeling language leads to more difficult access to the modeling language and thus, in the expert's experience, to less use of the modeling language in practice. The advantage is the unambiguousness in the interpretation and thus the reusability of the explicated knowledge. A lower level of detail in the specifications (e.g., allowing free text without specific formal specifications) leads to less unambiguity, but the access barrier to the use of the modeling language is lower, which is why the circle of users increases. From the workshops as well as other expert interviews, it became clear that the SSSE requires a multidisciplinary team with a variety of different actors. Therefore, the SemDaServ approach uses as few formal specifications for information and data models as possible. Nevertheless, further SysML diagrams can be used, which accordingly also bring the advantages of the multitude of specified specifications of SysML. In the interview, the level of detail of the specifications in the information and data model was confirmed as sufficient. In addition, the conclusiveness of the sequence of the SemDaServ process steps for running through the knowledge pyramid was confirmed.

The interview with expert 11 (cf. Table 4) focused on the broad applicability of the SemDaServ approach independent of the use case, role profiles of the actors, conclusiveness, and usefulness for practice. Expert 11 confirmed that the SemDaServ approach is generic enough to be used in an industry-independent manner. The role profiles described are appropriate and can already be found in practice in several companies. The version of the knowledge carrier matrix presented to expert 11 was not yet based on roles, but only noted the names of the knowledge carriers. This was changed at the suggestion of expert 11: In the SemDaServ version, in addition to the name, the knowledge carrier matrix primarily records the role and also the organization of the knowledge carrier. The conclusiveness of the approach and its usefulness for practice was confirmed.

The interview with expert 12 was focused on the suitability of the SemDaServ approach for the possibility of achieving a complete specification of all data. The question was whether knowledge-driven domain experts can identify all relevant data for a smart service in early development phases without having to fall back on previous data. The interview revealed that domain experts can identify a large part of the relevant data by naming the required information content and information flows. Nevertheless, it is required to have domain experts check statistical analyses of already existing data-especially correlation analyses-in the context of SemDaServ. This enables the discovery of relevant correlations that were previously unknown to the domain experts or that were simply forgotten. By having the revealed correlations checked by the domain experts, spurious correlations can be discovered and excluded from the data specification. Based on the interview with expert 12, the sub-process step Integrate statistical analysis results (see Section 3.2.2) was therefore added to the data specification process Clarify information needs.

5. Discussion

The SemDaServ approach should be adapted in practice depending on the specific requirements of the SSSE project as well as available resources (time, budget, staff, external experts). SemDaServ is theoretically applicable to all kinds of SSSE projects. For practical use, adapting SemDaServ to the particular SSSE project requirements is necessary to justify the expenses linked to the realization of SemDaServ. Indeed, conceptualizing SemDaServ in practice as a guiding framework rather than a rigid system makes its application more efficient. The four most important factors for adapting SemDaServ in practice are as follows:

1. Number of product and service components
2. Number and heterogeneity of actors to be involved
3. Requirements for the modeling depth
4. Method of operation (model-based or document-based)

For Factors 1 and 2, the guiding principle should be "as much as necessary, as little as possible", because these factors exponentially scale the effort related to SemDaServ's application. For example, assume that predictive maintenance of the aircraft engine's main ball bearings would be the most critical element of a power-by-the-hour smart service. Then it would make sense to focus the data specification on the physical component main ball bearings and the smart service component predictive maintenance. This makes the relevant part of the product structure and the service structure very small. The actors required to carry out the data specification process would be, in addition to the Core Team, a few domain experts for ball bearings, and data scientists with knowledge in the area of service life prediction. This reduction to the core elements makes the SemDaServ approach feasible in a lean way in this case. Similarly, the principle of "as simple as possible, as detailed as necessary" applies to Factor 3. For example, it is not necessary to formalize every detail of possible signal waveforms from sensors on the main bearings as part of the creation of the information and data model. It is much more important to specify that suitable sensors must be installed in the engine to monitor the condition of the main bearings. Factor 4 should be aligned to the usual approach within the company. While using a model-based approach has benefits such as traceability or automatic updates of linked elements, the document-based approach is more accessible to a larger set of stakeholders, as it usually does not require specialized knowledge regarding software tools. For example, for small projects, it may make more sense to perform the SemDaServ approach in a document-oriented manner using information and data models created in Microsoft Visio than to completely abandon the use of the SemDaServ approach if neither software licenses nor the know-how to use a model-oriented approach is available.

Regarding the working hypotheses the following conclusions are drawn from the evaluation presented in Section 4: WH1 (The probability of AI development with quality of results being in line with smart service requirements can be increased by a domain knowledge-driven data specification approach.) was confirmed in the interviews with the experts 7, 8, 9 (cf. Table 4 for looking up the IDs) as well as in both workshops. WH1 was not discussed in the remaining expert interviews because these expert interviews had a different thematic focus. The interviews and workshops revealed that a data-driven approach is currently used in practice for the development of AI components. This means that all available data is checked for its suitability regarding the realization of smart service requirements. Domain knowledge is of elementary importance here, since domain experts can use their knowledge to identify relevant data and distinguish causality from spurious correlation. If the available data is too small in scope or too low in quality, physical components of the SSS must be adapted, the quality requirements for the AI components must be reduced or, in the worst case, the SSS development project must be aborted. Data specification in early product development phases can reduce the probability of occurrence of the aforementioned scenarios. For illustration purposes, imagine the following synthetic example: Requirement 1 'The remaining lifetime of the main bearings must be known with an accuracy of more than 95%' and Requirement 2 'The number of sensors must be reduced as much as possible to save costs.' To meet Requirement 1, an ML model is trained based on data from engines already in use. The engine data used for training is selected so that the ball bearings used are comparable to the new engine model. Based on the data from already in-service engines, the resulting ML model meets Requirement 1. When testing the ML model on the data from the prototype of the engine to be developed, it is found that the 95% accuracy requirement is not met, as the new engine has fewer sensors in order to meet Requirement 2. In this situation, the quality of AI results (the accuracy of the ML model) is not in line with the smart service requirements. This is caused by an unfulfilled data need (missing sensor data). In the mentioned example, extensive product changes (adding the needed sensor as well as a redesign of affected components, electrical layout, etc.) and the need to redo the testing of all components (software and hardware) affected by the changes caused by the new sensor. Experts from the field of bearing technology would have known which data is required to predict the remaining life of a bearing. By using a domain knowledge-driven data specification approach, data needs can be discovered and cross-checked with SSS requirements. This can increase the probability of AI development with the quality of results being in line with smart service requirements. The extent to which this probability is increased is not part of WH1. Thus, WH1 can be confirmed.

WH2 (A clear understanding of relevant data for the development and operation of a smart service can be systematically generated by using domain knowledge to clarify information needs and derive data needs from information needs.) was discussed in all expert interviews and both workshops. As a result, WH2 can be partially confirmed. There was agreement that WH2 can be confirmed for small SSSE projects (e.g., predictive maintenance of a bearing) involving just the Core Team (cf. Table 1) and a handful of domain knowledge carriers. However, further research needs to be conducted to evaluate scalability for larger projects. It remains open up to which count of actors, as well as product and service components, the presented SemDaServ approach scalably leads to a clear understanding of the data relevant for the smart service. For this purpose, experiments are required to investigate the impact on individual process steps when scaling up the number of relevant actors, product, and service components. In addition, case studies on complex, industrial application examples are required to evaluate whether the presented SemDaServ approach may need to be given additional process steps or artifacts for larger SSSE projects.

WH3 (Domain knowledge relevant for AI training can be formalized using the SysML.) was confirmed in the expert interviews 6, 7, 8, 9, 11, and in both workshops. WH3 was not discussed in the remaining expert interviews because these expert interviews had a different thematic focus. Both workshops confirmed, that the SysML information model and data model of the SemDaServ approach are feasible to formalize the domain knowledge relevant for AI training. Expert 6 confirmed that the SysML elements used for the information model and data model are a valid choice to formalize domain knowledge relevant for AI training. Furthermore, 'SysML is designed to provide simple but powerful constructs for modeling a wide range of systems engineering problems. It is particularly effective in specifying requirements, structure, behavior, allocations, and constraints on system properties to support engineering analysis.' ([46] p. 1) Workshop two as well as interviews with experts 7, 8, 9, and 11 revealed, that these kinds of knowledge from the engineering domain (requirements, structure, behavior, allocations, constraints) are relevant for AI training. In workshop two, it was positively emphasized that the beneficiaries of the data specification—the data scientists, who were using their AI models on qualitatively and quantitatively sufficient data as well as a good semantic description of the data–can easily understand SysML due to its similarity to UML.

WH4 (Domain knowledge relevant for AI training can be formalized using a guided process.) was confirmed in the expert interviews 7, 8, 9, 10, 11, and both workshops. WH4 was not discussed in the remaining expert interviews because these expert interviews had a different thematic focus. According to the experts involved in the evaluation of WH4, the formalization of the domain knowledge relevant for AI training has not yet been described in practice as part of a standardized process. Different procedures established in practice for formalizing the domain knowledge relevant for AI training were therefore mentioned. As a result, the procedure differs depending on the industry, the size of the company, and the people involved. However, in both workshops and the expert interviews quoted for WH4, the following pattern emerged: the actors tasked with AI training (hereafter: AI engineers) first try to conduct data-based AI training through experiments. If this yields insufficient results, domain experts from the proximate company network are contacted. This is usually followed by an open interview of the domain expert to ask about relevant domain knowledge. If the AI engineer conducting the interview has little to no domain knowledge, it is difficult for the AI engineer to ask relevant questions. The open interview of domain experts is then usually repeated until the AI engineer has the impression that the domain knowledge relevant for the AI training is known. Finally, the formalization of the domain knowledge is mostly done in plain text or the form of diagrams (e.g., UML or entity-relationship diagrams). The described procedure of AI engineers can be described in a guided process by putting the mentioned steps into a logical order and consequently systematizing them. Thus, WH4 can be confirmed. Participants of workshop two further noted that the semantic data specification resulting from the application of the SemDaServ approach is very helpful for the data understanding and data preparation (especially feature engineering) steps of the widely used CRISP-DM process.

5.1. Limitations

The evaluation was conducted by discussing the SemDaServ approach with experts from industry as well as academia (workshops and interviews). Therefore, SemDaServ was qualitatively evaluated using expert experience and logic. This research approach is feasible to evaluate the applicability in practice, usefulness, and logical correctness of the SemDaServ approach. To evaluate the effectiveness and efficiency in real-world SSSE projects, experiments (e.g., A to B comparisons with professionals specifying data needs without any guidance, data-driven AI training without any data specification, etc.) are needed to quantify the efficiency and effectiveness of SemDaServ. Especially the impact of SemDaServ regarding cost, quality, and time on real-world SSSE projects cannot be quantified yet. Additionally, the uncertainty factor of the data specification resulting from the SemDaServ approach cannot be quantified yet. To overcome these limitations, a significant number of case studies are needed to measure the quality of the smart services developed using the specified data needs resulting from the application of the SemDaServ approach.

5.2. Future Research

The evaluation of the SemDaServ approach revealed the needs for detailing the following aspects: (1) An exemplary agenda for workshops necessary for the Clarify domain knowledge process step. (2) Guidelines on how to tailor the SemDaServ approach to different project types (new development vs CI/CD scenarios) (3) Recommendations on building successful Core Teams (cf. Table 1) and combinations of knowledge carriers (cf. Table 2), especially regarding feasible competence mixes. Future research is planned to address these aspects. Additionally, it is planned to research a model approach to size the data types, frequencies, and reliabilities to support the creation of the data model (process step Derive data needs). Furthermore, experiments measuring how the number of actors, product, and service components impact the overall resources (time, budget, scope of required domain knowledge) needed to realize SemDaServ are planed.

6. Conclusions

This article has presented the SemDaServ approach. SemDaServ is a systematic approach for semantic data specification in the context of AI-based SSS. In comparison to data-driven approaches, SemDaServ is driven by the knowledge of domain experts, who can define the data needs of a smart service in early development phases—even if no operational data of the embryonic SSS is available yet. The availability of operational data requires (virtual) prototypes of the SSS. Therefore, operational data of the SSS becomes available in late product development phases. If unfulfilled data needs are discovered late, costly iteration loops (e.g., returning to the requirements definition phase) and product changes (e.g., adding sensors with the resulting need for adaptation of data processing and data analysis) may be required. Hence, a goal of specifying the data needs of a smart service during early SSS development phases is the reduction of iteration loops in SSS development projects, which correlates with reduced costs and a faster time to market. The SemDaServ approach contributes to achieving this goal by providing a three-step process, five artifacts, as well as guidance on tools and IT systems supporting the realization of

SemDaServ in practice. The SemDaServ approach intends to improve the understanding of relevant data for the development and operation of smart services, guide the systematic formalization of domain knowledge relevant for AI training as part of smart service development, and increase the probability of AI development with quality of results being in line with smart service requirements. SemDaServ was validated by expert interviews and workshops. This qualitative evaluation of SemDaServ confirmed the applicability in practice, usefulness, and logical correctness of the SemDaServ approach. Based on the findings so far, we assume that SemDaServ contributes to reducing iteration loops during SSS development, resulting in fewer costs and development time. However, case studies and experiments are required and planned to quantify the effectiveness of SemDaServ.

Author Contributions: Conceptualization, M.P.; methodology, M.P.; validation, M.P.; formal analysis, M.P.; investigation, M.P.; resources, M.P. and R.S.; data curation, M.P.; writing—original draft preparation, M.P.; writing—review and editing, M.P. and R.S.; visualization, M.P. and R.S.; supervision, R.S.; project administration, M.P.; funding acquisition, M.P. and R.S. Both authors have read and agreed to the published version of the manuscript.

Funding: The research has not received external funding. The article processing charge was funded by the Open Access Publication Fund of TU Berlin.

Acknowledgments: We acknowledge support by the German Research Foundation and the Open Access Publication Fund of TU Berlin.

Conflicts of Interest: The authors declare no conflict of interest.

Abbreviations

The following abbreviations are used in this manuscript:

AI	Artificial intelligence
AutoML	Automated machine learning
BPMN	Business Process Modeling Language
CD	Continuous delivery
CI	Continuous integration
EOS	Engineering Operating System
IoT	Internet-of-Things
MBSE	Model-based systems engineering
ML	Machine learning
PDM	Product data management
PSS	Product service system
SemDaServ	Semantic Data Specification for AI-Based Smart Services
SSS	Smart service system
SSSE	Smart service systems engineering
SysML	Systems Modeling Language
UML	Unified Modeling Language

Appendix A

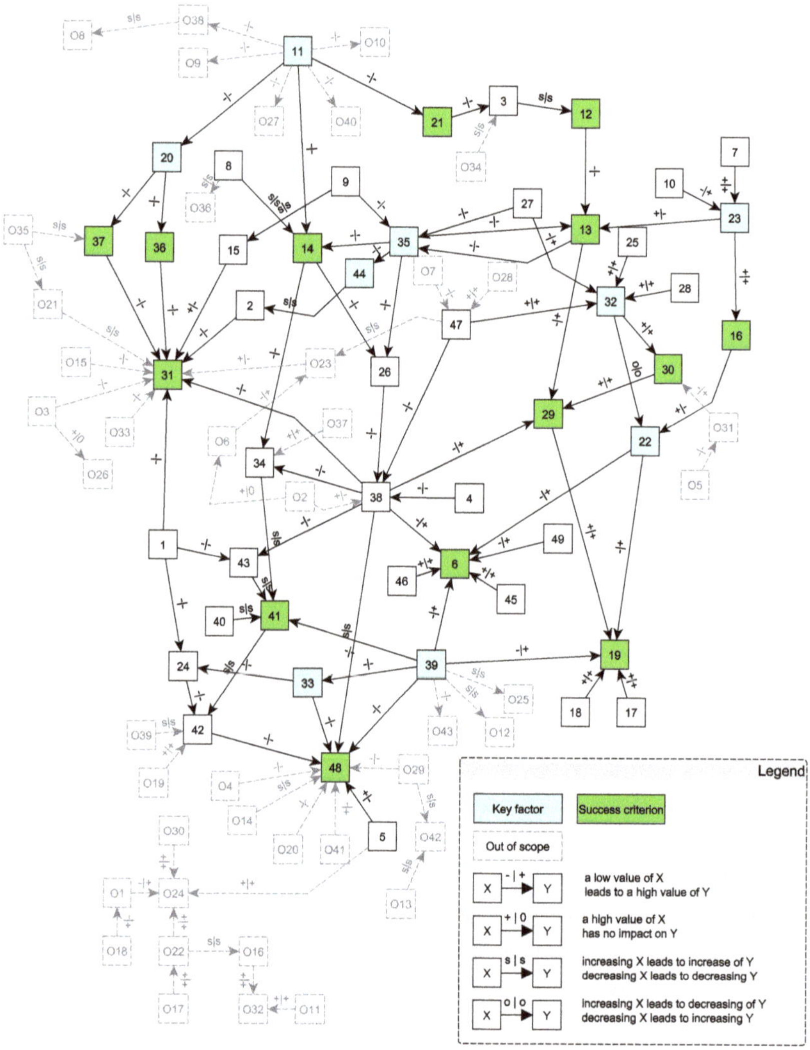

Figure A1. Reference model based on Design Research Methodology described in [23]. How to read the model: Take for example the connection 11 to O9. 11 stands for the degree of reusability of documented domain knowledge (looked up in Table A2). O9 stands for comprehensibility of the trained AI model (looked up in Table A1). 11 and O9 are linked with the label - | -. This means: Currently there is a low degree of reusability of documented domain knowledge and this leads to low comprehensibility of the trained AI model. As O9 is out of scope, the SemDaServ solution will not take this connection into account.

Table A1. Identified out-of-scope factors.

ID	Factor
O1	Agility of smart service development
O2	Assumed capabilities of data science tools to deal with low-quality data
O3	Availability of data scientists
O4	Availability/awareness of appropriate methods for service development
O5	Awareness of the added value of data analysis
O6	Capabilities of data science tools to deal with low-quality information
O7	Clarity regarding the ownership of the data
O8	Competitiveness of the company under consideration
O9	Comprehensibility of the trained AI model
O10	Contribution of domain knowledge to company productivity
O11	Degree of competitive advantage through differentiation by means of hybrid service bundles
O12	Degree of customer acceptance of the SSS
O13	Degree of customer integration in the development process
O14	Degree of customer satisfaction
O15	Degree of data literacy of actors involved
O16	Degree of the fulfillment of customer needs
O17	Degree of innovation of the smart service
O18	Degree of integration depth of smart service development methods into existing development processes, artifacts, and tools
O19	Degree of interdisciplinary collaboration
O20	Degree of management support
O21	Degree of transparency regarding the informative value of a data set
O22	Degree of uncertainty regarding customer needs, willingness to pay, market acceptance of the smart service
O23	Difficulty of data engineering
O24	Difficulty of smart service conception
O25	Duration of customer retention
O26	Duration of setting up a data engineering team
O27	Efficiency of domain knowledge generation
O28	Extent of manual data preparation
O29	Extent of testing to identify potential vulnerabilities of the SSS
O30	Individuality of the life cycles of the components of a SSS
O31	Investment in systematic the acquisition, processing, and preparation of data
O32	Level of margin
O33	Maturity of the AI-relevant IT infrastructure
O34	Professional experience of a data scientist in the target domain
O35	Quality of data science methods
O36	Quality of labels
O37	Quality of the analysis model
O38	Quality of the company's internal domain knowledge
O39	Quality of the product
O40	Reproducibility of ML algorithms from (scientific) publications
O41	Scope of the service spectrum
O42	Success rate of innovations
O43	Usefulness of the smart service

Table A2. Identified relevant factors.

ID	Factor	Key Factor?	Success Criterion?
1	Accuracy of fit of data selection	no	no
2	Availability of relevant data	no	no
3	Availability of domain knowledge required	no	no
4	Availability of synthetic data from (simulation) models	no	no
5	Complexity of the SSS	no	no
6	Cost of service development	no	yes
7	Degree of data-driven approach in the application of AI processes	no	no
8	Degree of human experience and skills	no	no
9	Degree of problem understanding with regard to the application domain	no	no
10	Degree of process-driven approach in the application of AI methods	no	no
11	Degree of reusability of documented domain knowledge	yes	no
12	Degree of systematicness in identifying relevant domain experts	no	yes
13	Degree of systematicness in linking domain knowledge and AI development	no	yes
14	Degree of utilization of relevant domain knowledge	no	yes
15	Difficulty of data analysis	no	no
16	Duration for identification of insufficient data situation	no	yes
17	Duration of adaptation of organizational processes	no	no
18	Duration of implementing changes in physical components	no	no
19	Duration until market maturity of the SSS	no	yes
20	Efficiency of domain knowledge application	yes	no
21	Efficiency of domain knowledge transfer	no	yes
22	Efficiency of smart service development methods	yes	no
23	Extent of trial and error approach to identifying relevant data	yes	no
24	Fit of requirements of existing system and new smart service	no	no
25	Heterogeneity of the data used	no	no
26	Information content of the data	no	no
27	Level of detail of problem specification	no	no
28	Number of data sources considered	no	no
29	Number of iteration loops in smart service development	no	yes
30	Number of redundancies of manual steps in data analysis	no	yes
31	Probability of success of the AI learning process	no	yes
32	Proportion of exploratory approach to data analysis	yes	no
33	Quality of collaboration between product and service development	yes	no
34	Quality of data analysis	no	no
35	Quality of data specification	yes	no
36	Quality of knowledge about data sources	no	yes
37	Quality of knowledge about relevant data	no	yes
38	Quality of relevant data	no	no
39	Quality of smart service development methods	yes	no
40	Quality of smart service development tools	no	no
41	Quality of the smart service	no	yes
42	Quality of the SSS	no	no
43	Quality of the trained AI model	no	no
44	Relevance of sensors in the product	yes	no
45	Risk of time-conditional data deviation	no	no
46	Risk of time-related model deviation	no	no
47	Scope of eligible data	no	no
48	Success of newly developed services on the market	no	yes
49	Transferability of trained AI models	no	no

Table A3. Identified success criteria for smart service data specification.

ID	Factor	Source
6	Cost of service development	[14,26,30]
12	Degree of systematicness in identifying relevant domain experts	[21]
13	Degree of systematicness in linking domain knowledge and AI development	Expert interview
14	Degree of utilization of relevant domain knowledge	Logical conclusion
16	Duration for identification of insufficient data situation	Expert interview
19	Duration until market maturity of the SSS	[26,29,30]
21	Efficiency of domain knowledge transfer	[14]
29	Number of iteration loops in smart service development	Logical conclusion
30	Number of redundancies of manual steps in data analysis	[27]
31	Probability of success of the AI learning process	[10,24,31]
36	Quality of knowledge about data sources	[31]
37	Quality of knowledge about relevant data	[24,31]
41	Quality of the smart service	[26,29,30]
48	Success of newly developed services on the market	[30]

Table A4. Identified key factors for smart service data specification.

ID	Key Factor	Source
11	Degree of reusability of documented domain knowledge	[28]
20	Efficiency of smart service development methods	[30]
22	Efficiency of the application of domain knowledge	[14]
23	Extent of trial and error approach to identify relevant data	Expert interview
32	Proportion of the explorative approach in data analysis	[27]
33	Quality of collaboration between product and service development	[15,29,30]
35	Quality of data specification	Logical conclusion
39	Quality of smart service development methods	[15,26,29,30]
44	Relevance of sensors in the product	Logical conclusion

Appendix B

Table A5. Mapping of functions and SemDaServ solution elements.

		Solution Elements												
		Process		Artifacts						Tools and IT Systems				
ID	**Function**	**Clarify Domain Knowledge Needs**	**Clarify Information Needs**	**Specify Data Needs**	**Smart Service Data Categories**	**Information Model**	**Data Model**	**Knowledge Carrier Matrix**	**Data Decision Matrix**	**Visualisation Tools**	**Modeling Tools**	**Text and Table Processing Tools**	**Data Science Tools**	**Enterprise IT**
100	Systematically specify data relevant to the smart service and their sources in the SSS context	X	X	X	X	X	X	X	X	X	X	X	X	X
200	Describe data relevant to smart services		X	X	X	X	X	X	X	X	X	X	X	X
210	Systematically describe relevant data and their sources		X	X		X	X		X	X	X	X	X	X
211	Describe relevant data		X	X		X	X		X	X	X	X	X	
212	Systematically ensure quality of data specification			X							X	X		X
213	Describe sources of relevant data		X	X		X	X			X	X	X	X	X
220	Describe data categories of smart services		X	X	X	X		X		X	X		X	
212	Collect data categories of smart services		X		X	X		X		X	X		X	
222	Document data categories of smart services in an extensible way		X	X	X					X	X			
223	Provide a system for describing data categories for smart services		X		X	X				X	X			
300	Support collaboration between product and service development	X	X	X	X	X	X	X	X	X	X	X	X	X
310	Extend existing smart service development methods	X	X	X	X	X	X	X	X	X	X	X		
311	Describe interface of existing smart service development methods to data specification	X			X	X	X	X	X			X		
312	Describe smart service development methods that can be used for data specification	X	X	X		X	X		X			X		
313	Tailor data specification process to meet needs					X	X			X	X	X		
320	Apply domain knowledge efficiently	X	X			X		X		X	X	X	X	X
321	Describe domain knowledge required for data interpretation	X	X			X				X	X	X		
322	Identify relevant domain knowledge and its sources	X						X		X	X	X	X	X
323	Document relevant domain knowledge in a reusable way	X	X			X				X	X			

References

1. Waring, J.; Lindvall, C.; Umeton, R. Automated Machine Learning: Review of the State-of-the-Art and Opportunities for Healthcare. *Artif. Intell. Med.* **2020**, *104*, 101822. [CrossRef] [PubMed]
2. Rapidminer. *50 Ways to Impact Your Business with AI*; Technical Report; RapidMiner, Inc.: Boston, MA, USA, 2020.
3. Industrial, M.D.; Software, A. Machine Learning Einfach Gemacht. *SPS-MAGAZIN* **2020**, *7*, 32–35.

4. Chauhan, K.; Jani, S.; Thakkar, D.; Dave, R.; Bhatia, J.; Tanwar, S.; Obaidat, M.S. Automated Machine Learning: The New Wave of Machine Learning. In Proceedings of the 2020 2nd International Conference on Innovative Mechanisms for Industry Applications (ICIMIA), Bangalore, India, 5–7 March 2020; pp. 205–212. [CrossRef]
5. Zöller, M.A.; Huber, M.F. Benchmark and Survey of Automated Machine Learning Frameworks. *arXiv* **2019**, arXiv:1904.12054.
6. Tuggener, L.; Amirian, M.; Rombach, K.; Lorwald, S.; Varlet, A.; Westermann, C.; Stadelmann, T. Automated Machine Learning in Practice: State of the Art and Recent Results. In Proceedings of the 2019 6th Swiss Conference on Data Science (SDS), Bern, Switzerland, 14 June 2019; pp. 31–36. [CrossRef]
7. Perrault, R.; Shoham, Y.; Brynjolfsson, E.; Clark, J.; Etchemendy, J.; Grosz Harvard, B.; Lyons, T.; Manyika, J.; Carlos Niebles, J.; Mishra, S.; et al. *Artificial Intelligence Index 2019 Annual Report*; Technical Report; Stanford University's Human-Centered Artificial Intelligence Institute (HAI): Stanford, CA, USA, 2019.
8. Elshawi, R.; Maher, M.; Sakr, S. Automated Machine Learning: State-of-The-Art and Open Challenges. *arXiv* **2019**, arXiv:1906.02287.
9. Chin, J. The Death of Data Scientists Will AutoML Replace Data Scientists? 2019. Available online: https://towardsdatascience.com/the-death-of-data-scientists-c243ae167701 (accessed on 8 April 2021).
10. Kozyrkov, C. Data Science... without Any Data?! 2020. Available online: https://towardsdatascience.com/data-science-without-any-data-6c1ae9509d92 (accessed on 8 April 2021).
11. Louis, P.; Russ, R. How to Develop Digital Products for Industrial Environments-The Data Science and Engineering Process in PLM. In Proceedings of the 9th International Conference on Data Science, Technology and Applications (DATA), Online, 7–9 July 2020. Available online: https://www.insticc.org/node/TechnicalProgram/data/2020/presentationDetails/99728 (accessed on 7 April 2021).
12. Marx, E.; Pauli, T.; Matzner, M.; Fielt, E. From Services to Smart Services: Can Service Engineering Methods Get Smarter as Well? In *WI2020 Zentrale Tracks*; GITO Verlag: Berlin, Germany, 2020; pp. 1067–1083. [CrossRef]
13. Tokarz, B.; Tokarz, B.; Fagundes, A.B.; Pereira, D.; Beuren, F.H. Product-Service Systems: A Literature Review on Assisting Development. *Int. J. Adv. Eng. Res. Sci.* **2020**, *7*, 41–51. [CrossRef]
14. Lee, J. *Industrial AI: Applications with Sustainable Performance*; Springer: Singapore, 2020. [CrossRef]
15. Anke, J. How to Tame the Tiger—Exploring the Means, Ends and Challenges in Smart Service Systems Engineering. In Proceedings of the Twenty-Eigtht European Conference on Information Systems (ECIS2020), Marrakech, Morocco, 15–17 June 2020; pp. 1–16.
16. Rosa, M.; Wang, W.M.; Stark, R.; Rozenfeld, H. A Concept Map to Support the Planning and Evaluation of Artifacts in the Initial Phases of PSS Design. *Res. Eng. Des.* **2021**. [CrossRef]
17. Shearer, C. The CRISP-DM Model: The New Blueprint for Data Mining. *J. Data Warehous.* **2000**, *5*, 13–22.
18. Feyyad, U. Data Mining and Knowledge Discovery: Making Sense out of Data. *IEEE Expert* **1996**, *11*, 20–25. [CrossRef]
19. SAS Institute Inc. SAS Help Center: Introduction to SEMMA. 2017. Available online: https://documentation.sas.com/doc/en/emref/14.3/n061bzurmej4j3n1jnj8bbjjm1a2.htm (accessed on 8 April 2021).
20. Azevedo, A.; Santos, M. KDD, SEMMA and CRISP-DM: A Parallel Overview. In Proceedings of the IADIS European Conference Data Mining, Amsterdam, The Netherlands, 24–26 July 2008.
21. Wang, W.M.; Preidel, M.; Fachbach, B.; Stark, R. Towards a Reference Model for Knowledge Driven Data Provision Processes. In *IFIP Advances in Information and Communication Technology*; Springer International Publishing: Basel, Switzerland, 2020; Volume 598, pp. 123–132. [CrossRef]
22. Roe, K.D.; Jawa, V.; Zhang, X.; Chute, C.G.; Epstein, J.A.; Matelsky, J.; Shpitser, I.; Taylor, C.O. Feature Engineering with Clinical Expert Knowledge: A Case Study Assessment of Machine Learning Model Complexity and Performance. *PLoS ONE* **2020**, *15*, e0231300. [CrossRef] [PubMed]
23. Blessing, L.T.; Chakrabarti, A. *DRM, a Design Research Methodology*; Springer: London, UK, 2009. [CrossRef]
24. Blei, D.M.; Smyth, P. Science and Data Science. *Proc. Natl. Acad. Sci. USA* **2017**, *114*, 8689–8692. [CrossRef]
25. Bundesministerium für Bildung und Forschung. Bekanntmachung der Richtlinie zur Förderung von Projekten zum Thema "Erzeugung von Synthetischen Daten für Künstliche Intelligenz". 2020. Available online: https://www.bmbf.de/foerderungen/bekanntmachung-3068.html (accessed on 8 April 2021).
26. Bullinger, H.J.; Scheer, A.W. Service Engineering—Entwicklung Und Gestaltung Innovativer Dienstleistungen. In *Service Engineering*, 2nd ed.; Springer: Berlin/Heidelberg, Germany, 2006; pp. 3–18. [CrossRef]
27. Deutsches Forschungszentrum für Künstliche Intelligenz GmbH (DFKI). Projekt Exdra–Idee, Übersicht, Ziele Und Ergebnisse. 2020. Available online: https://www.exdra.de/projekt/ (accessed on 8 April 2021).
28. Laroche, F.; Dhuieb, M.A.; Belkadi, F.; Bernard, A. Accessing Enterprise Knowledge: A Context-Based Approach. *CIRP Ann. Manuf. Technol.* **2016**, *65*, 189–192. [CrossRef]
29. Meyer, K.; Klingner, S.; Zinke, C. (Eds.) *Service Engineering*; Springer Fachmedien Wiesbaden: Wiesbaden, Germany, 2018. [CrossRef]
30. Richter, H.M.; Tschandl, M. Service Engineering–Neue Services Erfolgreich Gestalten Und Umsetzen. In *Dienstleistungen 4.0*; Springer Fachmedien Wiesbaden: Wiesbaden, Germany, 2017; pp. 157–184. [CrossRef]
31. Rogati, M. The AI Hierarchy of Needs | . 2017. Available online: https://hackernoon.com/the-ai-hierarchy-of-needs-18f111fcc007 (accessed on 8 April 2021).

32. Wellsandt, S.; Anke, J.; Thoben, K.D. Modellierung Der Lebenszyklen von Smart Services. In *Smart Service Engineering*; Springer Fachmedien Wiesbaden: Wiesbaden, Germany, 2017; pp. 233–256. [CrossRef]
33. Lünnemann, P.; Stark, R.; Wang, W.M.; Stark, R.; Manteca, P.I. Engineering Activities—Considering Value Creation from a Holistic Perspective. In Proceedings of the 2017 International Conference on Engineering, Technology and Innovation (ICE/ITMC), Madeira, Portugal, 27–29 June 2017; pp. 315–323. [CrossRef]
34. Hildebrand, K.; Gebauer, M.; Hinrichs, H.; Mielke, M. (Eds.) *Daten-Und Informationsqualität*; Springer Fachmedien Wiesbaden: Wiesbaden, Germany, 2018. [CrossRef]
35. Anke, J.; Poeppelbuss, J.; Alt, R. It Takes More than Two to Tango: Identifying Roles and Patterns in Multi-Actor Smart Service Innovation. *Schmalenbach Bus. Rev.* **2020**, *72*, 599–634. [CrossRef]
36. Poeppelbuss, J.; Durst, C. Smart Service Canvas–A Tool for Analyzing and Designing Smart Product-Service Systems. *Procedia CIRP* **2019**, *83*, 324–329. [CrossRef]
37. Exner, K.; Stark, R.; Kim, J.Y.; Stark, R. Data-Driven Business Model a Methodology to Develop Smart Services. In Proceedings of the 2017 International Conference on Engineering, Technology and Innovation (ICE/ITMC), Madeira, Portugal, 27–29 June 2017; pp. 146–154. [CrossRef]
38. Halstenberg, F.A.; Lindow, K.; Stark, R. Leveraging Circular Economy through a Methodology for Smart Service Systems Engineering. *Sustainability* **2019**, *11*, 3517. [CrossRef]
39. Müller, P.; Kebir, N.; Stark, R.; Blessing, L. PSS Layer Method–Application to Microenergy Systems. In *Introduction to Product/Service-System Design*; Springer: London, UK, 2009; pp. 3–30. [CrossRef]
40. VDI-Fachbereich Informationstechnik. Wissensmanagement im Ingenieurwesen–Grundlagen, Konzepte, Vorgehen. *VDI-Richtlinie* **2009**, *VDI 5610 Pt 1*, 1–28.
41. Exner, K.; Smolka, E.; Blüher, T.; Stark, R.; Blueher, T.; Stark, R. A Method to Design Smart Services Based on Information Categorization of Industrial Use Cases. *Procedia CIRP* **2019**, *83*, 77–82. [CrossRef]
42. Exner, K.; Preidel, M.; Gogineni, S.; Nickel, J.; Stark, R. Digitaler Zwilling Für Smart Services. *ProduktDaten J.* **2019**, *2*, 39–42.
43. Runkler, T.A. *Data Mining*; Springer Fachmedien Wiesbaden: Wiesbaden, Germany, 2015; Volume 53. [CrossRef]
44. English, L.P. *Improving Data Warehouse and Business Information Quality: Methods for Reducing Costs and Increasing Profits*; John Wiley & Sons, Inc.: New York, NY, USA, 1999.
45. Tavana, M.; Hajipour, V.; Oveisi, S. IoT-Based Enterprise Resource Planning: Challenges, Open Issues, Applications, Architecture, and Future Research Directions. *Internet Things* **2020**, *11*, 100262. [CrossRef]
46. Object Management Group. OMG Systems Modeling Language (OMG SysML™), Version 1.6. 2019. Available online: https://www.omg.org/spec/SysML/1.6/ (accessed on 10 April 2021).

applied sciences

MDPI

Article

Anticipating Future Behavior of an Industrial Press Using LSTM Networks

Balduíno César Mateus [1,2,*], Mateus Mendes [3,4,*], José Torres Farinha [3,5] and António Marques Cardoso [2]

1 EIGeS—Research Centre in Industrial Engineering, Management and Sustainability, Lusófona University, Campo Grande, 376, 1749-024 Lisboa, Portugal
2 CISE—Electromechatronic Systems Research Centre, University of Beira Interior, Calçada Fonte do Lameiro, P–62001-001 Covilhã, Portugal; ajmc@ubi.pt
3 Polytechnic of Coimbra, ISEC, 3045-093 Coimbra, Portugal; tfarinha@isec.pt
4 Institute of Systems and Robotics, University of Coimbra, 3004-531 Coimbra, Portugal
5 Centre for Mechanical Engineering, Materials and Processes—CEMMPRE, 3030-788 Coimbra, Portugal
* Correspondence: balduino.mateus@ubi.pt (B.C.M.); mmendes@isec.pt (M.M.)

Abstract: Predictive maintenance is very important in industrial plants to support decisions aiming to maximize maintenance investments and equipment's availability. This paper presents predictive models based on long short-term memory neural networks, applied to a dataset of sensor readings. The aim is to forecast future equipment statuses based on data from an industrial paper press. The datasets contain data from a three-year period. Data are pre-processed and the neural networks are optimized to minimize prediction errors. The results show that it is possible to predict future behavior up to one month in advance with reasonable confidence. Based on these results, it is possible to anticipate and optimize maintenance decisions, as well as continue research to improve the reliability of the model.

Keywords: time series prediction; LSTM prediction; deep learning prediction; predictive maintenance

Citation: Mateus, B.C.; Mendes, M.; Farinha, J.T.; Cardoso, A.M. Anticipating Future Behavior of an Industrial Press Using LSTM Networks. *Appl. Sci.* **2021**, *11*, 6101. https://doi.org/10.3390/app11136101

Academic Editors: Marlene Amorim, Yuval Cohen and João Reis

Received: 30 April 2021
Accepted: 25 June 2021
Published: 30 June 2021

1. Introduction

Modern processors, computers and high speed networks make it possible to acquire, transfer and store large quantities of data in real time. Acquisition and combination of data from different sensors makes it possible to gain an insightful view of the state of factories, industrial plants and other facilities. Large datasets can be constructed, stored and processed using information technologies such as Big Data, cloud computing, cutting-edge computing, and artificial intelligence tools. The Internet of Things (IoT) is a recent concept, which provides many benefits to different areas, such as maintenance and production management, because it facilitates the automation of tasks such as monitoring and maintenance. This results in the popularization of intelligent systems, which are highly dependent on Big Data [1] and are an important area of study, since they offer the tools and methods to acquire and process large volumes of data such as historical production processes, including many production and operating parameters.

Modern time-series and other data analysis techniques have been used with success for different tasks, such as freeway traffic analysis [2] and additive manufacturing [3]. Different approaches have also been proposed in the field of predictive maintenance [4,5]. Satisfactory results were obtained using Big Data records as support for PCA models, which resulted in a warning alarm several days before a potential failure happened [6].

Life cycle optimization has been an important concern for decades. A physical asset with proper maintenance will have a longer useful life with a greater return on investment for the organization [7].

Predictive maintenance requires good quality data. The information that is extracted from the online or offline data must be reliable, and so the results must be good enough to justify the investment in data collection and analysis. The process starts from the correct calibration of the reading sensors and equipment [8]. The data are then stored and processed using different models, such as Principal Component Analysis (PCA) and Neural Networks [9]. Maintenance planning involves the use of several algorithms, the most common being time series [10].

Maintenance of equipment in the industry becomes a sensitive and important point that affects the equipment's operating time and efficiency [5]. This makes maintenance one of the strategic points for the development and growth of competitiveness vis-à-vis competitors. Chen and Tseng studied the total expected cost of maintaining a flotation system, including the cost of lost production, the cost of repairs, and the cost of standby machines [11].

Daniyan et al. propose the integration of Artificial Intelligence (AI) systems, which will bring many benefits in diagnosing condition problems of industrial machines [12]. They highlight the viability of AI that combines the use of Artificial Neural Networks (ANNs) with a dynamic time series model, for fault diagnostics, to optimize the equipment intervention time.

Hsu et al. demonstrated that neural networks can be a great technology in the support and decision making of large and small companies [13]. There is a trend to use those tools in predictive maintenance systems with the aim of making the prediction systems more intelligent [14].

According to Jimenez et al., there is a great effort in the development of predictive models for application in predictive maintenance [15]. Ayvaz and Alpay apply Long Short-Term Memory (LSTM) neural network approaches to predict real production data, obtaining satisfactory results, superior to conventional models [16]. In their study to improve maintenance planning to minimize unexpected stops, they apply a new method that consists of the combined use of decomposition in empirical mode of ensemble and long-term memory. Their results showed a performance superior to other state of the art models.

LSTM networks use several ports with different functions to control neurons and to store information. The LSTM cell can retain important information for a longer period in which it is used. This property of information maintenance allows the LSTM to exhibit a good performance in the classification, processing, or forecasting of a complex dynamic sequences [17].

The present work uses different LSTM models to predict future trends of six variables, on a dataset containing three years of data samples grabbed in an industrial press, which aims to operate continuously with minimum downtime. Different data pre-processing techniques, network architectures and hyperparameters were tested in order to determine the models that best fit the data and provide the lowest prediction errors.

Section 2 contains a summary of related work. Section 3 describes the theory of the LSTM networks. Section 4 describes the methods used for the present work. Section 5 describes the results and validation of the predictive model. Section 7 draws some conclusions and suggestions for future work.

2. Related Work

2.1. Predictive Maintenance

In smart industries, predictive maintenance is one of the most used techniques to improve condition monitoring, as it allows one to evaluate the conditions of specific equipment in order to predict problems before failure [18]. For good performance of predictive models, it is important that the sensor data collected are of good quality. Deep neural models have been used with success to improve prediction for condition monitoring of industrial equipment.

Wang et al. [19] use a model of long short-term recurrent neural networks (LSTM-RNN) with the objective of predictive maintenance based on past data. The main objective of predictive maintenance is to make an accurate estimate of a system's Remaining Useful Life (RUL). Traditional systems are only able to warn the user when it is too late and the failure occurs, causing an unpredictable offline period during which the system cannot operate properly with a consequent waste of time and resources [20].

In order to assess the condition of a system, the predictive maintenance approach employs sensors of different kinds. Some examples are temperature, vibration, velocity or noise sensors, which are attached to the main components whose failure would compromise the entire operation of the system. In this sense, predictive maintenance analyzes the history of a system in terms of the measurements collected by the sensors that are distributed among the components, with the objective of extracting a "failure pattern" that can be exploited to plan an optimal maintenance strategy and thus reducing offline periods [21]. In a case related to the steel industry, Ref. [22] used neural networks for classification of maintenance activities, so that interventions are planned according to the actual status of the machine and not in advance. Using multiple neural networks to identify status and RUL at a higher resolution can be very difficult, as the system can predict failure classifications and may not be able to recognize neighboring states. One limitation arises from the need for maintenance records to label datasets and the need for large amounts of data of adequate quality with maintenance events, such as component failures.

When systems start to be very complex or the number of sensor measurements to manage is very large, it can be difficult to estimate a failure. For this reason, in recent years, machine learning techniques are used more and more to predict working conditions of a component. Mathew et al. [23] propose several approaches to machine learning such as support vector machines (SVMs), decision trees (DTs), Random Forests (RFs), and others that show which technique has the best performance in RUL forecast for turbofan engines.

A major challenge in operations management is related to predicting machine speed, which can be used to dynamically adjust production processes based on different system conditions, optimize production performance and minimize energy consumption [24]. Essien and Giannetti [25] use a deep convolutional LSTM encoder–decoder architecture model on real data, obtained from a metal packaging factory. They show that it is possible to perform combinations of LSTM with other networks to significantly improve the results.

2.2. Prediction with LSTM Models

LSTM neural networks achieved the best performance in a number of computational sequence labeling tasks, including speech recognition and machine translation [26]. There are a variety of engineering problems that can be solved using predictive neural models. Beshrand Zarzoura used neural network models to predict problems of suspended road bridge structures based on global navigation satellite system observations [27]. Sak et al. demonstrated that the proposed LSTM architectures exhibit better performances compared to deep neural networks (DNNs) in a large vocabulary speech recognition task with a large number of output states [28]. Chen et al. adopted LSTMs for predicting the failure of heavy truck air compressors [29]. They concluded that the use of LSTMs leads to more consistency in predictions over time compared to models that ignore history, such as random forest models.

Gosh et al. [30] presented an extension that they called Contextual LSTM (CLSTM). This model was also used for the forecasting of pollutants. There is also the proposal for a genetic long short-term memory (GLSTM), which has been used in the study of wind energy forecasting [31]. Guo et al. presented a combination method based on real-time prediction errors in which the support vector regression (SVR) and LSTM outputs are combined in the final results of the model's prediction, thus obtaining results of greater precision [32].

Ren et al. used a combination of a Convolution Neural Networks (CNNs) and LSTM in order to extract more in-depth information from data to predict the useful life of ion batteries [33]. Niu et al. used an LSTM and developed an effective speed prediction model to solve prediction problems over time [34]. Feng et al. report that the LSTM algorithm is superior and, according to them, it performs better than conventional neural network models [35].

The architecture of an LSTM network includes the number of hidden layers and the number of delay units, which is the number of previous data points that are considered for training and testing. Currently, there is no general rule for selecting the number of delays and hidden layers [36]. A deep LSTM can be built by stacking multiple LSTM layers, which generally works better than a single layer. Deep LSTM networks have been applied to solve many real-world sequence modelling problems [37]. The LSTM can also be used for planning studies [38], namely for planning the analysis of road traffic speed.

To produce a prediction model with good accuracy, it is necessary to optimize neural models' hyperparameters. While simple models can often produce good results with default hyperparemeters, the optimization process can greatly improve the results [39–41]. The selection of hyperparameters often makes the difference between underperformance and state-of-the-art performance. Optimization is often performed using machine learning algorithms, such as grid search, grey wolf optimization or particle swarm optimization. In the present prediction model, however, the hyperparameters were optimized manually, following a trial and error guided process, one variable at a time. This method was followed because it was the most convenient considering the limited computing power available.

2.3. LSTM with Encoder and Decoder

Experiments were performed with a predictive model based on the LSTM with encoder and decoder architecture. The model consists of two LSTMs, in which the first LSTM has the function of processing an input sequence and generating an encoded state. The encoded state compresses the information in the input stream. The second LSTM, called a decoder, uses the encoded state to produce an output sequence. Those input and output sequences can be of different lengths.

This technique has already been used to solve problems such as the prediction of vehicle trajectories based on deep learning [42]. This architecture [43] has shown great performance for tasks of translating from sequence to sequence. LSTM encoder–decoder models have also been proposed for learning tasks such as automatic translation [43,44]. There is the application of this model to solve many practical problems, such as the study of the equipment condition, applications in language translations, among others [45–47].

3. Theoretical Background

The present work uses LSTM networks, considering the referred different studies showing their usefulness for time series predictions [48,49]. The LSTM is a deep learning recurrent neural network architecture that is a variation of traditional recurrent neural networks (RNNs). It was introduced by Hochreiter and Schmidhuber in 1997. The most popular version is a modification refined by many works in the literature [50,51], which is called vanilla LSTM (hereinafter referred to as LSTM). The LSTM is excellent at handling time series data only with its network parameters. For example, weights and polarization are adjusted or optimized [52]. The primary modification of the LSTM when compared to the RNN architecture is the structure of the hidden layer [53]. The LSTM model is a powerful type of recurrent neural network (RNN), capable of learning long-term dependencies [54]. They became popular due to their power of representation and effectiveness in capturing long-term dependencies [55].

Many networks showed instability when dealing with exploding or vanishing gradient problems during learning. Those problems happen when the gradient of the error is too large or too small. If it is too large, it overflows and the errors cannot propagate properly through different layers during learning. If it is too small, it vanishes and the network does not learn. Different methods were proposed to solve those problems, known as a kind of of "door control" that is used in RNN models. For example, Gated Recurrent unit (GRU) algorithms [56,57], as the LSTMs [58,59], are to a large extent immune to the gradient problems and learn well.

The LSTM network structure is based on three ports whose function is to regulate the flow. Those ports are called the entrance door, the forget gate, and the exit door. The main port of entry is to regulate the entry of new memory data; the forget gate has the function of regulating the storage time in the network memory and the output port intends to regulate how much the value retained in memory influences the activation of the output block [60].

Kong et al. demonstrate some relevant conclusions such as (1) LSTM has a good predictive capacity; (2) their use can significantly improve the profit of service providers, so there is an opportunity when it comes to exploring the forecast in real time [61]. LSTM networks are the *de facto* gold standard for deep learning algorithms for analyzing time series data [55].

Figure 1 shows the internal architecture of an LSTM unit cell. According to [62,63], the internal calculation formulae of the LSTM unit are defined as follows:

$$i_t = \sigma(x_t U^i + h_{t-1} W^i + b_i) \tag{1}$$

$$f_t = \sigma(x_t U^f + h_{t-1} W^f + b_f) \tag{2}$$

$$o_t = \sigma(x_t U^o + h_{t-1} W^o + b_o) \tag{3}$$

$$a_t = tan(x_t U^C + h_{t-1} W^C + b_C) \tag{4}$$

where U^i, U^f, U^o and $U^C$are the weight matrices for mapping the current input layer on three ports and the state of the current input cell.

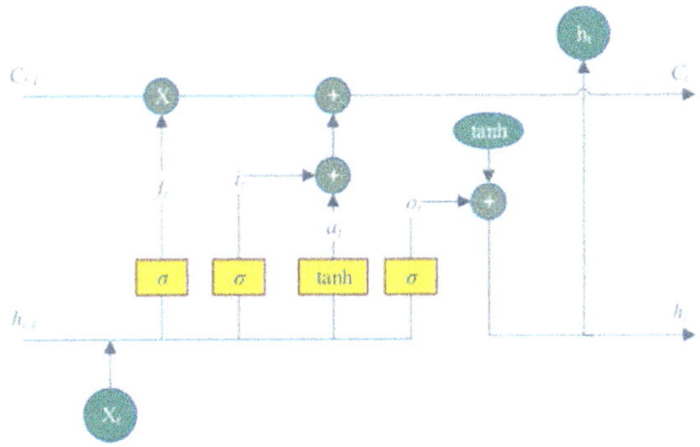

Figure 1. Detailed layout of a long short-term memory unit [63].

W^i, W^f, W^o and W^C are the weight matrices for mapping the previous output layer on three ports and the current state of the input cell. b_f, b_i, b_o, and b_c are polarization vectors for calculating the state of the door and the input cell. σ is the gate activation function, which is normally a sigmoid function. *tan* is the hyperbolic tangent function which is the activation function for the current state of the input cell.

Then, the current state of the output cell and the output layer can be calculated using the following equations.

$$C_t = \sigma(f_t \times C_{t-1} + i_t \times a_t) \tag{5}$$

$$h_t = tanh(C_t) \times o_t \tag{6}$$

To assess the quality of the prediction model, one of the most popular metrics is the Root Mean Square Error (RMSE), which is given by Equation (7):

$$RMSE = \sqrt{\frac{1}{n} \sum_{t=1}^{n} (Y_t - \hat{Y})^2} \tag{7}$$

where Y_t represents the desired (real) value and $\hat{Y}$ is the predicted (obtained from the model) value. The difference between Y and $\hat{Y}$ is the error between the value expected to obtain and the value actually obtained from the network. n represents the number of samples used in the test set.

The RMSE, however, is an absolute error. Therefore, there are also the Mean Absolute Percentage Error (MAPE) and the Mean Absolute Error (MAE). Those errors are given by the following formulae:

$$MAE = \frac{1}{n}\sum_{t=1}^{n}|Y_t - \hat{Y}_t| \quad (8)$$

$$MAPE = \frac{1}{n}\sum_{t=1}^{n}\frac{|Y_t - \hat{Y}_t|}{|Y_t|} \quad (9)$$

where Y_t represents the real value, $\hat{Y}_t$ the predicted value and n represents the total number of samples.

4. Data Preparation

Data are key to developing efficient modeling and planning. However, to be valuable, data need to be processed and structured before being analyzed.

4.1. The Problem

The main goal of the present work is to predict potential failures in an industrial drying press before they happen. Data come from six sensors installed in the press. Those sensors monitor the operation of the press, with a sampling period of one minute. The monitored variables are: (1) electric current intensity; (2) oil level at the hydraulic unit; (3) VAT pressure; (4) rotation speed; (5) temperature in the hydraulic unit; and (6) torque. The dataset contains six time series, one for each sensor, with the values stored in the database from 2016 to August 2020.

Figure 2 shows a plot of the six time series, before any processing is applied. These data present some upper and lower extremes, which may be discrepant data. Those discrepant samples may be due to reading errors or periods when the equipment was off or in another atypical state.

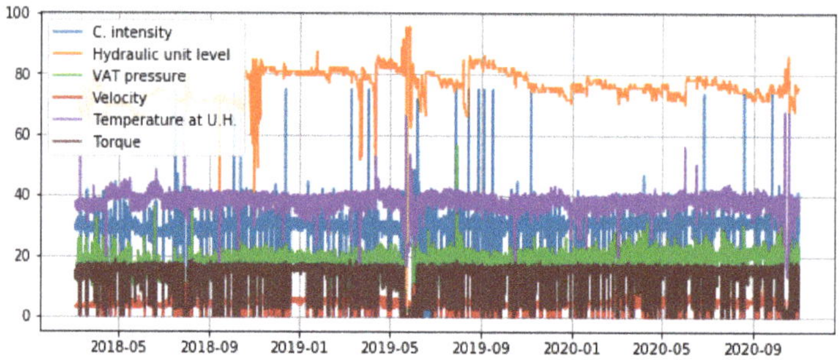

Figure 2. Plot of the original dataset values. The variables are electric current intensity, hydraulic unit oil level, VAT pressure, motor velocity, temperature at the hydraulic unit, and torque.

Some of the samples, such as those when the equipment was off but the sensors were still reading, can compromise the training of the machine learning models to be developed. Table 1 shows some statistical parameters such as mean, standard deviation (std), minimum, third quantiles, and maximum value.

Table 1. Statistical parameters of the dataset variables, before processing: C. intensity, hydraulic unit oil level, torque, VAT pressure, velocity, and temperature.

	C. Intensity	Hydraulic	Torque	VAT	Velocity	Temperature
mean	30.26	75.90	15.28	18.25	4.59	38.22
std	1.36	4.54	0.69	2.67	0.98	1.62
min	26.34	62.93	13.59	9.67	1.27	33.19
Q_1—25%	29.30	72.86	14.90	17.13	3.92	37.17
Q_2—50%	30.46	75.53	15.43	18.72	4.57	38.33
Q_3—75%	31.28	79.52	15.78	19.97	5.28	39.35
max	34.26	88.97	17.09	26.17	7.87	43.10

4.2. Cleaning Discrepant Data

In order to facilitate the training process, discrepant samples were identified and removed using the quantiles method. Samples which are beyond the $Q_1 - 3 \times std$ or $Q_3 + 3 \times std$ are replaced by the mean value. The extreme values were replaced with the average. Figure 3 shows the same variables after discrepant data samples were removed.

As the figure shows, the lines are now smoother and easier to read. Figure 4 shows that the samples are evenly distributed after the withdrawal of discrepant data.

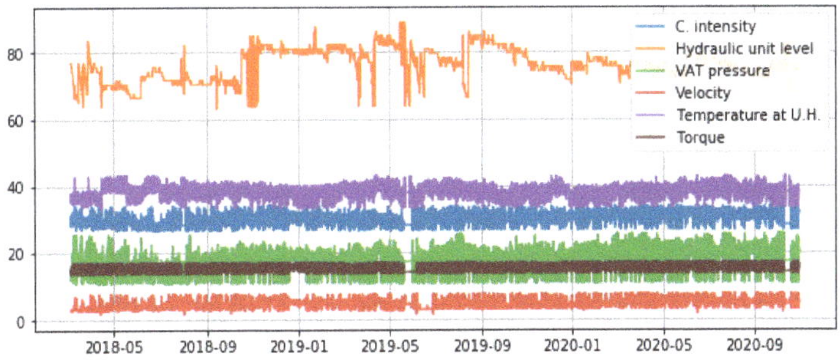

Figure 3. Plot of the dataset values after cleaning discrepant data. The variables are current intensity, hydraulic unit oil level, VAT pressure, velocity, temperature, and torque.

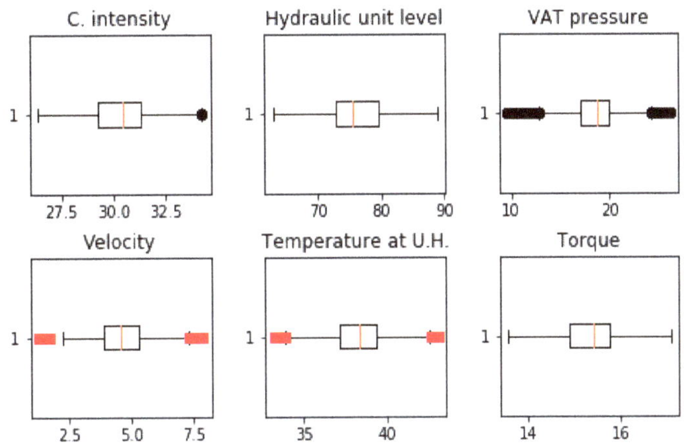

Figure 4. Distribution of data points of all the sensors, with lowly and highly discrepant data cleaned.

The predictive models to be used are robust and tolerant to noise. However, the cleaner data are expected to show better results. As an example, a provisional experiment to train a neural network LSTM model with a historical window of 70 samples and 40 LSTM unit cells showed higher and undetermined errors. The model was not able to learn or predict some variables, as shown in Table 2. With clean data, there were better and determinable results, as shown in Table 3. The tables show the MAPE and MAE for all input variables, as determined in the test set. They also show the RMSE, as calculated in the train and test sets, globally for all variables.

Table 2. Prediction results without cleaning discrepant data in the database, with a window of 70 samples and 40 LSTM units.

			Window 70 Days			
	C. Intensity	**Hydraulic**	**Torque**	**VAT**	**Velocity**	**Temperature**
MAPE	inf	8.46	inf	98.19	inf	11.59
MAE	3.52	6.57	24.73	10.53	14.88	4.21
	Train	**Test**				
RMSE	79.52	79.64				

Table 3. Forecast results with treatments in the database with 40 LSTM units.

			Window 70 Days			
	C. Intensity	**Hydraulic**	**Torque**	**VAT**	**Velocity**	**Temperature**
MAPE	2.52	3.02	2.44	13.10	inf	2.48
MAE	0.76	2.28	0.37	1.32	0.57	0.94
	Train	**Test**				
RMSE	1.71	1.97				

5. Experiments and Results

Experiments were performed with the aim of validating the model that has the best performance in predicting data from the industrial press. The tests are divided into two subsections, first with resampling of data to one sample per day and then with resampling for a sample each 12 h.

5.1. LSTM Models and Dataset Partition

After processing the data, experiments were performed with an LSTM model. The model included an encoder and decoder, with one hidden LSTM layer in the middle and a dense layer at the output. The model was used to train and predict, with six variables that represent data coming from the paper press sensors. The goal was to forecast the value of those variables with the highest possible level of confidence so that it brings added benefits in predictive maintenance.

Figure 5 describes the architecture of one of the network models used. The models were implemented in Python using the TensorFlow library and Keras.

The experiments were performed aiming to obtain a prediction for all variables one month in advance, from a window of a number of past samples.

The LSTM models received, as an input, a sequence consisting of the composition of a number of samples for each variable. The number of samples depended on the window size and the resampling rate used. The output sequence is composed of the values predicted for each of the variables.

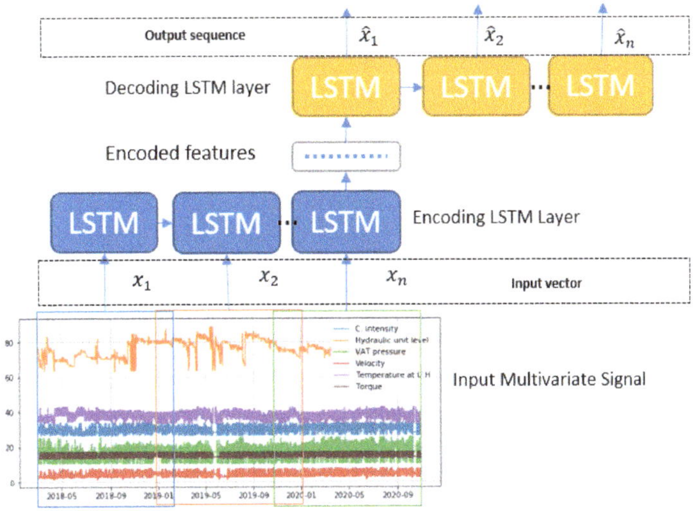

Figure 5. Model summary of one of the LSTM networks used. The model receives a window of n samples of each variable and predicts the value of those variables as predicted 30 days ahead.

To train and test the models, the dataset was divided into train and test subsets. Validation was performed using the test set, but those samples were not incorporated into the training set. The training set contained 85% of the samples and the test set the remaining 15% of samples. These values are adequate for convergence during learning. As an example, Figure 6 shows a learning curve for a model with 70 units in the middle layer and a window of 30 lag samples. The figure shows that learning converges and takes fewer than 10 epochs. The remainder experiments were performed using 100 epochs.

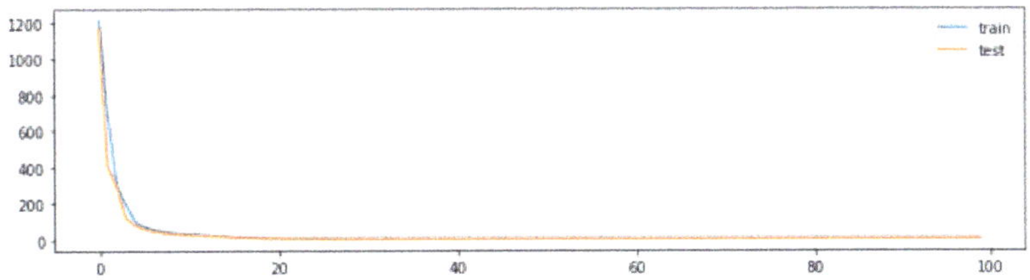

Figure 6. Example of learning curve, showing the loss measured during training of an LSTM model.

5.2. Experiments to Determine Historical Window Size and Number of LSTM Units Using One Sample per Day

The first experiments performed aimed to determine the best window size to use. The smaller the window, the smaller and faster the model that can be used. However, if the window is too small, it may be insufficient to make accurate predictions.

The original dataset had 1,445,760 data points, which is very large and would require a lot of memory and time to train and test. The experiments were performed after downsampling the data, so that there is only one sample per day. That sample is the average of 1004 original samples. The downsampled dataset is, therefore, less than the one thousand of the original dataset.

The results are measured in the test set. The figure above shows the MAPE and MAE measured for each variable. It also shows the global RMSE measured globally for the train and test sets.

As Figure 7 shows, models with windows of 40 and 50 samples allow better learning and produce smaller prediction errors.

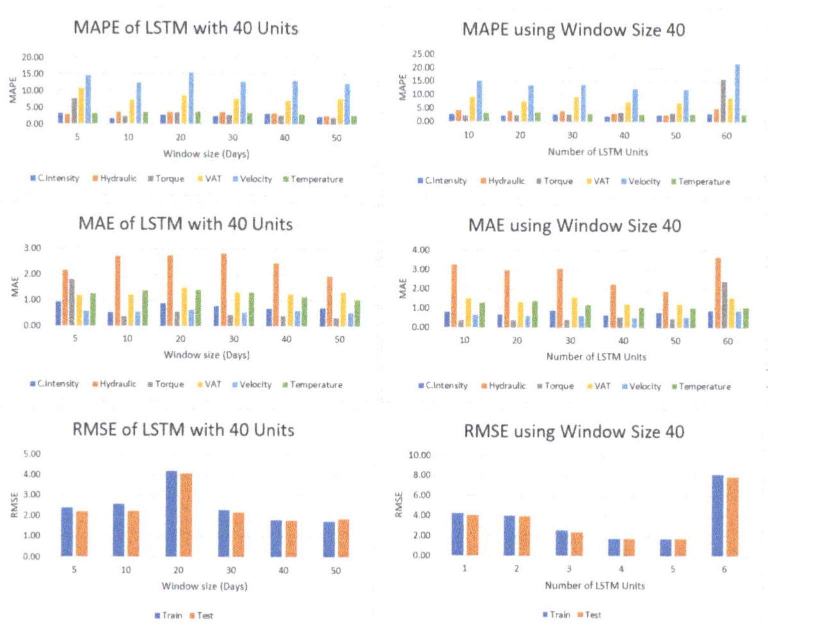

Figure 7. Results obtained with a different number of LSTM cells in the hidden layer, as well as different sliding window sizes, to predict values 30 days in advance with downsampling to one sample per day.

Additional experiments were performed to determine the best size for the number of cells in the hidden layer. For those experiments, a window of 40 historical samples was used, relying on the results of the previous experiments.

Figure 7 shows the results obtained for experiments with a window of 40 days and different numbers of hidden cells. As the results show, the model with the best performance is the one with 50 hidden cells.

After the results of the first experiments with one sample per day, additional experiments were conducted to determine if there was any considerable loss in downsampling from one sample per minute to one sample per day. A first experiment was performed, which consisted of halving the downsampling period from 24 to just 12 h. Therefore, the dataset doubled in size, since it contained two samples per day instead of just one.

5.3. Experiments to Determine Historical Window Size and Number of Unit LSTMs Using Two Samples per Day

According to the results shown in Figure 8, it is concluded that a window of 10 days (20 samples) shows the best performance. This shows that the model can exhibit approximately the same performance with even fewer input samples when compared to the models above. The models used for those experiments had 20 cells in the hidden layer.

Once the impact of the window size was determined, additional experiments were performed to gain a better insight into the impact of using more or less cells in the hidden layer. Figure 8 shows results of using different numbers of cells.

Figure 8. Results obtained with a different number of cells in the hidden layer, also using different window samples to predict values 30 days in advance with resampling for the two samples for a day.

5.4. Plot of One Result

Figure 9 shows plots of the results obtained using the model using 40 units in the hidden layer and a 10-day window of samples. As the figure shows, the forecasts in general follow the actual signals most of the time. However, there are still some areas where the actual signal diverges a small percentage from the prediction, namely for velocity and temperature. Most of the differences may be due to behaviors that are still difficult to capture due to the small dimension of the dataset. As more data will be collected, the neural models will probably be able to capture more patterns and offer more accurate predictions.

In addition to the graphs shown in Figure 9, in Tables 4 and 5, the magnitudes of the RMSE errors in the training set and test set are also presented. They were measured in the model validation dataset.

Table 4. The magnitude of RMSE errors in the test and training set, using one sample per day.

Window Size (Days)	Train	Test	Units	Train	Test
5	2.39	2.20	10	4.23	4.07
10	2.57	2.24	20	3.99	3.93
20	4.21	4.09	30	2.52	2.35
30	2.31	2.19	40	1.68	1.70
40	1.81	1.77	50	1.66	1.70
50	1.74	1.86	60	8.14	7.85

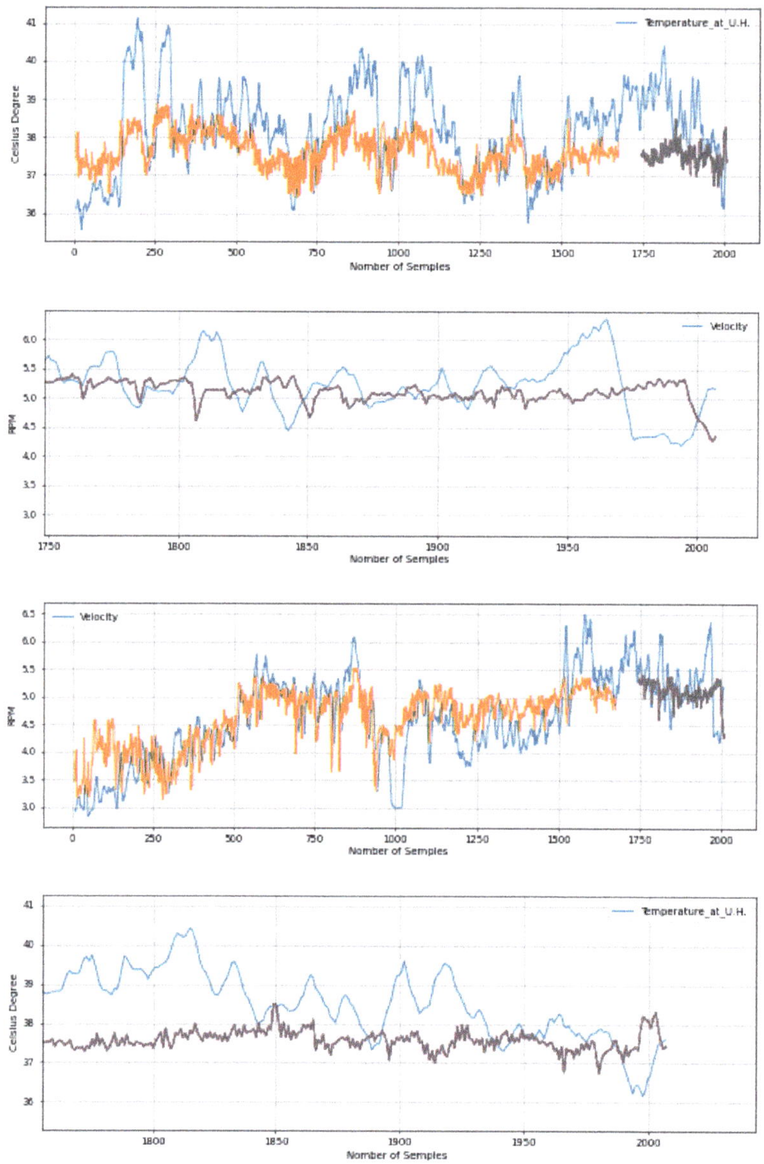

Figure 9. Variable forecast with a window of samples of 10 days, sampling rate two samples per day, and a network model with 50 units in the hidden layer. The blue lines show the actual value. The orange lines show the predictions during the training set and the gray lines show the predictions in the test set.

Table 5. The magnitude of RMSE errors in the test and training set, using two samples per day.

Window Size (Days)	Train	Test	Units	Train	Test
5	8.91	8.87	10	2.07	1.99
10	1.80	1.61	20	1.82	1.91
20	3.29	3.23	30	1.65	1.59
30	1.98	1.94	40	1.58	1.41
40	2.07	1.98	50	1.61	1.42
50	4.32	4.16	60	1.64	1.46

6. Discussion

Anticipating industrial equipment's future behavior is a goal that has been long sought after, for it allows predictive maintenance to perform the right actions at the right time. Therefore, the application of time series and other artificial intelligence models to forecast the equipment's state is a new and growing area of interest.

The present research uses a dataset of approximately 2.5 years of data of an industrial paper press. A procedure to clean the data is proposed and different experiments are described to use a deep neural model based on LSTM recurrent networks.

The method proposed is going to be applied in other industrial presses, aiming to improve predictive maintenance. Based on the state of the art and experiments, this architecture presents a good versatility, depending of course on the quality of data and hyperparameter settings.

The results show that it is possible to optimize neural models to forecast future values 30 days in advance. The model experimented uses as input a vector consisting of concatenation of a number of samples of all variables. The output is a vector with the predictions of all samples too. The performance of the models is generally better for some variables and worse for others. Those differences will be dealt with in future work.

An important conclusion is that the downsampling used might have been too aggressive. Experiments were performed using one sample per day and two samples per day. The models trained with two samples per day showed a better performance. Hence, more resolution is better for reducing errors and may allow for better learning. That is achieved at the cost of additional processing power. This is also another research question which will be dealt with in future work.

7. Conclusions

Predicting industrial machines' future behaviors is key for predictive maintenance success. The present research aims to find prediction models adequate for anticipating the future behavior of industrial equipment with good certainty.

The predictive model used was based on LSTM networks, with encoding and decoding layers as the input and output, respectively. In this study, different data pre-processing techniques, network architectures, and hyperparameters were tested, in order to determine the best models.

The predictive model used was based on LSTM network, with encoding and decoding layers as the input and output, respectively.

The results show that the model proposed is able to learn and forecast the behavior of the six variables studied: torque, pressure, current intensity, velocity, oil level and temperature. The best results were obtained using a window of samples of the last 10 days at two samples per day. The MAPE errors varied in the range of 2 to 17% for one of the best models for different variables.

Future work includes additional experiments to determine the optimal sampling rate and stabilize the results for optimal performance with all the variables. The predicted results will also be used to determine an expected probability of failure, using classification models. Other methods may also be used to deal with discrepant data. Later, the models developed will also be applied to other equipment.

Author Contributions: Conceptualization, J.T.F., A.M.C., M.M.; methodology, J.T.F. and M.M.; software, B.C.M. and M.M.; validation, J.T.F. and M.M.; formal analysis, J.T.F. and M.M.; investigation, B.C.M. and M.M.; resources, T.F., A.M.C. and M.M.; writing—original draft preparation, B.C.M.; writing—review and editing, J.T.F. and M.M.; project administration, J.T.F. and A.M.C.; funding acquisition, J.T.F. and A.M.C. All authors have read and agreed to the published version of the manuscript.

Funding: The research leading to these results has received funding from the European Union's Horizon 2020 research and innovation programme under the Marie Sklodowvska-Curie grant agreement 871284 project SSHARE and the European Regional Development Fund (ERDF) through the Operational Programme for Competitiveness and Internationalization (COMPETE 2020), under Project POCI-01-0145-FEDER-029494, and by National Funds through the FCT—Portuguese Foundation for Science and Technology, under Projects PTDC/EEI-EEE/29494/2017, UIDB/04131/2020, and UIDP/04131/2020.

Acknowledgments: This research is sponsored by FEDER funds through the program COMPETE—Programa Operacional Factores de Competitividade—and by national funds through FCT—Fundação para a Ciência e a Tecnologia—under the project UIDB/00285/2020. This work was produced with the support of INCD funded by FCT and FEDER under the project 01/SAICT/2016 nº 022153.

Conflicts of Interest: The authors declare no conflict of interest.

Abbreviations

The following abbreviations are used in this manuscript:

ARMA	Autoregressive Integrated Moving Average
CNN	Convolution Neural Networks
LSTM	Long Short-Term Memory
MAE	Mean Absolute Error
MAPE	Mean Absolute Percentage Error
RMSE	Root Mean Square Error
RNN	Recurrent Neural Networks

References

1. Sahal, R.; Breslin, J.; Ali, M. Big data and stream processing platforms for Industry 4.0 requirements mapping for a predictive maintenance use case. *J. Manuf. Syst.* **2020**, *54*, 138–151. [CrossRef]
2. Ahmed, M.S.; Cook, A.R. *Analysis of Freeway Traffic Time-Series Data by Using Box-Jenkins Techniques*; Transportation Research Board: Washington, DC, USA, 2020; ISBN 9780309029728.
3. Majeed, A.; Zhang, Y.; Ren, S.; Lv, J.; Peng, T.; Waqar, S.; Yin, E. A big data-driven framework for sustainable and smart additive manufacturing. *Robot. Comput. Integr. Manuf.* **2021**, *67*, 102026. [CrossRef]
4. Ferreiro, S.; Konde, E.; Fernández, S.; Prado, A. Industry 4.0: Predictive intelligent maintenance for production equipment. In *European Conference of the Prognostics and Health Management Society*; 2016; pp. 1–8. Available online: https://www.semanticscholar.org/paper/INDUSTRY-4-.-0-%3A-Predictive-Intelligent-Maintenance-Ferreiro-Konde/638c2b72a747ea4b82e098572be820083dca9c7a (accessed on 25 June 2021).
5. Wang, K. Intelligent predictive maintenance (IPdM) system—Industry 4.0 scenario. *WIT Trans. Eng. Sci.* **2016**, *113*, 259–268.
6. Yu, W.; Dillon, T.; Mostafa, F.; Rahayu, W.; Liu, Y. A global manufacturing big data ecosystem for fault detection in predictive maintenance. *IEEE Trans. Ind. Inform.* **2020**, *16*, 183–192. [CrossRef]
7. Pais, E.; Farinha, J.T.; Cardoso, A.J.M.; Raposo, H. Optimizing the Life Cycle of Physical Assets—A Review. *WSEAS Trans. Syst. Control* **2020**, *15*, 417–430. [CrossRef]
8. Martins, A.B.; Torres Farinha, J.; Marques Cardoso, A. Calibration and Certification of Industrial Sensors—A Global Review. *WSEAS Trans. Syst. Control* **2020**, *15*, 394–416. [CrossRef]
9. Rodrigues, J., Cost, I.; Farinha, J.; Mendes, M.; Margalho, L. Predicting motor oil condition using artificial neural networks and principal component analysis. *Eksploat. Niezawodn.* **2020**, *22*, 440–448. [CrossRef]
10. Torres Farinha, J. *Asset Maintenance Engineering Methodologies*; CRC Press: Boca Raton, FL, USA, 2018.
11. Chen, M.; Tseng, H. An approach to design of maintenance float systems. *Integr. Manuf.* **2003**, *14*, 458–467.
12. Daniyan, I.; Mpofu, K.; Oyesola, M.; Ramatsetse, B.; Adeodu, A. Artificial intelligence for predictive maintenance in the railcar learning factories. *Procedia Manuf.* **2020**, *45*, 13–18. [CrossRef]
13. Hsu, Y.Y.; Tung, T.T.; Yeh, H.C.; Lu, C.N. Two-Stage Artificial Neural Network Model for Short-Term Load Forecasting. *IFAC-PapersOnLine* **2018**, *51*, 678–683. [CrossRef]
14. Balduíno, M.; Torres Farinha, J.; Marques Cardoso, A. Production Optimization versus Asset Availability—A Review. *WSEAS Trans. Syst. Control* **2020**, *15*, 320–332. [CrossRef]

15. Jimenez, V.J.; Bouhmala, N.; Gausdal, A.H. Developing a predictive maintenance model for vessel machinery. *J. Ocean. Eng. Sci.* **2020**, *5*, 358–386. [CrossRef]
16. Ayvaz, S.; Alpay, K. Predictive maintenance system for production lines in manufacturing: A machine learning approach using IoT data in real-time. *Expert Syst. Appl.* **2021**, *173*, 114598. [CrossRef]
17. Yu, Z.; Moirangthem, D.S.; Lee, M. Continuous Timescale Long-Short Term Memory Neural Network for Human Intent Understanding. *Front. Neurorobot.* **2017**, *11*, 42. [CrossRef]
18. Aydin, O.; Guldamlasioglu, S. Using LSTM networks to predict engine condition on large scale data processing framework. In Proceedings of the 2017 4th International Conference on Electrical and Electronic Engineering (ICEEE), Ankara, Turkey, 8–10 April 2017; pp. 281–285. [CrossRef]
19. Wang, Q.; Bu, S.; He, Z. Achieving Predictive and Proactive Maintenance for High-Speed Railway Power Equipment with LSTM-RNN. *IEEE Trans. Ind. Inform.* **2020**, *16*, 6509–6517. [CrossRef]
20. Bruneo, D.; De Vita, F. On the Use of LSTM Networks for Predictive Maintenance in Smart Industries. In Proceedings of the 2019 IEEE International Conference on Smart Computing (SMARTCOMP), Washington, DC, USA, 12–15 June 2019; pp. 241–248. [CrossRef]
21. Dong, D.; Li, X.Y.; Sun, F.Q. Life prediction of jet engines based on LSTM-recurrent neural networks. In Proceedings of the 2017 Prognostics and System Health Management Conference (PHM-Harbin), Harbin, China, 9–12 July 2017; pp. 1–6. [CrossRef]
22. Bampoula, X.; Siaterlis, G.; Nikolakis, N.; Alexopoulos, K. A Deep Learning Model for Predictive Maintenance in Cyber-Physical Production Systems Using LSTM Autoencoders. *Sensors* **2021**, *21*, 972. [CrossRef]
23. Mathew, V.; Toby, T.; Singh, V.; Rao, B.M.; Kumar, M.G. Prediction of Remaining Useful Lifetime (RUL) of turbofan engine using machine learning. In Proceedings of the 2017 IEEE International Conference on Circuits and Systems (ICCS), Thiruvananthapuram, India, 20–21 December 2017; pp. 306–311. [CrossRef]
24. Düdükçü, H.V.; Taşkıran, M.; Kahraman, N. LSTM and WaveNet Implementation for Predictive Maintenance of Turbofan Engines. In Proceedings of the 2020 IEEE 20th International Symposium on Computational Intelligence and Informatics (CINTI), Budapest, Hungary, 5–7 November 2020; pp. 000151–000156. [CrossRef]
25. Essien, A.; Giannetti, C. A Deep Learning Model for Smart Manufacturing Using Convolutional LSTM Neural Network Autoencoders. *IEEE Trans. Ind. Inform.* **2020**, *16*, 6069–6078. [CrossRef]
26. Schmidhuber, J. Deep learning in neural networks: An overview. *Neural Netw.* **2015**, *61*, 85–117. [CrossRef]
27. Beshr, A.; Zarzoura, F. Using artificial neural networks for GNSS observations analysis and displacement prediction of suspension highway bridge. *Innov. Infrastruct. Solut.* **2021**, *6*. [CrossRef]
28. Sak, H.; Senior, A.; Beaufays, F. Long Short-Term Memory Based Recurrent Neural Network Architectures for Large Vocabulary Speech Recognition. *arXiv* **2014**, arXiv:1402.1128.
29. Chen, Z.; Liu, Y.; Liu, S. Mechanical state prediction based on LSTM neural netwok. In Proceedings of the 2017 36th Chinese Control Conference (CCC), Dalian, China, 26–28 July 2017; pp. 3876–3881. [CrossRef]
30. Ghosh, S.; Vinyals, O.; Strope, B.; Roy, S.; Dean, T.; Heck, L. Contextual LSTM (CLSTM) models for Large scale NLP tasks. *arXiv* **2016**, arXiv:1602.06291.
31. Shahid, F.; Zameer, A.; Muneeb, M. A novel genetic LSTM model for wind power forecast. *Energy* **2021**, *223*, 120069. [CrossRef]
32. Guo, J.; Xie, Z.; Qin, Y.; Jia, L.; Wang, Y. Short-Term Abnormal Passenger Flow Prediction Based on the Fusion of SVR and LSTM. *IEEE Access* **2019**, *7*, 42946–42955. [CrossRef]
33. Ren, L.; Dong, J.; Wang, X.; Meng, Z.; Zhao, L.; Deen, M. A Data-Driven Auto-CNN-LSTM Prediction Model for Lithium-Ion Battery Remaining Useful Life. *IEEE Trans. Ind. Inform.* **2021**, *17*, 3478–3487. [CrossRef]
34. Niu, K.; Zhang, H.; Zhou, T.; Cheng, C.; Wang, C. A Novel Spatio-Temporal Model for City-Scale Traffic Speed Prediction. *IEEE Access* **2019**, *7*, 30050–30057. [CrossRef]
35. Feng, M.; Zheng, J.; Ren, J.; Hussain, A.; Li, X.; Xi, Y.; Liu, Q. Big Data Analytics and Mining for Effective Visualization and Trends Forecasting of Crime Data. *IEEE Access* **2019**, *7*, 106111–106123. [CrossRef]
36. Palangi, H.; Deng, L.; Shen, Y.; Gao, J.; He, X.; Chen, J.; Song, X.; Ward, R. Deep Sentence Embedding Using Long Short-Term Memory Networks: Analysis and Application to Information Retrieval. *IEEE/ACM Trans. Audio Speech Lang. Process.* **2016**, *24*, 694–707. [CrossRef]
37. Rumelhart, D.E.; Hinton, G.E.; Williams, R.J. Learning representations by back-propagating errors. *Nature* **1986**, *323*, 533–536. [CrossRef]
38. Mao, Y.; Qin, G.; Ni, P.; Liu, Q. Analysis of road traffic speed in Kunming plateau mountains: A fusion PSO-LSTM algorithm. *Int. J. Urban Sci.* **2021**, 1–21. [CrossRef]
39. Hutter, F.; Lücke, J.; Schmidt-Thieme, L. Beyond Manual Tuning of Hyperparameters. *KI Künstliche Intell.* **2015**, *29*, 329–337. [CrossRef]
40. Khalid, R.; Javaid, N. A survey on hyperparameters optimization algorithms of forecasting models in smart grid. *Sustain. Cities Soc.* **2020**, *61*, 102275. [CrossRef]
41. Hutter, F.; Hoos, H.; Leyton-Brown, K. An Efficient Approach for Assessing Hyperparameter Importance. In Proceedings of the 31st International Conference on Machine Learning, Beijing, China, 21–26 June 2014; pp. 754–762.

42. Park, S.H.; Kim, B.; Kang, C.M.; Chung, C.C.; Choi, J.W. Sequence-to-Sequence Prediction of Vehicle Trajectory via LSTM Encoder-Decoder Architecture. In Proceedings of the 2018 IEEE Intelligent Vehicles Symposium (IV), Changshu, China, 26–30 June 2018; pp. 1672–1678. [CrossRef]
43. Cho, K.; van Merrienboer, B.; Gülçehre, Ç.; Bougares, F.; Schwenk, H.; Bengio, Y. Learning Phrase Representations using RNN Encoder-Decoder for Statistical Machine Translation. *arXiv* **2014**, arXiv:1406.1078.
44. Sutskever, I.; Vinyals, O.; Le, Q.V. Sequence to Sequence Learning with Neural Networks. *arXiv* **2014**, arXiv:1409.3215.
45. Wang, T.; Chen, P.; Amaral, K.; Qiang, J. An Experimental Study of LSTM Encoder-Decoder Model for Text Simplification. *arXiv* **2016**, arXiv:1609.03663.
46. Bengio, S.; Vinyals, O.; Jaitly, N.; Shazeer, N. Scheduled Sampling for Sequence Prediction with Recurrent Neural Networks. *arXiv* **2015**, arXiv:1506.03099.
47. Du, S.; Li, T.; Yang, Y.; Horng, S.J. Multivariate time series forecasting via attention-based encoder–decoder framework. *Neurocomputing* **2020**, *388*, 269–279. [CrossRef]
48. Gers, F.A.; Eck, D.; Schmidhuber, J. Applying LSTM to Time Series Predictable Through Time-Window Approaches. In *Neural Nets WIRN Vietri-01*; Tagliaferri, R., Marinaro, M., Eds.; Perspectives in Neural Computing; Springer: Berlin/Heidelberg, Germany, 2002; pp. 193–200._20. [CrossRef]
49. Meng, Q.; Wang, H.; He, M.; Gu, J.; Qi, J.; Yang, L. Displacement prediction of water-induced landslides using a recurrent deep learning model. *Eur. J. Environ. Civ. Eng.* **2020**. [CrossRef]
50. Sarikaya, R.; Hinton, G.E.; Deoras, A. Application of Deep Belief Networks for Natural Language Understanding. *IEEE/ACM Trans. Audio Speech Lang. Process.* **2014**, *22*, 778–784. [CrossRef]
51. Sundermeyer, M.; Schlüter, R.; Ney, H. LSTM neural networks for language modeling. In Proceedings of the Thirteenth Annual Conference of the International Speech Communication Association, Portland, OR, USA, 9–13 September 2012.
52. Hu, Y.; Sun, X.; Nie, X.; Li, Y.; Liu, L. An Enhanced LSTM for Trend Following of Time Series. *IEEE Access* **2019**, *7*, 34020–34030. [CrossRef]
53. Gers, F.A.; Schmidhuber, J.; Cummins, F. Learning to Forget: Continual Prediction with LSTM. In Proceedings of the 1999 Ninth International Conference on Artificial Neural Networks ICANN 99 (Conf. Publ. No. 470), Edinburgh, UK, 7–10 September 1999; pp. 850–855. [CrossRef]
54. Greff, K.; Srivastava, R.K.; Koutník, J.; Steunebrink, B.R.; Schmidhuber, J. LSTM: A Search Space Odyssey. *IEEE Trans. Neural Netw. Learn. Syst.* **2017**, *28*, 2222–2232. [CrossRef] [PubMed]
55. Hochreiter, S.; Schmidhuber, J. Long Short-Term Memory. *Neural Comput.* **1997**, *9*, 1735–1780. [CrossRef] [PubMed]
56. Li, C.; Jiang, P.; Zhou, A. Rigorous solution of slope stability under seismic action. *Comput. Geotech.* **2019**, *109*, 99–107. [CrossRef]
57. Li, C.; Hu, B.C.; Hu, D.; Xu, X.F.; Zong, X.C.; Li, J.P.; Wu, M.C. Stereoselective ring-opening of styrene oxide at elevated concentration by Phaseolus vulgaris epoxide hydrolase, PvEH2, in the organic/aqueous biphasic system. *Catal. Commun.* **2019**, *123*, 1–5. [CrossRef]
58. Qin, Y.; Li, K.; Liang, Z.; Lee, B.; Zhang, F.; Gu, Y.; Zhang, L.; Wu, F.; Rodriguez, D. Hybrid forecasting model based on long short term memory network and deep learning neural network for wind signal. *Appl. Energy* **2019**, *236*, 262–272. [CrossRef]
59. Zhang, Z.; Ye, L.; Qin, H.; Liu, Y.; Wang, C.; Yu, X.; Yin, X.; Li, J. Wind speed prediction method using Shared Weight Long Short-Term Memory Network and Gaussian Process Regression. *Appl. Energy* **2019**, *247*, 270–284. [CrossRef]
60. Zhao, R.; Yin, Y.; Shi, Y.; Xue, Z. Intelligent intrusion detection based on federated learning aided long short-term memory. *Phys. Commun.***2020**, *42*, 101157. [CrossRef]
61. Kong, X.; Kong, D.; Bai, L.; Xiao, J. Online pricing of demand response based on long short-term memory and reinforcement learning. *Appl. Energy* **2020**, *271*, 114945. [CrossRef]
62. Li, Y.; Lu, Y. LSTM-BA: DDoS Detection Approach Combining LSTM and Bayes. In Proceedings of the 2019 Seventh International Conference on Advanced Cloud and Big Data (CBD), Suzhou, China, 21–22 September 2019; pp. 180–185. [CrossRef]
63. Alameer, Z.; Fathalla, A.; Li, K.; Ye, H.; Jianhua, Z. Multistep-ahead forecasting of coal prices using a hybrid deep learning model. *Resour. Policy* **2020**, *65*, 101588. [CrossRef]

applied sciences

MDPI

Article

A Conceptual Model Proposal to Assess the Effectiveness of IoT in Sustainability Orientation in Manufacturing Industry: An Environmental and Social Focus

Adriane Cavalieri [1,2,*], João Reis [1,3] and Marlene Amorim [1]

[1] Department of Economics Management Industrial Engineering and Tourism, GOVCOPP, Campus Universitário de Santiago, University of Aveiro, 3810-193 Aveiro, Portugal; reis.joao@ua.pt (J.R.); mamorim@ua.pt (M.A.)

[2] Divisão de Avaliações e Processos Industriais, Instituto Nacional de Tecnologia, Ministério da Ciência, Tecnologia e Inovações, Rio de Janeiro 20081-312, Brazil

[3] Industrial Engineering and Management, EIGeS, Campo Grande, Lusofona University, 1749-024 Lisbon, Portugal

* Correspondence: adriane.cavalieri@int.gov.br

Abstract: The scientific literature reveals that there is a gap oriented towards empirical study of the relationship between the Internet of Things (IoT) and sustainability in manufacturing industries. This paper aims to fill this gap by proposing a new conceptual model (CM) for evaluating the effectiveness of IoT technologies in relation to their orientation towards socio-environmental sustainability and the circular economy approach. The research methodology for developing the CM follows the PRISMA protocol, and the data are obtained from the Web of Science (WoS) and Elsevier Scopus databases, focusing on the relationship between IoT and sustainable manufacturing. The PRISMA methodology results in six articles whose statements contribute to the development of the CM. The statements are identified, categorized and organized from the selected articles and divided into dimensions, namely: IoT technology and environmental and social context. The CM incorporates these dimensions and their constructs and indicators to support the assessment of the effectiveness of IoT technologies in relation to socio-environmental sustainability and the circular economy approach. The result of this study is a CM whose objective is to guide organizations in the use of IoT technologies applied to the production and supply chain, in order to create advances in the field of sustainability and the circular economy. The CM will be validated and applied in a manufacturing industry in the next publication. The paper contributes to management practices as it explores the knowledge of performance measurement and evaluation in the context of IoT, sustainability and the circular economy approach.

Keywords: Internet of Things; sustainable manufacturing; environmental sustainability; social sustainability; circular economy; conceptual model; performance measurement and assessment system; production process; supply chain

Citation: Cavalieri, A.; Reis, J.; Amorim, M. A Conceptual Model Proposal to Assess the Effectiveness of IoT in Sustainability Orientation in Manufacturing Industry: An Environmental and Social Focus. *Appl. Sci.* **2022**, *12*, 5661. https://doi.org/10.3390/app12115661

Academic Editor: Luis Javier Garcia Villalba

Received: 2 May 2022
Accepted: 31 May 2022
Published: 2 June 2022

1. Introduction

Individuals, society and governments are pushing the manufacturing industry towards the triple bottom line (TBL), which relates to social, economic and environmental sustainability, aiming to protect present and future generations. A sustainable orientation must define the commitment of the manufacturing industries, where the approach of eco-friendly processes, products and services is no longer sufficient from an economic sustainability perspective [1].

Manufacturing can be divided into discrete manufacturing, process and service industries, including activities from customer to factory and vice versa, throughout the manufacturing chain. Manufacturing is of prime importance for the maintenance of the quality of human life and for service and product delivery, contributing to the world economy. On the other hand, from the point of view of environmental and social sustainability, manufacturing has a major impact on the ecosystem and on working conditions, taking into account the consumption of raw material and energy, the greenhouse effect, the generation of waste, the release of toxic materials, floating plastic and product end-of-life implications [2].

The TBL was proposed by Elkington in an article published in 1998 [3]. The author argues that manufacturing industries should focus on the relationship between economic performance (such as measures of the company's financial performance), environmental performance (aspects such as minimizing environmental waste and improving efficient consumption of resources) and social performance (relating to the well-being of employees and the community) [4]. The approach that develops manufacturing industries towards the TBL is known as sustainable manufacturing (SM) [5].

The definition of SM provided by the US Department of Commerce on the OECD website is: "Manufacturing processes that minimize negative environmental impacts, conserve energy and natural resources, are safe for employees, communities and consumers and are economically sound" [6] (p. 1). However, the Organization for Economic Co-operation and Development (OECD) notes that there is no single common definition of SM. This is an approach oriented towards reducing business risks in any manufacturing operation and maximizing the opportunities that arise from improvements in its processes and products [7]. The OECD website also mentions that in 2011, a Sustainable Manufacturing Toolkit was launched that aimed "to provide a practical starting point for businesses around the world to improve the efficiency of their production processes and products in a way to contribute to sustainable development and green growth" [7] (p. 1).

Since manufacturing is the source of all goods for life, transportation, entertainment, production, safety and health, SM is one of the most important issues for sustainable development [2]. The implementation of SM depends on the alignment of the strategic business plan with the balance between social, economic and environmental sustainability to achieve real benefits from its adoption. However, most of a company's focus is on monetary gains, without a commitment to environmental protection and societal well-being [5].

Despite the fact that economic performance continues to be the dominant objective of companies, they have begun to realize the importance of social issues from the perspective of sustainability. For this reason, they adopt specific practices and measures to obtain a competitive advantage within that perspective, using methods such as customer management, the sharing of information, the practice of transparency and traceability, corporate sustainability reports, corporate social involvement, standardization and monitoring, life cycle assessment, well-being and equity of employees, job stability, sustainable supplier management and the sustainable development of partners [4].

In fact, the technology used in sustainable manufacturing enhances sustainability and represents the most positive contribution to environmental, social and economic prospects [2]. In the context of recent literature, the advent of Industry 4.0, made possible by digital technologies such as the Internet of Things, big data and analytics and artificial intelligence, is perceived as a facilitator of sustainable manufacturing practices and sustainability performance [8–10]. On the other hand, the authors in [8–10] also highlighted some environmental and social sustainability gaps.

There are only a few peer-reviewed articles that have explored Industry 4.0 from a sustainability point of view, highlighting themes such as critical success factors for environmentally sustainable manufacturing, developing a framework for a sustainable Industry 4.0, digitization and the circular economy and cloud manufacturing as an alternative for sustainable manufacturing [10]. Some studies that refer to the relationship between digital technologies (Internet of Things, cloud computing, big data and analytics) and sustainability have inconsistent conclusions, mainly in terms of environmental sustainability, as they have mostly been based on a qualitative view [9].

There is a lack of studies on the effect of each Industry 4.0 technology on the circular economy approach, with respect to themes such as input reduction, consumption, reuse, recovery, recycling and waste and emissions reduction [8]. Moreover, researchers should explore the benefits and challenges within organizations using open-ended or multiple-choice research questions on how to implement and adopt the Internet of Things (IoT) in supply chains, capturing the practical insights of practitioners who are directly involved in IoT adoption and operations [11]. Future work should limit data collection by applying the terms IoT and sustainable intelligent manufacturing, waste valorization, circular supply chain management, zero waste, sustainable manufacturing and/or waste management, targeting a specific industrial sector [12]. There is a lack of knowledge and a limited number of publications dealing with performance measurements in relation to Industry 4.0 [13].

Therefore, the present study aims to fill these gaps by providing a conceptual model (CM) whose objective is to assess the effectiveness of the IoT orientation towards environmental and social sustainability in the operations of manufacturing industries and/or in their supply chains. In this regard, the research question to be discussed concerns how the scientific literature related to IoT, socio-environmental sustainability and the circular economy contributes to the development of the CM with regard to performance measurement and assessment.

The CM is developed via the claims of the scientific literature that discusses the effectiveness of the actions of IoT technologies for environmental and social sustainability. The CM considers the current level of performance in relation to what must be achieved and how it must be achieved, together with what has been assessed and what has not been assessed, in a general way, not measuring performance against a well-defined goal, as highlighted by the survey by Melnyk [14]. The intent of the assessment is to help the organization to engage employees in realizing the performance of IoT technologies. The evaluation focuses on environmental and social sustainability and should not include many restrictions on how to achieve these goals, given the dynamics and the turbulent environment that may lead to the determination of new measures [14]. Therefore, the assessment is oriented towards the progress and success of sustainability within the business context.

This paper contributes to knowledge about the measurement and evaluation of performance in relation to the effect of IoT technologies on sustainability and circular economy approaches in production operations and supply chains. The CM should help the organization to engage employees in the assessment and measurement of the effectiveness of IoT technologies, with a focus on socio-environmental sustainability and the circular economy.

The paper is organized as follows. Section 2 describes the research methodology for developing the CM related to "IoT and sustainable manufacturing". Section 3 presents the results as a mapping of the selected sources by PRISMA (preferred reporting items for systematic review and meta-analysis), a categorization of the statements of the selected sources, a synthesis of the statements and the CM itself. Section 4 presents a discussion of the results. Section 5 presents the theory and managerial contributions, Section 6 reveals the research limitations and Section 7 presents some suggestions for future research.

2. Methodology

The authors of this study acknowledge that the meaning of "conceptual model" comes from the definition of a "conceptual framework" (CF), which is related to a "network" of concepts that are interconnected and together provide a comprehensive understanding of a real-life phenomenon. The concepts that are part of the conceptual framework support one other and articulate their respective phenomena [15]. Jabareen [15] presents the main features of the conceptual framework. The CF is called a conceptual model (CM) when it contains the methodological assumption of assessing the "real world" and uses variables or factors [15].

The study presents a CM that contains the methodological assumption of assessing the "real world" with regard to constructs, factors, indicators and their definitions, focusing on the effectiveness of IoT technologies for sustainable manufacturing (environmental and social sustainability).

The development of the CM follows a methodology adapted from Jabareen as follows [15]:

1. Mapping of the selected sources: carrying out a systematic literature review applying the PRISMA process, focusing on the IoT and sustainable manufacturing (environmental and social sustainability) and the identification of contents or statements related to empirical facts and practices.
2. Categorizing the selected sources:
    - 2.1 Extensive reading and categorization of selected content by reading selected literature and categorizing the content into dimensions and representative constructs with each dimension.
        - 2.1.1 Identify and name concepts: review selected content allowing concepts to emerge from the literature.
        - 2.1.2 Deconstruct and categorize the concepts: identify the main attributes, characteristics, assumptions and roles of concepts and, later, organize and categorize them according to their features.
    - 2.2 Integration of concepts: integrate and group concepts that have similarities to a new one, manipulating the concepts to give a reasonable number.
3. Synthesis, resynthesis and making sense: conducting an iterative process that includes repetitive synthesis and resynthesis, until the researcher recognizes a CM that makes sense.

The methodology is illustrated in Figure 1.

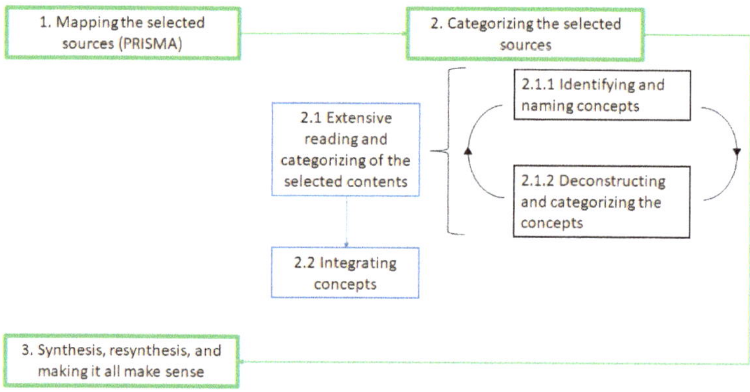

Figure 1. CM development methodology.

3. Results

3.1. Mapping the Selected Sources: PRISMA

The publications eligible for the design of the CM were mapped via a systematic literature review using the PRISMA process (preferred reporting items for systematic reviews and meta-analyses) [16]. PRISMA employs structured and explicit methods, with the following phases: (1) identification phase, (2) screening phase, (3) eligibility phase and (4) inclusion phase, to identify, select and critically evaluate the relevant research. The main benefit is to minimize bias, as this can make it difficult to conduct and interpret the review.

The article by Malek and Desai [5] presents a systematic literature review to map the literature in relation to sustainable manufacturing. These authors adopted the terms ("Sustainable Manufacturing" OR "Sustainable Production" OR "Sustainable Operations") as keywords to select the publications. Following their work, this research considered the same keywords for the Web of Science (WoS) and Elsevier's Scopus databases to ensure the identification of high-quality scientific articles on sustainable manufacturing. The research on WoS and Scopus was conducted on 14 April 2022.

3.1.1. Identification Phase

The articles were identified through the WoS and Scopus databases. The search began in WoS and Scopus with the exact phrases in "TOPIC" or "TITLE-ABS-KEY" ("Sustainable Manufacturing" OR "Sustainable Production" OR "Sustainable Operations") AND ("Internet of Things"), resulting in 82 (eighty-two) documents and 416 (four hundred and sixteen) documents, respectively.

3.1.2. Screening Phase

An additional refinement was made in relation to the types of documents, to maintain the quality of the present study, including journal articles, early access and reviews without defining the range of the years of the publications and considering only articles in English. The application of these criteria resulted in 51 (fifty-one) articles (WoS) and 275 (two hundred and seventy-five) articles (Scopus).

Further refinement was performed by considering WoS's subject categories. Thus, this stage generated 26 (twenty-six) articles, since the following categories were excluded: Agronomy; Chemistry Analytical; Chemistry Multidisciplinary; Electrochemistry; Energy Fuels; Engineering Chemical; Engineering Electrical Electronic; Engineering Mechanical; Food Science Technology; Instruments Instrumentation; Materials Science Multidisciplinary; Mathematics; Mathematics Interdisciplinary Applications; Physics Applied; Telecommunications. The selected categories and respective numbers of articles were Automation Control Systems (1), Computer Science Interdisciplinary Applications (4), Engineering Environmental (4), Engineering Industrial (6), Engineering Manufacturing (9), Environmental Sciences (10), Environmental Studies (5), Green Sustainable Science Technology (9), Management (2), Multidisciplinary Sciences (1) and Operations Research Management Science (7).

Further refinement was performed by considering the Scopus subject areas. Thus, this stage generated 80 (eighty) articles, as the following categories were excluded: Agricultural and Biological Sciences; Arts and Humanities; Biochemistry, Genetics and Molecular Biology; Chemical Engineering; Chemistry; Decision Sciences; Earth and Planetary Sciences; Economics, Econometrics and Finance; Energy; Health Professions; Materials Science; Mathematics; Medicine; Multidisciplinary; Physics and Astronomy; Psychology; Social Sciences. The selected categories and respective numbers of articles were Business, Management and Accounting (7), Computer Science (54), Engineering (55) and Environmental Science (6).

3.1.3. Eligibility Phase

The abstracts were checked. The last refinement criterion was applied in relation to the abstracts of the articles, where the selection was based on articles related to the "production process" and "environmental–social" sustainability.

From WoS, this step generated 5 (five) articles that were read in their entirety. However:

- Two articles were discarded: one was related to life cycle assessment (LCA) and other article concerned lean manufacturing and healthcare. Both subjects were out of the scope of this work.

From SCOPUS, this step generated 11 (eleven) articles that were read in their entirety. However:

- Three articles were duplicates of articles in WoS. Two of these were discarded as mentioned earlier, and the article by Li et al. [17] was selected to contribute to the study.
- Five articles were not considered in the research. Two articles were discarded, as one was concerned with manufacturing process modeling and other was out of the industry context. One article was not free and another proposed the design of a

business maturity scheme for companies implementing Industry 4.0. Finally, another article focused on manufacturing resiliency and sustainability.

3.1.4. Inclusion Phase

Suitable full texts should be selected to contribute to the qualitative synthesis of the research. A total of 6 (six) articles were selected to contribute to the design of the CM for manufacturing organizations.

The PRISMA results are shown in Figure 2.

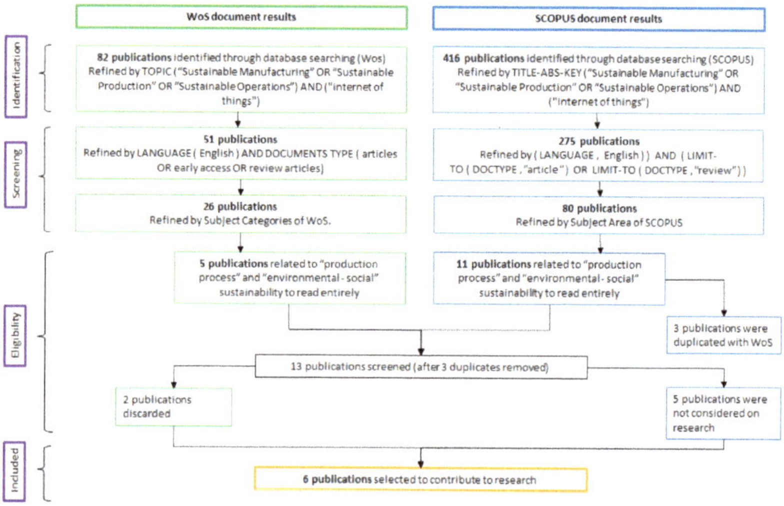

Figure 2. PRISMA process: (1) identification phase; (2) screening phase; (3) eligibility phase; (4) inclusion phase.

The selected sources supported the lack of a comprehensive understanding of Industry 4.0 technologies and sustainable manufacturing in relation to an empirical point of view, as demonstrated by their suggestions for future research, for example, the development of a model to assess simultaneously the capabilities of both sustainability aspects and Industry 4.0 [18], the relationship between organizational performance and digitalization of environmental sustainability practices [19], exploring the impact of enabling technologies on sustainability pillars for manufacturing industries in developing countries [20] and research on the effects of the emerging technological field of Industry 4.0 on sustainable manufacturing [21].

3.2. *Categorizing the Selected Sources*

The phase of categorizing the selected sources was developed with the support of Cavalieri's research [22,23].

The PRISMA methodology resulted in six articles, in which the statements were related to empirical facts and practices regarding IoT, social–environmental sustainability and the circular economy approach. The statements were identified, categorized and organized according to their attributes into dimensions and their representative constructs, and then grouped into factors to be assessed by the indicators, as follows:

- Dimensions: the three principal dimensions to be assessed were IoT technology, environmental approaches and social approaches.
- Constructs:

i. The seven constructs for IoT technology were: IoT expectations, IoT technology capacity, IoT technologies integration, IoT-based process management, IoT data, IoT challenges and IoT barriers.
ii. The four constructs for environmental approaches were: company engagement, performance measurement methodology, performance indicators implementation and environmental sustainability and circular economy practices.
iii. The four constructs for social approaches were: company engagement, performance measurement methodology, performance indicators implementation and social sustainability practices.

- Factors to be assessed/measured by the indicators, which should fit the statements and their definitions related to the construct.

3.3. *Synthesis and Resynthesis: The Statements and Their Dimensions, Constructs and Factors*

The integration and grouping process of the statements resulted in dimensions and constructs being categorized and organized according to their attributes. The statements of the selected articles were organized and grouped as follows:

3.3.1. IoT Technology

- IoT Technology Expectation

Top management chooses to implement IoT technology because it is expected to be beneficial in the digitalized world or because IoT technology is seen as an agent of improvement or an agent of transformation that perpetually manifests shock waves throughout the organization [19].

- IoT Technology Capacity

The IoT technology supports the management of a collection of large amounts of data for the production process and for data analysis and data mining [17], as a sophisticated and advanced technological device for massive data storage, retrieval, processing and analysis [18]. After transferring large amounts of data through the cloud, data analysis is completed and useful information is produced [20] which can be used to guide production decision-making [17].

The use of IoT technology enables the development of smart manufacturing via the interrelationship between the smart constituent elements of the company, such as smart products, smart facilities (sensors, data storage equipment, software), physical entities (parts, machinery) and networking components (interfaces, wired and wireless network protocols) [17]. The complex manufacturing network supports real-time management through the integration of internal business departments (vertical integration) and/or the integration between the company and the supply chain (horizontal integration) [17].

- IoT Technologies Integration

The "intelligent factory" uses information and communication technologies such as platforms and applications to integrate the production area with other company departments, distributors and customers, giving rise to more transparent supply chains [21]. The digitization and interconnection of industrial processes enabled by IoT technologies is facilitated by data analytics, machine learning and artificial intelligence [21]. Machines can trade and interact to reconfigure themselves for the dynamic nature of production, and the new smart system is integrated with existing systems in a compatible manner [18]. The entire factory can be wirelessly interconnected, monitored and controlled [20].

Production processes are supported by networked IoT technologies for data collection, exchange and analysis [18]. Smart network connections employing IoT technologies are established between different subsystems within the company, including sensors, actuator control, management and the manufacturing area (vertical integration), and different companies in the supply chain can share and exchange information (horizontal integration). Furthermore, different product-oriented (or package) processes can be established throughout the product life cycle starting from customer needs and product design to product maintenance and recycling (end-to-end integration) [18].

- IoT-Based Process Management

IoT technologies increase cooperation by sharing information and collaboration within the supply chain. They support the monitoring and control of the production process through data collection, providing a reference for making business decisions through big data analysis, allowing information to be obtained and shared to facilitate collaboration between people and things [17].

IoT technologies are also used to understand the status of the supply chain by obtaining real-time information from all nodes in the supply chain. Furthermore, IoT technologies facilitate the interconnection of physical and virtual space (widespread deployment of distributed devices embedded with computing, identification, communication and sensing capabilities) [17].

- IoT Data

IoT technology supports decision-making with high-quality data from customer relationship management, warehousing management, production management and the supply chain, considering the set of interconnected processes that cover the entire product life cycle and the entire company operation [17].

- IoT Challenges

Companies may face difficulties regarding the implementation of the identification and sensing of "smart objects". Sensing technologies include radio-frequency identification (RFID), wireless sensor networks (WSNs), near-field communication (NFC) and Bluetooth technology (BT). In addition, there are difficulties in collecting data for the identification of "smart objects", which are embedded in computing and communication resources, and problems in the management of "smart objects" because they are numerous, heterogeneous and dynamic [17].

Data transfer over network technology is considered a problem for company decision makers. The full operation of the transfer of data by the network technology requires addressing, routing, end-to-end transmission, gateways and traffic characterization. Network technologies depend on wired technologies, wireless technologies, cellular networks and satellite communication technology [17].

- IoT Barriers

There are organizational, technological, governmental and ecosystem maturity barriers [20]. Organizational barriers include lack of a senior management support system, resistance from the top management system, low perceptions regarding the digital revolution, risky investment in technologies, unavailability of a digital strategy, unavailability of a data-based service system and fluctuations in production size. Technological barriers include the high cost of technology, the unavailability of I4.0 standards, the unavailability of a data security system, low IT levels, the unavailability of IT infrastructure and service centers and the quantity of parts to be produced. The governmental and ecosystem maturity barriers include the unavailability of government policies, lack of support from government, the low maturity of the manufacturing industry, the unavailability of a technology ecosystem and the lack of consultants and trainers in the area.

3.3.2. Environmental Approach

- Company Engagement

Environmental challenges and the concern for sustainability are key issues that companies consider when developing their strategy [21]. A reliable definition for sustainable manufacturing practice develops sustainability awareness among companies and their supply chains, and between companies and their customers [18]. Environmental sustainability principles should be incorporated into companies' business models to help them understand whether environmental sustainability initiatives could lead to better performance, regardless of social responsibility aspects [19].

An integrated smart and sustainable business model can be based on company-specific strategies [18] with regard to the relationship between environmental sustainability and digital transformation [19]. Digital technologies offer organizations opportunities to develop new business models focused on the environment, incorporating environmentally sustainable practices justified by digital transformation [19], for example, the company may rely on the IoT for carrying out sustainable business practices in relation to reducing carbon emissions and minimizing solid waste discarded into the environment [19].

Digital transformation is a hot topic for discussion among top-level management, with respect to how environmental sustainability practices can become a part of the strategic decision-making process [19]. Consumers demand "environmentally friendly" products, and companies perceive new business possibilities through Industry 4.0 technologies [21].

- Performance Measurement Methodology

Digital technologies are used to develop new performance measurement methods for "sustainable and smart manufacturing" [18]. The sustainability performance of IoT manufacturing should follow a guideline and a standard for environmental sustainability assessment metrics, which should be agreed among employees [18].

The existing tools and methods establish a reliable approach for "environmental sustainability and smart manufacturing" [18]. Data-driven smart algorithms focus on sustainable manufacturing, sustainable supply chains and sustainable product end-of-life and life cycle assessments [18]. Different types of sensors result in the development of specific performance criteria to mitigate negative effects on the environment without detriment to competitiveness [21].

- Performance Indicators Implementation

Clean manufacturing processes, driven by digital technology, can reduce costs without harming the environment and without negative impacts on the ecosystem [19].

Smart business processes, which rely on cleaner and more sustainable mechanisms seen from the economic, environmental and social points of view, may offer several favorable circumstances simultaneously, such as can reducing operating costs, improving profitability and shop-floor employee safety and reducing the environmental impact of the business [19]. In addition, seen from the economic and environmental point of view, they may offer increased production rates, effective utilization of resources, reduction of carbon dioxide (CO_2) emissions and waste reduction [20].

The IoT represents an opportunity to drive sustainable manufacturing, enabling the use of environmentally friendly, abundant and locally available resources [18]. The IoT enables all types of data collection and analysis from industrial processes, easily helping to avoid unnecessary manufacturing steps [21]. IoT technologies allow the company to improve the impact of the process on the environment, eliminating waste throughout the value chain, enhancing sustainable consumption, eliminating harmful waste discarded into the environment [19], reducing scrap on the shop floor [20] and contributing to reducing the entry of virgin resources, the generation of waste [18,21] and CO_2 emissions [20].

The interconnection of processes allowed by IoT technologies causes an increase in the development of performance indicators [21]. The company obtain higher-quality data generated from IoT to support decision makers with information from production management on topics such as raw materials, energy consumption, water consumption, water waste, solid waste, by-products [17], the use of packaging [21] and air pollution [19], and the reduced consumption of materials results in less dependency on natural resources [20].

Power consumption can be reduced due to the improved precision of data monitoring via IoT technologies [20,21]. On the other hand, data centers consume large amounts of energy and resources, impacting the environment negatively, as monitored by IoT technologies [24]. There is an additional environmental liability measurement associated with Industry 4.0 as a consequence of the materials required for electrical devices, which are sometimes scarce and may require intensive extraction and processing efforts, which may negate the environmental advantage of the Industry 4.0 context [18].

- Environmental Sustainability and Circular Economy Practices

Digital technologies are used to develop new ways of coping with waste [19]. IoT technologies improve manufacturing process efficiency regarding the 6R design ("reduce", "reuse", "recycle", "recover", "redesign" and "remanufacture"), in order to save natural resources [18,20]. Regarding the improvement of the economic and ecological flows of resources, IoT technologies enable collaboration and partnerships among a company's stakeholders with respect to "closing the loops" by reusing raw materials, sharing raw materials, reusing waste, sharing waste [21] and allowing the reutilization of materials in a remanufacturing process [20]. Industry 4.0 technologies assist in raw materials purchasing from suppliers when needed (the raw material or semi-finished production material is requested on demand) [24].

The incorporation of different types of sensors allows greater transparency of operations, which adds intelligence to processes to mitigate negative effects on the environment and throughout the supply chain, reducing the losses generated along the entire chain [21]. The IoT supports information and communication technologies such as platforms and applications that are employed within the "intelligent shop floor", helping to reduce energy consumption, solid waste, the use of packaging, by-products [21], the use of raw materials, water consumption and water waste [17]. These technologies are employed to integrate the production area with distributors and customers, helping to reduce waste, energy and the use of packaging [21]. The IoT sensors provide real-time monitoring information for better air quality [19].

The utilization of IoT technologies ensures a dynamic interconnection among energy providers, the company and market demand, which leads to better energy management [18]. Continuous monitoring through smart devices increases the visibility and awareness of energy consumption by using real-time problem solving [21].

3.3.3. Social Approach

- Company Engagement

System integration promotes communication between different levels of the company (and between manufacturing plants), which supports the development and strength of the company's values and corporate culture [21].

A digital culture, with associated training, may be a challenge for companies [20], especially at the early stage of Industry 4.0 implementation. Many people are afraid that digital solutions and digital technologies may result in a loss of jobs [20]. Some employees have lost their jobs due to insufficient knowledge of digital technologies [20], and some employees have damaged sensors and interface devices or refused to follow the instructions [20]. On the other hand, there are digital technology solutions developed by companies to address career sustainability issues arising from machines replacing humans [18] and to ensure a safer workplace, leading to a decrease in workplace accidents and an increase in employee morale, as well as making work easier [20].

The increased use of digital technologies creates new jobs with a different profile [20], where the major challenge is finding and retaining creative people and people with strong analytical skills [20]. As digital technologies develop dynamically, training keeps employees up to date [20].

- Performance Measurement Methodology

There should be a guideline for determining the performance of smart industries with regard to social sustainability [18]. The existing tools and methods should establish a reliable approach for "social sustainability and smart manufacturing", together with standard social sustainability assessment metrics regarding the IoT technologies implementation agreed upon by the company, as mentioned by Sartal [21] in relation to environmental sustainability.

- Performance Indicators Implementation

Employees should continuously adapt to the new restrictions imposed on job options due to industrial innovation, and they should be able to understand the information and use information from various sources related to various subjects to maintain a career and upgrade their abilities to perform new tasks, via continuous education [18].

New skilled and trained employees are needed to apply IoT technologies effectively [18]. New profiles of employees are immediately required for positions related to the application of digital technologies [21]. Manual work is reduced in favor of cognitive and analytical skills, fundamentally linked to information technologies and data analysis [21].

- Social Sustainability Practices

IoT technologies trigger the development of jobs in different areas, for example, automation engineering, control system configuration, artificial intelligence and software engineering, as well as reducing most types of lower-skilled jobs [20].

Smart grids allow machines to communicate and make small decisions without human intervention [18]. Machine communication and negotiation pave the way and increase the demand for new jobs, where humans are focused on designing, developing and maintaining this network of machines [18].

IoT technologies offer employees better and safer working conditions [18]. The IoT helps to improve equipment and operator safety through better maintenance solutions and by providing real-time hazard warnings [21].

In the smart shop floor, machines work hand in hand with humans, observing them and learning from them in a way very similar to an apprentice, complementing humans rather than replacing them, offering labor career sustainability [18]. However, it is still argued that IoT technologies lead to a shrinking of the human workforce, thus reducing job opportunities and increasing unemployment. This may result in resistance against adopting Industry 4.0 initiatives [18].

A company can implement big-data-driven systems and IoT technologies for a better division of labor between humans and smart machines, to address the security, privacy and ethical issues introduced by smart manufacturing networks [18]. Digital technologies allow collaborative networks for employees (shop-floor employees and managers) to exchange their knowledge and experiences with the supply chain [21], as typical activities in any manufacturing environment (e.g., analysis, cooperation, creativity) continue to be carried out by human workers [21].

The synthesis of the statements and their dimensions, constructs and related factors to be assessed/measured are summarized in Figure 3.

3.3.4. The Conceptual Model

The CM provides an interpretative approach to the current state of the art described in the literature, where the systematic literature review plays a key role in establishing knowledge. The iterative and repetitive synthesis process resulted in the following dimensions, constructs, indicators and indicator definitions (see Tables 1–3).

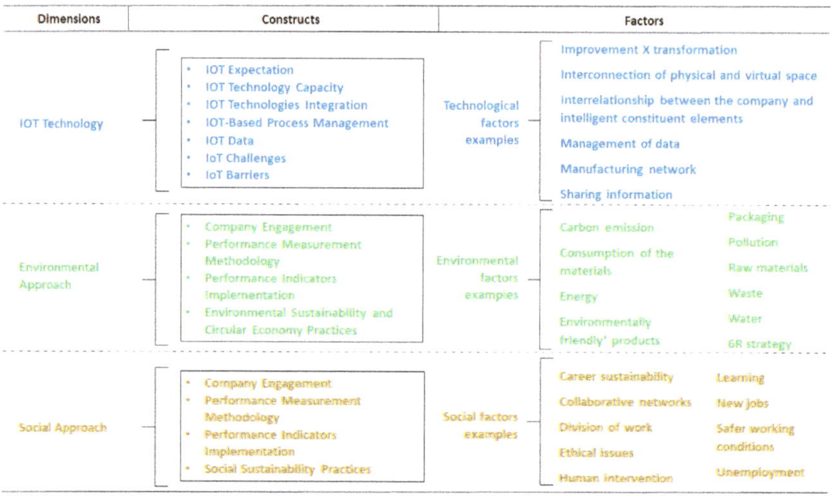

Figure 3. The synthesis of the statements and their dimensions, constructs and factors.

Table 1. IoT Technology.

Dimension	Construct	Indicators	Indicator Definitions	Source
IoT Technology	IoT expectations	• Company leadership's view of IoT.	• The viewpoint of top managers and managers in relation to IoT technology perspectives, which influences their purpose of IoT implementation.	[19]
	IoT technology capacity	• Level of technological sophistication. • Level of manufacturing network. • Level of data management. • Interrelationship among the company's intelligent constituent elements.	• The company's potential to innovate regarding IoT technologies within its operations and in its supply chain.	[17,18,20]
	IoT technologies integration	• Connections among the company's intelligent network. • Networked processes access and use. • Compatibility of the digital system. • Level of shop-floor interconnection.	• The company's intelligence regarding the interconnection of the IoT technologies within its operations and in its supply chain, which enables the identification, selection, analysis and management of relevant information on potential events or problems with real-time responses.	[18,20,21]
	IoT-based process management	• Level of IoT contribution to process management (production–company supply chain)	• The company's purpose of IoT implementation within its operations and in its supply chain.	[17]

Table 1. *Cont.*

Dimension	Construct	Indicators	Indicator Definitions	Source
	IoT data	• Level of data route between the internal and external company processes considering customer, warehousing, brewhouse process, fermentation process, beer processing and supply chain.	• The company's data flows regarding IoT technology within its operations and in its supply chain to support decision makers, which influences the performance measurement implementation.	[17]
	IoT challenges	• Data access and utilization of "smart objects". • Transference and data analysis results.	• The company's issues when operationalizing the IoT.	[17]
	IoT barriers	• Organizational/technological/governmental and ecosystem maturity	• The difficulties that company faces in implementing IoT.	[20]

Table 2. Environmental Approach.

Dimension	Construct	Indicators	Indicator Definitions	Source
Environmental Approach	Company engagement	• Development of environmental sustainability strategy. • Development of environmental sustainability and digital transformation integration strategy. • Development of environmental sustainability and digital transformation politics. • Definition of sustainable manufacturing practices. • Development of new business model via environmental sustainability and IoT integration. • Implementation of sustainable manufacturing and IoT technologies integration practices.	• The company commitment to environmental sustainability and digital transformation relationships in its own operation and in its supply chain.	[18,19,21]
	Performance measurement methodology	• Development of environmental sustainability assessment methodology. • Guidelines for the environmental sustainability performance. • Definition of tools and methods for "environmental sustainability and smart manufacturing" performance. • Development of data-driven smart algorithms for design of "environmental sustainability and smart manufacturing".	• The development of procedures to measure the resource consumption (water use, raw materials, energy), the design for 6R, by-products and the pollution generated by the company and its supply chain based on IoT technologies.	[18,21]
	Performance indicators implementation	• Environmental sustainability assessment metrics. • Performance measurements for "environmental sustainability and smart manufacturing". • Performance metrics for additional environmental liability.	• The assessment of the resource consumption (water use, raw materials, energy), the design for 6R, by-products and the pollution generated by the company and its supply chain based on IoT technologies.	[17–21,24]

Table 2. *Cont.*

Dimension	Construct	Indicators	Indicator Definitions	Source
	Environmental sustainability and circular economy practices	• Platforms and applications employment within the company and in its supply chain. • Environmental sustainability and smart manufacturing design for 6R. • Records of environmental sustainability and smart manufacturing improvement process. • Monitoring information of the operations and the supply chain through smart devices.	• The digital technology (IoT technologies) and environmental approach as integrated practices to mitigate and/or eliminate resource consumption (water use, raw materials, energy), by-products and pollution, and to improve the design for 6R, by the company and its supply chain.	[17–21,24]

Table 3. Social Approach.

Dimension	Construct	Indicators	Indicator Definitions	Source
Social Approach	Company engagement	• Development of social sustainability strategy. • Development of training program for digital technologies. • Development of program for career sustainability. • Politics for a safer workplace. • Politics for job retention. • Politics for bilateral communication.	• The company commitment to social sustainability and digital transformation relationships in its own operation and in its supply chain.	[18,20,21]
	Performance measurement methodology	• Development of social sustainability assessment methodology. • Definition of tools and methods for the "social sustainability and smart manufacturing" performance. • Guidelines for the social sustainability performance.	• The development of procedures to measure human factors in relation to IoT technologies implementation in the company and its supply chain.	[18,21] [1]
	Performance indicators implementation	• Valorization of worker adaptation. • Valorization of self-learning. • Valorization of continuous learning. • Assessment metrics for job sustainability. • Assessment of the new skills and new profiles. • Implementation of social sustainability and smart manufacturing performance metrics.	• The assessment of human factors in relation to IoT technologies implementation in the company and its supply chain.	[18,21]
	Social sustainability practices	• Valorization of cognitive and analytical human skills. • Valorization of the human work. • Human autonomy and mediation. • New kind of working conditions. • Concerns regarding unemployment. • Collaborative networks. • Bilateral communication.	• The digital technology (IoT technologies) and social approaches as integrated practices to boost the human factors in the company and in its supply chain.	[18,20,21]

[1.] This indicator definition is an insight from reference [21].

4. Discussion

An effective way of monitoring and evaluating performance is the introduction of key performance indicators (KPIs) that fit the strategic intentions of the company [25]. Performance measures applied with Industry 4.0 technologies should be able to capture local contexts and a wide range of phenomena from the external context and analyze a large amount and variety of data [26]. In this regard, performance measures should be autonomous and heterogeneous in detecting data and planning information to support the management of the production process and the supply chain [26].

IoT technology is an example of an Industry 4.0 technology that is employed to achieve smarter manufacturing and performance measurement. It is believed to be a critical step in industry [27]. The use of IoT for shop-floor management is facilitated by the fact that the technology can be installed in a limited area such as on a production line, in a storage area or on a packing line [27].

IoT technologies are generally employed to monitor environmental conditions in industry, for example using low-cost sensors to collect the necessary data within production facilities, e.g., "temperature, humidity, air pressure, air quality (carbon monoxide, liquid petroleum gas, smoke), lightning and noise" [25] (p. 286). Some requirements should be met to make these solutions viable, consisting of the three constraints of scalability, adaptability and cost-effectiveness. Scalability refers to the applicability to different sizes of installations, as well as the subsequent adjustment to any size changes. Adaptability means that the system should be easily adaptable according to the prevailing environmental conditions in the production area, through a quick and simple exchange of the employed sensors. Another requirement is cost-effectiveness, for example using common sensors in the plant [25].

Most companies still aim for monetary gains without a commitment to environmental protection and the well-being of society. The main purpose of KPIs in production systems is to improve quality and efficiency, reduce costs and lead times and increase flexibility and profitability. Results are presented quantitatively and compared with the performance target to understand how plant productivity should be increased [13].

Some researchers are applying the ISA-95 and ISO-22400 standards as a support for developing and implementing a performance measurement system referring to the IoT-based production performance model [13,27], in relation to the definition of manufacturing processes and performance indicator formulas, respectively.

ISO-22400 defines the application of KPIs and sub-KPIs and their formulas, corresponding elements and benefits, from thirty-five KPIs oriented towards a manufacturing execution system (MES)—a software package combining multiple execution management components into single and integrated solutions focused on the management of shop-floor operations such as material delivery and consumption, as well as production progress [27]. On the other hand, the ISA-95 standard describes entities at the shop-floor level, where information technologies and operation technologies interact, developing an automated interface between the company and the control systems [13]. In this regard, the IoT device detects a product on the production line, and its data such as "time", "quantity", "location", "value" and "status" are sent to the MES. Then, these data are aligned with the production performance model, which consists of the three subparts of actual equipment, actual produced material and actual consumed material [27].

The CM contributes to emphasizing the balance between social and environmental sustainability in the business context to achieve the benefits of adopting sustainable manufacturing in the production process and supply chain; that is, it goes beyond monitoring the environmental conditions of the industry, as mentioned earlier. In other words, the CM is concerned with reducing or eliminating environmental hazards, to preserve natural resources and employee/community well-being.

The objective of the CM is to assess the performance of the strategy at the shop-floor level and in the corresponding supply chain, considering the IoT technology dimension, the environmental sustainability dimension and the social sustainability dimension.

For instance, in relation to the IoT technology dimension, the CM aims to assess the point of view of managers and top managers in relation to IoT technology perspectives, which influences their IoT implementation purposes. The company's potential for innovation in IoT technologies lies in its operations and supply chain. The company's "smartness" and "responsiveness" also lies in the interconnection between the IoT technologies of its operations and supply chain, which allows the identification, selection, analysis and management of relevant information regarding potential events or problems with real-time responses. Thus, the company's data flows regarding IoT technology, within its operations and across its supply chain, support decision makers and influence the performance measurement implementation.

With regard to the dimension of environmental sustainability, the CM proposes to assess the company's commitment to the relationship between environmental sustainability and digital transformation in its own operation and in its supply chain. At this level, the development of procedures should be carried out to measure resources consumption (i.e., usage of water, raw materials and energy), the design for 6R, by-products and the pollution generated by the company and its supply chain, based on IoT technologies. Digital technology (IoT technologies) and environmental approaches as integrated practices must exist to mitigate and/or eliminate resource consumption (water use, raw materials and energy), by-products and pollution, and to improve the design for 6R, by the company and its supply chain.

Regarding the dimension of social sustainability, the CM recommends assessing the company's commitment to social sustainability and digital transformation in its operations and in the supply chain. It is also related to the development of procedures to measure human factors in relation to the implementation of IoT technologies in the company and its supply chain, as well as the assessment of the human factors in relation to the implementation of IoT technologies in the company and its supply chain. Digital technology (IoT technologies) and social approaches as integrated practices enhance human factors in the company and its supply chain.

Finally, the IoT technology dimension is directly related to the environmental and social sustainability dimensions that affect the results of the associated indicators. In addition, these indicators must be aligned with the KPIs oriented towards the productivity category in the production process and in the supply chain. For example, we refer to the ISA-95 and ISO-22400 standards, economic sustainability, the transformation to the triple bottom line (TBL) and circular economy approaches.

5. Theoretical and Managerial Contributions

This paper contributes to the scientific literature regarding:

- The measurement and evaluation of performance in Industry 4.0 within the scope of sustainability and the circular economy.
- The effect of IoT technologies in approaching the circular economy on themes such as input reduction, consumption, reuse, recovery, recycling and waste and emissions reduction.
- Exploring the benefits and challenges within organizations on how to implement and adopt the IoT and environmental and social sustainability in its operations and supply chains.

This paper contributes to the business and management context regarding:

- The CM, which should help the organization to engage employees in assessing the effectiveness of IoT technologies with a focus on socio-environmental sustainability.
- The focus on socio-environmental sustainability, which can lead to new or revised measures that improve the organization's sustainability performance.

6. Research Limitations

The limitation of this research is that the CM was not validated, used as a management tool to assess the real world, or applied as a pilot study.

7. Suggestions for Future Research

The suggestions for future research are twofold, as they allow mitigation of some of the limitations of this article but also provide new and exciting avenues of research, as follows:

- The validation of the CM, according to Jabareen [15] (p. 54), to certify "whether the proposed framework and its concepts make sense not only to the researcher but also to other scholars and practitioners (...) is a process that starts with the researcher, who then seeks validation among 'outsiders'". The researches can receive feedback, new insights and comments from expert opinions—the "outsiders"—by consensus methods such as the Delphi Method "to gather general agreement on topics that do not yet have empirical evidence to support future decisions or actions; often, these topics are ambiguous or controversial" [28] (p. 663). The Delphi method has advantages for obtaining consensus from other methods as "it eliminates the bias and influence that can occur in face-to-face meetings as the respondents are to remain anonymous, (...) the ranking of each item by the entire response group helps make the ultimate conclusions more reliable than a single meeting, (...) does not require specified meeting times" [28] (p. 666).
- The translation of the statements into a management tool to assess whether IoT technologies are oriented towards socio-environmental sustainability and circular economy approaches in manufacturing industries. The management tool can be a questionnaire using a five-point Likert scale via the online platform SurveyMonkey and/or interviews. The results should contribute to the management practices as an input to the planning and implementation of IoT technologies oriented towards sustainability and the circular economy approach. In addition, the results contribute to the scientific–academic environment, because there is a demand for empirical studies on, for example, the impacts of digital transformation on the environmental and social domains of sustainability, the relationship between organizational performance and digitalization of environmental sustainability practices and digital transformation strategies integrated with sustainability pillars in manufacturing.
- The application of this management tool in a pilot study aimed at a specific industrial sector to investigate, for example, the differences in the socio-environmental effectiveness of the IoT in small, medium and large organizations in a certain sector.

Author Contributions: Conceptualization, A.C.; methodology, A.C.; formal analysis, A.C.; investigation, A.C.; writing—original draft preparation and editing, A.C.; review, J.R. and M.A.; supervision, J.R. and M.A. All authors have read and agreed to the published version of the manuscript.

Funding: This research received no external funding.

Institutional Review Board Statement: Not applicable.

Informed Consent Statement: Not applicable.

Data Availability Statement: Data sharing is not applicable to this article.

Acknowledgments: Adriane Cavalieri would like to register that she appreciates the support of the University of Aveiro in enabling postdoctoral work, on behalf of João Reis and Marlene Amorim.

Conflicts of Interest: The authors declare no conflict of interest.

References

1. Xavier, A.; Reyes, T.; Aoussat, A.; Luiz, L.; Souza, L. Eco-Innovation Maturity Model: A Framework to Support the Evolution of Eco-Innovation Integration in Companies. *Sustainability* **2020**, *12*, 3773. [CrossRef]
2. Garetti, M.; Taisch, M. Sustainable Manufacturing: Trends and Research Challenges. *Prod. Plan. Control* **2012**, *23*, 83–104. [CrossRef]
3. Hallinger, P. Analyzing the intellectual structure of the Knowledge base on managing for sustainability, 1982–2019: A meta-analysis. *Sustain. Dev.* **2020**, *28*, 1493–1506. [CrossRef]
4. Mathiyazhagan, K.; Mani, V.; Mathivathanan, D.; Rajak, S. Evaluation of Antecedents to Social Sustainability Practices in Multi-Tier Indian Automotive Manufacturing Firms. *Int. J. Prod. Res.* **2021**, 1–22. [CrossRef]
5. Malek, J.; Desai, T.N. A Systematic Literature Review to Map Literature Focus of Sustainable Manufacturing. *J. Clean. Prod.* **2020**, *256*, 120345. [CrossRef]
6. Howard, M.C. Sustainable Manufacturing Initiative (SMI): A True Public-Private Dialogue. Available online: https://www.oecd.org/sti/ind/45010349.pdf (accessed on 30 September 2021).

7. OECD. *About Sustainable Manufacturing and the Toolkit*; Organisation for Economic Co-operation and Development: Paris, France; Available online: http://t4.oecd.org/innovation/green/toolkit/aboutsustainablemanufacturingandthetoolkit.htm#:~{}:text=The%20OECD%20Sustainable%20Manufacturing%20Toolkit%20aims%20to%20provide,to%20contribute%20to%20sustainable%20development%20and%20green%20growth (accessed on 30 September 2021).
8. Laskurain-Iturbe, I.; Arana-Landín, G.; Landeta-Manzano, B.; Uriarte-Gallastegi, N. Exploring the Influence of Industry 4.0 Technologies on the Circular Economy. *J. Clean. Prod.* **2021**, *321*, 128944. [CrossRef]
9. Li, Y.; Dai, J.; Cui, L. The Impact of Digital Technologies on Economic and Environmental Performance in the Context of Industry 4.0: A Moderated Mediation Model. *Int. J. Prod. Econ.* **2020**, *229*, 107777. [CrossRef]
10. Sharma, M.; Joshi, S. Digital Supplier Selection Reinforcing Supply Chain Quality Management Systems to Enhance Firm's Performance. *TQM J.* **2020**. [CrossRef]
11. Haddud, A.; DeSouza, A.; Khare, A.; Lee, H. Examining Potential Benefits and Challenges Associated with the Internet of Things Integration in Supply Chains. *JMTM* **2017**, *28*, 1055–1085. [CrossRef]
12. Cavalieri, A.; Reis, J.; Amorim, M. Circular Economy and Internet of Things: Mapping Science of Case Studies in Manufacturing Industry. *Sustainability* **2021**, *13*, 3299. [CrossRef]
13. Tambare, P.; Meshram, C.; Lee, C.-C.; Ramteke, R.J.; Imoize, A.L. Performance Measurement System and Quality Management in Data-Driven Industry 4.0: A Review. *Sensors* **2022**, *22*, 224. [CrossRef] [PubMed]
14. Melnyk, S.A.; Bititci, U.; Platts, K.; Tobias, J.; Andersen, B. Is Performance Measurement and Management Fit for the Future? *Manag. Account. Res.* **2014**, *25*, 173–186. [CrossRef]
15. Jabareen, Y. Building a Conceptual Framework: Philosophy, Definitions, and Procedure. *Int. J. Qual. Methods* **2009**, *8*, 49–62. [CrossRef]
16. Moher, D.; Liberati, A.; Tetzlaff, J.; Altman, D.G.; The PRISMA Group. Preferred Reporting Items for Systematic Reviews and Meta-Analyses: The PRISMA Statement. *BMJ* **2009**, *339*, b2535. [CrossRef]
17. Li, K.; Zhou, T.; Liu, B. Internet-Based Intelligent and Sustainable Manufacturing: Developments and Challenges. *Int. J. Adv. Manuf. Technol.* **2020**, *108*, 1767–1791. [CrossRef]
18. Abubakr, M.; Abbas, A.T.; Tomaz, I.; Soliman, M.S.; Luqman, M.; Hegab, H. Sustainable and Smart Manufacturing: An Integrated Approach. *Sustainability* **2020**, *12*, 2280. [CrossRef]
19. Feroz, A.K.; Zo, H.; Chiravuri, A. Digital Transformation and Environmental Sustainability: A Review and Research Agenda. *Sustainability* **2021**, *13*, 1530. [CrossRef]
20. Pasi, B.N.; Mahajan, S.K.; Rane, S.B. The Current Sustainability Scenario of Industry 4.0 Enabling Technologies in Indian Manufacturing Industries. *Int. J. Prod. Perform. Manag.* **2021**, *70*, 1017–1048. [CrossRef]
21. Sartal, A.; Bellas, R.; Mejías, A.M.; García-Collado, A. The Sustainable Manufacturing Concept, Evolution and Opportunities within Industry 4.0: A Literature Review. *Adv. Mech. Eng.* **2020**, *12*, 168781402092523. [CrossRef]
22. Cavalieri, A.; Macedo-Soares, T.D.v.A.; Thiollent, M. *Avaliando o Desempenho da Universidade*; Editora PUC-Rio; Edições Loyola: São Paulo, Brazil, 2004; Volume 18, ISBN 85-15-02999-5.
23. Cavalieri B., A.M. *Avaliação do Desempenho da Universidade no Brasil: Um Instrumento de Auto-Avaliação Focando no Ensino e na Gestão*; Programa de Engenharia de Produção, 2001; Tese, Universidade Federal do Rio de Janeiro (COPPE/UFRJ): Rio de Janeiro, Brazil, 2001.
24. Waibel, M.W.; Steenkamp, L.P.; Moloko, N.; Oosthuizen, G.A. Investigating the Effects of Smart Production Systems on Sustainability Elements. *Procedia Manuf.* **2017**, *8*, 731–737. [CrossRef]
25. Mörth, O.; Eder, M.; Holzegger, L.; Ramsauer, C. IoT-Based Monitoring of Environmental Conditions to Improve the Production Performance. *Procedia Manuf.* **2020**, *45*, 283–288. [CrossRef]
26. Lopes, M.A.; Martins, R.A. Mapping the Impacts of Industry 4.0 on Performance Measurement Systems. *IEEE Latin Am. Trans.* **2021**, *19*, 1912–1923. [CrossRef]
27. Hwang, G.; Lee, J.; Park, J.; Chang, T.-W. Developing Performance Measurement System for Internet of Things and Smart Factory Environment. *Int. J. Prod. Res.* **2017**, *55*, 2590–2602. [CrossRef]
28. Waggoner, J.; Carline, J.D.; Durning, S.J. Is There a Consensus on Consensus Methodology? Descriptions and Recommendations for Future Consensus Research. *Acad. Med.* **2016**, *91*, 663–668. [CrossRef] [PubMed]

applied sciences

MDPI

Article

Artificial Intelligence Synergetic Opportunities in Services: Conversational Systems Perspective

Shai Rozenes [1] and Yuval Cohen [2,*]

[1] Department of Industrial Engineering and Technology Management, Holon Institute of Technology, Holon 5810201, Israel
[2] Department of Industrial Engineering, Afeka Tel-Aviv College of Engineering, Tel Aviv 6998812, Israel
* Correspondence: yuvalc@afeka.ac.il; Tel.: +972-545398152

Abstract: The importance of this paper is its discovery of the unused synergetic potential of integration between several AI techniques into an orchestrated effort to improve service. Special emphasis is given to the conversational capabilities of AI systems. The paper shows that the literature related to the use of AI in service is divided into independent knowledge domains (silos) that are either related to the technology under consideration, or to a small group of technologies related to a certain application; it then discusses the reasons for the isolation of these silos, and reveals the barriers and the traps for their integration. Two case studies of service systems are presented to illustrate the importance of synergy. A special focus is given to the conversation part of these service systems: the first case presents an application with high potential for integrating new AI technologies into its AI portfolio, while the second case illustrates the advantages of a mature application that has already integrated many technologies into its AI portfolio. Finally, the paper discusses the two case studies and presents inclusion relationships between AI capabilities to facilitate generating a roadmap for extending AI capabilities with synergetic opportunities.

Keywords: artificial intelligence; service; technology integration; conversational systems; technology maturity; chatbot; robo-chef; synergy; technology roadmap

Citation: Rozenes, S.; Cohen, Y. Artificial Intelligence Synergetic Opportunities in Services: Conversational Systems Perspective. *Appl. Sci.* **2022**, *12*, 8363. https://doi.org/10.3390/app12168363

Academic Editor: Juan Francisco De Paz Santana

Received: 24 July 2022
Accepted: 18 August 2022
Published: 21 August 2022

1. Introduction

This paper uncovers synergetic opportunities for integrating bundles of several different AI specializations in various services with a special focus on conversational systems. For this purpose, we use an extensive literature review and two case studies. In the two case studies, special attention is given to the analysis of conversational capabilities. The case studies are discussed, and future research opportunities are extracted and listed in the conclusion section.

The idea of using Artificial Intelligence (AI) for service is not new [1]; however, there is considerable overlapping and blur between AI implementation in services and in the industry. For coherent analysis of this paper, we find it useful to describe the following hierarchy of AI techniques, tools, methods, and implementations into three distinct levels: (1) General AI techniques, (2) domain specialization AI techniques, (3) application tailored AI solutions. Each of these categories will be briefly discussed next and illustrated in Figure 1.

1. The fundamental AI techniques could serve almost any purpose, and any application specialty. Some examples of pure AI techniques are pattern recognition, data mining (DM), machine learning (ML), deep learning (DL), rule-based reasoning, fuzzy logic, expert systems, etc.
2. The domain specialization AI techniques, generate a specific domain specialization (for example, natural language processing (NLP)) mostly by adjusting and improving one or more of the pure AI techniques (e.g., NLP may use pattern recognition, machine

learning or deep learning); these domain specializations may possibly integrate other non-AI techniques as well (for example, statistics and statistical inference).

3. The application-tailored bundles; are already solutions for specific needs based on use cases.

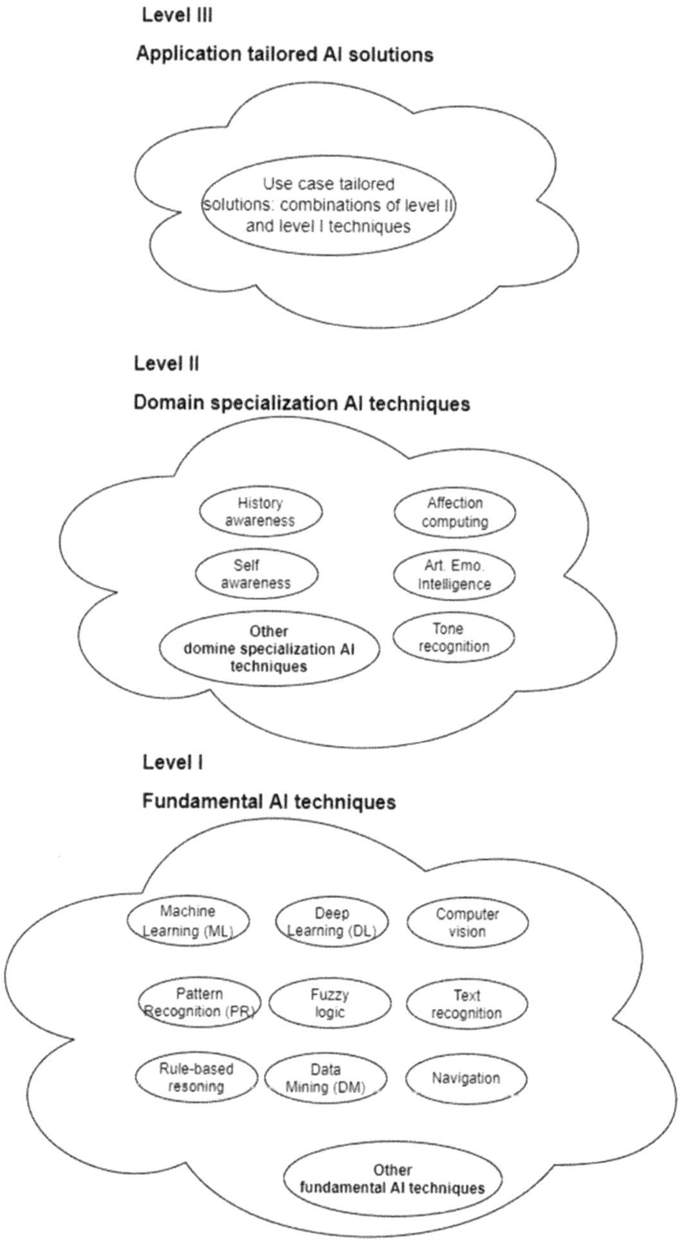

Figure 1. Hierarchy of specialization in AI tools and techniques.

In the AI toolbox, fundamental AI techniques are the prevalent familiar tools, and using any of them as an independent decision is mostly unrelated to the synergies we shall discuss. The domain specialization techniques, on the other hand, have a broad potential for synergies. The synergies related to domain specialization techniques stem from the integration between domain specialization techniques themselves. The synergies are also related to adding new fundamental technique/s to a domain specialization.

AI domain specialization developed in many directions: natural language processing (NLP), case-based reasoning (CBR), speech and tone recognition, face and emotion recognition, gesture recognition, collaborative systems and autonomous systems—to name a few [2]. Thus, each direction brought with it a specialization and specialists that focus on their field of specialty without mastering other AI fields [3]. For example, it is extremely rare to find affection computing experts that also specialize in autonomous systems; however, there are some AI fields that are closer than others to certain other AI fields. To visualize these relationships, in the service context, we map them to clusters as shown in Figure 2.

Figure 2 groups the AI domain specializations, level II in Figure 1, into clusters of major AI specializations and their relationships. In the context of service provision, the main identified AI clusters are:

- Speech-related cluster—AI techniques that focus on speech analysis and generation.
- Text analysis cluster—AI techniques that focus on analyzing different types of text.
- Emotional recognition cluster—AI technique that focuses on emotions recognition and analysis.
- Computer vision cluster—AI techniques that focus on various methods of analysis pictures, photos and videos.
- Collaborative cluster—AI techniques that focus on collaboration between human operators and digital machines.
- Awareness cluster—AI techniques that focus on various awareness capabilities such as self-awareness and context awareness.

A remarkable phenomenon is the usage of Gesture recognition in three different clusters. Namely, the Emotion recognition cluster, Computer vision cluster, and Collaborative cluster.

In terms of the AI analysis in those fields, there are several overlapping cases, where a field may belong to more than one cluster.

The relationships in Figure 2 are both reflected by adjacency and common AI fields. For example, tone recognition is part of both Speech related cluster and Emotion recognition cluster. Another example is the adjacency of the Text analysis cluster to Speech related cluster, which points at their relative closeness.

The use of AI in service is divided into narrow specializations.

AI field is characterized by the narrow specialization of AI experts [3,4]. Experts have a deep understanding of their narrow field of experience, but know very little about other AI fields; this phenomenon is also known as sectorial silos [5]. Gupta et al. [3] and Meunier and Bellais [5] supported the idea that these sectorial silos are limiting, and wider approach should be adopted.

Several papers deal with information silos, their drawbacks, and the advantages of breaking them, for example [6–8]. Gupta et al. [3] state that there is a common need to go beyond the development of AI in sectorial silos, so as to understand the impacts AI might have across society. Miriyev A. and Kovač M. [4] state that: "An education methodology is needed for researchers to develop a combination of skills in physical artificial intelligence."

Martínez-Plumed et al. [9] while dealing with the futures of artificial intelligence technologies, developed a TRL (technology readiness levels) methodology for evaluating the maturity level of each AI technique.

The rest of this paper is structured as follows:

The introduction is followed by a literature review section of the related literature; The next section describes a case study on Robo-chef to illustrate a case where a large potential remains to be realized. A second case study follows on a mature technology of chatbots, which illustrates the advantage of integrating numerous AI fields across several clusters for an advantageous integrative system. A discussion section follows, and the last section is a summary and conclusion, with some insights for future research.

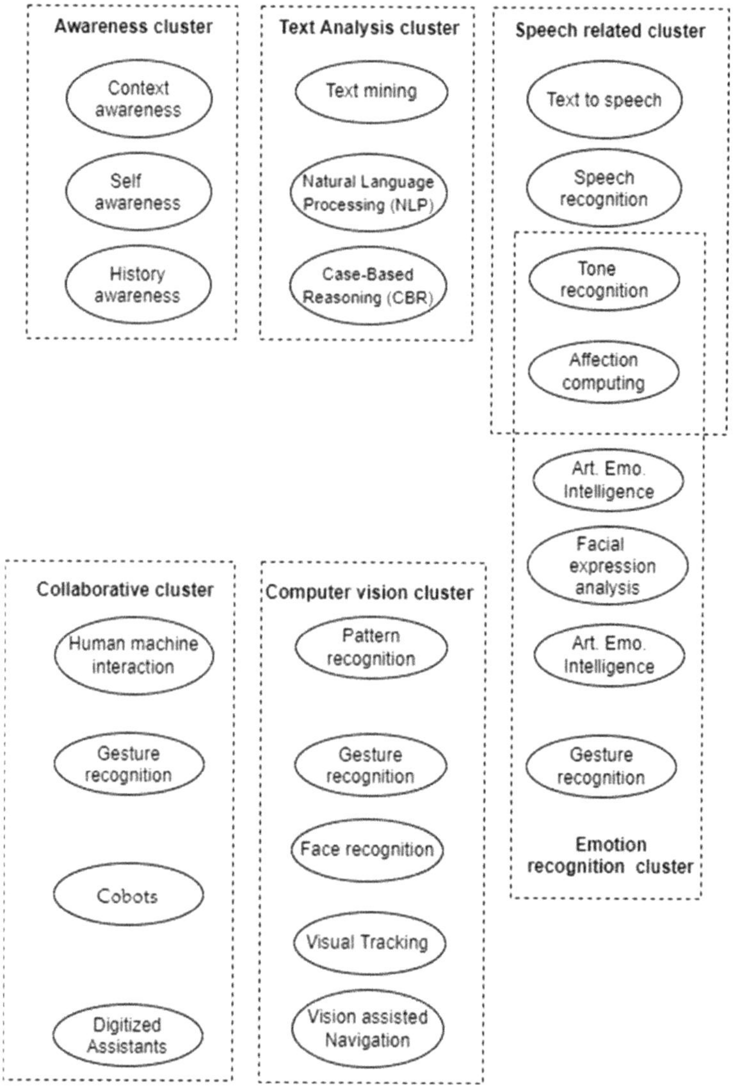

Figure 2. Clusters of major AI domain specializations in services and their relationships.

2. Literature Review

This section reviews the literature related to AI deployment in services, the papers that advocate the integration of several AI techniques or technologies in relation to services, and the literature related to the case studies.

2.1. AI Deployment in Services

Artificial intelligence (AI) is increasingly reshaping services by performing various tasks, constituting a major source of innovation [10]. The deployment of AI in services is typically attributed to encounters with customers. For example, Li et al. [11] identified four modes of AI technology-based service encounters: AI-supplemented, AI-generated, AI-mediated, and AI-facilitated encounters. Smart technologies and connected objects are rapidly changing the organizational frontline. Yet, our understanding of how these technologies infuse service encounters remains limited [12]. Robinson et al. [13] categorized several types of services, interspecific service (AI-to-human), inter AI service (AI-to-AI), and introduced the concept of counterfeit service; they also proposed a research agenda focused on the implementation of AI in dyadic service exchanges. AI is frequently used for integrating robotics into services [14,15]. Belk [16] examined ethical issues related to integrating AI and robotics in services.

2.2. Advocating Integration of Several AI Techniques or Technologies in Services

Numerous papers advocated the integration of several AI techniques. In all of these articles the integration yields improved synergic results.

Some examples are as follows: Benbya et al. [17] in their editorial article, stated that "artificial intelligence (AI) technologies offer novel, distinctive opportunities and pose new significant challenges to organizations that set them apart from other forms of digital technologies". Chen and Decary [18] provide a guide to understand the fundamentals of major AI technologies such as, machine learning, natural language processing, AI voice assistants and medical robotics, as well as their proper use in healthcare; they also provide practical recommendations to help decision-makers develop an AI strategy that can support their digital healthcare transformation.

Androutsopoulou et al. [19] addressed the transformation of communication between citizens and government via chatbots guided by AI; they advocated the integration of natural language processing, machine learning and data mining technologies, and leverages existing data of various forms (with the possibility of using expert systems).

Elfatih et al. [20] advocated the integration of different AI technologies in automotive 5G communication, such as machine learning and swarm intelligence algorithms; they also advocated using Google's Kubemeter project as an open source, enables to improve the community and sharing machines between applications. The sharing machines require ensuring that two applications do not try to use the same ports [21].

Vocke et al. [22] advocated the integration of the current technological solutions available in the field of artificial intelligence. In addition, they discussed the next step to integrate AI technologies with current methods for optimizing the innovation process.

2.3. Literature as a Background to the Robo-Chef Case Study

A search for robotic chefs (on Google scholar) found only very few relevant papers. For example, searching for robo-chef yields 19 results (June 2022), of which two are citations only, two not in English, and 5 published before 2017. Therefore, this review includes some background work on robots in somewhat similar environments.

Rosete et al. [23] reviews the literature on service robots in the hospitality industry. Afsheen et al. [24] presents a self-sufficient robo-waiter with some navigation capability; however, the communication is only done by the user on the keyboard attached to the robo-waiter, and wirelessly sent to the kitchen; this is a clear case of limited use of technology: no NLP, no speech recognition, no vocal communication ...

Al-Sayed [25] mentions robo-chefs as part of the developing technologies in the future kitchen. Sener and Yao [26] discuss the theoretical learning process of a robo-chef. Garcia-Haro et al. [27] discuss service robots in catering applications and mention robo-chefs and one of the robot types. Zhu and Chang [28] dealt with the motions of the robotic chef and their effect on food quality. Bollini et al. [29] presented a robot that identifies ingredients placed on the table and operates according to a set of natural language instructions.

2.4. Literature for the Chatbot Case Study

The research on chatbots has proliferated in recent years, as the usage of chatbots dramatically increased and almost became ubiquitous [30,31]. The large majority of chatbots are confined to written text messages, as text gives an answer to the vast range of service issues that are raised by the customers [32,33]; this reliance on text has spawned research and implementations of natural language processing (NLP) and sentiment analysis based on text [34].

Okuda and Shoda [35] describe an AI-based chatbot service for the financial industry; they apply AI to generate a service thesaurus by applying ML on the text in FAQ, and call-center response-manuals.

Sidaoui et al. [36] evaluated customer experience during the conversation with a chatbot.

Chen et al. [37] classify and measure the service quality of AI chatbots in frontline service; they developed seven dimensions for service quality measurement that could be described as follows:

- Understanding the explicit and implicit meaning, and the emotional implication of the text;
- Close human-AI collaboration;
- Human-like behavior (including empathy, and social cues);
- Continuous improvement (including learning and updates);
- Personalization;
- Culture adaption;
- Responsiveness and simple.

Bulla et al. [38] review a plethora of issues and applications of AI Based Medical Assistant Chatbots; they present concurrent technology applications and identify issues to be amended in future years. Varitimiadis et al. [39] Presented a distributed and collaborative multi-chatbot system for guidance in museums.

Borsci et al. [40] developed a chatbot usability scale for interaction with AI-based chatbots; they developed two measuring tools: (i) A diagnostic tool in the form of a checklist. (ii) A 15-item questionnaire with high reliability.

Erickson and Kim [41] check the compatibility chatbots with a knowledge management system and concluded that while the implementation of this combination is rare, the merits of this integration are highly attractive. Chao et al. [42] stated that the bottleneck of service provision has shifted from system development to the establishment of an in-depth domain knowledge base. Mydyti, H., and Kadriu [43] studied how chatbots can be implemented in the domains of banking, e-commerce, tourism, and call centers, and discussed the benefits and challenges of chatbots in driving the digital transformation of businesses.

Chatbots are not only a low-cost solution for helping burnt-out human service providers, but their scalability (ability to increase the answering capacity) and their autonomous operation enables increasing service availability and performance [44].

3. Case Study 1: Robo-Chef

This Robotic Chef is an intelligent robotic arm which is able to cook food dishes in an ordinary home environment or restaurants. The robotic arm recognizes the utensils and ingredients required for the particular recipe [45]. Robotic cooking is a difficult task, as the translation from raw recipe instructions to robotic actions involving precise motions and tool-handling is challenging [46]. Robotic chefs are starting to replace human chefs in the restaurant industry [28].

The aim of the case study is to point at the potential of integrating various technologies into the Robo-chef functionality. In particular, the potential of using conversational capabilities which currently are missing form most Robo-chefs will be highlighted. Such integration will bring Robo-chef closer to the look and feel of human beings, and their behavior and reactions could be even more effective—as advanced robotic and navigation abilities combined with access to vast knowledge, deep learning, and other artificial intelligence technologies could enhance their ability to converse and guide the user.

The literature about technologies integration in robo-chefs is very limited and concentrates in a limited number of applications. For example, Zhu and Chang [28] examined the robotic chef anthropomorphism on food quality prediction. Bollini et al. [29] presented a robot that initialized with a set of ingredients placed on the table and a set of natural language instructions describing how to use these ingredients in cooking a plate-like cookies, a salad, or a meatloaf.

Park et al. [47] describe five different robot chef systems, none of which has speech recognition, voice recognition, CBR, gesture recognition, machine learning and Cobots capabilities; however, they mentioned implicit sensing capabilities and it was not clear how these were achieved.

Li et al. [11] lists the following AI characteristics for service robots: personification, autonomy, deep learning, complex interaction, people-oriented, understanding of aesthetics, and emotional abilities; however, except for the complex interaction, none of these abilities are mentioned in the literature about Robo-chefs.

We did not find evidence for vast adaptation of robot chefs in the food industry; moreover, we did not find evidence of wide usage of the following technologies with Robo-chefs:

1. Voice/speech recognition;
2. Emotion recognition;
3. Face recognition;
4. Navigation;
5. Gesture recognition;
6. Cobots capabilities.

Synergy Opportunities for Robo-Chef

We divide the opportunities for Robo-chef improvements into two parts: (1) conversational capabilities, (2) fundamental AI capabilities.

While Robo-chefs currently do not possess the same conversational capabilities as service systems such as chatbots, it is inevitable that its maturity trajectory will eventually lead to the addition of these capabilities. Therefore, we start from discussing the improvement opportunities for Robo-chef that come from conversational capabilities.

Synergy potential of Conversational AI capabilities:

1. Speech communication potential: the Robo chef could get instructions from the human chef while the human chef is busy; this has the potential for activating the robo-chef without immediate closeness and while the chef's hands are occupied in other activities. Speech instructions are easy and flowing, with the ability for passing much more information and exerting tighter control on the robo-chef; this would make the robo chef more flexible and easier to guide.
2. Gesture recognition: collaborative work with humans is the hallmark of the new digital age. Therefore, a robo chef should be able to collaborate with a human chef. Using gesture recognition, the human chef can efficiently signal the robo—chef several important instructions such as: (1) stop current activity, (2) increase or decrease the flames, (3) operate faster or slower, (4) wait, (5) start stirring etc.
3. Face and sentiment recognition: These abilities are currently missing form Robo-chefs, but greatly improve the conversational capabilities of many other service AI systems (e.g., chatbots). Thus, they hold the same potential for Robo-chefs.

Synergy potential of fundamental AI Capabilities

1. Computer vision potential: certain robo-chefs currently have ability to verify the readiness of the food they cook and its location; however, there is no evidence of using vision capabilities for identifying silverware and cookware and bringing them to the cooking arena, as well as removing them for washing and cleaning.
2. Navigation potential: If robo-chefs could navigate the clattered kitchen, this would enable them to move from place to place, to bring pots, pans mixers and other large

cookware from different parts of the kitchen; this dramatically increases the robo-chef's independence and efficiency.

3. Machine learning (ML): ML is a very efficient tool for identifying patterns and their effects, Identify the correct combination of dosages that would make a recipe a great success. ML can identify repeating situations and can infer when and what to do, to improve the process. For example: (1) when to bring hot or cold water to the chef, (2) when to bring salt or certain spices to the chef, (3) when to change the oven temperature and how to control it, etc.

4. Case Study 2: Chatbot

The aim of the case study is very different from the Robo-waiter case, since chatbots are much more developed and matured, especially in the capabilities of the conversational system. The conversational capabilities in chatbots are much more prevalent with wide usage across all industries; this maturity led many research projects to propose integration with more technologies to increase the synergy and improve the chatbot performances; this strengthens the claim of this paper regarding the contribution and synergy of integrating technologies in various services. Chatbots represent a unique tool that has extraordinary maturity and can enlighten the path for future progress of all other service tools. The very basic core of chatbots uses text-related tool and NLP [34].

4.1. Chatbot Adoption of AI Technologies

In the following paragraphs we describe several conversational AI technologies that were integrated into chatbots in research or implementations for the benefit of service.

4.1.1. Voice Recognition and Text to Speech Chatbots

The integration of voice recognition into chatbot functionality was mentioned in a research on the use of chatbots for distance education as early as 2005 [48]. A computing architecture for full voice input and output is offered by du Preez, et al. [49]. Voice recognition with text to speech technology is mentioned several times in a review by Satu et al. [50], and a survey by Abdul-Kade and Woods [51]. Shakhovska, et al. [52] describes the development of a speech-to-text chatbot interface based on Google API. Kumar et al. [53] proposed a voice recognition-based educational chatbot for visually impaired people. Using voice recognition in medical services chatbots is described in Athota et al. [54], Tjiptomongsoguno [55] and Kadam et al. (2021). A clear contribution of the voice recognition addition was found or implied in all of the above cases.

In all these cases, the chatbot used NLP analysis, and voice, and speech technologies.

4.1.2. Tone Recognition and Chatbots

In early chatbot design, the focus was merely on producing coherent responses and using grammatically correct sentences [56–59]. Nowadays, more important is not only what is said by a chatbot, but also how it is expressed linguistically [60]. Users prefer chatbots that use language that is structurally correct and has a logical style [61]. So, the use of tone analysis became more popular in the recent research. Johnson et al. [62] uses tone recognition for its proposed chatbot; they mention the ability of IBM's Watson system for tone recognition and mood analysis: "Tone analyzer service documentation", in IBM.com while citing and its integration with a chatbot (https://www.ibm.com/watson/developercloud/doc/toneanalyzer/Retrieved—24 May 2022).

Lee et al. [63] developed a system that pre-processes speech with sound data enhancing method in speech emotion recognition and transform the sound into a spectrogram that applied to recognize the five emotions, which are peace, happy, sad, angry and fear.

Sheth et al. [64] stated that an intelligent chatbot has the ability to leverage a microphone tone analyzer service to analyze speech tonality and sentiment.

4.1.3. Gesture Recognition and Chatbots

Gesture recognition technology integration into chatbots is another researched combination that is still not widely implemented, but is mentioned in many research papers. Most of these papers also include voice and speech recognition. The idea to use gesture recognition for human-computer interaction is not new (e.g., [65]) and especially for chatbots [66]; however, the actual case studies and pioneering implementations of this technology came much later. Johnson et al. [62] report integrating gesture recognition capabilities with a chatbot using capabilities of two external systems: (1) IBM Watson and (2) cleverbot. An advanced chatbot with the abilities of face recognition and hand gesture recognition is described in Gopinath et al. [67].

Several recent papers suggested integrating sign language and chatbots for serving people with hearing disabilities. Pardasani et al. [68] report their experience of integrating American sign language based on fingers and hand gestures. The system they devised has also a full audio interface. Huang, Wu and Kameda [69] propose a new design of a chat bot system for people with Hearing or Speech Disorder (PHSD) with Leap Motion gesture recognition. Fledgling use of Gesture recognition in chatbots was mentioned in a medical chatbot applications [70] and in a Human-Resource (HR) management application [71].

4.1.4. Face and Sentiment Recognition and Chatbots

The integration of face recognition into chatbot functionality is another example of technology specialization (in addition for using core chatbot text and NLP technologies); however, while some cases added this technology separately (e.g., Angeline et al. [72]; Ahmed et al. [73]), many of the presented cases of chatbot usage of face-recognition are also using voice recognition (e.g., [74,75]).

A prevalent use of face and facial expressions recognition for chatbots is for sentiment analysis. Some examples are: Lee et al. [76] uses facial expression analysis in its counseling service, using emotional response generation. Devaram [77] empathic chatbot uses facial recognition for identifying feelings of its human customers. Lee et al. [76] use deep neural network with its facial recognition for emotion recognition. Silapasuphakornwong and Uehira [78] utilize facial recognition along with voice emotion recognition for elderly emotion monitoring. Huang and Chueh [79] even go further to analyze the facial expression of pats for veterinary consultation.

4.1.5. Case Based Reasoning

Case-based reasoning (CBR) is an artificial-intelligence technique that categorizes experience into "cases" and correlates the current problem to a similar "case". The integration of Case Based Reasoning (CBR) in chatbots is now prevalent in many organizations [80]. The combination of CBR and chatbots is very natural as CBR is based on text processing. The integration of CBR in chatbots is mentioned as early as 2007 [81] for a chatbot that was used in the educational environment. An additional case of an educational chatbot that integrates CBR is mentioned in Buyrukoğlu, and Yilmaz [82]. In many cases CBR is used for solving customer problems. For example, handling of customer complaints [83].

4.1.6. Avatar Technology and Chatbots

Advances in computer technology have fostered the proliferation of virtual characters, often called avatars, that are representation of users, controlled by a human or software, that have an ability to interact [84]. Three-dimensional avatars can be added to make the chat bot more appealing. The avatar is certainly capable of displaying emotions and moods in the form of the facial expression of the conversation that was spoken so the subject gets more interesting [74]. Przegalinska et al. [85] conducted research on anthropomorphizing chat bots using avatars; their recommendations are to focus on the three new trust-enhancing features of chatbots that transparency, integrity, explain ability that allow for greater control.

4.1.7. Context and Client History Analysis and Chatbots

Many organizations store valuable data and information about their customers. In many cases this data is related to Customer Relationship Management (CRM) [86]; this data is a treasure trove for chatbot communication with the customers. Inferring the customer situation can be significantly improved by analyzing their history. For example, A client who has many recent complaints in their history file deserves special attention; and repeated claims should be analyzed and, in some cases, referred to a human manager.

To continue the above discussion, few papers describe the advantages of holistic system with all the above technologies. For example, Angga, et al. [74] describe a chatbot with 3D avatar, full voice interface, and facial expression analysis. Trappey et al. [2] integrates virtual reality (VR) and Case Based Reasoning (CBR) with other technologies. Knickerbocker et al. [87] advocated the heterogeneous integration of IoT, AI and advanced computing technologies for healthcare.

5. Capabilities Evolution of the Major AI Specializations in Conversational Services

Some papers advocate the integration of technologies for overall better communication experience that leads to improved customer satisfaction. In this section we propose an evolutionary perspective for describing and illustrating AI capabilities relationships. The proposed relationships convey inclusion of capabilities. For example, "Text to Speech" capability includes both capabilities of "Text recognition" and "Speech recognition"; this evolutionary description is a theoretical description, not necessarily related to materializing a specific application. In practice, in some cases several levels of the hierarchy could be bypassed (for example by using deep-learning, instead of machine learning). Our approach is illustrated and summarized in Figure 3.

The main considerations of this approach are: (1) the realization that AI capabilities are built in evolutionary manner with hierarchical capabilities. (2) the realization that performing a service function is the main goal of AI deployment in service provision. (3) therefore, relating AI technology to a service function is a key for assessing its importance. (4) however, immature AI technology, or the unavailability of a certain AI technology are serious barriers that prevent this AI integration in service provision.

Based on Figure 2, we analyzed the capability evolution of the various AI technologies for decision-making in conversational service context and developed the following capabilities evolution chart; this chart could be used for generating an evolutionary plan for effective and efficient AI integration process in conversational service systems.

Figure 3 presents the capabilities' hierarchy of the various AI technologies in conversational service context. For example, "Face recognition" capabilities include the capabilities of "Visual pattern recognition". Figure 3 shows the input-related capabilities on its top level, and downward hierarchy, of progressively advanced processing capabilities leading to the outputs at the bottom level.

While Figure 3 focuses on the AI integration in conversational service systems, it is important to mention that performing non-conversational service functions may also be important in service provision, leading to a different dependencies scheme. For example, for Robo-Chef some tactile and navigation capabilities are more important than the emotion recognition capabilities. Therefore, nowadays these capabilities are more developed in Robo-Chefs than the emotion recognition capabilities. In the long-range, we may see integration of mature AI technologies even if their function is less significant. In this regard, even if a function is very important, but the current AI technology is immature, it forms a serious obstacle that prevent this AI integration in the service provision.

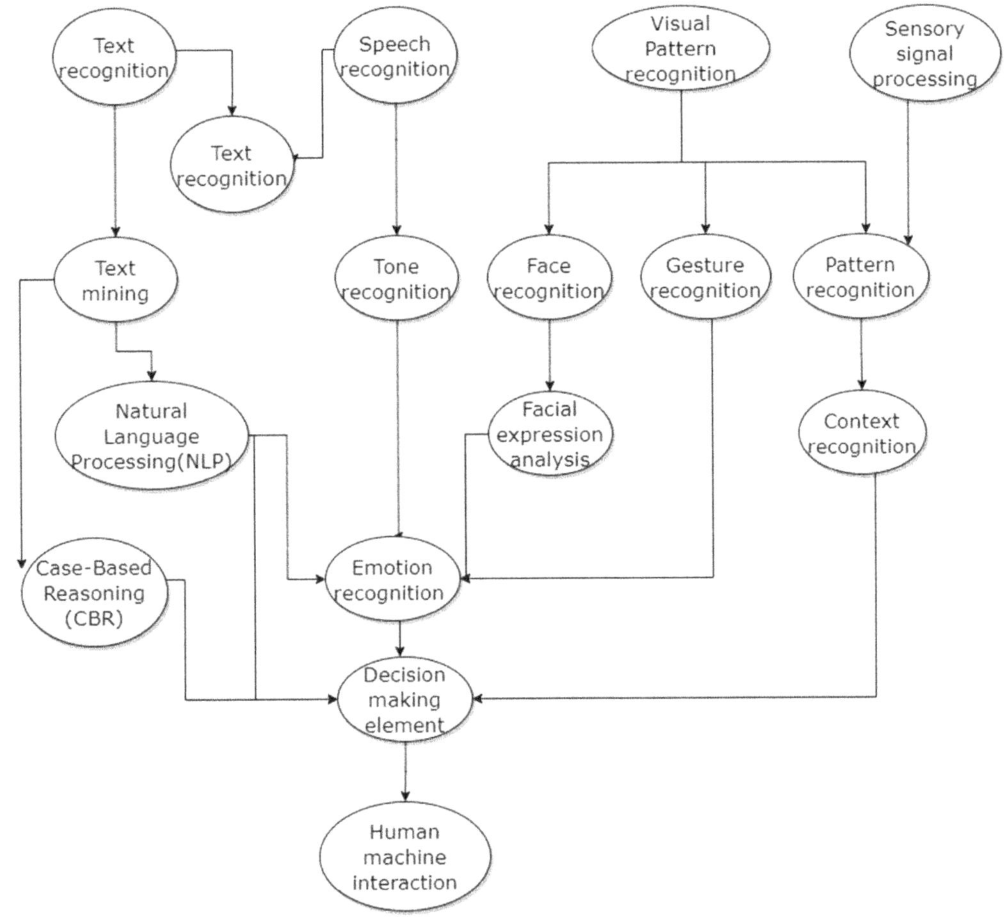

Figure 3. Capabilities evolution of the major AI specializations in conversational support service systems.

6. Discussion

So-far, our discussion was generic, and we did not deal with specific implementations by a specific user, or a specific company. In this section we try to portray the approach that can utilize the information presented thus far, for the benefit of implementers. Specific implementation is always dependent upon the use case, product requirement, and market demand; it is therefore, that the requirement elicitation must be done so that the needs of the systems would be clear, prior to the decision on the AI framework to be developed; it is therefore assumed that at least a preliminary use-case analysis is already done, and the functional requirements of the system are already defined. From this point, we propose a sequential approach for generating an AI technology integration plan; this approach is illustrated and summarized in Figure 4.

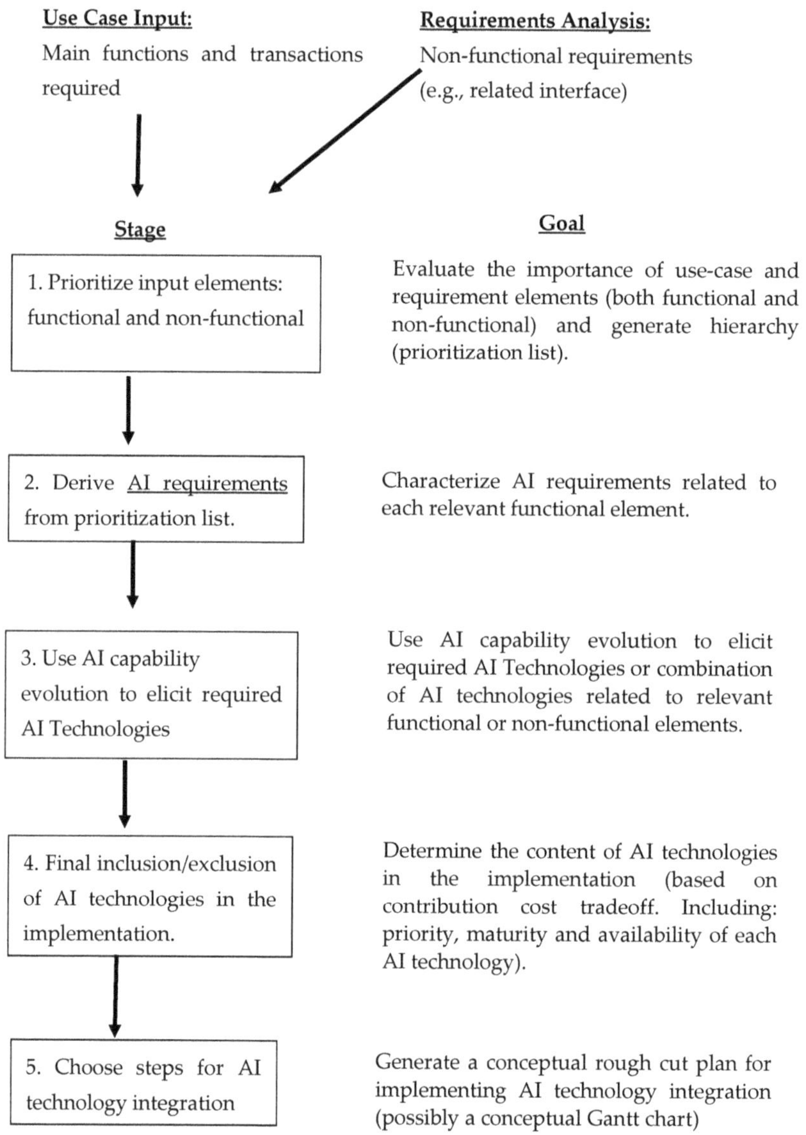

Figure 4. Proposed process for generating AI technology integration plan.

The main considerations of this approach are: (1) the realization that different services may have vastly different characteristics and functional requirements. (2) the realization that performing a service function is the main goal of AI deployment in service provision. (3) therefore, relating AI technology to a service function is a key for assessing its importance. (4) however, immature AI technology, or the unavailability of a required AI technology are serious barriers that hamper this AI integration in service provision.

Thus, we now describe the stages of generating an AI integration plan, after getting the service's main functions and transactions from a preliminary use-case analysis, and some non-functional requirements (mainly related to the interface).

1. The first stage is to evaluate and prioritize the importance of elements from a preliminary use-case analysis (both functional and non-functional) and generate an importance hierarchy (prioritization list) of these requirements.
2. The second stage is to derive AI requirements from the prioritization list (of functional and non-functional elements); this is to define the major outcomes required from the AI technology capabilities.
3. The third stage is to use AI capability evolution (Figure 3) to elicit required AI technologies, or combination of AI technologies, related to relevant functional or non-functional elements. In some cases, there is more than one way to achieve the same capability—For example, given available training data, one can build a single deep learning architecture for emotion recognition based on raw text and speech data, without building the intermediate modules illustrated in Figure 3. At this stage we show all alternatives to be chosen in the next stage.
4. The fourth stage is to determine the content of AI technologies in the implementation (based on contribution cost tradeoff. Including: priority, maturity and availability of each AI technology). At this stage, at most, only one AI alternative is chosen (e.g., deep learning vs. machine learning).
5. The fifth stage is to generate a conceptual rough-cut plan for implementing AI technology integration (possibly a conceptual Gantt chart).

Figure 4 describes and summarizes the proposed process for generating an AI technology integration plan; however, it would take several case studies to test this approach and come up with insights as to its strengths and weaknesses.

6.1. Simple Illustrative Example

We use a simple chatbot for illustration purposes only. Specifically, we use administrative chatbot of an eye-care-center which gives information: (1) about the center services, (2) appointment availability, (3) various forms, (4) procedures to be followed.

Stage 1: A quick analysis of the use-case and requirements reveals heavy dependency on text communication; however, it is clear that many of the clients have real eye-sight problem, so that the option of speech communication is crucial. The communications scope is limited in a way that can keeps it structured; it is assumed that dealing with emotions is less important.

Stage 2: AI Requirements:

- "Heavy dependency on text communication" → Human machine interaction through text leading to natural language understanding.
- "Speech communication is crucial" → Speech interaction ability.
- "Structured communication" → Easy text mining.

Stage 3: Required AI Technologies:

From the stage 2 it is clear that NLP is needed for the implementation. So, from Figure 3 we conclude that: "text mining" is needed as well as "text recognition".

From stage 2 it is clear that Speech interaction ability is required. Therefore, from Figure 3: "text to speech", "speech recognition", and "text recognition" are needed.

Stage 4: Final inclusion/exclusion of AI technologies

From previous stages it is clear that most of the AI technologies are fully required. Therefore, the included technologies are as follows:

"Text recognition"
"Text mining"
"Speech recognition"
"Text to speech"

Stage 5: Steps for AI technology integration

The outcome of stage 4 leads to the following AI implementation plan:

"Text recognition" → "Text mining"
"Speech recognition" → "Text to speech"

Note that the implementation is done with two parallel progress paths.

6.2. Limitations and Potential Benefits of the Proposed Approach

6.2.1. Limitations

The limitations of this study are as follows:

1. The study focused on conversational service systems, therefore is may not fully reflect all the situations and practices of other domains.
2. The study did not consider the point that deep learning may outperform classic machine learning methods because deep learning automatically "combines" raw data features instead of requiring feature engineering.
3. The study contains only 2 case studies, so there may be points that the study overlooks which may appear in other case studies.
4. The study gives a time snapshot that may be short lived in our dynamic changing technological world.

6.2.2. Potential Benefits

The benefits of this study are as follows:

1. The benefit of this study is its discovery of unused synergetic potential of integration between several AI techniques into an orchestrated effort to improve service.
2. The study tackles the problem of AI knowledge silos in service provision; it discusses the reasons for the isolation of these silos, and reveals the barriers and the traps for their integration.
3. The study described a roadmap of AI clusters in the service domain.
4. The study illustrates the synergetic use of AI technologies in a mature case study, and the lack of major AI synergy in a less matured second case study.
5. The paper presents a novel evolutionary inclusion model of conversational AI capabilities.
6. The paper presents a novel sequential approach for generating AI implementation plan.

7. Conclusions

This paper examined the potential of integrating several AI techniques or technologies for performing better service and increasing customer satisfaction related to the service encounters. The paper maps the major AI clusters and analyze dependencies between the major elements of AI capabilities. Two different case studies are presented. One of the case studies shows the rich integration of AI technologies in a mature chatbot application, while the other case study reveals a very narrow use of AI integration in less mature applications such as Robo-Chef; it was shown that while research literature often advocates such integration, the actual integration of various technologies is very slow and, in some cases, non-existent; it is therefore, that we propose an evolutional approach in the discussion section.

Future research may include maturity model developments for specific environments; case studies related to integrating technologies in the service industry; and scorecard dashboard development based on quantitative data analysis.

A barrier to the integration of technologies is the privacy of the customer and the user. The user and the customers must first agree to either be seen or be heard in the computerized system.

Author Contributions: Conceptualization, Y.C. and S.R.; methodology, S.R. and Y.C.; formal analysis, S.R.; investigation, Y.C.; writing—original draft preparation, S.R. and Y.C.; writing—review and editing, Y.C. and S.R.; visualization, S.R. All authors have read and agreed to the published version of the manuscript.

Funding: This research received no external funding.

Institutional Review Board Statement: Not applicable, the study not involve humans or animals.

Informed Consent Statement: Not applicable.

Data Availability Statement: Not applicable.

Conflicts of Interest: The authors declare no conflict of interest.

References

1. Gomi, T. New AI and Service Robots. *Ind. Robot.* **2003**, *30*, 123–138. [CrossRef]
2. Trappey, A.J.; Trappey, C.V.; Chao, M.-H.; Wu, C.-T. VR-Enabled Engineering Consultation Chatbot for Integrated and Intelligent Manufacturing Services. *J. Ind. Inf. Integr.* **2022**, *26*, 100331. [CrossRef]
3. Gupta, S.; Langhans, S.D.; Domisch, S.; Fuso-Nerini, F.; Felländer, A.; Battaglini, M.; Tegmark, M.; Vinuesa, R. Assessing Whether Artificial Intelligence Is an Enabler or an Inhibitor of Sustainability at Indicator Level. *Transp. Eng.* **2021**, *4*, 100064. [CrossRef]
4. Miriyev, A.; Kovač, M. Skills for Physical Artificial Intelligence. *Nat. Mach. Intell.* **2020**, *2*, 658–660. [CrossRef]
5. Meunier, F.-X.; Bellais, R. Technical Systems and Cross-Sector Knowledge Diffusion: An Illustration with Drones. *Technol. Anal. Strateg. Manag.* **2019**, *31*, 433–446. [CrossRef]
6. Miller, L.C.; Jones, B.B.; Graves, R.S.; Sievert, M.C. Merging Silos: Collaborating for Information Literacy. *J. Contin. Educ. Nurs.* **2010**, *41*, 267–272. [CrossRef]
7. De Gregorio, G.; Ranchordás, S. Breaking down Information Silos with Big Data: A Legal Analysis of Data Sharing. In *Legal Challenges of Big Data*; Edward Elgar Publishing: Cheltenham, UK, 2020.
8. Charbonneau, D.H.; Priehs, M.; Hukill, G. Beyond Knowledge Silos: Preserving and Sharing Institutional Knowledge in Academic Libraries. *Knowl. Silos Preserv. Shar. Inst. Knowl. Acad. Libr.* **2016**, 1–8.
9. Martínez-Plumed, F.; Gómez, E.; Hernández-Orallo, J. Futures of Artificial Intelligence through Technology Readiness Levels. *Telemat. Inform.* **2021**, *58*, 101525. [CrossRef]
10. Huang, M.-H.; Rust, R.T. Artificial Intelligence in Service. *J. Serv. Res.* **2018**, *21*, 155–172. [CrossRef]
11. Li, M.; Yin, D.; Qiu, H.; Bai, B. A Systematic Review of AI Technology-Based Service Encounters: Implications for Hospitality and Tourism Operations. *Int. J. Hosp. Manag.* **2021**, *95*, 102930. [CrossRef]
12. De Keyser, A.; Köcher, S.; Alkire, L.; Verbeeck, C.; Kandampully, J. Frontline Service Technology Infusion: Conceptual Archetypes and Future Research Directions. *J. Serv. Manag.* **2019**, *30*, 156–183. [CrossRef]
13. Robinson, S.; Orsingher, C.; Alkire, L.; De Keyser, A.; Giebelhausen, M.; Papamichail, K.N.; Shams, P.; Temerak, M.S. Frontline Encounters of the AI Kind: An Evolved Service Encounter Framework. *J. Bus. Res.* **2020**, *116*, 366–376. [CrossRef]
14. Wirtz, J.; Patterson, P.G.; Kunz, W.H.; Gruber, T.; Lu, V.N.; Paluch, S.; Martins, A. Brave New World: Service Robots in the Frontline. *J. Serv. Manag.* **2018**, *29*, 907–931. [CrossRef]
15. Belanche, D.; Casaló, L.V.; Flavián, C.; Schepers, J. Robots or Frontline Employees? Exploring Customers' Attributions of Responsibility and Stability after Service Failure or Success. *J. Serv. Manag.* **2020**, *31*, 267–289. [CrossRef]
16. Belk, R. Ethical Issues in Service Robotics and Artificial Intelligence. *Serv. Ind. J.* **2021**, *41*, 860–876. [CrossRef]
17. Benbya, H.; Pachidi, S.; Jarvenpaa, S. Special Issue Editorial: Artificial Intelligence in Organizations: Implications for Information Systems Research. *J. Assoc. Inf. Syst.* **2021**, *22*, 10. [CrossRef]
18. Chen, M.; Decary, M. Artificial Intelligence in Healthcare: An Essential Guide for Health Leaders. *Healthc. Manag. Forum* **2020**, *33*, 10–18. [CrossRef] [PubMed]
19. Androutsopoulou, A.; Karacapilidis, N.; Loukis, E.; Charalabidis, Y. Transforming the Communication between Citizens and Government through AI-Guided Chatbots. *Gov. Inf. Q.* **2019**, *36*, 358–367. [CrossRef]
20. Elfatih, N.M.; Hasan, M.K.; Kamal, Z.; Gupta, D.; Saeed, R.A.; Ali, E.S.; Hosain, M.S. Internet of Vehicle's Resource Management in 5G Networks Using AI Technologies: Current Status and Trends. *IET Commun.* **2022**, *16*, 400–420. [CrossRef]
21. Pokhrel, S.R. Software Defined Internet of Vehicles for Automation and Orchestration. *IEEE Trans. Intell. Transp. Syst.* **2021**, *22*, 3890–3899. [CrossRef]
22. Vocke, C.; Constantinescu, C.; Popescu, D. Application Potentials of Artificial Intelligence for the Design of Innovation Processes. *Procedia CIRP* **2019**, *84*, 810–813. [CrossRef]
23. Rosete, A.; Soares, B.; Salvadorinho, J.; Reis, J.; Amorim, M. Service Robots in the Hospitality Industry: An Exploratory Literature Review. In *International Conference on Exploring Services Science*; Springer: Berlin/Heidelberg, Germany, 2020; pp. 174–186.
24. Afsheen, S.; Fathima, L.; Khan, Z.; Elahi, M. A Self-Sufficient Waiter Robo for Serving in Restaurants. *Int. J. Adv. Res. Dev.* **2018**, *3*, 57–67.
25. Al-Sayed, L. Technologies at the Crossroads of Food Security and Migration. In *Food Tech Transitions*; Springer: Berlin/Heidelberg, Germany, 2019; pp. 129–148.
26. Sener, F.; Yao, A. Zero-Shot Anticipation for Instructional Activities. In Proceedings of the IEEE/CVF International Conference on Computer Vision, Seoul, Korea, 27 October–2 November 2019; pp. 862–871.
27. Garcia-Haro, J.M.; Oña, E.D.; Hernandez-Vicen, J.; Martinez, S.; Balaguer, C. Service Robots in Catering Applications: A Review and Future Challenges. *Electronics* **2020**, *10*, 47. [CrossRef]
28. Zhu, D.H.; Chang, Y.P. Robot with Humanoid Hands Cooks Food Better? Effect of Robotic Chef Anthropomorphism on Food Quality Prediction. *Int. J. Contemp. Hosp. Manag.* **2020**, *32*, 1367–1383. [CrossRef]

29. Bollini, M.; Tellex, S.; Thompson, T.; Roy, N.; Rus, D. Interpreting and Executing Recipes with a Cooking Robot. In *Experimental Robotics: The 13th International Symposium on Experimental Robotics*; Desai, J.P., Dudek, G., Khatib, O., Kumar, V., Eds.; Springer International Publishing: Berlin/Heidelberg, Germany, 2013; pp. 481–495, ISBN 978-3-319-00065-7.
30. Adamopoulou, E.; Moussiades, L. An Overview of Chatbot Technology. In *IFIP International Conference on Artificial Intelligence Applications and Innovations*; Springer: Berlin/Heidelberg, Germany, 2020; pp. 373–383.
31. Rapp, A.; Curti, L.; Boldi, A. The Human Side of Human-Chatbot Interaction: A Systematic Literature Review of Ten Years of Research on Text-Based Chatbots. *Int. J. Hum.-Comput. Stud.* **2021**, *151*, 102630. [CrossRef]
32. Hien, H.T.; Cuong, P.-N.; Nam, L.N.H.; Nhung, H.L.T.K.; Thang, L.D. Intelligent Assistants in Higher-Education Environments: The FIT-EBot, a Chatbot for Administrative and Learning Support. In Proceedings of the 9th International Symposium on Information and Communication Technology, Danang City, Vietnam, 6–7 December 2018; pp. 69–76.
33. Yarovyi, A.; Kudriavtsev, D. Method of Multi-Purpose Text Analysis Based on a Combination of Knowledge Bases for Intelligent Chatbot. In Proceedings of the CEUR Workshop Proceedings, Vulnius, Lithuania, 8 December 2021; Volume 2870, pp. 1238–1248.
34. Locke, S.; Bashall, A.; Al-Adely, S.; Moore, J.; Wilson, A.; Kitchen, G.B. Natural Language Processing in Medicine: A Review. *Trends Anaesth. Crit. Care* **2021**, *38*, 4–9. [CrossRef]
35. Okuda, T.; Shoda, S. AI-Based Chatbot Service for Financial Industry. *Fujitsu Sci. Tech. J.* **2018**, *54*, 4–8.
36. Sidaoui, K.; Jaakkola, M.; Burton, J. AI Feel You: Customer Experience Assessment via Chatbot Interviews. *J. Serv. Manag.* **2020**, *31*, 745–766. [CrossRef]
37. Chen, Q.; Gong, Y.; Lu, Y.; Tang, J. Classifying and Measuring the Service Quality of AI Chatbot in Frontline Service. *J. Bus. Res.* **2022**, *145*, 552–568. [CrossRef]
38. Bulla, C.; Parushetti, C.; Teli, A.; Aski, S.; Koppad, S. A Review of AI Based Medical Assistant Chatbot. *Res. Appl. Web Dev. Des.* **2020**, *3*. [CrossRef]
39. Varitimiadis, S.; Kotis, K.; Pittou, D.; Konstantakis, G. Graph-Based Conversational AI: Towards a Distributed and Collaborative Multi-Chatbot Approach for Museums. *Appl. Sci.* **2021**, *11*, 9160. [CrossRef]
40. Borsci, S.; Malizia, A.; Schmettow, M.; Van Der Velde, F.; Tariverdiyeva, G.; Balaji, D.; Chamberlain, A. The Chatbot Usability Scale: The Design and Pilot of a Usability Scale for Interaction with AI-Based Conversational Agents. *Pers. Ubiquitous Comput.* **2022**, *26*, 95–119. [CrossRef]
41. Erickson, M.; Kim, P. Can chatbots work well with knowledge management systems? *Issues Inf. Syst.* **2020**, *21*, 53–58.
42. Chao, M.-H.; Trappey, A.J.C.; Wu, C.-T. Emerging Technologies of Natural Language-Enabled Chatbots: A Review and Trend Forecast Using Intelligent Ontology Extraction and Patent Analytics. *Complexity* **2021**, *2021*, 5511866. [CrossRef]
43. Mydyti, H.; Kadriu, A. The Impact of Chatbots in Driving Digital Transformation. *Int. J. E-Serv. Mob. Appl. IJESMA* **2021**, *13*, 88–104. [CrossRef]
44. Um, T.; Kim, T.; Chung, N. How Does an Intelligence Chatbot Affect Customers Compared with Self-Service Technology for Sustainable Services? *Sustainability* **2020**, *12*, 5119. [CrossRef]
45. Ban, P.; Desale, S.; Barge, R.; Chavan, P. Intelligent Robotic Arm. In *ITM Web of Conferences*; EDP Sciences: Les Ulis, France, 2020; Chapter 32, p. 01005.
46. Danno, D.; Hauser, S.; Iida, F. Robotic Cooking Through Pose Extraction from Human Natural Cooking Using OpenPose. In *Intelligent Autonomous Systems 16*; Ang, M.H., Jr., Asama, H., Lin, W., Foong, S., Eds.; Springer International Publishing: Berlin/Heidelberg, Germany, 2022; pp. 288–298.
47. Park, S.Y.; Kim, S.; Leifer, L. "Human Chef" to "Computer Chef": Culinary Interactions Framework for Understanding HCI in the Food Industry. In *International Conference on Human-Computer Interaction*; Springer: Berlin/Heidelberg, Germany, 2017; pp. 214–233.
48. Heller, B.; Proctor, M.; Mah, D.; Jewell, L.; Cheung, B. Freudbot: An Investigation of Chatbot Technology in Distance Education. In *EdMedia+ Innovate Learning, Publisher: Association for the Advancement of Computing in Education (AACE))*; Association for the Advancement of Computing in Education (AACE): Waynesville, NC, USA, 2005; pp. 3913–3918.
49. Du Preez, S.J.; Lall, M.; Sinha, S. Sinha An Intelligent Web-Based Voice Chat Bot. In Proceedings of the IEEE EUROCON 2009, St. Petersburg, Russia, 18–23 May 2009; pp. 386–391.
50. Satu, M.S.; Parvez, M.H. Review of Integrated Applications with Aiml Based Chatbot. In *2015 International Conference on Computer and Information Engineering (ICCIE)*; IEEE: Piscataway, NJ, USA, 2015; pp. 87–90.
51. Abdul-Kader, S.A.; Woods, J.C. Survey on Chatbot Design Techniques in Speech Conversation Systems. *Int. J. Adv. Comput. Sci. Appl.* **2015**, *6*, 72–80.
52. Shakhovska, N.; Basystiuk, O.; Shakhovska, K. Development of the Speech-to-Text Chatbot Interface Based on Google API. In *MoMLeT*; CEUR-WS: Aachen, Germany, 2019; pp. 212–221.
53. Kumar, M.N.; Chandar, P.L.; Prasad, A.V.; Sumangali, K. Android Based Educational Chatbot for Visually Impaired People. In Proceedings of the 2016 IEEE International Conference on Computational Intelligence and Computing Research (ICCIC), Chennai, India, 15–17 December 2016; pp. 1–4.
54. Athota, L.; Shukla, V.K.; Pandey, N.; Rana, A. Chatbot for Healthcare System Using Artificial Intelligence. In Proceedings of the 2020 8th International Conference on Reliability, Infocom Technologies and Optimization (Trends and Future Directions) (ICRITO), Noida, India, 4–5 June 2020; pp. 619–622.

55. Tjiptomongsoguno, A.R.W.; Chen, A.; Sanyoto, H.M.; Irwansyah, E.; Kanigoro, B. Medical Chatbot Techniques: A Review. *Proc. Comput. Methods Syst. Softw.* **2020**, *1294*, 346–356. [CrossRef]
56. Perrachione, T.K.; Del Tufo, S.N.; Gabrieli, J.D. Human Voice Recognition Depends on Language Ability. *Science* **2011**, *333*, 595. [CrossRef]
57. Anand, A.; Shanmugam, R. Voice Speech and Recognition—An Overview. In Proceedings of the 3rd International Conference on Computing Informatics and Networks, Delhi, India, 29–30 July 2020; Springer: Berlin/Heidelberg, Germany, 2021; pp. 347–356.
58. Todkar, S.P.; Babar, S.S.; Ambike, R.U.; Suryakar, P.B.; Prasad, J.R. Speaker Recognition Techniques: A Review. In Proceedings of the 2018 3rd International Conference for Convergence in Technology (I2CT), Pune, India, 6–8 April 2018; pp. 1–5.
59. Kabir, M.M.; Mridha, M.F.; Shin, J.; Jahan, I.; Ohi, A.Q. A Survey of Speaker Recognition: Fundamental Theories, Recognition Methods and Opportunities. *IEEE Access* **2021**, *9*, 79236–79263. [CrossRef]
60. Chaves, A.P.; Doerry, E.; Egbert, J.; Gerosa, M. It's How You Say It: Identifying Appropriate Register for Chatbot Language Design. In Proceedings of the 7th International Conference on Human-Agent Interaction, Kyoto, Japan, 6–10 October 2019; pp. 102–109.
61. Jain, M.; Kumar, P.; Kota, R.; Patel, S.N. Evaluating and Informing the Design of Chatbots. In Proceedings of the 2018 Designing Interactive Systems Conference, Hong Kong, China, 9–13 June 2018; pp. 895–906.
62. Johnson, A.; Roush, T.; Fulton, M.; Reese, A. Implementing Physical Capabilities for an Existing Chatbot by Using a Repurposed Animatronic to Synchronize Motor Positioning with Speech. *Int. J. Adv. Stud. Comput. Sci. Eng.* **2017**, *6*, 20.
63. Lee, M.-C.; Chiang, S.-Y.; Yeh, S.-C.; Wen, T.-F. Study on Emotion Recognition and Companion Chatbot Using Deep Neural Network. *Multimed. Tools Appl.* **2020**, *79*, 19629–19657. [CrossRef]
64. Sheth, A.; Yip, H.Y.; Iyengar, A.; Tepper, P. Cognitive Services and Intelligent Chatbots: Current Perspectives and Special Issue Introduction. *IEEE Internet Comput.* **2019**, *23*, 6–12. [CrossRef] [PubMed]
65. Iurgel, I. From Another Point of View: Art-E-Fact. In *International Conference on Technologies for Interactive Digital Storytelling and Entertainment*; Springer: Berlin/Heidelberg, Germany, 2004; pp. 26–35.
66. Montero, C.A.; Araki, K. Enhancing Computer Chat: Toward a Smooth User-Computer Interaction. In *International Conference on Knowledge-Based and Intelligent Information and Engineering Systems*; Springer: Berlin/Heidelberg, Germany, 2005; pp. 918–924.
67. Gopinath, D.; Vijayakumar, S.; Harish, J. Analyze of Facial Expression and Hand Gestures Using Deep Learning. In *AIP Conference Proceedings*; AIP Publishing LLC: Melville, NY, USA, 2022; Volume 2444, p. 030001.
68. Pardasani, A.; Sharma, A.K.; Banerjee, S.; Garg, V.; Roy, D.S. Enhancing the Ability to Communicate by Synthesizing American Sign Language Using Image Recognition in a Chatbot for Differently Abled. In Proceedings of the 2018 7th International Conference on Reliability, Infocom Technologies and Optimization (Trends and Future Directions) (ICRITO), Noida, India, 29–31 August 2018; pp. 529–532.
69. Huang, X.; Wu, B.; Kameda, H. Development of a Sign Language Dialogue System for a Healing Dialogue Robot. In Proceedings of the 2021 IEEE International Conference on Dependable, Autonomic and Secure Computing, International Conference on Pervasive Intelligence and Computing, International Conference on Cloud and Big Data Computing, International Conference on Cyber Science and Technology Congress (DASC/PiCom/CBDCom/CyberSciTech), Virtual Conference, 25–28 October 2021; pp. 867–872.
70. Fadhlallah, G.M. A Deep Learning-Based Approach for Chatbot: Medical Assistance a Case Study. Master's Thesis, University of Mohamed Khider—BISKRA, Khider, Algeria, 2021.
71. AbdElminaam, D.S.; ElMasry, N.; Talaat, Y.; Adel, M.; Hisham, A.; Atef, K.; Mohamed, A.; Akram, M. HR-Chat Bot: Designing and Building Effective Interview Chat-Bots for Fake CV Detection. In Proceedings of the 2021 International Mobile, Intelligent, and Ubiquitous Computing Conference (MIUCC), Cairo, Egypt, 26–27 May 2021; pp. 403–408.
72. Angeline, R.; Gaurav, T.; Rampuriya, P.; Dey, S. Supermarket Automation with Chatbot and Face Recognition Using IoT and AI. In Proceedings of the 2018 3rd International Conference on Communication and Electronics Systems (ICCES), Coimbatore, India, 15–16 October 2018; pp. 1183–1186.
73. Ahmed, S.; Paul, D.; Masnun, R.; Shanto, M.U.A.; Farah, T. Smart Home Shield and Automation System Using Facebook Messenger Chatbot. In Proceedings of the 2020 IEEE Region 10 Symposium (TENSYMP), Dhaka, Bangladesh, 5–7 June 2020; pp. 1791–1794.
74. Angga, P.A.; Fachri, W.E.; Elevanita, A.; Agushinta, R.D. Design of Chatbot with 3D Avatar, Voice Interface, and Facial Expression. In Proceedings of the 2015 international conference on science in information technology (ICSITech), Yogyakarta, Indonesia, 27–28 October 2015; pp. 326–330.
75. Margreat, L.; Paul, J.J.; Mary, T.B. Chatbot-Attendance and Location Guidance System (ALGs). In Proceedings of the 2021 3rd International Conference on Signal Processing and Communication (ICPSC), Coimbatore, India, 13–14 May 2021; pp. 718–722.
76. Lee, D.; Oh, K.-J.; Choi, H.-J. The Chatbot Feels You-a Counseling Service Using Emotional Response Generation. In Proceedings of the 2017 IEEE international conference on big data and smart computing (BigComp), Jeju, Korea, 13–16 February 2017; pp. 437–440.
77. Devaram, S. Empathic Chatbot: Emotional Intelligence for Empathic Chatbot: Emotional Intelligence for Mental Health Well-Being. *arXiv* **2020**, arXiv:201209130.
78. Silapasuphakornwong, P.; Uehira, K. Smart Mirror for Elderly Emotion Monitoring. In Proceedings of the 2021 IEEE 3rd Global Conference on Life Sciences and Technologies (LifeTech), Nara, Japan, 9–11 March 2021; pp. 356–359.

79. Huang, D.-H.; Chueh, H.-E. Chatbot Usage Intention Analysis: Veterinary Consultation. *J. Innov. Knowl.* **2021**, *6*, 135–144. [CrossRef]
80. Alsarayreh, S. The Impact of Technology on Knowledge Retention: A Systematic Review. *Int. J. Inf. Technol. Lang. Stud.* **2021**, *5*, 38–46.
81. Leonhardt, M.D.; Tarouco, L.; Vicari, R.M.; Santos, E.R.; da Silva, M.D.S. Using Chatbots for Network Management Training through Problem-Based Oriented Education. In Proceedings of the Seventh IEEE International Conference on Advanced Learning Technologies (ICALT 2007), Niigata, Japan, 18–20 July 2007; pp. 845–847.
82. Buyrukoğlu, S.; Yilmaz, Y. A Novel Semi-Automated Chatbot Model: Providing Consistent Response of Students' Email in Higher Education Based on Case-Based Reasoning and Latent Semantic Analysis. *Int. J. Multidiscip. Stud. Innov. Technol.* **2021**, *5*, 6–12.
83. Lee, C.-H.; Wang, Y.-H.; Trappey, A.J. Ontology-Based Reasoning for the Intelligent Handling of Customer Complaints. *Comput. Ind. Eng.* **2015**, *84*, 144–155. [CrossRef]
84. Miao, F.; Kozlenkova, I.V.; Wang, H.; Xie, T.; Palmatier, R.W. An Emerging Theory of Avatar Marketing. *J. Mark.* **2022**, *86*, 67–90. [CrossRef]
85. Przegalinska, A.; Ciechanowski, L.; Stroz, A.; Gloor, P.; Mazurek, G. In Bot We Trust: A New Methodology of Chatbot Performance Measures. *Digit. Transform. Disrupt.* **2019**, *62*, 785–797. [CrossRef]
86. Saravanan, D.; Kaur, P. Customer Relationship Management in Banking in the UK Industry: Case of Lloyds Bank. *ECS Trans.* **2022**, *107*, 14325.
87. Knickerbocker, J.U.; Budd, R.; Dang, B.; Chen, Q.; Colgan, E.; Hung, L.W.; Kumar, S.; Lee, K.W.; Lu, M.; Nah, J.W.; et al. Heterogeneous Integration Technology Demonstrations for Future Healthcare, IoT, and AI Computing Solutions. In Proceedings of the 2018 IEEE 68th Electronic Components and Technology Conference (ECTC), San Diego, CA, USA, 29 June 2018; pp. 1519–1528.

applied sciences

MDPI

Article

Artificial Intelligence-Based Technological-Oriented Knowledge Management, Innovation, and E-Service Delivery in Smart Cities: Moderating Role of E-Governance

Syed Asad Abbas Bokhari [1] and Seunghwan Myeong [2,*]

[1] The Center of Security Convergence & eGovernance, Inha University, Nam-gu, Incheon 22212, Korea
[2] Department of Public Administration, Inha University, Incheon 22212, Korea
* Correspondence: shmyeong@inha.ac.kr; Tel.: +82-1057071108

Abstract: The fundamental goal of this research is to investigate the quantitative relationship between technology-oriented knowledge management, innovation, e-governance, and smart city performance using knowledge management-based service science theory and diffusion of innovation theory. Previous research has found a connection between knowledge management, innovation, e-governance, and e-service delivery. We believe these are not only direct connections but also contextual and interactive relationships, so we explored the significance of innovation as a mediator between knowledge management and e-service delivery. Furthermore, we investigated the moderating impact of e-governance on the relationship between innovation and e-service delivery. A survey questionnaire was administered to the population of public officers, entrepreneurs, and citizens, from metropolitan cities for data sampling, and SPSS was applied to analyze data of 569 participants collected from South Korea, Pakistan, Japan, and Bangladesh. We discovered from the analysis that the direct relationships are contextual because innovation mediates the relationship between knowledge management and e-service delivery, and e-governance plays a moderating role in the relationship between innovation and e-service delivery. Based on the outcomes from quantitative analysis, all our proposed hypotheses in this study were supported significantly.

Keywords: technology-oriented knowledge management; innovation; e-governance; e-service delivery; smart city performance

Citation: Bokhari, S.A.A.; Myeong, S. Artificial Intelligence-Based Technological-Oriented Knowledge Management, Innovation, and E-Service Delivery in Smart Cities: Moderating Role of E-Governance. *Appl. Sci.* **2022**, *12*, 8732. https://doi.org/10.3390/app12178732

Academic Editor: Dimitris Mourtzis

Received: 5 August 2022
Accepted: 27 August 2022
Published: 31 August 2022

1. Introduction

The recognition of "resources" or "capabilities" that permit organizations to identify, generate, convert, and disseminate knowledge is critical to realizing the successes and failures of knowledge management (KM) within corporations. The structural, technical, and cultural elements that enable KM's intensification of social capital are termed KM infrastructure [1,2]. The innovation facet is related to the technologically enabled affiliations that emerge within organizations [3], and organizations can ambitiously be organized by a 'smart city' [4]. The presence of norm and trust mechanisms, as well as collaborative learning environments, is signified by the institutional and cultural dimensions.

The appraisal of the KM infrastructure that allows the institutions to identify, develop, transform, and disseminate knowledge is crucial in understanding the strengths and weaknesses of KM initiatives and their impact on different elements.

Numerous scholars have stressed the significance of knowledge systems and applications in knowledge management [5,6]. Previous KM research has been segmented in that it has described a few components of KM performance but has not offered a comprehensive viewpoint of KM impact on other organization attributes such as innovation performance and smart city performance. Most researchers have examined the association between KM enablers, procedures, or outcomes in exclusion. For instance, Gold et al. [7] proposed that the infrastructure of knowledge (culture, technology, structure) and the process of knowledge (attainment, adaptation, submission, and security) have a direct influence on organizational effectiveness. However, they ignored the correlation between knowledge management and innovation. While Lee et al. [8] demonstrated the cooperative relationships between knowledge management enablers, knowledge creation procedures, knowledge management transitional outcomes, and organizational performance, their research did not contemplate the entire knowledge process and its direct and indirect impact on performance.

Currently, the emphasis on innovation- and technology-led evolution is on innovation hubs and inventive centers, smart technological localities, and Living Laboratories that test innovative products [9]. KM has taken power from the confines of the corporate world and enlarged into other socio-economic fields such as education and governance [10]. Major global institutions, including the UN, the World Bank, the EU, and the Organization for Economic Cooperation and Development (OECD), have incorporated knowledge management frameworks into their domestic and global strategic planning. It has become obvious that there is a significant association between knowledge management and urban development, as city activities can be deliberately created to enable knowledge cultivation. Many scholars are looking into 'knowledge cities' [11] and knowledge-based smart city development [12]. Integrated knowledge and innovation are crucial determinants of the smart city's rhetoric and execution. Recent technology capabilities would never have the same impact on smart cities if they had never been entrenched in knowledge and innovation [13]. The extensive knowledge market was essential for the implementation of the paradigm of cities; it is one of two intellectual components that comprise the contemporary concepts about a smart city, its implementation, and enhanced performance.

The term "smart city" is frequently linked with the notion of a digital city, with the extensive use of technology, especially its performance in governance, surveillance, mobility, education, health, and telecom infrastructure [14]. Nevertheless, the idea of a smart city extends beyond technology to include other predictors of innovation and governance, such as technological innovation, institutional innovation, social innovation, e-governance, e-government, and smart governance issues [15,16]. Considering the importance of city governance and administration, as well as collaboration between different stakeholders, to meet the optimum city performance, innovation, expansion, sustainable development, and liveability [17], we aim to investigate how smart governance affects smart city performance directly and also moderates the association between innovation and city performance.

The main objective of our study is to examine the relationship between technology-oriented knowledge management, innovation, e-governance, and smart city performance with the help of knowledge management that is based on service science theory [18] and diffusion of innovation theory [19], as service science theory discusses the use of knowledge that is collected through citizen and artificial intelligence can help to improve and optimize city's service delivery. Diffusion of innovation theory refers to the procedure by which people espouse a new concept, product, practice, and ethos. Further, we will investigate the indirect mediating role of innovation in the relationship between technology-oriented KM and smart city performance and the indirect moderating role of e-governance in the relationship between innovation and smart city performance. Previous scholars examined the direct impact of knowledge management on innovation [20,21], the impact of innovation on smart city performance [22], and the effect of e-governance on smart city performance [23,24], but only a few explored the indirect relationship between these constructs [25]. Our study will contribute to the existing literature by investigating indirect associations to know-how innovation that mediates the relationship between the integration KM and city performance and how e-governance strengthens the relationship between innovation and smart city performance.

The subsequent section briefly outlines the literature on KM, innovation, e-governance, and smart city performance. Next, Section 3 describes the research method that was used to find relevant outcomes for this study. Finally, Section 4 describes the research findings, while Section 5 discusses the recommended next steps for smart city research from the perspective of knowledge management. Section 6 concludes with policy implications and a conclusion.

2. Background and Hypotheses

2.1. Technological-Oriented KM, Innovation, and Smart City Performance

For numerous eras, the practice of knowledge management (KM) has attracted the attention of researchers and experts alike. Academics and professionals have focused their efforts on the discussion of how to effectively employ KM in contemporary organizations to achieve better outcomes [6,8]. The fundamental KM approach and its application to accomplish benefits of performance and competitive advantages are critical success factors in this context [26,27]. Considering the significance of technological innovation and knowledge sharing in our economic system, knowledge management will hold a significant role in the corporate in the future [28]. Consequently, the digital revolution and the increased high-tech innovations in various disciplines will absorb tedious tasks, abandoning only complicated operations for highly competent, primarily white-collar workers [29]. Concurrently, new forms of knowledge are developed because of such new technologies, leading to new prerequisites for administering knowledge [30]. Previous literature suggests one of the main approaches of KM, which is referred to as technology-oriented KM, and it follows a codified strategy to find explicit knowledge that is stashed in external databases [31]. Digitization can effectively process enormous amounts of heterogeneous data, knowledge, and information by employing AI and associated technologies. There are two aspects that distinguish AI applications, which determine our understanding of knowledge and how it is managed in institutions. First, AI algorithms can process data and discover trends autonomously, perhaps more effectively than people. As a corollary, these evolutionary computations can instantly develop important types of knowledge from data [30].

Smart city governments are constantly under pressure to enhance public service delivery with a citizen-friendly approach to digital transformation. Local governments in smart cities are constantly interested in improving the citizen-friendly delivery of public services in the age of technology revolution to enhance efficiency. Instead of focusing on a specific range of services for target markets, as is common in the private sector, municipal government services must manage a broad, diverse array of services that must be delivered to all inhabitants [32]. Even though distinctive clusters of residents will have unique attributes and expectations, access to public services and information must be guaranteed [33], while the cost efficiency of service delivery must be sustained.

Knowledge sharing is critical to the principle of Knowledge Alignment because knowledge integration cannot be easily accomplished without sharing. Consequently, numerous previous researchers found no association between Knowledge Stock and Knowledge Integration [34], which is not surprising given that the level of expertise does not indicate proclivity to share. It is consistent with prior research, which discovered that knowledge had little or no direct impact on performance [35]. Subject Matter Experts may be reluctant to share their knowledge with non-domain professionals for various reasons, including power, language differences, and time constraints [36]. On the contrary, most organizations claim that an effective and efficient KM process will benefit organizational performance. As a result, knowledge management is widely accepted as an important predictor of organizational innovation or performance [37]. However, there are some differences in the outcomes of KM sub-processes or sub-dimensions and organizational performance.

Performance is a common thread in most disciplines, such as social science and management, and it is significant to academics and practitioners. Although the relevance of the notion of performance is broadly accepted, the intervention of performance in study designs is perhaps one of the most difficult issues that is encountered by academic researchers today. With the quantity of literature on the subject constantly growing, there appears to be little hope of achieving alliance on basic terminology and interpretations. Some people have expressed their dissatisfaction with this concept. Consequently, smart city performance should be included in electronic service delivery by smart cities in this study [38]. From a traditional standpoint, organizational performance is usually associated with economic performance [39], and the financial benefits of organizational effectiveness are strongly tied to the company's performance [40]. Darroch's [37] analysis employs contrasting and individually introspective performance indicators, such as "Our company is more profitable than the industry average," and individual introspective performance indicators, such as "We are more profitable than we were five years ago." These performance indicators include both financial and non-financial indicators.

Nevertheless, similar to any other organizational resource, effective technology-oriented knowledge management through artificial intelligence should contribute to key attributes of smart city performance, such as e-service delivery [41].

Furthermore, as smart cities improve their AI-based knowledge management, they can achieve optimal e-services solutions to satisfy the needs of their citizens [30]. Smart cities can acquire and use knowledge more productively with increased AI-based knowledge management capabilities, resulting in above-average performance. Thus, we propose:

Hypothesis 1. *Higher the AI-based technology-oriented knowledge management, the higher the likelihood that a smart city offers e-service delivery to citizens.*

When considering the association between Knowledge Management and innovativeness, we first begin with Schumpeter. According to him, integrating established theoretical and physiological ingredients is known as an innovation [42]. Specifically, innovation is the process of combining an organization's existing knowledge capital to generate new knowledge. Consequently, an innovative business's ultimate focus is reorganizing current knowledge assets while researching new knowledge [43]. Knowledge exploration and manipulation have been proven to contribute to the innovativeness of an organization and its performance [44]. Numerous studies on the significance of Knowledge Management in innovation has been undertaken. The outcomes of Du Plessis [21] supported the crucial importance of knowledge management in knowledge processing capability and hence in the incidence and interactivity of innovation. Huergo [45] presents statistical evidence supporting the positive effect of technology management on an organizations' innovation success. Brockman and Morgan [46] argue that KM techniques such as "innovative information use," "efficient information gathering," and "shared interpretation" improve the efficiency and innovativeness of new products. Theoretical approaches provide vague arguments about a particular emphasis on "demand-driven" or "collaborative" knowledge management techniques. Incredibly strong relations in a knowledge-sharing community may constrain the innovation process due to redundancy [47]. On the other hand, a shared knowledge base enhances intellectual capital within the society [48].

Knowledge management systems, particularly ICT elements, emerge to enhance the efficiency and at least perceived progress [49]. It is compatible with the outcomes of knowledge management in businesses, which unearth statistical evidence proving enterprises with superior knowledge management employ their resources effectively, increasing innovation [21]. The findings of previous case studies offer conflicting results too. Darroch et al.'s findings are an excellent illustration. Darroch [37] discovered no substantial advantages. A further component of the KM-innovation connection is how knowledge management influences distinctive forms of innovation. According to Darroch and McNaughton [50], different kinds of innovation demand different resources and a unique knowledge management strategy, such as technology-oriented knowledge management. They examined the impact of knowledge management on three different kinds of innovation. As per their observations, diverse KM initiatives are significant for different innovations. Consequently, we believe that different knowledge management will influence different aspects of innovation success, as well as the velocity, reliability, and magnitude of innovation success. Hence, we propose:

Hypothesis 2. *Higher the AI-based technology-oriented knowledge management, the higher the likelihood that a smart city will have more innovation success.*

Innovation is a modern concept, discipline, or artifact that a person or entity perceives as novel. When an innovation emanates, diffusion occurs, which implies interacting or distributing the innovation reports to the intended group [51]. According to the theory of diffusion of innovations, diffusion of innovation emerges when potential consumers become informed of the innovation, analyze its significance, and decide, based on their assessment, to incorporate or reject the innovation and demand evidence of the deployment or disapproval decision [51]. These mechanisms eventually occur through a platform among citizens (consumers). Diffusion of innovation considers individual and societal elements that influence an adoption decision or abandon a particular innovation. Rogers contends that cognitive and social factors, as well as environmental and contextual aspects, may influence the diffusion of innovation.

Service innovation, defined as "new developments in service processes involved in delivering core products and services" [52], can be defined as a group of enhanced efficiency for delivering existing services or products [53]. E-service innovation focuses on services that are provided mostly through digitized network connectivity, demonstrating the types of companies that employ internet technologies to optimize service delivery and adapt the services that suit the client's demands. E-service innovation improves value by facilitating service providers to leverage digital strategies for improving customer–healthy relationships and reducing service output uncertainty [54]. External data can be consolidated with digital knowledge acquired through the internet and other useful information to maximize the effectiveness of service delivery [55]. E-service innovation can be investigated by identifying the qualities that distinguish it from all other innovations for improved service delivery [56]. Consequently, e-service innovations can encourage organizations to provide enhanced customer value while improving e-service delivery.

Another relationship that is investigated in this study is the link between innovation and smart city performance, which is a city's capacity to provide e-service delivery. Previous research established a significant positive association between innovation and performance [37,57,58]. Hence, we proposed the following hypotheses on this basis:

Hypothesis 3. *Higher the innovation, the higher the likelihood that a smart city will provide e-service delivery.*

Hypothesis 4. *Innovation mediates the relationship between AI-based technology-oriented knowledge management and e-service delivery.*

2.2. Moderating Role of E-Governance

E-governance is defined as "the public sector's use of information and communication technologies to improve information and service delivery, encouraging citizen participation in the decision-making process, and making government more accountable, transparent and effective ... its objective is to engage, enable and empower the citizen" [59]. Citizens, corporations, governments, and institutions all benefit from e-governance. Citizens get benefits from electronic services that are affordable, convenient, instantaneous, efficient, transparent, and equitable around the clock; businesses take advantage of lower time in registration of new business set-up, get assistance in undertaking e-commerce business, superior compliance to regulatory standards to conduct business, convenient and more transparent while doing business with government through e-tendering, and preventing corruption during finance clearing from government compensation by employing e-banking. Government institutions benefit from up-to-date information for proper policy decisions and regulatory control; quick handling of provided data for improved decision-making; efficient management; stronger propagation of regulatory norms; improved results in regulatory mechanisms such as taxation; higher performance in social sectors such as health, education, and social welfare; and developing a positive impression of dynamic modern government in public.

Smart city governments constantly look for modern techniques to provide the quality of public services. E-Government is one indication of a drastic transformation in service delivery to citizens, in which unique information and communication technologies (ICT), mechanisms, organizational structures, and management systems are launched to promote public significance and generate positive change in people's lives [60]. During this evolution, a significant number of innovations were implemented. Compared to the corporate sector, where organizations attempt to maximize competitiveness to generate profit, government institutions strive to innovate to generate better performance. Further, public sector services are poised to generate public performance and improve desired public outcomes. The three main principles of public sector innovations are novelty, execution, and implications, which lead to better public outcomes such as reliability, performance, transparency, and user satisfaction [61].

Service delivery innovation is among the best-acclaimed innovations in public sector organizations in Eu countries; according to the 2010 European Union's Yardstick, 66 percent of organizations across the EU-27 report experienced incorporated innovations in public services [62,63]. System and governance strategies for innovation have been identified as the most prevalent, particularly at the domestic level. Environmental challenges, increasing population, and poverty have highlighted the use of creative and innovative approaches to the challenges confronting public services in European cities. As novel approaches to address the most complex urban challenges, modern e-governance frameworks, organizational techniques, and transparency have been proposed [64]. Technology innovation has recently boosted governments' capabilities to perform the necessary methodologies and procedures to achieve this [65].

ICT has been invented to provide an intensifying range of services, provide people access to online platforms, and mitigate service delivery costs. These activities fall under the umbrella of e-government, which aims to "enable and improve the efficiency with which government services and information are provided to citizens, employees, businesses, and government agencies" [66]. In terms of communication channels for the delivery of government services, the online channel is likely to be the top priority for governments, owing to its cost-effectiveness [67]. As a result, governments are interested in their citizens' adoption of the online service delivery channel. Consequently, the essence of government portals must concentrate on those unique requirements and strive to satisfy "consumers" (inhabitants, citizens, and enterprises) [68]. Considering these requirements, governments must choose an online service delivery model that integrates structure and content to improve performance. Hence, we propose our hypotheses as follows:

Hypothesis 5. *Higher the implementation of e-governance in a smart city, the higher the likelihood that a smart city offers e-service delivery to citizens.*

Several previous studies have utilized governance as moderating variable to investigate their constructs, for example, moderating the role of governance mechanisms on the relationship between ESG disclosure and firm performance [69]; moderating the role of governance on the relationship between free cash flow and earning management [70]; moderating role of governance heterogeneity on the relationship between psychological ownership, knowledge sharing, and entrepreneurial orientation [71]; and moderating role of governance environment on the relationship between risk allocation and private investment [72]. We assume that e-governance is best suited to be applied as a moderating variable to investigate the relationship between innovation and smart city performance. Hence, we propose:

Hypothesis 6. *Relationship between innovation and smart city performance is strengthened with the moderating impact of e-governance.*

3. Research Methodology

3.1. Sampling

Increasingly, researchers are combining mixed-method approaches to establish a deeper level explanation for this phenomenon that is under investigation, improve the validity of the results, and explain conflicting outcomes [53]. This study used a quantitative survey technique to collect data for testing the proposed research model and hypotheses. The quantitative survey was carried out from January 2022 to May 2022. Following that, interviews were performed. We interviewed public officers in target cities in Pakistan in April 2022 to help interpret and understand the statistical results, thereby strengthening the outcomes. The data were acquired from a sample of South Korea, Pakistan, Bangladesh, and Japan public officials and citizens that were directly or indirectly involved in public service delivery decision-making. This assessment threshold was developed on the assumption that senior officials and citizens would necessitate the presence of some system to ensure knowledge management. The most qualified individuals in each department were identified and requested to respond to the survey, presuming that they would be qualified to comment on the transmission of knowledge throughout the organization instead of one or two departments.

The survey's administration took place in three stages. After identifying the population of public officers, entrepreneurs, and citizens, from metropolitan cities with a population of 600,000 or more in South Korea, Pakistan, Japan, and Bangladesh, a pre-notification mail describing the objective of the study and proclaiming the impending influx of the survey was sent to targeted respondents. The justification for choosing these four countries was that South Korea and Japan are East Asian developed economies with strong e-governance and e-services for their citizens [73]. In contrast, Pakistan and Bangladesh are South Asian emerging economies striving to design and implement such governance and services [74], so it is essential to evaluate respondents' perceptions from different geographic areas from the same continent. According to our best knowledge and observation, only a few studies have yet been undertaken in the comparative sense of such Asian regions [75].

Two weeks later, a set of questionnaires was forwarded to the targeted respondents, including shared online on different social media websites. The effective usable sample size was 569. Although very few experimental investigations on knowledge management were identified in the existing literature, it is hard to determine how age, education, experience, or nationality may have influenced the findings. To test for quasi-bias, a spontaneous cross-section of 90 participants who had not responded was chosen and delivered a short survey questionnaire to fill. The brief questionnaire was completed by 24 (26.7 percent) of this group. ANOVA analyses reported no difference in the mean replies from early, late, or non-respondents and thus no substantial variation between each segment of the respondents. Table 1 describes the respondents' age, education, experience, and nationality characteristics.

Table 1. Personal characteristics of the survey respondents.

Characteristic	Category	N	%
Age	18 to 30 years	297	52
	31 to 40 years	188	33
	41 to 50 years	58	10
	More than 50 years	26	05
Education	PhD degree	55	10
	Master's degree	174	30
	Bachelor's degree	340	60
Experience	1 to 10 years	176	31
	11 to 20 years	326	57
	21 to 30 years	60	11
	More than 30 years	7	01
Nationality	South Korea	380	67
	Japan	31	05
	Pakistan	109	19
	Bangladesh	49	09

3.2. Construct Measurement

A survey questionnaire was constructed to evaluate the four possible phenomena that were under study: (a) technology-oriented knowledge management (KM); (b) innovation; (c) e-governance; and (d) smart city performance. All of the variables were assessed with components that had previously been substantiated in research. The survey questionnaire items were paraphrased to address the perspective of this study explicitly.

3.2.1. Knowledge Management

Knowledge management was adapted from [76], which designed three scales to evaluate KM behaviors and practices: acquiring, disseminating, and responding to knowledge. There were eight factors that captured those:

- processes for acquiring knowledge about traffic violations through the database (KM1)
- processes for acquiring knowledge about our citizens' behavior through AI (KM2)
- process for acquiring knowledge about new services (KM3)
- process for acquiring knowledge about competitors within our private industry (KM4)
- feedback from projects through the database to improve subsequent projects (KM5)
- processes for exchanging knowledge with our private business partners (KM6)
- process for benchmarking performance through the database (KM7)
- teams that are devoted to identifying best practices for services (KM8)

3.2.2. Innovation

This paper employs the adapted [77] typology of Innovation. In this context, *Innovation* is defined as creating groups with different areas of expertise (INN1), knowledge sharing within groups (INN2); knowledge sharing between groups (INN3); encouragement to question and reflect on the decisions (INN4); availability of physical resources to acquire new knowledge to develop new ideas (INN5); allocate time for idea generation through knowledge sharing (INN6); new or significantly improved methods of producing services (INN7); the acquisition of advanced machinery, equipment, and computer hardware for the development of new or significantly improved services (INN8); the acquisition of software for the development of new or significantly improved services (INN9); and the acquisition of existing knowledge, copyrighted works, patented and non-patented inventions, and other types of knowledge from other cities (INN10).

3.2.3. E-Governance

We adapted the measurement scale [78] to determine e-governance for this study. *E-governance* is defined in this context as a strategy of local government for e-government (EG1), a citizen's right to require digital communication (EG2); businesses right to require digital communication (EG3), public authority's right to require digital communication from other parts of the public sector (EG4), utilization of ICT project budget thresholds/ceilings to structure its governance processes (EG5), public services or procedures that are mandatory to use online (EG6), government priority to increase the number of mandatory online services that are aimed at citizens (EG7), government priority to increase the number of mandatory online services that are aimed at businesses (EG8), and the main national citizen portal for government services (EG9).

3.2.4. Smart City Performance

We utilized Eeservice delivery to measure the construct of smart city performance. The measurement scales that were used by [33] for e-service delivery were adapted to investigate this variable here. We measured e-service delivery in this perspective as the ease of enrolment of voting online for the first time in government elections (ESD1), ease of lodging personal income tax return online (ESD2), ease of renewing international passport online (ESD3), ease of renewing personal driving license online (ESD4), ease of making an official declaration of theft of personal goods to the relevant police online (ESD5), ease of obtaining a copy of a birth certificate for self electronically (ESD6), ease of obtaining a copy of a marriage certificate for self electronically (ESD7), and ease of renewal of registration for a motor vehicle online (ESD8).

3.3. Analysis

The survey data were analyzed employing IBM SPSS Statistics 23 and SmartPLS 3, a multi-regression modelling approach that has gained prominence due to its precision and effectiveness. The multi-regression technique includes a regression estimation procedure, depicting quantitative and qualitative latent constructs while enforcing fundamental criteria on scale items, sample size, and redistributive assumptions. We performed an analysis in stages: (1) we evaluated the measurement model by restricting our indicators to a sequence of confirmatory factor analysis (CFA); and (2) we developed a structural model to investigate our hypotheses. SPSS 23 [79] was used for statistical analysis to substantiate the indicators and investigate the hypotheses.

To ensure that the answers were truly representative, the stimulatory effects of nonrespondent bias were mitigated by distinct participants to a sample of nonrespondents that were predicated on personal characteristics such as age, education, and experience. At the 5% level of significance, the chi-square test results found no significant difference between the three respondent groups for age ($\chi^2 = 70.323$, $p < 0.01$), education ($\chi^2 = 484.580$, $p < 0.01$), gender ($\chi^2 = 4.937$,$p < 0.01$), and experience ($\chi^2 = 423.907$, $p < 0.01$). Consequently, we asserted that this study was not concerned with nonresponse bias.

Another potential source of concern is the presence of common technique bias. By separating predictors and criterion construct objects throughout a lengthy survey question and assuring survey confidentiality, we reduced typical technique bias. The Harman one-factor test was used to look for common approach bias [80]. An unrotated confirmatory factor analysis of all the elements that were employed in this study reveals five elements with eigenvectors that were greater than one, which explains about 73% of the variation. The first (largest) component accounted for 18% of the variance. As multiple factors were collected and no single criterion accounted for more than 52% of the variation, common technique bias was not identified as a significant concern.

A convergent validity test was employed to create a measurement model of the entire self-rating scales using confirmatory factor analysis (CFA). After that, the modification index was used to select objects from the factors. The element with the highest modification index score was eliminated first, followed by the next component, until the intended goodness of fit was accomplished. Most goodness-of-fit predictors surpassed the defined cut-off criterion, but a few factor loadings were below the minimum standard of 0.5. Therefore, we excluded them from acquiring valid data for our model. The factor loadings of all factors of estimated parameters are validated to be higher than the critical value point of 0.5 [15]. We are now at the crucial stage of determining whether the conceptual framework we have defined is legitimate after it has been explained and delivered all the necessary reliability and validity tests. It was achieved by ascertaining the goodness-of-fit benchmark for the model fit. The potential to ascertain how well the model fits into the variation structure of the dataset is regarded as the goodness of fit. The CFA evaluation and research framework represent the data well based on quantitative assessment criteria. Cronbach's alpha coefficients were employed to evaluate the reliability of the metrics, and construct correlation was applied to estimate the sample's validity. The items for each variable were created using previous research. These indices have the potential to provide definitive evidence about construct reliability and validity above the threshold of 0.50.

Figure 1 illustrates our research framework, in which technology-oriented KM is depicted as an independent variable, smart city performance dependent, and innovation mediating and e-governance as a moderating variable. Our conceptual framework suggests a direct impact of technologically-oriented KM on smart city performance, which is e-service delivery, but with the integration of innovation, the direct linear relationship was transformed into a mediating relationship. Furthermore, e-governance was introduced as a moderating variable between innovation and smart city performance. Statistical mediation and moderation analysis employ three fundamental techniques: (1) causal stages, (2) coefficient difference, and (3) coefficient product [81].

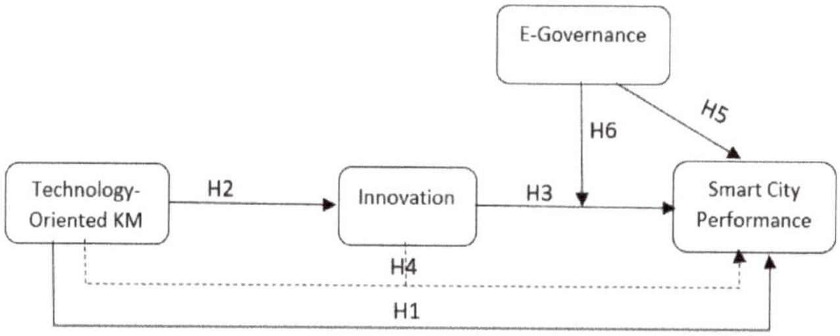

Figure 1. Research framework of AI-based KM on innovation and e-service delivery.

4. Results

Table 2 displays the item measures' standardized loading outcomes and other benchmarks, as well as the reliability and validity indicators. All of the components in the reliability analysis had factor loadings varying from 0.637 to 0.895, suggesting they were suitable for the rest of the assessment. The composite reliability indicators of all of the first-order components range from 0.903 to 0.953, which is greater than the recommended threshold of 0.70 [82]. Furthermore, the average variance that was extracted was greater than the 0.50 threshold that was suggested by [82]. The descriptive and discriminant validity of the measurements is shown in Table 3. For better discriminant validity, the square root of a construct's average variance must be greater than the square root of the construct's comparisons with the other components [83]. The findings also suggested that our components met this threshold, proving discriminant validity. An investigation of cross-loadings revealed appropriate discriminant validity as well.

Table 2. Construct reliability and validity Using CR, AVE, Cronbach's' Alpha, and KMO Test.

Item	Standardized Factor Loadings	Composite Reliability	Average Variance Extracted (AVE)	Cronbach Alpha	KMO and Bartlett's Test
	Cronbach Alpha = 0.971			KMO & Bartlett's Test = 0.815	
KM1	0.742				
KM2	0.807				
KM3	0.895				
KM4	0.870				
KM5	0.852	0.953	0.717	0.943	0.934
KM6	0.872				
KM7	0.875				
KM8	0.850				
INN1	0.717				
INN2	0.678				
INN3	0.819				
INN4	0.823				
INN5	0.817				
INN6	0.656	0.929	0.569	0.910	0.928
INN7	0.792				
INN8	0.637				
INN9	0.809				
INN10	0.764				

Table 2. *Cont.*

Item	Standardized Factor Loadings	Composite Reliability	Average Variance Extracted (AVE)	Cronbach Alpha	KMO and Bartlett's Test
EG1	0.720				
EG2	0.759				
EG3	0.805				
EG4	0.743				
EG5	0.650	0.917	0.553	0.897	0.906
EG6	0.732				
EG7	0.784				
EG8	0.735				
EG9	0.753				
ESD1	0.735				
ESD2	0.761				
ESD4	0.813				
ESD4	0.686	0.903	0.540	0.840	0.798
ESD5	0.672				
ESD6	0.665				
ESD7	0.776				
ESD8	0.757				

Table 3. Descriptive statistics, mean, standard deviation, and correlations between variables.

	N	Mean	Std. D	Edu	Gen	Exp	KM	Inn	EGov	ESD
Edu	569	2.293	1.477	1						
Gen	569	1.453	0.498	0.073	1					
Exp	569	2.489	0.695	0.037	0.157 **	1				
KM	569	3.522	0.819	0.109 **	0.049	0.305 **	1			
Inn	569	3.592	0.683	0.108 **	0.095 *	0.313 **	0.929 **	1		
EGov	569	3.851	0.602	0.102 *	0.081	0.210 **	0.715 **	0.841 **	1	
ESD	569	3.797	0.625	0.095 *	0.034	0.318 **	0.668 **	0.771 **	0.614 **	1

** Correlation is significant at the 0.01 level (2-tailed); * Correlation is significant at the 0.05 level (2-tailed).

We employed IBM SPSS Statistics 23 with the bootstrap technique to examine the proposed model. An evaluation of the conceptual framework, which included the coefficients of the correlation between the constructs, substantiated the hypothesized impacts and the R-square values, which suggest the proportion of the variation in the dependent constructs is expressed by their forebears. The control constructs (Model 1) were joined into the analysis model first, preceded by the main variables (Model 2), two-way interaction effect (Model 3), and moderating effects (Model 4), as suggested by [84]. Consequently, we simulated both the interactive (Models 3 and 4) and main effects on innovation (Model 2). The findings of the structural equation model analysis are demonstrated below. We concentrated on Model 3 and Model 4 because the speculated complex interactions are statistically significant.

Figure 2 illustrates the Model 4 and Model 5 paths and their significance. Technology-oriented knowledge management had a significant impact on innovation ($\beta = 0.766$, $p < 0.01$) and e-service delivery ($\beta = 0.370$, $p < 0.01$). This factor accounted for 64.9% of the variation in innovation and 65.3% of the variation in e-service delivery. Consequently, H1 and H2 are supported. H3 was supported by the fact that innovation had a significant impact on e-service delivery ($\beta = 0.935$, $p < 0.01$). The outcomes for the three control variables in the study exhibit that the respondents' gender, education, age, and experience have no impact on innovation, e-governance, or e-service delivery.

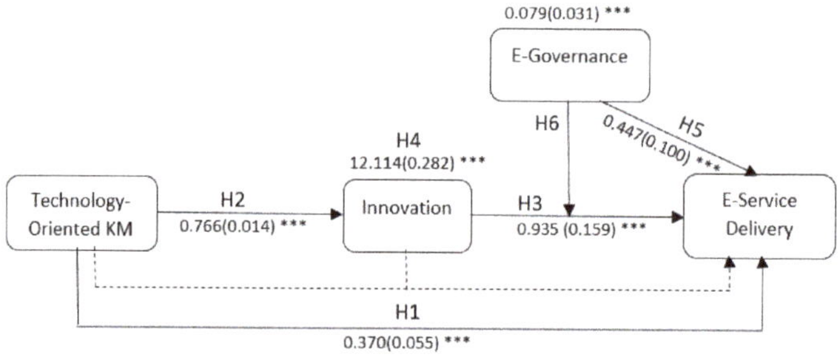

Figure 2. Research outcomes from multiple regression analysis. *** Impact of Technology Oriented KM, Innovation, and E-governance on E-Service Delivery.

We investigated the interaction effect of innovation on technology-oriented KM and e-service delivery and discovered a significant interactive effect (β = 12.114, $p < 0.01$). We further examined the interaction impact of e-governance between innovation and e-service delivery and found a strong significant moderating effect (β = 0.447, $p < 0.01$). This result corroborates our hypothesis that complementarity is essential in the suggested framework. Although the complementarity of internal and external dynamics may expedite synergic innovation, few investigations have been made to test this correlation. Therefore, we designed to simulate both the interactive and main impacts of innovation. When these interaction terms were included, the R^2 for innovation increased to 0.653. Model 5 was explained by applying multiple-regression modeling to explore the mediating role of innovation when knowledge management was a predictor variable and e-service delivery was considered an observed variable. The results in Table 5 revealed (β = 12.114, $p < 0.01$) a significant positive and indirect relationship between knowledge management and e-service delivery, hence, H4 is strongly supported.

The results of the moderating analysis are shown in Model 4 of Table 4. The findings demonstrate a direct positive relationship between e-governance and e-service delivery (β = 0.447, $p < 0.01$), strongly supporting our proposed H5. It indicated a significant and positive direct relationship between e-governance and e-service delivery. Moreover, we hypothesized that e-governance would play a moderating role in the relationship between innovation and e-service delivery. The findings (β = 0.079, $p < 0.01$) provided strong support for our hypothesis H6 as an indirect moderating relationship between innovation and e-service delivery. The outcomes showed a substantial and progressive direct and indirect relationship between e-governance and e-service delivery; e-governance plays a critical positive and significant moderating role between innovation and e-service delivery.

It is important to understand the essence of the variables, so we have explained the essence of the variables and their indicators in Table 5. In Model 1, the control variables were included; Model 2 explains independent variables, which are AI-based KM and innovation; Model 3 describes the moderating variable of e-governance; Model 4 indicates our moderating test of e-governance between the relationship of innovation and e-service delivery; and finally, Model 5 explains the mediating role of innovation between AI-based KM and e-service delivery. All of the six hypotheses that were analyzed in the five models were substantially supported. Further, a summary of the results regarding the development of technology-oriented knowledge management and its impact on e-service delivery, along with the mediating role of innovation and the moderating role of e-governance, are given in Table 6 below.

Table 4. Multiple regression analysis—the effect of AI-based KM, innovation, and e-governance on e-service delivery.

Variables	Dependent Variable: E-Service Delivery				DV: Innovation
	Model 1	Model 2	Model 3	Model 4	Model 5
Independent Variables					
(Constant)	4.500 (0.1118) ***	1.207 (0.139) ***	1.398 (0.144) ***	2.309 (0.379) ***	1.066 (0.080) ***
Education	0.043 (0.017) ***	0.005 (0.011)	0.006 (0.011)	0.004 (0.011)	0.006 (0.007)
Gender	0.099 (0.050) **	0.172 (0.033) ***	0175 (0.032) ***	0.177 (0.032) ***	0.064 (0.021) ***
Exp	0.300 (0.036) ***	0.100 (0.024) ***	0.091 (0.024) ***	0.086 (0.024) ***	0.026 (0.016) ***
Knowledge Mgt.		0.309 (0.053) ***	0.388 (0.055) ***	0.370 (0.055) ***	0.766 (0.014) ***
Innovation		1.027 (0.063) ***	1.283 (0.086) ***	0.935 (0.159) ***	
E-Governance			0.223 (0.051) ***	0.447 (0.100) ***	
Moderating effect					
Innovation x E-Governance				0.079 (0.031) ***	
Mediating effect					
Knowledge Mgt. → Innovation → E-Service Delivery				*(Sobel Test)*	12.114 (0.282) ***
N	569	569	569	569	569
R	0.344	0.798	0.805	0.808	0.931
R^2	0.118	0.637	0.649	0.653	0.866
Std. Error	0.588	0.378	0.372	0.370	0.250
F Models	25.316 ***	197.424 ***	172.968 ***	150.738 ***	912.608 ***
Durbin-Watson	1.704	1.993	2.032	2.045	1.882

** Correlation is significant at the 0.01 level (2-tailed); *** Correlation is significant at the 0.001 level (2-tailed).

Table 5. Characteristics of the evaluation models of artificial intelligence-based technological-oriented knowledge management, innovation, and e-service delivery in smart cities.

	Essence	Indicators	Results (Effects)
Model 1	Control Variables	Constants, Education, Gender, and Experience	Strongly Supported
Model 2	Independent Variables	AI-based KM and Innovation	Strongly Supported
Model 3	Moderating Variable	E-Governance	Strongly Supported
Model 4	Moderating Test	Innovation x E-Governance	Strongly Supported
Model 5	Mediating Test	AI-based KM, Innovation, and E-Service Delivery	Strongly Supported

Table 6. Generalization of the hypotheses of artificial intelligence-based technological oriented knowledge management, innovation, and e-service delivery in smart cities.

	Essence	Results (Effects)	Factors of Influence	
			Positive	Negative
Hypothesis 1	AI-based technology-oriented knowledge management → E-service Delivery	Supported	Direct impact	-
Hypothesis 2	AI-based technology-oriented knowledge management → Innovation success	Supported	Direct impact	-
Hypothesis 3	Innovation → E-service Delivery	Supported	Direct impact	-
Hypothesis 4	AI-based technology-oriented knowledge management → Innovation → E-service Delivery	Supported	Mediating impact	-
Hypothesis 5	E-governance → E-service Delivery	Supported	Direct impact	-
Hypothesis 6	Innovation → E-governance → E-service Delivery	Supported	Moderating impact	-

5. Discussion

According to the knowledge management-based service science theory by [18] and the diffusion of innovation theory of [19], a city government should integrate its technological resources and competencies to manage acquired knowledge and enhance e-service delivery through technological innovation. Following the theoretical framework, the findings corroborate our hypothesis that enhancing innovation must be driven by the interaction effects of knowledge management and city performance. Hess and Rothaermel [85] explored the role of innovation on a city's performance to determine when and how technology-oriented sources are substitutive. This paper advances a research gap by examining the interaction effects of technology-oriented knowledge management and e-service delivery on innovation and the contextual role of e-governance between innovation and e-service delivery. City governments must implement diverse approaches regarding e-service offering and e-service delivery protocols by ensuring innovation and e-governance, fostering good e-governance with innovation.

Table 4 shows a diverse range of results. All the correlations between knowledge management, innovation, e-governance, and smart city performance indicators were positive and statistically significant. Table 4 provides evidence that several independent knowledge management elements do not correlate with different aspects of performance measures. One plausible interpretation of these findings is that comparative performance metrics may struggle from a halo effect, wherein city governors sensationalize their own cities' effectiveness. Besides that, knowledge management is not the only factor that influences performance, and other factors, such as the city's innovative or e-government environment, may substantially impact performance. The relationship between knowledge management and innovation was theoretically established in the literature, but statistical evidence was inadequate.

Consequently, in this study, a city that is proficient in knowledge management attributes is more innovative. According to a common assumption, intangible knowledge is more complicated for contenders to access and replicate. Therefore, this type of knowledge has a tremendous opportunity to transform competitive advantages [86], improving performance. The findings that are presented in this study are significant because they demonstrate that knowledge is just as essential as what we do with that knowledge to be innovative.

Smart cities with well-developed technology-oriented knowledge management behavioral patterns are more likely to generate greater performance (i.e., e-service delivery) and develop incremental innovations supporting our proposed H1 and H2 substantially. Moreover, municipalities with well-developed innovations and technology are more strongly predictive of e-service delivery, with the fact that technological innovation is critical for providing electronic services in smart cities, supporting our assertion in H3. These conclusions are also supported by an analysis of individual knowledge management factors. Our empirical analysis not only suggests that knowledge management has a significant and positive influence on innovation and innovation had a significant positive effect on smart city performance, but the findings also revealed that knowledge management has a significant indirect effect on smart city performance through innovation, supporting our projected H4 substantially, suggesting that cities with more information technology can enhance performance by maximizing the e-services that they provide to their citizens.

Furthermore, our statistical analysis recommended that e-governance substantially and positively impacts smart city performance; therefore, our proposed H5 was supported significantly. The findings also supported H6 and proved that the e-governance factor strengthens the direct relationship between innovation and performance; hence this moderating relationship is also confirmed. In the context of smart cities through innovation, we investigated the role of e-governance in boosting e-service delivery and its implications on citizen satisfaction. According to the study findings, e-governance has the potential to strengthen the association between innovation and e-service delivery. There is a significant disparity in the expectations and perceptions of ordinary citizens in the cities regarding service delivery, which has harmed residents' satisfaction over the years. Considering the overall adverse effect of the predominant dilemma, there is an imperative need in developing cities that lack innovation to implement e-governance in all public agencies [87].

Further direction, strategic purposes, and measures to implement these strategic purposes are explained in Table 7.

Table 7. Directions and means of development of technology-oriented knowledge management based on artificial intelligence, innovations, and the provision of electronic services in smart cities.

Parameters (Directions)	Strategic Purposes	Means (Measures) of Implementation of Strategic Purposes
Artificial Intelligence-based Technological-Oriented Knowledge Management	○ Disaster management [88] ○ Technological innovation and revolution [89,90] ○ Firm growth and performance [91] ○ Enhance business process [92]	○ Strategic planning, mitigation and preparedness activities, rehabilitation ○ Knowledge sharing, application and storage, learning and decision-making ○ Competitive advantage ○ Leadership support, adequate funds, functional support
Innovation	○ Service innovation [52] ○ E-services innovation [54,93] ○ Technological innovation [89]	○ Incorporation of product innovation and introduction of new products/services ○ User interaction with products/services ○ User/customer experience ○ Acquisition of knowledge, software, and hardware to develop new services
E-Governance	○ Provision of E-services [94] ○ Public development [95]	○ Investment in ICT ○ Incorporation of private and non-profit IT projects ○ E-administration ○ Transparency between public-private businesses
E-Service Delivery	○ Healthcare [96] ○ Education [97] ○ Social services [98] ○ Other E-services [41]	○ Decision-making about public healthcare ○ Culture of education and provide practical tools to adapt management process ○ Renew registration for a motor vehicle online ○ Renew a driver's license online ○ Renew an international passport online ○ obtain a copy of a birth/marriage certificate for self electronically
Smart Cities (considering the total impact according to the selected parameters)	○ Smart economy ○ Smart governance ○ Smart environment [99] ○ Smart mobility ○ Smart living	○ Innovative business approach, R&D expenditures, labor market productivity, and city's economic role in the national/international market ○ Use of ICT and participation of people in decision-making process ○ Responsible resource management and sustainable urban planning ○ Efficient transportation system ○ Citizen's quality of life

6. Conclusions

This study demonstrates that direct and indirect driving forces are mutually advantageous. Furthermore, analyzing their interaction can help to model the relationships between knowledge management, innovation, e-governance, and e-service delivery. Smart cities should manage the knowledge that is acquired through artificial intelligence and develop new information technology-based e-services through innovation. Furthermore, innovation mediates the relationship between knowledge management and e-service delivery, while e-governance moderates the relationship between innovation and smart city performance.

6.1. Theoretical Implications

Organizations make decisions about what operations the organization will engage in, how those operations will be carried out, what resources will be necessary, which resources will be disbursed to different functions, and, eventually, which resources will be used [100]. In this context, this study contends that knowledge that is acquired through artificial intelligence serves several functions:

1. Technological-oriented knowledge can be both an intangible and tangible resource [101] that can be used for better decision-making.
2. Acquiring knowledge favors any decision-making regarding utilizing resources to provide electronic services.
3. A competency in knowledge management empowers everyone within a city government to capitalize the most assistance from the knowledge and other capabilities [100].
4. Effective, efficient, and constructive knowledge management contributes significantly to innovation.
5. Innovation through KM has a stronger influence over e-service delivery when a smart city has a high degree of e-governance.

Constructive knowledge management was developed as a coordinating mechanism by presenting substantial evidence with a proclivity for establishing innovation capabilities were more likely to have well-developed knowledge management policies and attitudes. It is reasonable to suggest that most smart cities have knowledge management capabilities and ensure the effective utilization of other accessible resources. This finding provides early evidence for [100] concepts by demonstrating the importance of knowledge management as a coordinating mechanism when formulating innovation capabilities. Furthermore, we discovered substantial evidence for the notion that a smart city that was developing dynamic innovations had well-developed knowledge management policies and behaviors, as well as credible evidence that enhanced smart city performance and knowledge management co-existed.

Technology-oriented knowledge management was found to directly impact e-service delivery and innovation, while innovation had a direct effect on e-service delivery. When e-governance was added as a moderator, it not only directly impacted e-service delivery but also strengthened the relationship between innovation and e-service delivery. These findings are significant because empirical support is provided for the existing knowledge management-based service science theory [18] and the diffusion of innovation theory of [19], and, more importantly, empirically evidenced development of e-governance as a moderator between the innovation and e-service delivery is yet another contribution to the literature of innovation and applied sciences.

6.2. Managerial Implications

Knowledge management has been heralded as a novel discipline. The understanding of the concept of knowledge management is frequently systematic with the advent of information technology as a remedy for knowledge acquisition. This study addresses a broader knowledge management framework by utilizing previously discovered knowledge management elements that are characteristics of an organization that manages knowledge effectively [76]. The study also demonstrates the significance of effective knowledge management. Consequently, smart city managers should develop initiatives to improve knowledge management attitudes and behaviors because a city that manages knowledge effectively will be more innovative. Furthermore, smart city governors should develop and implement an e-governance system to improve e-service delivery to smart city citizens through innovative technologies.

6.3. Limitations and Future Research

Similar to most empirical research, this study has certain limitations that must be considered when interpreting, extending, and generalizing the findings. Since this research was performed in Asian countries such as South Korea, Pakistan, and Japan, the attributes of the analyzed respondents may not extend to those in other cultures and countries that differ from those that were mentioned. Consequently, further investigation into cross-continent differences in social mechanisms that are designed to address innovation in e-service delivery is warranted. Finally, because participation in this survey was discretionary, consciousness variance was unavoidable. The Harman one-factor test was used to rule out any potential issues. According to the results of the test, each major construct describes roughly equal variance, denoting that our data do not have an elevated common method variance.

According to the findings of this study, smart cities that effectively manage knowledge were more innovative and outperformed in delivering e-services. The study also discovered that knowledge management influenced innovation and that innovation influenced performance positively, and e-governance significantly impacted performance and moderated the relationship between innovation and performance. One of the core themes of this study is that effective knowledge management facilitates the extraction of high-quality e-services from certain resources. Future research is needed to strengthen and expand this assumption by investigating the facilitating importance of knowledge management in greater depth.

Author Contributions: S.A.A.B., conceptualization, methodology, validation, formal analysis, investigation, and writing—original draft preparation; S.M., conceptualization, methodology, writing—review and editing, and funding acquisition. All authors have read and agreed to the published version of the manuscript.

Funding: This work was supported by the Ministry of Education of the Republic of Korea and the National Research Foundation of Korea (NRF-2019S1A5C2A03081234).

Institutional Review Board Statement: Not applicable.

Informed Consent Statement: Not applicable.

Data Availability Statement: Not applicable.

Conflicts of Interest: The authors declare no conflict of interest.

References

1. Chuang, S.-H. A resource-based perspective on knowledge management capability and competitive advantage: An empirical investigation. *Expert Syst. Appl.* **2004**, *27*, 459–465. [CrossRef]
2. Halawi, L.A.; Aronson, J.E.; McCarthy, R.V. Resource-based view of knowledge management for competitive advantage. *Electron. J. Knowl. Manag.* **2005**, *3*, 75.
3. Lee, D.; van den Steen, E. Managing know-how. *Manag. Sci.* **2010**, *56*, 270–285. [CrossRef]
4. Bergh, J.V.D.; Viaene, S. Key Challenges for the Smart City: Turning Ambition into Reality. In Proceedings of the 2015 48th Hawaii International Conference on System Sciences, Washington, DC, USA, 5–8 January 2015.
5. Abualoush, S.; Masadeh, R.; Bataineh, K.; Alrowwad, A. The Role of Knowledge Management Process and Intellectual Capital as Intermediary Variables between Knowledge Management Infrastructure and Organization Performance. *Interdiscip. J. Inf. Knowl. Manag.* **2018**, *13*, 279–309. [CrossRef]
6. Ajanaku, O.J. Knowledge management infrastructure and processes on effectiveness of nursing care. In Proceedings of the 2018 12th International Conference on Research Challenges in Information Science (RCIS), Nantes, France, 29–31 May 2018.
7. Gold, A.H.; Malhotra, A.; Segars, A.H. Knowledge Management: An Organizational Capabilities Perspective. *J. Manag. Inf. Syst.* **2001**, *18*, 185–214. [CrossRef]
8. Lee, S.; Kim, B.G.; Kim, H. An integrated view of knowledge management for performance. *J. Knowl. Manag.* **2012**, *16*, 183–203. [CrossRef]
9. Komninos, N. Intelligent cities: Towards interactive and global innovation environments. *Int. J. Innov. Reg. Dev.* **2009**, *1*, 337. [CrossRef]
10. Angelidou, M. Smart cities: A conjuncture of four forces. *Cities* **2015**, *47*, 95–106. [CrossRef]
11. Carrillo, F. *Knowledge Cities*; Routledge: London, UK, 2006.
12. Sotarauta, M. *Leadership and the City: Power, Strategy and Networks in the Making of Knowledge Cities*; Routledge: London, UK, 2015.
13. Komninos, N. Intelligent cities: Variable geometries of spatial intelligence. *Intell. Build. Int.* **2011**, *3*, 172–188. [CrossRef]
14. Bernardo, M.d.R.M. Smart city governance: From e-government to smart governance. In *Smart Cities and Smart Spaces: Concepts, Methodologies, Tools, and Applications*; IGI Global: Hershey, PA, USA, 2019; pp. 196–232.
15. Bokhari, S.A.A.; Myeong, S. Use of Artificial Intelligence in Smart Cities for Smart Decision-Making: A Social Innovation Perspective. *Sustainability* **2022**, *14*, 620. [CrossRef]
16. Lopes, N.V. Smart governance: A key factor for smart cities implementation. In Proceedings of the 2017 IEEE International Conference on Smart Grid and Smart Cities (ICSGSC), Singapore, 23–26 July 2017.

17. Silva, B.N.; Khan, M.; Han, K. Towards sustainable smart cities: A review of trends, architectures, components, and open challenges in smart cities. *Sustain. Cities Soc.* **2018**, *38*, 697–713. [CrossRef]
18. D'Aniello, G.; Gaeta, M.; Orciuoli, F.; Sansonetti, G.; Sorgente, F. Knowledge-Based Smart City Service System. *Electronics* **2020**, *9*, 965. [CrossRef]
19. Kaminski, J. Diffusion of innovation theory. *Can. J. Nurs. Inform.* **2011**, *6*, 1–6.
20. Carneiro, A. How does knowledge management influence innovation and competitiveness? *J. Knowl. Manag.* **2000**, *4*, 87–98. [CrossRef]
21. du Plessis, M. The role of knowledge management in innovation. *J. Knowl. Manag.* **2007**, *11*, 20–29. [CrossRef]
22. Anthopoulos, L.G. *Understanding Smart Cities: A Tool for Smart Government or an Industrial Trick?* Springer International Publishing: Cham, Switzerland, 2017. [CrossRef]
23. Lombardi, P.; Giordano, S.; Farouh, H.; Yousef, W. Modelling the smart city performance. *Innov. Eur. J. Soc. Sci. Res.* **2012**, *25*, 137–149. [CrossRef]
24. Kumar, V. E-governance for smart cities. In *E-Governance for Smart Cities*; Springer: Berlin/Heidelberg, Germany, 2015; pp. 1–43.
25. Haider, S.A.; Kayani, U.N. The impact of customer knowledge management capability on project performance-mediating role of strategic agility. *J. Knowl. Manag.* **2020**, *25*, 298–312. [CrossRef]
26. Jennex, M.E. Towards understanding knowledge management strategy. In Proceedings of the International Conference on Information Systems, Munich, Germany, 15–18 December 2019.
27. Oluikpe, P. Developing a corporate knowledge management strategy. *J. Knowl. Manag.* **2012**, *16*, 862–878. [CrossRef]
28. Davenport, T.H.; Ronanki, R. Artificial intelligence for the real world. *Harv. Bus. Rev.* **2018**, *96*, 108–116.
29. de Grip, A.; Borghans, L.; Smits, W. Future developments in the job level and domain of high-skilled workers. In *Towards a Transparent Labour Market for Educational Decisions*; Routledge: London, UK, 2018; pp. 21–56.
30. Fteimi, N.; Hopf, K. *Knowledge Management in the Era of Artificial Intelligence-Developing an Integrative Framework*; Otto-Friedrich-Universität: Bamberg, Germany, 2021. Available online: https://aisel.aisnet.org/ecis2021_rip/20/ (accessed on 15 July 2022).
31. Maier, R.; Remus, U. Implementing process-oriented knowledge management strategies. *J. Knowl. Manag.* **2003**, *7*, 62–74. [CrossRef]
32. Wang, L.; Bretschneider, S.; Gant, J. Evaluating web-based e-government services with a citizen-centric approach. In Proceedings of the 38th Annual Hawaii International Conference on System Sciences, Washington, DC, USA, 3–6 January 2005.
33. Gouscos, D.; Laskaridis, G.; Lioulias, D.; Mentzas, G.; Georgiadis, P. An approach to offering one-stop e-government services—Available technologies and architectural issues. In *Electronic Government*; Springer: Berlin/Heidelberg, Germany, 2002; pp. 264–271.
34. Reich, B.H.; Gemino, A.; Sauer, C. Knowledge management and project-based knowledge in it projects: A model and preliminary empirical results. *Int. J. Proj. Manag.* **2012**, *30*, 663–674. [CrossRef]
35. Faraj, S.; Sproull, L. Coordinating Expertise in Software Development Teams. *Manag. Sci.* **2000**, *46*, 1554–1568. [CrossRef]
36. Maqsood, T. Knowledge Management in Project-based Companies: An Organic Perspective. *Int. J. Manag. Proj. Bus.* **2009**, *2*, 318–320. [CrossRef]
37. Darroch, J. Knowledge management, innovation and firm performance. *J. Knowl. Manag.* **2005**, *9*, 101–115. [CrossRef]
38. Saha, P.; Nath, A.; Salehi-Sangari, E. Success of government e-service delivery: Does satisfaction matter? In Proceedings of the International Conference on Electronic Government, Bilbao, Spain, 31 August 2010.
39. Richard, P.J.; Devinney, T.M.; Yip, G.S.; Johnson, G. Measuring Organizational Performance: Towards Methodological Best Practice. *J. Manag.* **2009**, *35*, 718–804. [CrossRef]
40. Ahmed, S.; Fiaz, M.; Shoaib, M. Impact of knowledge management practices on organizational performance: An empirical study of banking sector in Pakistan. *FWU J. Soc. Sci.* **2015**, *9*, 147–167.
41. Erastus, L.R.; Jere, N.R.; Shava, F.B. A secure smart city infrastructure framework for E-service delivery within a developing country: A case of windhoek in Namibia. In Proceedings of the Fifth International Congress on Information and Communication Technology, London, UK, 20–21 February 2021.
42. Schumpeter, J.A. The analysis of economic change. *Rev. Econ. Stat.* **1935**, *17*, 2–10. [CrossRef]
43. Yao-Sheng, L. The effects of knowledge management strategy and organization structure on innovation. *Int. J. Manag.* **2007**, *24*, 53.
44. Hall, R.; Andriani, P. Managing Knowledge for Innovation. *Long Range Plan.* **2002**, *35*, 29–48. [CrossRef]
45. Huergo, E. The role of technological management as a source of innovation: Evidence from Spanish manufacturing firms. *Res. Policy* **2006**, *35*, 1377–1388. [CrossRef]
46. Brockman, B.K.; Morgan, R.M. The Role of Existing Knowledge in New Product Innovativeness and Performance. *Decis. Sci.* **2003**, *34*, 385–419. [CrossRef]
47. Alavi, M.; Leidner, D.E. Knowledge Management and Knowledge Management Systems: Conceptual Foundations and Research Issues. *MIS Q.* **2001**, *25*, 107–136. [CrossRef]
48. Nonaka, I.; Toyama, R.; Konno, N. SECI, Ba and Leadership: A Unified Model of Dynamic Knowledge Creation. *Long Range Plan.* **2000**, *33*, 5–34. [CrossRef]
49. OECD. *The Learning Government: Introduction and Draft Results of the Survey of Knowledge Management Practices in Ministries/Departments/Agencies of Central Government*; OECD: Paris, France, 2003.

50. Darroch, J.; McNaughton, R. Examining the link between knowledge management practices and types of innovation. *J. Intellect. Cap.* **2002**, *3*, 210–222. [CrossRef]
51. Rogers, E.M. *Diffusion of Innovations*; Simon and Schuster: New York, NY, USA, 2010.
52. Oke, A. Innovation types and innovation management practices in service companies. *Int. J. Oper. Prod. Manag.* **2007**, *27*, 564–587. [CrossRef]
53. Chuang, S.-H.; Lin, H.-N. Co-creating e-service innovations: Theory, practice, and impact on firm performance. *Int. J. Inf. Manag.* **2015**, *35*, 277–291. [CrossRef]
54. Tsou, H.-T.; Chen, J.-S. The influence of interfirm codevelopment competency on e-service innovation. *Inf. Manag.* **2012**, *49*, 177–189. [CrossRef]
55. Kim, N.; Pae, J.H. Utilization of new technologies: Organizational adaptation to business environments. *J. Acad. Mark. Sci.* **2007**, *35*, 259–269. [CrossRef]
56. Xu, H.; Sharma, S.K.; Hackney, R. Web services innovation research: Towards a dual-core model. *Int. J. Inf. Manag.* **2005**, *25*, 321–334. [CrossRef]
57. Vázquez, R.; Santos, M.L.; Álvarez, L.I. Market orientation, innovation and competitive strategies in industrial firms. *J. Strateg. Mark.* **2001**, *9*, 69–90. [CrossRef]
58. Li, T.; Calantone, R.J. The impact of market knowledge competence on new product advantage: Conceptualization and empirical examination. *J. Mark.* **1998**, *62*, 13–29. [CrossRef]
59. UNESCO. *Defining E-Governance*; UNESCO: Paris, France, 2005.
60. Contini, F.; Lanzara, G. *ICT and Innovation in the Public Sector: European Studies in the Making of E-Government*; Springer: Berlin/Heidelberg, Germany, 2008.
61. Daglio, M.; Gerson, D.; Kitchen, H. Innovating the public sector: From ideas to impact. *Building Organ. Capacit. Public Sect. Innov.* **2014**, *19*, 2020.
62. Arundel, A.; Hollanders, H. A Taxonomy of Innovation: How Do Public Sector Agencies Innovate? Results of the 2010 European Innobarometer Survey of Public Agencies. 2011. Available online: https://www.researchgate.net/publication/279639116_A_taxonomy_of_innovation_How_do_public_sector_agencies_innovate_Results_of_the_2010_European_Innobarometer_survey_of_public_agencies (accessed on 13 May 2022).
63. Paskaleva, K.; Cooper, I.; Concilo, G. Co-producing smart city services: Does one size fit all? In *Smart Technologies for Smart Governments*; Springer: Berlin/Heidelberg, Germany, 2018; pp. 123–158.
64. Organization of Economic Co-operation and Development. *Together for Better Public Services: Partnering with Citizens and Civil Society*; OECD Publishing: Paris, France, 2011.
65. Osborne, S.P.; Radnor, Z.; Vidal, I.; Kinder, T. A Sustainable Business Model for Public Service Organizations? *Public Manag. Rev.* **2014**, *16*, 165–172. [CrossRef]
66. Carter, L.; Belanger, F. Citizen adoption of electronic government initiatives. In Proceedings of the 37th Annual Hawaii International Conference on System Sciences, Big Island, HI, USA, 5–8 January 2004.
67. Ebbers, W.; Pieterson, W.; Noordman, H. Electronic government: Rethinking channel management strategies. *Gov. Inf. Q.* **2008**, *25*, 181–201. [CrossRef]
68. Kubicek, H.; Hagen, M. Integrating e-commerce and e-government. The case of Bremen Online Services. *Law Electron. Commer.* **2001**, *12*, 177–196.
69. Albitar, K.; Hussainey, K.; Kolade, N.; Gerged, A.M. ESG disclosure and firm performance before and after IR: The moderating role of governance mechanisms. *Int. J. Account. Inf. Manag.* **2020**, *28*, 429–444. [CrossRef]
70. Nekhili, M.; Ben Amar, I.F.; Chtioui, T.; Lakhal, F. Free Cash Flow And Earnings Management: The Moderating Role Of Governance And Ownership. *J. Appl. Bus. Res. (JABR)* **2015**, *32*, 255–268. [CrossRef]
71. Pittino, D.; Martínez, A.B.; Chirico, F.; Galván, R.S. Psychological ownership, knowledge sharing and entrepreneurial orientation in family firms: The moderating role of governance heterogeneity. *J. Bus. Res.* **2018**, *84*, 312–326. [CrossRef]
72. Wang, H.; Liu, Y.; Xiong, W.; Song, J. The moderating role of governance environment on the relationship between risk allocation and private investment in PPP markets: Evidence from developing countries. *Int. J. Proj. Manag.* **2019**, *37*, 117–130. [CrossRef]
73. Park, J.; Hisanaga, N.; Kim, Y. Transfer of occupational health problems from a developed to a developing country: Lessons from the Japan-South Korea experience. *Am. J. Ind. Med.* **2009**, *52*, 625–632. [CrossRef]
74. Jamil, S. Artificial Intelligence and Journalistic Practice: The Crossroads of Obstacles and Opportunities for the Pakistani Journalists. *J. Pract.* **2020**, *15*, 1400–1422. [CrossRef]
75. Chaudhary, G.M.; Hashmi, S.H.; Khan, M.A. Exchange Rate and Foreign Trade: A Comparative Study of Major South Asian and South-East Asian Countries. *Procedia-Soc. Behav. Sci.* **2016**, *230*, 85–93. [CrossRef]
76. Darroch, J. Developing a measure of knowledge management behaviors and practices. *J. Knowl. Manag.* **2003**, *7*, 41–54. [CrossRef]
77. Chausset, J.; Namara, L.M. Measuring Organization Innovation in Colloboration with a Swedish Consultancy Firm. 2014. Available online: https://odr.chalmers.se/handle/20.500.12380/199817 (accessed on 23 May 2022).
78. OECD. *Government at a Glance 2015*; OECD: Paris, France, 2015.
79. Roni, S.M.; Djajadikerta, H.G. *Data Analysis with SPSS for Survey-Based Research*; Springer: Singapore, 2021. [CrossRef]
80. Podsakoff, P.M.; MacKenzie, S.B.; Lee, J.-Y.; Podsakoff, N.P. Common method biases in behavioral research: A critical review of the literature and recommended remedies. *J. Appl. Psychol.* **2003**, *88*, 879–903. [CrossRef]

81. Hair, J.F. *Multivariate Data Analysis: A Global Perspective*, 7th ed.; Prentice Hall: Upper Saddle River, NJ, USA, 2009.
82. Segars, A. Assessing the unidimensionality of measurement: A paradigm and illustration within the context of information systems research. *Omega* **1997**, *25*, 107–121. [CrossRef]
83. Coleman, R.L.; Herzog, T.J.; Chan, D.W.; Munroe, D.G.; Pappas, T.C.; Smith, A.; Zhang, Z.; Wolf, J. Validation of a second-generation multivariate index assay for malignancy risk of adnexal masses. *Am. J. Obstet. Gynecol.* **2016**, *215*, 82.e1–82.e11. [CrossRef]
84. Bokhari, S.A.A.; Aftab, M. Personality traits and social loafing among employees working in teams at small and medium enterprises: A cultural perspective data from emerging economies. *Data Brief* **2022**, *42*, 108085. [CrossRef]
85. Hess, A.M.; Rothaermel, F.T. When are assets complementary? star scientists, strategic alliances, and innovation in the pharmaceutical industry. *Strateg. Manag. J.* **2011**, *32*, 895–909. [CrossRef]
86. Foss, N.J. Knowledge-Based Approaches to the Theory of the Firm: Some Critical Comments. *Organ. Sci.* **1996**, *7*, 470–476. [CrossRef]
87. Naz, R. E-Governance for Improved Public Service Delivery in Fiji. *J. Serv. Sci. Manag.* **2009**, *02*, 190–203. [CrossRef]
88. Oktari, R.S.; Munadi, K.; Idroes, R.; Sofyan, H. Knowledge management practices in disaster management: Systematic review. *Int. J. Disaster Risk Reduct.* **2020**, *51*, 101881. [CrossRef]
89. Lee, V.H.; Leong, L.Y.; Hew, T.S.; Ooi, K.B. Knowledge management: A key determinant in advancing technological innovation? *J. Knowl. Manag.* **2013**, *17*, 848–872. [CrossRef]
90. Russ, M. Knowledge Management for Sustainable Development in the Era of Continuously Accelerating Technological Revolutions: A Framework and Models. *Sustainability* **2021**, *13*, 3353. [CrossRef]
91. Hitt, M.A.; Ireland, R.; Lee, H.-U. Technological learning, knowledge management, firm growth and performance: An introductory essay. *J. Eng. Technol. Manag.* **2000**, *17*, 231–246. [CrossRef]
92. Chatterjee, S.; Ghosh, S.K.; Chaudhuri, R. Knowledge management in improving business process: An interpretative framework for successful implementation of AI–CRM–KM system in organizations. *Bus. Process Manag. J.* **2020**, *26*, 1261–1281. [CrossRef]
93. Ciuchita, R.; Mahr, D.; Odekerken-Schröder, G. "Deal with it": How coping with e-service innovation affects the customer experience. *J. Bus. Res.* **2019**, *103*, 130–141. [CrossRef]
94. Bannister, F.; Connolly, R. Defining e-governance. *e-Serv. J. J. Electron. Serv. Public Priv. Sect.* **2012**, *8*, 3–25. [CrossRef]
95. Madon, S. e-Governance for Development. In *E-Governance for Development*; Springer: Berlin/Heidelberg, Germany, 2009; pp. 53–70.
96. El Morr, C.; Subercaze, J. Knowledge management in healthcare. In *Handbook of Research on Developments in e-Health and Telemedicine: Technological and Social Perspectives*; IGI Global: Hershey, PA, USA, 2010; pp. 490–510.
97. Sallis, E.; Jones, G. *Knowledge Management in Education: Enhancing Learning & Education*; Routledge: London, UK, 2013.
98. Gabbay, J.; le May, A.; Jefferson, H.; Webb, D.; Lovelock, R.; Powell, J.; Lathlean, J. A case study of knowledge management in multiagency consumer-informedcommunities of practice': Implications for evidence-based policy development in health and social services. *Health* **2003**, *7*, 283–310. [CrossRef]
99. Colldahl, C.; Frey, S.; Kelemen, J.E. Smart Cities: Strategic Sustainable Development for an Urban World. 2013. Available online: https://www.diva-portal.org/smash/record.jsf?pid=diva2:832150 (accessed on 18 May 2022).
100. Penrose, E.; Penrose, E.T. *The Theory of the Growth of the Firm*; Oxford University Press: Oxford, UK, 2009.
101. Hall, R. A framework linking intangible resources and capabiliites to sustainable competitive advantage. *Strat. Manag. J.* **1993**, *14*, 607–618. [CrossRef]

MDPI
St. Alban-Anlage 66
4052 Basel
Switzerland
Tel. +41 61 683 77 34
Fax +41 61 302 89 18
www.mdpi.com

Applied Sciences Editorial Office
E-mail: applsci@mdpi.com
www.mdpi.com/journal/applsci

www.ingramcontent.com/pod-product-compliance
Lightning Source LLC
Chambersburg PA
CBHW061449210926
51850CB00008B/1660